RFID Applied

RFID Applied

Jerry Banks
Manuel Pachano
Les Thompson
David Hanny

BICENTENNIAL
1807
WILEY
2007
BICENTENNIAL

JOHN WILEY & SONS, INC.

For general information about our other products and services, please contact our Customer Care Department within the United States at (800) 762-2974, outside the United States at (317) 572-3993 or fax (317) 572-4002.

Wiley also publishes its books in a variety of electronic formats. Some content that appears in print may not be available in electronic books. For more information about Wiley products, visit our web site at www.wiley.com.

Library of Congress Cataloging-in-Publication Data:

RFID applied / by Jerry Banks . . . [et al.].
    p. cm.
  Includes bibliographical references.
  ISBN: 978-0-471-79365-6 (cloth)
  1. Inventory control—Automation. 2. Radio frequency identification systems. I. Banks, Jerry.
  TS160.R435 2007
  658.7'87—dc22

                                      2006030753

Printed in the United States of America

10 9 8 7 6 5 4 3 2 1

To the new generation; Danny and Zack Lazega,
Emma and Grace Mailman.

To Mary Ann, my loving wife, for her endless support, and
to my patient daughters Hollie, Madison, Keagan, Cheyenne, and Averi.

To my beautiful and loving wife, Teresita, for her unconditional support
and love; to my sons, Manny and Danny, for their amusing questions;
and to my father and mother, Manuel and Carmen,
to whom I owe my existence and education.

To my wife, Meredith, for her never ending patience, support,
and love, and to my mother and father, Debby and Robert,
for their years of encouragement.

Contents

Foreword

Radio frequency identification seems, at first blush, very simple. A tag transmits a unique serial number via radio waves to an interrogator, or reader, allowing you to identify the object or person to which it is attached. But the more you get into RFID, the more you realize it is a complex technology—with different standards, frequencies and protocols, different applications and different data-sharing standards—that makes using it for business benefits a challenging endeavor.

In *RFID Applied*, the authors tackle this complex subject successfully, enabling business people to figure out how and where it can be used to improve efficiencies and increase sales. The book consists of three parts and two appendixes. Part A explains RFID. Early chapters in that part help readers get up to speed on the basics: They describe what RFID is, how it evolved, and the different characteristics of the various types of RFID technologies, including active (battery-powered) and passive (no battery) low-, high- and ultrahigh-frequency systems.

The rest of Part A goes into more depth, which will give readers the knowledge they need to begin a successful deployment. Some of the material is technical, but the strength of *RFID Applied* is the authors' refusal to gloss over some of the more complex aspects of RFID. Chapter 4, "Beyond the Basics," covers some technical material such as data modulation schemes and anticollision algorithms in clear, understandable language. Chapter 6, "The Business Case for RFID," explains the costs of RFID systems components and how to calculate the potential return on investment. It also offers a sample business case that is very instructive.

Chapter 7, "Industry Standards," explains the highly complicated web of standards bodies that have an influence on RFID systems. And Chapter 9, "Integration," provides valuable insights into how RFID systems are linked to corporate networks so they can feed the back-end software applications that make use of the data. The authors ably explain the importance of data logging, data filtering, synchronization and other networking tasks that are key to making an RFID system work.

As a bonus, the authors have included the invaluable Parts B and C. Part B explains how RFID is being applied in key industries: automotive, cattle ranching, health care, manufacturing, marine terminal operation, the military, payment transactions, retailing, transportation, and warehousing and distribution. While less in-depth than Part A of the book, Part B provides a high-level view for those who want to understand how RFID is being applied in specific industries.

Part C provides background information on RFID adoption in 10 countries: Australia, China, France, Germany, Japan, Singapore, South Korea, Spain, the United Kingdom and the United States. This overview gives readers a high-level view of what's happening with RFID globally.

RFID is truly a complicated subject, and *RFID Applied* does an excellent job of providing both high-level insights and the detailed information that businesspeople need to put RFID to work in their operations today.

Mark Roberti
Editor, *RFID Journal*

January 15, 2007

Preface

RFID Applied is just that. It's about the application of RFID. If you want a book about electrical and computer engineering you need another source. Let's say that you have been asked to lead an effort at your company to use RFID in your supply chain. You have heard about RFID because so much has been written on the topic since Wal-Mart and the US DoD made their proclamations that shippers attach RFID tags to their deliveries. This book is for you!

The book was written by three people with experience in the application of RFID to real life situations. A fourth author had a lot of experience writing books, and that was his contribution to the mix. In addition, many, many people from approximately twenty nations pitched in to help to complete this book in a timely fashion.

One of the authors is a frequent speaker on supply chain management. He noticed that, beginning in 2004, more and more of his PowerPoints had mention of RFID on them. So, discussion of RFID went from virtually zero at the beginning of 2004 to an hour by the beginning of 2005. The literature was filled with the birthing pains of extensive use of RFID (the evolution of standards, the lack of people with expertise in the area, the shakeout of the many providers, and so on.) He decided that a book on applications was needed. One thing led to another leading to this book.

The intended reader is a person with BS degree in engineering, science, management/business, or computer science. Computational aids are useful in only a few places. Mostly, what you will need is the ability to think in terms of systems, and some common sense.

The book is organized into three parts and two appendices. Part A is the textual material. There are ten chapters in Part A plus a short epilogue. We carry this theme of "ten" throughout the book. Part B discusses applications of RFID in ten areas. Part C describes RFID activity in ten nations of the world. Appendix A presents ten unique applications. Appendix B presents ten useful websites.

Consider Part A, the textual material. In Chapter 1, we set the stage for RFID, describing some systems that the reader may have encountered. We talk about the infrastructure of RFID; the tags, the readers, the middleware (i.e., software that is needed to make the system a reality). We provide a roadmap for implementing RFID.

In Chapter 2, we trace the roots back to radar, then going forward through the barcode era (which still exists and will continue to exist). Exchanging data between computers (EDI) is introduced. The internet makes it possible to accomplish global data synchronization using standards forwarded by the EPC Global Network.

Chapter 3 provides the basics of RFID. It is a primer on tags and readers. It discusses many kinds of tags. To use RFID properly please study this chapter thoroughly. For those interested in further depth, proceed to Chapter 4.

With so much interest in RFID, there have been lots of advances in hardware (readers and tags), software, and data collection & exchange. These advances are discussed in Chapter 5.

Much has been written in the literature about the return on investment (ROI), or, lack thereof, for using RFID. In Chapter 6, methods for computing the ROI are given. A thorough example helps in understanding the nuances of this computation.

In order for tags to communicate with readers throughout the world, standards have been developed. These standards continue to evolve. Chapter 7 discusses these standards.

Chapter 8 is a very thorough look at the components of an RFID system, and by extension, a business system. This chapter examines how the individual components work together.

Chapter 9 describes the various layers that make up a real world RFID solution and how each of these layers communicates with others. The chapter also addresses many of the issues faced with building an RFID system that can meet the needs of a large enterprise with discussions on system management, network layout, security, and data modeling.

There have been lots of challenges to RFID appearing in the popular media (even the daily news). People are concerned that their privacy or security will be invaded. Chapter 10 discusses issues associated with this situation.

The Epilogue contains a reprise; where we are in the rapidly evolving area of RFID as of the date of our writing. And, the Epilogue contains our vision of the future; where we believe RFID is headed.

The book has a website at www.RFIDAppliedBook.com. That website contains a lot of useful information. It is updated frequently by the authors. It will become the basis of the next edition of the book. (We hope that there are many editions of the book!) Please help us by using that website and providing information, feedback, and errata.

Jerry Banks
David Hanny
Manuel Pachano
Les Thompson

February 1, 2007

Acknowledgments

RFID Applied is an international effort. Contributors from some 20 nations made it possible. The authors want to thank those who have contributed so much time and effort to bringing the book to reality.

Chapter 4, "Beyond the Basics," was the combined effort of Manos Tentzeris, professor of Electrical and Computer Engineering, and his team from the Georgia Institute of Technology in Atlanta, Georgia. Professor Tentzeris is from Greece. The team consisted of Mr. Amin Rida, a graduate student from Lebanon; Mr. Antonio Ferrer-Vidal, a research engineer from Spain; Mr. Li Yang, a graduate student from China; Mr. Sabri Serkan Basat, a graduate student from Turkey; Mrs. Chika Umolu, an undergraduate student at the time of contribution and from Nigeria. Professor Tentzeris and his team also contributed to Chapter 10, "The Issue of Privacy and Security.

Chapter 7, "Industry Standards," was contributed by Yoon Seok Chang, professor of Air Transport, Transportation & Logistics at Korea Aerospace University, formerly Hankuk Aviation University. He is also a director of Ubiquitous Technology Application Research Center (UTAC) at HAU and Adjunct Professor, Department of Industrial Engineering, KAIST.

Part B, "Applications in 10 Areas," was coordinated by Professor Henry Lau, Department of Industrial and Manufacturing Systems Engineering, The University of Hong Kong, and his colleagues Bill Chan, Albert Ko, and Wilburn Tsang, as well as Vicky Wong from the Deutsche Bank AG, Hong Kong Branch.

Part C, "RFID Activities in 10 Countries," was coordinated by Wong Tack Wai at The Logistics Institute–Asia Pacific in Singapore. The 10 countries and the contributors are as follows:

RFID in Australia   BGee Shekar
                                   Neugen Solutions
                                   Sydney, Australia

RFID in China

Wang Shujun
Beijing Economic Information Centre
Beijing, China

Lin Zhuo
Beijing Bureau of Quality and Technical
     Supervision
Beijing, China

Wang Dong
Shanghai JiaoTong University
Shanghai, China

Tan Jie
Institute of Automation, Chinese Academy of
     Sciences
Beijing, China

Jason Liu
China EPC WG, China Association for
     Standardization
Beijing, China

RFID in France

Hervé Astier
Brooks Software, A division of Brooks
     Automation, Inc.
Drôme, France

RFID in Germany

André Hanisch
Fraunhofer Institute for Factory Operation and
     Automation
Magdeburg, Germany

RFID in Japan

Tatsuya Inaba
Keio University
Kanagawa, Japan

Jin Mitsugi
Keio University
Kanagawa, Japan

Jun Murai
Keio University
Tokyo, Japan

Shin'ichi Konomi
Center for Spatial Information Science, University
     of Tokyo
Tokyo, Japan

RFID in Singapore	Robert De Souza The Logistics Institute–Asia Pacific Singapore
	Mark Goh The Logistics Institute–Asia Pacific Singapore
	Wong Tack Wai The Logistics Institute–Asia Pacific Singapore
RFID in South Korea	Yoon Seok Chang Korea Aerospace University (Formerly Hankuk Aviation University) Hankuk, South Korea
RFID in Spain	Andrés García Higuera Engineering School, University of Castilla La Mancha Ciudad Real, Spain
RFID in the United Kingdom	Gabriel Fregoso Brooks Software Reading, United Kingdom (Currently: Zapopan, Jalisco, Mexico)
RFID in the United States	Gisele Bennett Georgia Tech Research Institute Georgia Institute of Technology Atlanta, Georgia

Appendix B, "10 Useful Web Sites," was contributed by Sergio Torres, Descartes Systems Group, Atlanta, Georgia. Sergio Torres is from Mexico.

Trademarks

Airbus is a registered trademark of Airbus Industries.

Aironet is a registered trademark of Cisco Systems, Inc.

American Express is a registered trademark of the American Express Company.

AMQM is a trademark of Lynsoe Systems.

BarrelTrak is a trademark of TagStream, Inc.

BizTalk is a registered trademark of Microsoft Corporation.

BMW is a registered trademark of Bayerische Motoren Werke AG.

Boeing is a trademark of the Boeing Management Company.

Campbell's is a registered trademark of the Campbell Soup Company.

CardWeb.com is a registered trademark of CardWeb.com, Inc.

ChartFX is a trademark of Software FX, Inc.

Checkpoint is a registered trademark, Checkpoint Systems, Inc.

Coca-Cola is a registered trademark of the Coca-Cola Company.

ContentMaster is a trademark of Itemfield, Inc.

Crystal Reports is a registered trademark of Business Objects SA.

Edgeware is a trademark of the GlobeRanger Corporation.

EPC (Electronic Product Code) is a trademark of EPCglobal.

EPCglobal, Inc. is a trademark of EPCglobal, Inc.

Excel is a registered trademark of Microsoft Corporation.

FedEx is a registered trademark of the FedEx Corporation.

GlobeRanger is a trademark of GlobeRanger Corporation.

Goodyear is a trademark of the Goodyear Tire & Rubber Company.

GS1 US is a trademark of GS1 US.

GTAG is a trademark of Uniform Code Council, Inc. and EAN International.

IBM is a registered trademark of the IBM Corporation.

ISO is registered trademark of ISO Properties, Inc.

Jetsons is a trademark of Hanna-Barbera Productions Incorporated.

KEELOQ is a registered trademark of Microchip Technology, Inc.

Marks & Spencer is a registered trademark of Marks and Spencer Group Plc.

MasterCard is a registered trademark of MasterCard International Incorporated.

McDonald's is the registered trademark of the McDonald's Corporation.

Microchip is a registered trademark Microchip Technology, Inc.

μ-Fiber Microwire is a trademark of Demodulation Inc.

NASCAR is a registered trademark of the National Association for Stock Car Racing, Inc.

NetWeaver is a registered trademark of SAP.

Nokia is a registered trademark of the Nokia Corporation.

Omron is a registered trademark of the Omron Tateisi Electronics Company.

Paramount Farms is a trademark of Paramount Farms Incorporated.

PeopleSoft is a registered trademark of Oracle Corp.

Philips is a registered trademark of Philips Semiconductors Incorporated.

Plexiglas is a registered trademark of Altuglas, International.

RadioShack is a trademark of the Radio Shack Corporation.

SAP is a registered trademark of SAP AG.

SAP NetWeaver is a registered trademark of SAP AG.

Self-Adaptive Silicon is a registered trademark of Impinj, Inc.

Sensormatic is a registered trademark, Sensormatic Electronics Corporation.

SkyeModule M0 is a trademark of SkyTek Incorporated.

SkyeModule M1 is a trademark of SkyTek Incorporated.

Speedpass is a trademark Exxon Mobil Corporation.

SUBWAY is a registered trademark of a registered trademark of Doctor's Associates Inc.

Tag-IT is a trademark of Texas Instruments, Inc.

Texas Instruments is a trademark of Texas Instruments Incorporated.

Uniform Code Council, Inc. is a trademark of GS1 US, Inc.

UPC (Universal Product Code) is a trademark of United Pan-Europe Communications.

Viagra is a registered trademark of Pfizer, Inc.

Visa is a registered trademark of Visa International.

Wal-Mart is a registered trademark of Wal-Mart Stores Incorporated.

WBIMB is a registered trademark of International Business Machines Corporation.

WebSphere is a registered trademark of International Business Machines Corporation.

WebSphere Business Integration Broker is a registered trademark of International Business Machines Corporation.

WebSphere RFID Device Infrastructure (WRDI) is a trademark of International Business Machines Corporation.

RFID Applied

The Stage Is Set

At some point in your life, you probably have used one of those credit-card-style security badges to gain entrance to a building, or driven past a toll road on one of those nonstop, boothless lanes. If so, you have experienced RFID applied.

1.1 What Is RFID?

In the simplest form, and as its name implies, radio frequency identification, or RFID, is the process and physical infrastructure by which a unique identifier, within a predefined protocol definition, is transferred from a device to a reader via radio frequency waves. It has taken many years of development to come up with a functional system, but the basic principle is not much different than that of the well-known barcode: Encode an identifier number in a machine-readable form that can be accessed quickly and reliably, with no human translation. However, it is not fair to say that RFID is just a glorified barcode transferred via radio frequency waves. The very nature of RFID, the fact that it is based on a microprocessor containing a data memory space, allows RFID chips to be applied in many instances that could not have been ever imagined with barcodes.

Imagine a world where a company has no problem finding inventory in a warehouse, or ensuring that the products it ships concur with the shipping order, or determining that the products received are all in the shipment, or avoiding stock-outs on the sales floor, or knowing the current stage of production of a particular product, or simply finding assets on its premises. This is the promise of RFID—a technology that can enable these situations to happen. If this is your idea of a perfect world, this book is for you, the business practitioner who needs to learn and understand how RFID can improve your business from a practical perspective.

The stage is set for RFID. In fact, it has been set for a while. People have been using RFID technology for many years, and mostly without noticing it. Everyday use of RFID technology has become common. It is so common, in fact, that until recently, many industries didn't even really think about its potential. It was a forgotten technology that had just a few, ubiquitous applications. Many businesses thought that the technology was either not robust enough for enterprise-wide deployment or not cost-effective enough to generate positive *returns on investments* (ROIs) in those deployments. The point of this book is to present a case of why this technology is important and how we see it changing the future of industry by supporting huge increases in automation, productivity, effectiveness, and cost-saving opportunities, eventually positively affecting the holy grail of the business world: a prosperous bottom line.

1.2 RFID Systems in the Real World

Before we get deep into the components that make up an RFID infrastructure, it will help to relate some examples of real-life implementation of RFID systems. As mentioned, RFID has been around for quite a while and there are many RFID applications that are used on a daily basis. Five of these are shown in the following paragraphs. Part B and Appendix A of this book go into greater detail about some of these, as well as other examples.

1.2.1 Toll Roads

This is probably one of the most common RFID applications used by millions of people on a daily basis. Many toll roads offer the option of a fast lane in which the driver does not have to stop at the toll booth to pay. Instead, the driver attaches a small device to (usually) the windshield that allows the driver to proceed through the fast lane at a reasonable speed (usually the speed limit). This small device, an *RFID tag*, is read by a *reader*, installed in the fast lane, as the car passes by (these terms are defined in the next section). The *reader* sends a signal to an *RFID-enabled system* with the unique identifier of the tag as well as other pertinent information such as date and time. This RFID-enabled system then uses a *database* to associate the tag identifier with the proper automobile and ultimately with the bill code associated with that automobile.

1.2.2 Newborn-Infant Tracking

Many hospitals have faced the erroneous swap of newborns with parents, creating great emotional distress for the parents as well as major legal liabilities. Some innovative hospitals started looking for a way to identify babies and to properly match them with their parents. RFID provides a great mechanism to ensure that the right baby is put in the arms of the right mother. Both the baby and the mother are affixed with a secure wristband that carries an RFID tag. The tag's unique identities are electronically associated with the baby and the mother at the time that the wristbands are put on (usually a few minutes after birth). From that moment until discharge time, the RFID wristbands are checked to ensure that the right baby is with the right mother.

1.2.3 High-Value Asset Tracking and Management

Although tracking every asset with RFID within, say, a warehouse, may be too daunting a task given today's technology, it may be very feasible to just track selected high-value items where the ROI of the RFID infrastructure makes sense. That is exactly what some companies are doing today. A good example of this is the recent move of some aerospace companies to start tagging high-valued engine components and tracking them not only within the manufacturing plants and warehouses but also in the field. The U.S. Navy has run pilot tests with a special type of RFID infrastructure that is capable of sensing temperature, humidity, and pressure. In these pilot tests, the Navy applied RFID tags to containers carrying high-valued engines in order to know not only their location within plants and warehouses but also to determine when the different characteristics (temperature, humidity, and pressure) changed outside the allowable tolerances. The RFID tags would send information to an asset management system whenever the sensors inside the containers detect a potentially dangerous situation; for example, too high a temperature or too high a humidity level. These pilot tests also proved the ability to transmit location information even when deployed in the field by being offered the capability of the RFID tags communicating with information systems via satellite or cell phone.

1.2.4 Gasoline Payment

A few major oil companies are bringing to market a new, more convenient way to pay for gas. This method employs an RFID tag with a unique identifier that is transferred to the pump via the RFID reader. Once the unique identifier has been read, the back-end information system matches this unique identifier and relates it to the person at the gas pump, providing all of the information to complete the sale. Preference information, such as to what credit card the consumer uses and whether or not the consumer wants a receipt, is stored in the consumer's profile and used at the point of sale (gas pump). Figure 1-1 shows Mobil's Speedpass.

1.2.5 Attraction-Park Children Positioning

A common problem that almost every parent has experienced to some degree is losing a child in a public venue. This is usually a very frightening situation. To alleviate this problem, some attraction parks have established a child-tracking system in which an RFID-enabled bracelet is placed on the child's wrist (see Figure 1-2). RFD readers strategically set throughout the park grounds provide complete coverage so that the child can be found

Figure 1-1 Exxon Mobil's Speedpass RFID solution (Courtesy of CardWeb.com, Inc.).

using various location determining methods (for example, triangulation). This information is secured by the park's information system and is provided only to the person responsible for the child.

1.3 RFID Systems—RFID Infrastructure

The simplest RFID system (or infrastructure, as it is commonly referenced) has three major components, as depicted in Figure 1-3:

- An RFID tag
- An RFID reader
- A predefined protocol definition (format) for the information transferred

Figure 1-2 RFID-based bracelets (Courtesy of Texas Instruments, Inc.).

Tag   Reader

Figure 1-3 Simple RFID system.

An optional component, based on the topology of the RFID infrastructure, is what is termed a *signpost* and is discussed in Section 1.3.3. Also, it is important to note that the third component is not a physical component but rather an agreed methodology that allows for the interpretation of the information transferred between the other two components (the RFID tag and reader).

Real-world systems are often more complex than that shown in Figure 1-5 in many respects. One of the promises of RFID is the ability to tie together different organizations, whether they are from within the same enterprise (for example, the manufacturing deparent and the distribution department of a company) or different enterprises (for example, suppliers and customers of an enterprise). The ability to have real-time information across these organizations can bring tremendous value to both parties, but this shared information must be understood by all participants of the information chain. To this effect, RFID systems must be expanded from the simplest form to incorporate other elements that enable the information chain.

These real-world systems employ one or more of the following components:

- RFID middleware and database
- RFID-enabled applications

The addition of these components enables an RFID solution that can interact with enterprise-wide as well as interenterprise information systems. Additionally, as the industry matures, RFID self-governing bodies lead the way for the creation of hardware, software, and data standards that increase the efficiencies of these components. Figure 1-4 shows the interaction of the components.

But before we get to the description of this collaborative environment, it is important to extend our depiction of the basic RFID system.

1.3.1 Tags

Let's start with the tag. The tag is composed of two essential elements and one optional component:

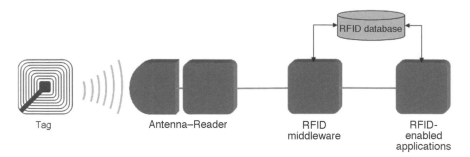

Figure 1-4 Extended RFID infrastructure.

- An integrated circuit,
- An antenna,
- Memory (optional)

The integrated circuit (or IC) contains a microprocessor, memory, and a transponder. The microprocessor processes the information coming from the reader and, at a minimum, accesses the memory to provide the unique identifier for the tag. On this topic, by definition, each tag contains a unique identifier within the predefined protocol definition that makes it different from every other tag in a specific set.

The antenna is used to communicate with the reader and extends the range of this communication. Antenna design varies quite drastically based on the environment and application of the tag. A good antenna design will enable proper communication between the tag and the reader, yielding a very reliable system. Conversely, poor antenna design or incorrect choice of antenna design may negate communication between these components, thus creating high levels of misreads (very poor reliability).

As we will see later in this chapter, some tags provide the ability to remember information sent by the reader. The memory is used for this purpose.

Tags come in three basic flavors:

- Passive tags
- Active tags
- Semi-active tags

They can also be read-only or provide read-write capability.

1.3.1.1 Passive Tags

Passive tags have no built-in power source. Power is provided by the radio frequency wave created by the reader that induces in the antenna a tiny but sufficient electrical current to activate the tag. When the tag comes into the range of the radio frequency wave field created by the reader, it uses that energy to power up its internal components and to communicate with the reader. The advantages of these tags are that they are inexpensive to manufacture, are very small in size, and require no internal power supply. The drawback is that the range of operation (in terms of the distance from the reader) is limited to only a few meters. Figure 1-5 shows various types of passive tags. The antenna configurations vary widely based on the application of the tag. Different configurations work differently based on the constraints of the environment in which the tag will be used. Much experimentation is required to design an effective antenna. In practice, this is usually performed on a trial-and-error basis.

1.3.1.2 *Active Tags*

Active tags have an internal power source (a battery) that provides the necessary power for the operation of the tag over a period of time. Because active tags beep (in their respective radio frequency) at specified intervals, the battery life is determined by the frequency of the beeps. The higher the beeping frequency (number of beeps in a given period), the shorter the battery life. These tags are constantly beeping (or "chirping," as it is commonly called) and therefore are not required to be within the power field of the reader to be detected. Because they use an internal battery, their signal strength is a lot higher than passive tags and therefore can be read from a further distance. This is one of the advantages of active tags. In open-field environments with minimal interference, active tags can be detected more than 1.5 km away from the reader. The downside of active tags is usually twofold: the cost and the size of the tag. Because they must have a self-contained power source, the cost of the tag is bounded on the lower end by the cost of the battery, which by itself is usually more than the cost of a passive tag. Similarly, the battery takes space, and therefore the tag

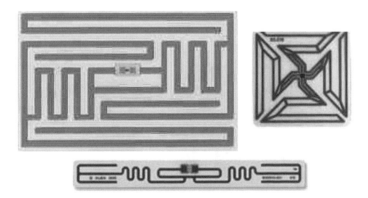

Figure 1-5 Passive RFID tags.

must allocate real estate for the battery. This increases its size dramatically when compared to a passive tag. Figure 1-6 depicts various active tags.

1.3.1.3 Semi-Active Tags

One of the problems with active tags is that their use is bounded by the life of the batteries that power them. Furthermore, frequently beaconing (or, chirping) reduces the life of the battery, so in environments where there is a need for real-time or pseudo-real-time reads, these tags may not last for a sufficient amount of time. A semi-active tag is a combination of a passive and an active tag. The passive component of the tag gets energized as it comes into the electromagnetic field of a reader. As it energizes, it triggers the active component of the tag to send an RFID signal. The benefit is that the battery is only used when triggered by the passive component of the tag, and it then returns to "sleep" mode after a predetermined amount of time, thus halting the battery drain. The signal travels further than if it were originated from a passive tag component, thus, the range of the tag is much higher.

1.3.1.4 Read/Write Tags

Another classification of RFID tags is whether they are *read-only* (RO) tags or they can be *read-write* (RW) tags. RO tags, as their name implies, can only be read by the reader. In other words, the communication between the

Figure 1-6 Active RFID tags (Courtesy of RF-Code, Inc.).

reader and the tag is unidirectional. These tags are encoded with their unique identity at manufacturing time or at initial setup time.

RW tags provide the capability of not only reading information from the tag by the reader but also the ability for the reader to send (write) information to the tag at any time. These types of tags contain a memory space used to store the information sent by the reader. This memory space can vary from just a few bytes to hundreds of kilobytes (KB) and much higher memory capacity is expected in the future.

Whether a tag is RO or RW depends primarily on the type of application in which it will be used. Some applications do not require the tag to hold any information, as it is only used as an identifier. Other applications require information, such as an asset maintenance history, to be maintained by the tag

1.3.2 Readers

Readers are the electronic components that transmit and/or receive the radio frequency waves used to communicate with the tags. Chapter 4 provides more information concerning the types of readers and the physics behind them, but for now it is important to put forth a basic understanding of readers and their components. A reader has two main elements:

- An antenna
- An IC board with at least
- A microprocessor
- Memory
- A radio frequency transponder

1.3.2.1 Antennas

Antennas are the required conduit to receive and transmit radio frequency waves. Much like the radio in a car requires an antenna to receive a signal, a reader must use the antenna to communicate with the tag. Antennas come in a variety of forms and are tuned for the specific environment in which they will be deployed. Figure 1-7 shows some different antenna configurations.

The critical importance of the use of the appropriate antenna cannot be understated in a specific environment for the success or failure of the communication between the tag and the readers. Many otherwise great RFID deployments have failed because of the selection of improper antennas.

1.3.2.2 Reader IC Board

The IC board in the reader processes the necessary information to communicate with the tag. It also uses its transponder to handle the radio frequency communication with the tags. There is a great deal of complexity associated with handling the communication with the tags. Because of this,

Figure 1-7 Different types of reader antennas (Courtesy of Texas Instruments, Inc.).

readers have microprocessors that allow them to handle a variety of situations when communicating with tags.

One of these situations is what is called a *collision*. A collision occurs when two tags are trying to communicate at exactly the same time with the reader. Since tags are self-contained entities that don't know about other tags (although this is not always true, as we will see when we discuss RFID self-forming networks later in the chapter), they send information to the reader on their own schedule. Because a reader only has one channel of communication, it must handle simultaneous communication (i.e., the collisions) in specific ways. We go into more detail on collisions in Chapter 4. As collision mechanisms develop over time, the microprocessor provides a versatile solution to handle this type of circumstance.

1.3.3 Signpost

A *signpost* is a special transmitter, usually using infrared technology, that can provide granular location information in an RFID infrastructure. Signposts came into being out of necessity. One of the current limitations of general RFID infrastructures is that it is very hard to pinpoint the location of tags due to what is called *RF signal bleeding*. To explain this, consider the following example. Assume that your RFID infrastructure spans multiple floors within a building. Because of the geography of the building, it may be impossible to stop RF signals from being read in the floors above and below a tag. In fact, in three-dimensional space, the closest reader to a tag may be located on the floor above or below it. In an RFID infrastructure, it is almost impossible to discern that a further reader on the same floor as the tag should be used as the correct reader instead of the reader on the floor above or below the tag.

To solve this problem, some vendors have devised a signpost that operates in the infrared spectrum as opposed to operating in the radio frequency spectrum. One very important characteristic of infrared signals is that they require line of sight to be detected—think of a typical TV remote control; if you put your hand in front of its infrared light-emitting bulb, you cannot control the TV. The advantage of the signpost is that it is very inexpensive, so you can put them in many locations in an RFID infrastructure. The tags can read the signal being emitted by the signpost and append it to their ID, thus telling the reader where the tag is. Since infrared requires line of sight, as long as the signpost is enclosed in a "room" (the field covered by the reader), the RFID infrastructure can discern, with granularity, where tags are located.

1.3.4 RFID Information

Traditionally, different vendors of RFID solutions had different methodologies for communicating between readers and tags. Every vendor created what was thought to be the most efficient and complete mechanism for communication. The result was that readers and tags from different vendors could not communicate, thus limiting the possibility of creating complex RFID solutions. In the last few years, several organizations have attempted to create a single standard of communication to facilitate the rapid growth of RFID solutions. Entities such as Massachusetts Institute of Technology's (MIT) Auto-ID lab and the ISO Standards body have provided a platform where teams of RFID providers and users come together to create a standard for interindustry RFID communication. This is thought to be the only means by which RFID can penetrate industrial solutions on a major scale. These standards address many, if not all, aspects of RFID communication, from how the reader and the tags communicate with each other to what information is provided by the RFID infrastructure to the consumer applications.

1.3.4.1 EPC Standards

The Electronic Product Code (EPC) standard was developed by the Auto-ID Center at MIT with the collaboration of academic and industry personnel and currently administered by EPCglobal, Inc. The standard provides a mechanism to uniquely identify every product ever manufactured or to be manufactured. The commonly known Universal Product Code (UPC) provided a mechanism to uniquely identify every *type* of product manufactured but did not allow for the identification of every instance of each of the product types. The EPC does provide for the identification of every instance.

As one can imagine, there are billions, if not trillions of products manufactured in the world (imagine every can of soda, shoe, pencil, and so forth having its own unique EPC numbers). So, the protocol definition to uniquely identify each product must account for the large number of diverse products and instances. To do this, the EPC standard cleverly partitions the manufacturer and product number in a way that is compact and sensible. The key to this protocol definition is the centralized body that dispenses the EPC numbers according to the predefined protocol, much like the GS1 US dispenses the UPC numbers. Figure 1-8 shows an example of an EPC encoding schema. The standards are discussed in much greater detail in Chapter 7.

1.3.4.2 ISO Standards

Another global body in charge of providing different types of industry standards is the well-known International Organization for Standardization (ISO®). This organization, made up of over 140 members from over 90 nations, provides nation-neutral standards that help people from all continents do business with each other on a common platform. ISO has been working on RFID for years; it has released and is currently working on standards to define the communication protocol of RFID components as well as data elements and data interfaces for dealing with RFID information.

Many European businesses opt for ISO as an alternative to what is perceived by some as a U.S.-biased organization, EPCglobal, Inc. However, there is a movement within these organizations to provide a unified standard for true worldwide cooperation.

1.3.5 Self-Forming RFID Networks

A special type of RFID network infrastructure is what's called a *self-forming network.* This infrastructure is made up of tags that can act, beyond their normal capabilities, as relay transceivers that can not only transmit their own information but also relay the information they receive from other tags, thus extending the reading range.

Figure 1-9 shows a pictorial representation of a self-forming network. What is unique about these RFID infrastructures is that the self-forming network can recognize a tag when it comes into the "read" field of the infrastructure, since the tags have the capability to, by using a predefined protocol, recognize other tags and relay their information. The result of this

Figure 1-8 EPC-based information (Courtesy of EPC Global).

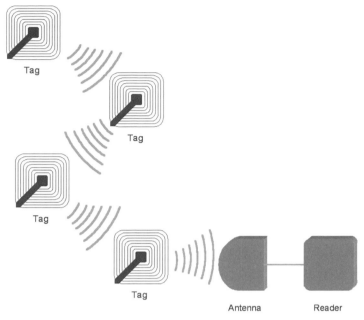

Figure 1-9 Self-forming network.

is that the actual read range of the RFID infrastructure can be extended if there are tags that can relay the information of themselves as well as other tags.

1.3.6 RFID Middleware and Database

Middleware refers to the software component in charge of converting low-level RFID hardware information into usable event information. In other words, the middleware component interfaces with the RFID hardware components (i.e., the readers) and is responsible for translating machine information into information related to tag events. Tag event information refers to the logical events that are mapped to the actual physical events. Although different RFID systems can handle different types of events, there is at least one event that is universal to all RFID systems: "Tag seen by a reader."

This particular event signals the fact that the reader detected a tag. The tag ID is the minimum information reported by the middleware. Usually, this information is also combined with other useful information, such as:

- Tag ID
- Reader ID
- Date/time stamp

The middleware acts as the standard mechanism of communication with readers. This is important because it allows computer information systems and applications to use a higher-level communication methodology with the RFID infrastructure without having to understand the lower-lever issues required to communicate with the RFID hardware.

More sophisticated RFID systems can handle others events. For example:

- Status of tag memory
- Tag sensor information (assumes sensors embedded in tag)
- Tag battery level (applicable to active tags)
- Tag position (assumes GPS or other location feed)
- Tag into zone
- Tag out of zone

Another benefit of middleware components is that they provide for the use of one single mechanism to communicate with different RFID infrastructures. For example, some RFID applications require the capability of deploying both active and passive tags into an environment to provide the proper data capture level. Middleware allows the receiving information systems to just use a single communication protocol to talk to both types of RFID infrastructures. This greatly reduces the IT requirements for this type of RFID solution.

Because RFID systems tend to generate huge amounts of tag event information, it is important to provide a mechanism that allows asynchronous communication with the RFID system. The middleware component makes use of an RFID database to keep track of the different types of tag events generated by the infrastructure and then to analyze correlated events to provide higher-level logical events. An example of this may be the "tag into zone" event. This is in reality a logical event that is composed of a sequence of physical events.

To illustrate this example, let's assume that we want to know when an active tag, beeping at an interval of once every two seconds, came into a specific zone. Furthermore, let's assume that this zone is defined by a room that is 100 percent covered by a reader. Figure 1-10 shows a picture of this scenario. When the tag is out of the room, the reader cannot detect anything and thus reports nothing. As soon as the tag enter the room, the reader informs the middleware that Tag X has been seen. In our example, the reader will detect the beep from the tag every two seconds and will report that information to the middleware (every two seconds). If the tag is left in the room for a period of 10 hours, the reader would have sent 18,000 messages (30 messages/minute × 60 minutes/hour × 10 hours) to the middleware telling it that it saw the tag all of those times. An information system is probably not ready to handle that kind of volume of data, nor is it interested in handling it. The middleware can greatly improve this process by being a bit smart and providing just the logical information of interest to the information system—that is, an asset went into the room. As long as

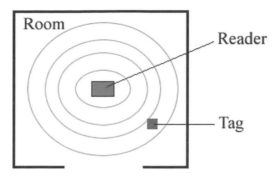

Figure 1-10 "Tag into zone" event.

the tag is still in the room, it is not really necessary to keep telling the information system that the tag it is still in the room, unless, of course, the information system is interested in verifying that the tag is indeed in the room.

The "tag into zone" event is composed of the following physical events:

- A tag is detected by a reader covering a zone.
- The tag continues to be detected by the same reader for some period of time.

In this case, the middleware is probably using the RFID database to check the tag id and the date/time stamp received from the reader and comparing it against what is in the database. For example, assume that the same tag had been seen by the same reader within the last few instances, but it had not been seen previously. It can be assumed that the tag came into the zone, thus reporting a "tag into zone" event to the information system. From then on, the "seen" event reported by the same tag, can be properly ignored and not communicated to the information system. So, in this example, the information system would only receive one message from the middleware ("tag into zone"), as opposed to 18,000 messages stating that reader Y saw tag X.

1.3.7 RFID-Enabled Applications

In actuality, RFID applications are not truly part of an RFID infrastructure but rather the recipient of the information provided by the RFID infrastructure. However it is important to mention them in this section, since these applications are the consumers of the information and act upon this information. These applications could be any system that uses the RFID information and processes it in some way. Following are examples of these:

- Warehouse management systems (WMS)
- Transportation management systems (TMS)

- Production scheduling systems
- Order management systems (OMS)
- Order entry systems (OES)
- Inventory management systems
- Asset management systems

These applications must be written (or re-written, in many cases) to accept real time data pertinent to the RFID infrastructure.

1.4 RFID in the Enterprise

With the basics of RFID explained, practitioners of industry will demand to know how and where does RFID fit in the enterprise. As illustrated in Section 1.2, there are already many applications where RFID creates a lot of value, whether by providing a cost savings opportunity, improving service levels, or actually increasing revenue.

Before implementing an RFID solution, there are many questions that must be answered. Business managers will want to consider, among other items:

- Compatibility of the solution with the environment
- The potential ROI
- The risk factors associated with using new or newer technology
- The IT capability to handle RFID-generated massive volumes of data
- The state of readiness of systems interacting with the RFID solution (or, infrastructure)
- Applicability of the RFID solution as opposed to other less technically challenging solutions

In many instances an RFID solution will be much more appropriate if combined with other technologies, such as bar codes, in order to provide a fail-safe, redundant solution. In other instances, RFID solutions may not be the most appropriate because of environmental, economic, or safety reasons. The point is that in every instance a detailed feasibility analysis must be conducted in order to determine the viability of an RFID solution. This section contains a list of questions and issues that should help the practitioner determine if RFID is the most appropriate solution for the problem at hand.

1.4.1 Why, When, and Where RFID?

The three basic questions to determine whether RFID should be considered as a potential solution are *why, when,* and *where* should an enterprise deploy

RFID. These are considered "strategic" questions, and their answers should be clearly understood before asking the operational questions of *how* should the enterprise deploy an RFID solution? They are considered strategic because their responses will dictate whether or not an enterprise will embark into a, more than likely, long-term project that will require considerable (and specialized) resources, money, and time. If these answers are not clearly understood before commencing the project, project members will face uncertainty throughout the project and the possibility of project failure increases rather dramatically. The *how* question should be a surrogate to the strategic questions. It is not to say that it is any less important, but it is not sufficient. To illustrate this point, think of an asset-tracking project where the price of the tags is too high compared to the products being tracked. In this case, an implementation engineer may know exactly how to implement the RFID-based asset tracking solution, but it would not make sense from an ROI point of view.

Although *why, where,* and *when* questions are a good staring point, they should be broken down into more detailed questions for proper analysis. The following is a list of questions that expands on these strategic questions and is useful in making a high-level determination on the viability of an RFID solution:

- What is the value provided by the RFID solution?
  - Cost reduction
  - Revenue generation
  - Productivity or process improvement
  - Marketing differentiator
  - Service improvement
  - Vendor/supplier mandate
  - Quality assurance
- Do individual objects need to be uniquely identified?
  - If there is no need to track objects, it may be doubtful that an RFID solution would be useful.
- Is the environment where objects need to be tracked a closed-loop environment or an open environment?
  - This may dictate the type of RFID technology to be used in terms of the infrastructure required.
- Is there a need for real time or near-real-time data capture?
  - If not, there may be other less sophisticated solutions that may provide the necessary results at a lower cost.
- What are the physical characteristics of the objects to be tracked?
  - Characteristics such as size, liquid content, metal content radio frequency interference, and others will dictate the type of RFID solution to be used.

- What is the universe of objects to be tracked?
  - How many?
  - What types?
  - Over what area?
- Are the interfacing information systems able to handle massive volumes of RFID-based information?
  - Typically, RFID systems generate huge amounts of information for processing by other systems. It is important to understand how these other systems will face such amounts of data.

As we will see in Chapter 6, one of the most important steps in the determination of the applicability of RFID solutions is the computation of the ROI. This is many times an elusive subject, since the components of the computation are sometimes soft (qualitative) and sometimes hard (quantitative). This is especially true when the benefits of an RFID solution are more qualitative than quantitative, as, for example, in the case of improved customer service or marketing differentiation.

1.4.2 A Road Map to Implementation

The implementation of an RFID solution deals primarily with the *how* question. Once the strategic questions (*why, where,* and *when*) have been clearly addressed, the implementation teams must put in place a project plan that will cover every aspect of the installation and operation of the RFD solution. As any other project, implementing an RFID solution requires detailed analysis of the problem at hand and the proposed solution. The following is a high-level implementation guideline:

- *Identification of problem at hand*
  - Documentation of problem characteristics and issues
  - Identification of parties involved in the problem (vendors, customer, partners, etc.)
  - Identification of the environment involved in the problem (physical characteristics of environment)
    - High metal content; this will create interference and limit the range of RFID.
    - High water or liquid content; water, or liquids for that matter, block and deflect radio frequencies, this increases misreads of RFID signals.
    - High radio frequency areas; areas in which there is a high concentration of electro-magnetic waves (microwaves, radio-broadcasting, TV signal emitters, etc.) will create interference with the RFID signal thus limiting the reliability of the system.
    - Areas where there is radio wave sensitive equipment, such as medical telemetry equipment, electronically controlled explosives, sen-

sitive navigation systems, and so forth, can be affected by RFID signals.
  - All these will have a profound effect on the type of RFID solution applicable.
- Identification of IT systems involved in the problem (input, output, consumer, and transactional IT systems and interfaces)
- Identification of high-risk issues
  - Time-driven constraints related to infrastructure deployment-building requirements, if any
- *Business case analysis*
  - Identification of cost components
  - Identification of benefits
  - ROI analysis
- *Definition of solution implementation team*
  - Business process owners
  - User representative members
  - Information technology members
  - Facilities manager members
  - Vendor/provider members
- *Design of solution*
  - Documentation of solutions components
    - Infrastructure specification (wired, wireless, mixed)
    - Readers (with associated hardware)
    - Tags (with associated hardware)
    - Antennas (with associated hardware)
    - Custom casing for components
    - Cabling
    - Wireless equipment
    - Power requirements and power supply points
    - Computer hardware such as servers, backups, uninterruptible power supplies
    - Local or wide area network requirements (port drops, etc.)
    - Communication requirements (satellite, cell-phone, etc.)
  - Documentation of business process requirements
    - Process changes
    - Process additions
    - Process eliminations
  - RFID event definitions
    - One of the most important aspects of an RFID solution is the issue of what events need to be tracked.
  - Definition and documentation of IT requirements and interfaces
    - Data generation systems—systems that provide information to the RFID infrastructure
    - RFID database contents—systems that maintain transient RFID event information

- RFID history data warehouse—systems that maintain historical RFID event information
- Processing systems—systems that convert or enhance RFID event information
- RFID data consuming systems—systems that utilize RFID event information to provide decision support capability
- Catalog of vendors available for RFID solution
  - This may be the hardest task given the fact that the industry is in its infancy. Market hype tends to be emphasized over practical experience, although many of the RFID solutions deployed are the first of their kind.
- *Pilot test phase—Selection of problem subset to test solution*
  - Definition of pilot test's objectives. The pilot test may have multiple objectives, for example:
    - Testing of new technology or multiple competing technologies
    - Testing of coverage area
    - Testing of environmental fit; how well does the RFID solution work in a specific environment?
    - Testing of system reliability
    - Testing of system interfacing
    - Testing of data processing scalability (given the huge amounts of data produced by the RFID infrastructure)
  - Definition of pilot's scope such as
    - Objects to track
    - Coverage area
    - Events
    - Interfacing information systems
    - Personnel
    - Business processes
  - Setup of baseline against which results will be measured
    - This process is extremely important to understanding the success or failure of the pilot test. This also dictates the clear definition (as stated previously) of the pilot test's objective.
- *Adjustment of solution based on pilot test's feedback*
  - Stress test solution for abnormal situations
    - Power failure
    - Network failure
    - Server failure
    - Extraneous tags
    - Reader failure
    - Tag failure
  - Adjustment of infrastructure (antenna positioning, reader strength and setting, tag enclosures, etc.)
- *Roll out of solution in phased approach*
  - Schedule of rollout:

- Personnel
- Coverage area
- Products tagged
- Events tracked
- Business process change requirements
- *Normal operation*
  - Continuous improvement methodology

Past, P... Fu...

plane's radio transponder. If the air-
...s expected to transmit a reply to the
...de that identified the incoming air-
...responded with the wrong code or
...tish military would consider the in-
...t (Wikipedia, 2005c). The IFF system
...fire between airplanes and between
...is still in use today by most military
...more data is transmitted than a sin-
...same as it was in the 1940s.
...pplication of radio communications
...id-1900s. Engineers quickly learned
...d receive radio waves, and with this
...gineer was born. Most engineers re-
..."black art" due to the inherent com-

Some form of Radio Frequency Ide...f RF technology caused by dynamic
longer than most realize. It all began...gnetic fields. As with most challeng-
laid the foundation for RFID by refi...rld tackled this new technology head
netism and creating new ways of co...ed a paper entitled "Communication
able advancements in and outside o...an discovered that radio waves could
into what we today recognize as RF...y to power a remote transmitter. The

As RFID exists today, we have d...omagnetic energy harvested from the
tified numerous applications for the...f and generate a radio transmission
RFID may evolve into something tha...ry is the foundation for today's pas-
day, our understanding of the fund...
applications are conceived. ...peded the development of practical

This chapter will discuss the pro...tag could become the device as we
discovery of the fundamental princip...to be made in the field of electronics.
most forward thinking applications...at Bell Labs by John Bardeen, Walter
RFID do not stand alone, and there a...pedia, 2005d). In 1948, Raytheon Cor-
nologies and standards that will als...ally available CK722 contact transistor
...the transistor paved the way for the
...lutionized circuit etching technologies.
...bled the development of small, and

2.1 Traditional Uses of ...ID tags.

...le to design and implement practical
James Clerk Maxwell (1831 to 1879), ...ag was in a manageable form factor.
published the first theories on elect...ns were related to security and sur-
Electricity and Magnetism" in 1873 ...spring up in the late 1960s and early
built upon the collective works of ...(EAS) is one of the most basic appli-
Maxwell's formulas are referred to ...y transmit an "I am here" signal when
tions accurately describe the phenom...to the RF energy source to power the
well theorized that electromagnetic ...es not uniquely identify an asset, but
in the form of a wave. In 1888, the G...is in a certain location given the EAS
(1857 to 1894) was the first to prove...(Landt and Catlin, 2001). These appli-

cations are in use today in almost any business where merchandise shrinkage can be a problem. EAS tags can be found in books, in compact disc cases, and attached to clothing. These tags trigger an alarm or notify store security when they are detected at one of the store's exits. In EAS solutions, the power source is usually in a portal configuration in which a high-gain antenna is placed on each side of the exit. When the tag passes between the two antennas, the tag receives enough power to transmit the "I am here" signal, which triggers the alarm. EAS has also been applied to monitoring assets such as munitions and personnel. The first commercial EAS applications were developed by two companies, Checkpoint® and Sensormatic®, in the late 1960s and early 1970s. Both Checkpoint and Sensormatic are still major players in the EAS solution market.

Even though RFID tags and readers were successfully being built and used throughout the 1960s, they were not very practical because of their size. RFID technology became more practical when Intel Corporation introduced the 4004 microprocessor in 1971. The Intel 4004 was the world's first single-chip microprocessor. Although the Intel 4004 did not revolutionize RFID components overnight, the microprocessor did spark a technological revolution. The race was on to build smaller and faster integrated circuits. The speed at which microchip manufacturing and design knowledge advanced was on an exponential scale. Engineers could not get enough of these small, versatile chips. With this new technology in their tool belts, engineers were now able to build more sophisticated RFID solutions than they had even dreamed about just a few years earlier. As microprocessors became smaller and smaller, RFID tags and readers became more and more advanced. New tags were built with peripheral functionality such as temperature and humidity sensors and extra onboard memory for storing information other than an identification number.

In 1978, Matt Lezin and Tom Wilson successfully implanted RFID tags under the skin of dairy cows. The tags they employed contained peripheral functionality in addition to standard identification. Their tags could not only identify a cow but could also measure and transmit its body temperature. A cow implanted with one of these tags could be monitored for possible health issues, ovulation cycles, and feeding patterns (Eagle, 2002). Since Lezin and Wilson tagged the first cow, a wide variety of animals have been tagged including fish, monkeys, cats, and dogs. Many pet owners have traded their pet's metal identification tags for a subdermal microchip tag, and many city governments are now mandating that pets be electronically tagged. Today, these tags can store more than a pet's identification number. The most advanced tags can store a pet's unique identifier, name, address, and vaccination record.

The United States Department of Defense (DoD) was the first major entity to throw fuel on the RFID fire. The DoD was one of the early adopters of the technology because of potential logistics rewards. The first DoD field trials tagged assets at the shipping container level. Containers are logistical units that contain collections of items to be transported. Containers may be loaded on a ship and then dumped on a beachhead with a platoon. It was believed that container-level granularity would result in a huge logistics advantage in both war and peace. As the tags became more sophisticated, so did the ways in which the DoD utilized the technology. More advanced tags with onboard memory could be updated to report a container's manifest when queried. Both handheld and portable readers could not only identify the container but interrogate its contents.

Investigation and adoption of RFID in the commercial sector came after the DoD started using the technology. With the computer revolution, the world became a lot smaller and businesses were feeling the impact. The information age allowed companies to conduct business easily with customers and suppliers in other parts of the nation and around the world. Orders and sales volume were up, and supply chain and order fulfillment logistics became more and more important as the information age increased the pace of business. Barcodes filled the gap for many years, but now industries are beginning to recognize the benefits of RFID and the real-time capabilities that it offers. Companies like Gillette helped pioneer RFID in the retail space by making large contributions to the Auto-ID Center at MIT. When Wal-Mart mandated that its top 100 suppliers must provide RFID-tagged containers by the end of 2006, the retail world quickly took notice. Soon after Wal-Mart's mandate, many other companies such as Best Buy followed suit. Even though Wal-Mart was the first retail giant to make such a mandate, it was not the first, non-DoD company to implement RFID. Companies around the world have field-tested and implemented RFID solutions ranging from food produce monitoring to hospital workflow management.

Highway 407 in Toronto, Canada, was the first fully electronic toll road. It was completed in 1991 by Raytheon Company. Motorists that use the 407 Express Toll Route have a transponder installed in their vehicle. The transponder is really nothing more than an RFID tag. The transponder replies to queries received from readers placed along the toll road. As a vehicle travels along the highway, the vehicle will pass near the toll readers. These readers request the tag's identification number, which is associated with the car and, most importantly, a bank account. The associated bank account is automatically debited the toll amount as the motorist makes use of the highway. The Canadian Ministry of Transportation has also installed video cameras along the highway as a fail-safe method to capture an image of any vehicle's license plate that does not have a transponder installed or if the transponder is malfunctioning. Raytheon Company was not the first to think of this application. In May of 1974, Fred Sterzer of RCA filed a U.S. patent (#4,001,822) entitled "Electronic license plate for motor vehicles." Oklahoma opened the first hybrid electronic toll road in 1991, and it utilized electronic identification technology for express lane tolls only and collected all other tolls through traditional tollbooths. Since 1991, many hybrid toll roads have been opened, but the opening of a 100 percent electronic toll road is a testament to the reliability of the technology.

2.2 Comparison to Barcodes

As RFID quietly matured for over 30 years, another technology revolutionized supply chain management and logistics in general. This technology was the barcode. Today, everyone takes the barcode for granted, but without barcodes, almost every business market in the world would move at a snail's pace.

2.2.1 History

The Smithsonian Institute in Washington, D.C., has a pack of Wrigley's chewing gum on display (Tracey, 2005). This pack of gum is the first barcode labeled product ever scanned by a barcode reader. This momentous event occurred in June 26, 1974, at Marsh's supermarket in Tory, Ohio (Adams Communications, 2005).

Barcodes proliferated to virtually every industry on the globe, and the barcode became a world-changing technology. Much like RFID, the barcode was invented years before it was implemented in a commercial solution. U.S. patent #2,612,994 was issued on October 7, 1952, to Bernard Silver and Norman Joseph Woodland. The patent was entitled "Classifying apparatus by method." Four years earlier, Silver and Woodland began investigating how to automatically identify a product in a checkout line after Silver overheard a conversation between one of the deans at Drexel Institute of Technology, in Philadelphia, and a local food chain owner (Adams Communications, 2005). Twenty-two years later the first barcode was scanned.

2.2.2 Basics

A barcode is nothing more than data encoded into an image. The image employs high-contrast regions, such as black lines on a white background, to represent the encoded data. Virtually any type of data can be encoded in a barcode including unique identification numbers and text. When a barcode is scanned, it is translated from a printed or etched image on a product or piece of paper to a digital format that can be used by a computer. The first step in scanning a barcode is to transfer the image into a computer or handheld device for processing. There are many different types of devices that can scan a barcode. These devices include (TechTarget, 2006) described as follows:

1. *Pen wand.* A pen wand works by placing the pen at one end of the barcode and then sliding the pen, at a constant rate, to the opposite

side. It is important to note that the pen wand must be moved at a constant rate in order to read the barcode accurately and efficiently.

2. *Slot scanner.* The slot scanner works much like the pen wand except that the item to be scanned slides over a stationary scanner. The item to be scanned slides through a scanning slot that ensures the item is positioned correctly. As with the pen wand, the barcode may not be recognized accurately if the item is not slid through the slot at a constant rate.

3. *Camera.* The camera takes a picture of the barcode, and then image processing software decodes the image. Cameras are much better than the previous two devices because a camera can read the barcode at any orientation and the image may be sampled many times by taking multiple pictures of the barcode. Each decoded image can then be compared against the other samples to identify faulty reads and, thus, reduce errors.

4. *CCD (charge-coupled device).* CCD barcode readers work much like cameras in that they are essentially taking a picture of the barcode. The difference is that CCD works by counting photons, or units of light. The CCD is divided into a grid of photon collectors. By processing the photon saturation at each grid point, the CCD can determine which parts of the image are dark and which are light. The CCD is much cheaper than a camera and can sample the barcode image faster. The CCD scanner is most times preferable over the camera scanner.

5. *Laser.* A laser scanner is what most people think of when they imagine a barcode reader because it is employed in most grocery store checkout lanes. The laser scanner is the most mechanically advanced reader in that it has more moving parts than all the other devices. A laser reader uses a vibrating mirror to sweep the laser's focal point across the barcode. The darker regions absorb more of the laser light than the lighter regions. The reader samples the reflected light as the laser sweeps across the barcode image to determine the contrasting areas of the image; less reflected light equates to a darker part of the image and more reflected light equates to a lighter part of the image. Laser scanners can read barcodes more than 6 m away depending on their focal length and the barcode's size.

2.2.3 Barcode Standards

The contrasting regions of a barcode can be arranged in many different image formats. The first image format created by Silver and Woodland was a bull's-eye shape. Today, most barcodes come in one of two basic formats—one-dimensional or two-dimensional—and there are also two types of two-dimensional barcodes: matrix and stacked. Figures 2-1, 2-2, and 2-3 are barcode encodings of the text "RFID Applied".

RFID Applied

Figure 2-1 Code 128B 1D barcode created with Barbecue.

Barcodes also have multiple data formats encoded into the image. Figure 2-1 is in Code 128B format, Figure 2-2 is in PDF417 format, and Figure 2-3 is in Quick Response (QR) format. A Code 128B formatted barcode can encode alphanumeric data of variable length, and a PDF417 formatted barcode can encode up to 1.1 kilobytes of data. Some barcodes, such as the QR barcode, can be damaged such that up to 30 percent of the image is completely gone and no data will be lost (Denso Wave, 2003). Many other formats exist for different applications of the barcode. Most barcode scanners today can read multiple encodings. The most common barcode format in North America is the Universal Product Code format, and it is used for retail product identification. UPC was the barcode format printed on the pack of Wrigley's gum mentioned earlier. The International Article Numbering (IAN) system, formerly known as the European Article Number (EAN), is the international equivalent to the UPC.

For any proposed system to become a standard it must be regulated by a standards body. There are two organizations that regulate barcode standards. The organization that regulates the format and issuing of barcodes in the United States is the GS1 US™ organization. GS1 US was formally known as the Uniform Code Council, Inc.® (UCC). The GS1 organization, formally known as EAN International, is the global counterpart to GS1 US. The GS1/GS1 US organization is also referred to as the EAN-UCC system. The EAN-UCC system developed the Global Trade Identification Number (GTIN). The GTIN is a family of global data structures that includes all UCC/EAN standardized barcodes. The standardization of barcode formats allowed the barcode to become the global technology that it is today. RFID must achieve the same level of standardization if it is to become a global force equivalent to that of the barcode.

GS1 formed EPCglobal, Inc., specifically for RFID standardization and assignment of unique identifiers for RFID tags. The EPCglobal, Inc. standards are discussed in more detail in Chapter 7. EPCglobal, Inc. created a standard format called the Electronic Product Code (EPC) for RFID tags that is to serve as the base format for RFID tag data. The EPC is a meta-coding scheme that is designed to meet the needs of many differ-

Figure 2-2 PDF417 2D barcode created with Barbecue.

Figure 2-3 QR Code barcode created with QR Draw Pro.

ent industries (EPCglobal, 2005a). The EPC standard is somewhat backward-compatible with the standard GTIN format. EPC accommodates the standard GTIN by creating a Serial GTIN (SGTIN). The legacy GTIN only identifies a class of products, while an SGTIN adds an encoded serial number to uniquely identify an individual product (EPCglobal, 2005a). The EPC standard provides for backward compatibility with many of the legacy barcode formats.

2.2.4 Speed

Some of the most advanced RFID readers can identify up to 60 different RFID tags at approximately the same time, while a barcode reader can identify only one item at a time. The ability to sample many RFID tags in the same time period it takes to scan one barcode can greatly save time and increase throughput for most logistical processes.

2.2.5 Visibility

An even more amazing fact is that an RFID reader does not need a direct line of sight to read tags. The RFID reader can even be located in a completely different room than the tags it is reading. There are types of materials through which an RF signal cannot pass. Materials that are impervious to RF signals are said to be opaque to RF, while those materials that allow RF signals to pass through are transparent to RF. RF waves that operate at different frequencies can penetrate different types of materials. This concept is explained in more detail in Chapters 3 and 4.

Unlike RFID, barcode technology must be able to physically "see" the barcode image in order to retrieve the encoded data. The concepts of opaque and transparent materials are directly applicable to the light emitted by a barcode scanner because light also travels in the form of a wave. Because light cannot pass through objects such as walls, cardboard, or paper, the barcode scanner must have line of sight to the barcode image if it is to successfully reflect light off of the barcode.

2.2.6 Implementation

Barcodes are a globally proven technology that is easy to use, and barcodes are fairly cheap compared to RFID tags and infrastructure required to support an RFID-based solution. Barcodes have an advantage over RFID tags in that the data encoded into the barcode is usually printed underneath the barcode image (see Figure 2-1). A user does not need any special equipment to pick up a can of soup and read the UPC printed on the back, but special RFID reader hardware must be used to read an RFID tag's data. The ultimate solution would be to label all RFID tags with a barcode that mirrors the RFID tag's data. Using this technique, a logistical process becomes even more flexible by enabling practitioners to read RFID tagged products using an RFID reader, pick up a single product and scan it with a barcode scanner, or simply read the number printed under the barcode. As with any new technology, there are growing pains. Architecting business solutions where barcodes and RFID work together will allow businesses to more easily migrate to new RFID-centric business processes while maintaining backward compatibility and overall flexibility.

2.2.7 Cost

The cost comparison between RFID and barcodes can be staggering initially before the return on investment is understood. It is easy to compare barcode versus RFID hardware costs, but the return on investment is a complex issue. Chapter 6 covers the business case for RFID in detail. Barcode technology has become a ubiquitous technology that equates to a very competitive market for barcode hardware. Most barcode hardware is sold at competitive prices. This is not the case with RFID readers. Readers are sophisticated pieces of hardware with several integrated internal components such as digital signal processors, general-purpose microprocessors, and sensitive RF transceivers. This level of advanced technology comes with a price.

RFID tag prices versus barcode label prices are exponentially different for two basic reasons. First, RFID tags incorporate some advanced electronics, while a barcode is nothing more than ink on a piece of paper. Second, creating an RFID tag is much more expensive than printing a barcode. A piece of paper and a low-cost black-and-white printer is all that is needed to create a barcode. In contrast, the most basic RFID tag has a very small integrated circuit and an antenna. Beyond the hardware is any software that operates the integrated circuit. Most RFID tags have a barcode printed on them.

Table 2-1 shows a high-level overview of the five comparisons made earlier in this chapter.

2.3 Electronic Data Interchange

The statement "the world is getting smaller every day" has become somewhat of a cliché, but it has never been truer when RFID is considered.

Table 2-1 RFID to Barcode Comparison

	Speed	Range	Visibility	Implementation	Cost
Barcode	One at a Time	< 6 meters	Line of Sight	Easy	Low to Medium
RFID	Multiple at a Time	< 180 meters	RF Transparent Materials	Challenging	Medium to High

Because of RFID, any object in the world can become a piece of data! As this data is amassed and more and more objects are tagged, it becomes important to be able to access the data efficiently and interpret it in meaningful ways. An RFID tag is useless unless it is associated with a physical object. When an RFID tag is associated with an object, the association is usually stored in a database or some form of catalog or directory for later retrieval. Once the association is made, it must be able to be queried by RFID applications that interpret the RFID data in a useful way. Discovery services, such as EPCglobal's Object Name Service (ONS), allow businesses to retrieve tag to object associations. The ONS specification is discussed in more detail in Chapter 8. Regardless of the how this data is accessed or stored; the data must be available to RFID applications for quick access. Quick access usually equates to a local or cached copy of the data. The way in which this data is synchronized across all enterprises is a great example of electronic data interchange.

Electronic data interchange (EDI) is the term applied to how data is organized and transmitted among disparate computer systems. Sharing data electronically, across a large enterprise and between completely separate businesses, enables commerce to happen at a much faster pace than in the past. Business-to-business (B2B) EDI solutions have matured greatly since the data was first stored electronically. Imagine a world where information was stored in a hard-copy format, such as paper or microfiche. To transmit this data from one business to another, there was a considerable physical effort involved, and the cataloging and access of this data could be very costly. The next step in EDI evolution was to store the information electronically on disk, tape, or any other digital media. Electronic storage allowed for easy categorization and searching, but the media of choice would still have to be physically moved if the data was to be transferred to another system.

When computer networks began to emerge, the data could then be transmitted across a network to other systems. This was a major step because this transfer could happen automatically without any physical effort. Batches of data could be transmitted across the network on a regular schedule. As the networking technology became fast enough to support real-time data transfers, accurate and up-to-date data availability allowed businesses to make split-second decisions based on the latest data, where data from batch EDI systems may be days, weeks, or even months old.

Every industry has its own jargon. For example, a computer programmer may talk about bytes and bits, while a horse breeder would use words like pedigree and sire. It is important that like businesses agree on standards to describe the parts of their industry that are unique to them. This example extends to business data as well. If a horse breeder wanted to transmit a horse's pedigree to another breeder electronically, it would be useful to have a standard pedigree format that both breeders' computer systems understood. When businesses use the same format to describe their data, they are essentially talking the same language, and when businesses talk the same language, they can easily communicate. The American National Standards Institute (ANSI) Accredited Standards Committee (ASC) X12 has a catalog of over 325 EDI formats for a wide range of industries. The ASC X12 organization has been developing EDI formats for over 25 years (ASC X12, 2005). The EPCglobal Network defines a language called the Physical Markup Language (PML). This language provides a standardized vocabulary for describing RFID-related data (Floerkemeier et al., 2003). EPCglobal has proposed a new standard that will supersede PML. The new standard, named EPC Information Services (EPCIS), is still in development and is part of the EPC Global architecture specification. The data interchange format specification of EPCIS will replace PML once development and testing of the new standard has concluded.

Even though businesses may communicate with the same language, it does not imply that their computer systems know how to communicate. There are many different computer architectures: IA64, MIPS, SPARC, ARM, and so on. Each computer architecture formats data in a different way. The format that one computer system uses to represent an integer number may be interpreted as a decimal number by another. Computer scientists have been working to resolve these issues for many years, but the explosion of the Internet and networked systems has been a tremendous catalyst for this effort. Today there are many standards that allow computer systems to agree on how data should be formatted. The most recognized format today is called the Extensible Markup Language (XML). XML is the basis for many data formats used every day by millions of people. The Hypertext Markup Language (HTML), the language used to describe Web pages, is a subset of the XML standard. XML itself is a subset of the Standard Generalized Markup Language (SGML) standard. Using XML, businesses can transfer documents between one another using other transfer protocols such as File Transfer Protocol (FTP) or Hypertext Transfer Protocol (HTTP), to name a few. The EPCglobal Network's Physical Markup Language specification is formatted using XML. Figure 2-4 is an example of a PML document that describes a temperature reading from an RFID tag with advanced functionality (Floerkemeier et al., 2003).

Computer system architects are faced with many decisions when designing a computer system or application. One of the most critical decisions is how to format, process, and publish data. System architects tend to favor a data model that most efficiently matches the data requirements for the solution. When a system's data must be shared with other computer systems, the data model chosen may not be portable across system boundaries. Luckily, most industries have a standard data model that should be employed by system designers, but sometimes standards are not available or must be modified or ignored in favor of system performance and scalability. In the case where an industry standard is not an option, third-party software, also known as middleware, must be employed to perform the work

```
<?xml version="1.0" encoding="utf-8" ?>
<pmlcore:Sensor>
        <pmluid:ID>urn:epc:1:124.162.37</pmluid:ID>
        <pmlcore:Observation>
                <pmlcore:DateTime>2005-11-06T13:04:34-06:00</pmlcore:DateTime>
                <pmlcore:Data>
                        <pmlcore:XML>
                                <TemperatureReading xmlns="http://sensor.example.org/">
                                        <Unit>Celsius</Unit>
                                        <Value>5.3</Value>
                                </TemperatureReading>
                        </pmlcore:XML>
                </pmlcore:Data>
        </pmlcore:Observation>
</pmlcore:Sensor>
```

Figure 2-4 Sample RFID tag temperature sensor XML document.

of integrating the systems. The third-party software's responsibility is to transform data from one format into another. For example, one bank may understand Interactive Financial Exchange (IFX) format, while another only understands Open Financial Exchange (OFX) format. The transformation software would convert an IFX document to an OFX document or vice versa by mapping one data field in the input document to the appropriate data field in the output document. IBM Corporation's WebSphere Business Integration Messaging Broker® (WBIMB), Microsoft Corporation's BizTalk®, and Itemfield Corporation's ContentMaster™ are a small subset of the multitude of data transformation and business integration solutions available.

EDI must be applied to RFID in order to accomplish the goals of RFID. How EDI is used is dependent on the industry that is hosting the RFID solution. For logistics-based solutions, EDI enables an advanced shipping notice (ASN) or electronic bill of lading to be transmitted ahead of a shipment. The advanced notice informs the receiving business about the items to expect in the next shipment. When the electronic shipping notice is received from the source of the shipment, the receiver may set up their systems to automatically accept the RFID-tagged items into inventory when they arrive. The system may also perform an audit of the shipment to ensure that the correct items were delivered. RFID EDI can also be applied to businesses that have multiple campuses that require data synchronization or aggregation. Each campus may record only information about the RFID tags currently located on-site. The enterprise, however, requires information from all the campuses for decision-making and reporting purposes. Using EDI, each campus can report RFID information to a central data repository that represents the enterprise-wide RFID footprint, thus giving the business RFID visibility across all campuses. Taking this example a bit further, the business may use the enterprise-wide RFID data to automatically generate purchase requests to its suppliers to replenish depleted stock items or re-order needed supplies by using an electronic purchase order. The electronic purchase order could then be routed to the correct supplier with the help of EDI.

EDI increases a business's ability to make fast decisions by providing the business with real-time information harvested from across the enterprise. Businesses are also able to automate many of the interactions with their customers and suppliers. When businesses automate their systems with EDI they

- Decrease labor costs
- Provide better service to their customers
- Create growth opportunities
- Give their employees more time to focus on the future of the business and less on the day-to-day issues

As mentioned earlier, EDI can be implemented in a batch or real-time architecture. Providing real-time data on which decisions can be based is the goal of RFID. New computer system architectures are being invented to address this need. The concept of a "service-oriented architecture" (SOA) has become the headline of many information technology (IT) publications. The primary idea behind SOA is that businesses can offer services that can be consumed by other businesses electronically. The services are presented in such a way that there is no real interdependency between the businesses other than the service contract. Using a form of EDI, one business can use another business's service to accomplish a task. Based on the earlier example, Company A may need to order some materials from one of its suppliers, Company B. If Company B offers a "reorder service," then company A can simply use that service to automatically order the materials needed without any human interaction between the companies.

In the same spirit of SOA, publish and subscribe (Pub-Sub) architectures also offer loosely coupled data delivery. In a Pub-Sub architecture, data is published to a common location based on an internal or external event. Once the data is published, it can then be accessed by multiple clients as needed without any effort on the part of the data source. An example of an external event would be the completion of nightly batch processing. A Pub-Sub architecture may publish the batch results for clients to access the next day, such as bank account balances that are updated nightly based on the previous day's transaction postings. An external event may be generated by the client requesting data. In this model, data is published on demand, but once published, it is accessible by any clients interested in the data.

2.4 Internet

The Internet was spawned from an early government computer network called Advanced Research Projects Agency Networks (ARPANET). ARPANET was started in 1969 after several years of computer connectivity research and was originally only accessible by the government, military, research facilities, and universities. The Internet, as it exists today, is made up of interconnected computers and networks of computers and became accessible to commercial entities in 1995. The Internet allows connected computers to communicate by routing data through an Internet Protocol (IP), packet switched network. IP is a way in which information is addressed and sent from computer to computer on the Internet. Computers connect to the Internet through many different interfaces including hardwired connections such as copper wire or fiber-optic cable or using over-the-air (OTA) interfaces such as 802.11x and satellite links. 802.11x is a wireless networking standard that allows computers to communicate using radio waves. The most common flavors of 802.11x are 802.11A, 802.11B, and 802.11G. Most laptop computers today come equipped with wireless connectivity using one or more of the 802.11x standards so that laptops can seamlessly roam between the different types of networks.

The Internet is an example of a wide area network (WAN) and also bears the distinction of being the world's largest WAN. A WAN usually connects computers or computer networks that span a large geographic area. The definition of "a large geographic" area is subjective, but it is usually quantified in kilometers. Many companies have an internal network called an intranet. An intranet by definition is only accessible by the computers inside an organization. Today, an intranet is more of a logical distinction because most intranets are connected in some way to the Internet. An organization's intranet is sometimes called a local area network (LAN), unless it connects computers in different buildings or cities; then it is most often called a WAN. As mentioned earlier, an organization may expose all or portions of its intranet to the Internet, thus becoming a part of the Internet. To manage security, an organization's IT department may install software such as a "firewall" to manage data traffic between the company's intranet and the Internet. A *firewall* is a piece of software that regulates the entry and exit points to a network. If a computer is secured by a firewall, it is said to be "behind the firewall."

IT departments also create network buffer zones, called demilitarized zones (DMZs) that provide even more security. If a computer must be able to be accessed from the external Internet, an organization can place computers inside the DMZ such as Web servers and FTP servers. The computers in the DMZ sometimes act as a data proxy to other computers inside the organization's internal network by marshaling data from one computer to another after verifying that the data is safe.

Each computer on the Internet is assigned an IP address. This address allows the computer to send and receive data across the Internet. Some computers have registered names that make addressing easier. For example, the IP address 216.109.112.135 maps to "yahoo.com." Another way to say this is yahoo.com "resolves to" the IP address 216.109.112.135. The identifier "yahoo.com" is the domain name for the company Yahoo! The mapping of the IP address to the domain name is stored in a globally accessible database called a domain name server (DNS). When a computer wants to communicate with yahoo.com, it first queries the DNS for yahoo.com's IP address.

Once a computer has the IP address, it can easily send messages to yahoo.com. DNS also provides a level of abstraction that can be beneficial. Because of the abstraction of the domain name from the IP address, the IP address can change without the other computers or users ever knowing. The DNS is simply updated with the new IP address and the domain name will automatically map to the correct computer on the Internet. EPCglobal's ONS is built on top of DNS.

RFID tags are addressable by a uniform resource identifier (URI) as are pieces of data on the Internet such as documents and images. An image may have a URI of "http://www.theexample.com/images/rfidtagpic.jpg," while an EPC labeled RFID tag would have a URI of "urn:epc:id:sgtin: 0614141.100734.1245." ONS provides the mapping from the EPC to the detailed information about the tagged object located somewhere on the Internet (EPCglobal, 2005b). ONS is discussed in more detail in Chapter 8.

Now that computers are capable of communicating with any other computer connected to the Internet, businesses have a great resource. The Internet provides a global framework for businesses to leverage. The ever-increasing level of connectivity allows an RFID-enabled industry to track a product from the raw materials stage to when a customer purchases the finished product and maybe even further. In industries where freshness of the product is of the utmost importance, like seafood, meat, and produce, tracking the product from harvest to the store shelf or display case is extremely valuable. Using advanced RFID tags with peripheral functionality such as temperature, products can be monitored throughout their journey to enforce quality standards. The Internet backbone enables the end-to-end visibility needed to monitor the product on each step of its journey.

When physical objects become visible around the globe and can be tracked at the click of a button, security becomes paramount. Civil rights groups and conspiracy theorists have already begun pointing out ways in which this technology could be abused by hackers and governments around the world. The U.S. State Department bolstered opposition to RFID technology when it started placing RFID tags in all U.S. passports as of October 2006. The tag contains a digital picture of the person as well as the passport data (Krim, 2005). Many civil rights groups believe that the U.S. government is attempting to leverage the Internet connectivity found across most of the country to track citizens. The issues regarding privacy are discussed in more depth in Chapter 10.

There will always be predators that will attempt to steal information to make a profit. Today, hackers break into computer systems across the Internet using several different techniques that exploit a security hole. There are serious concerns that hackers may be able to steal private information, such as passport data, by setting up their own RFID reader so that they can sniff data from an innocent victim as he or she passes. Because of these concerns, sensitive RFID data must be secured just as any other sensitive data is secured today on the Internet. There are three steps to providing robust security:

- Authentication
- Authorization
- Encryption

First, a user or computer system, also known as a principal, must be authenticated before it can attempt to access secured data. In order for a principal to be authenticated, the principal must provide the correct credentials that prove that the principal is who it says it is. The most common example is when a user types in a user name and password when logging into a computer, the user is requesting to be authenticated based on the user's user name and password credentials. Next, the user must be authorized to access the data. Authorization is the process of granting access to the data based on the requestor's identity. The last step is to transmit the data to the requestor in ciphertext, also called encrypted, format. Only the receiving user or system should be able to decrypt the requested data into plaintext, also called decrypted, format.

In most cases, a tag number is meaningless unless it can be mapped to a physical object; therefore, the mapping information must be secured, not the tag number. In other cases, the tag number can be used to track an object or a person as in the case of U.S. RFID-enabled passports. Privacy advocates are becoming increasingly wary of all of the possible ways that RFID could be abused if implemented incorrectly. Cryptography and data security expert Bruce Schneier has raised a red flag about many of the flaws in the technology today from a security perspective. Schneier revealed a security hole in the anticollision algorithm employed by most RFID tags. Anticollision algorithms govern when tags transmit. If all the tags transmit at the same time, readers would have trouble receiving and distinguishing which signal came from what tag. The details of anticollision algorithms are discussed in more depth in Chapter 4. The security-flawed algorithm uses a unique collision identification number, different from the tag's RFID number, to determine when a tag is to transmit. By analyzing how an RFID tag responds when queried, the RFID tag can be identified using the collision identifier. The resolution to this problem is found in the ISO 14443A specification. ISO 14443A is another anticollision algorithm that uses random transmission times to reduce collisions rather than unique anticollision identifiers (Schneier, 2005). Tags that transmit in a random pattern do not contain unique collision identifiers that can be used to identify the tags.

Schneier acknowledges that the U.S. State Department has done an exceptional job at designing the security for the new e-Passports. The only way that a hacker could potentially take advantage of the anticollision algorithm flaw would be to place a rogue reader within 10 centimeters of the passport while a border agent was querying the passport's RFID chip data. Even then, the hacker would not be able to read the data that was transmitted. The hacker would only be able to obtain the unique identifier for the anticollision algorithm. It would be much easier to steal the passport to get the information.

When an RFID tag has onboard memory that stores sensitive information, it must be secured using the steps detailed above. Microchip® uses a cryptography technique called KEELOQ® to secure transmitted data between tags and readers. KEELOQ generates an encryption key using a nonlinear algorithm that changes the key for every transmission. The key is then used to encrypt data before it is transmitted to ensure transmission security. Other encryption algorithms such as Data Encryption Standard (DES), Triple DES (3DES), and Advanced Encryption Standard (AES) are also used to encrypt data stored in onboard tag memory.

Each beacon from an RFID tag generates a piece of data that must be recorded in a database. As billions of tags are produced and released into circulation, the amount of data generated every day becomes staggeringly vast. For this data to be considered useful, it must not only be stored, but it also must be accessible. Companies such as Yahoo! and Google have made fortunes providing solutions for searching through the tremendous amounts of data found today on the Internet. Searches that find correlations between locations, product types, and so on will all provide meaningful information to businesses and entire industries.

Networks must be built with RFID traffic in mind in order to provide the scalability required to handle the tremendous data load that could arise. An architecture is said to be "scalable" if it can perform under a heavy load. With thousands of tags, each transmitting up to several times a second, an underequipped or ill-prepared network could easily be brought to its knees. Much of the burden of building scalable architectures falls on the shoulders of the software architects that are charged with routing this data to the correct location, be it a database or another computer system. It is up to the software developers to deliver this data in the most concise way possible so that the network is not burdened with unnecessary data. Data transport mechanisms such as multicasting provide a framework that allows a single server to send data to multiple clients at once. Using multicasting, a server broadcasts data to a common location. All clients that want to receive data "listen" for data at this common location. When the data source broadcasts the data, it is sent to all the listeners by the underlying data transport layer. The converse data transport mechanism uses point-to-point delivery. Point-to-point delivery sends data from the server to a single client. If there were 100 clients, this could equate to 1,000 bytes of total data transmitted by the server if each message was 10 bytes in size. A multicast-based solution would only transmit 10 bytes. This is how scalable solutions are architected.

2.5 EPCglobal Network

The EPCglobal Network was started as an academic research project at the Auto-ID Center at MIT in conjunction with five other leading research centers around the globe. The Auto-ID Center researchers understood that the EPCglobal Network research project needed to be standardized in order for it to become successful. To accomplish this task, the nonprofit organization EPCglobal, Inc. was founded in November of 2003 as a joint venture between EAN International and the Uniform Code Council to facilitate the adoption of the EPCglobal Network. As discussed earlier in this chapter, UCC and EAN have years of experience in delivering and managing global standards such as barcodes. EPCglobal's mission is to "[drive] global adoption and effective implementation of the EPCglobal Network." As of November of 2003, the MIT Auto-ID Center is no longer involved in the administrative functions of the EPCglobal Network and participates in a research capacity only. EPCglobal Inc. is an industry-driven organization. Professionals in industry and education can join and participate in the development and management of the technologies and standards that comprise the EPCglobal Network.

2.5.1 EPCglobal, Inc. Organization

EPCglobal, Inc. imposes strict processes for submission, standardization, and enhancement to EPCglobal Network technologies. Figure 2-5 depicts the EPCglobal, Inc. organization chart. EPCglobal is organized such that new requirements and enhancements can easily flow through the organization.

The EPCglobal board of governors is made up of representatives from EAN, UCC, and several RFID industry pioneering companies and governmental organizations. The EPCglobal president reports to the board of governors to ensure that the standardization effort is progressing as planned and heading in the correct direction. The Architecture Review Committee (ARC) is responsible for prioritizing and reviewing all proposed standards and enhancements to existing standards. The ARC is the technical arm of the president. The staff aids in the promotion of the EPC standards. The

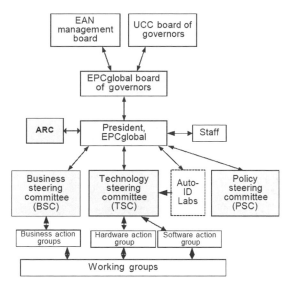

Figure 2-5 EPCglobal, Inc. organization chart (*Source:* Reprinted by permission of GS1 US).

staff helps with the day-to-day operations of EPCglobal, as well as improves existing EPC standards.

The Business (BSC), Technology (TSC), and Policy (PSC) Steering Committees are in charge of their respective action groups and work groups. The action and work groups are discussed later in this chapter. The BSC focuses on the development of RFID as it relates to individual industries such as manufacturing, health care, and defense, to name a few. The TSC deals with the software, hardware, physics, and other engineering-type issues related to RFID. Interacting with the public on issues like privacy and education is the responsibility of the PSC.

The Auto-ID labs are where the technology is researched, created, developed, and tested. Auto-ID labs have been formed around the world. The first Auto-ID lab was the Auto-ID Center at MIT, where the EPCglobal standards and technology originated.

The working groups are where the real serious work is done. These groups are tasked with work items such as requirements gathering, documentation, and software/hardware development. The working groups are managed by their respective action groups.

2.5.2 Standards Process

The standards development process has two serial tracks. The first is the submission track. The submission track includes three stages that must be completed before graduating to the standards track:

1. Requirements definition

2. Architecture assessment
3. Standards requirements and plan

The standards track proceeds through six stages before the initial proposal becomes a standard:

1. Working group formation
2. Initial technical development
3. Action group review
4. Prototype and test
5. Committee review
6. Board ratification

From each track, several artifacts are produced. For example, the submission track may produce application standards, while the standards track may produce a new International Organization for Standards (ISO) or World Wide Web Consortium (W3C) standard. Detailed information about each track can be found at *www.epcglobalinc.org*. Tables 2-2 and 2-3 show an overview of the submission and standards tracks, respectively. The tables indicate the development process steps, in which the EPCglobal organization participates during each step, and the artifacts of each step (EPCglobal, 2005c).

EPCglobal, Inc. is an industry-driven organization made of up three different action groups: Hardware, Software, and Business. Companies that are interested in participating in one or more of the action groups must first be an EPCglobal subscriber. Companies that subscribe to EPCglobal get the benefits of being able to influence the standards created by the organization and share ideas and experiences with other RFID companies. Professionals that wish to become an EPCglobal subscriber must first sign and submit the appropriate EPCglobal Intellectual Property (IP) Policy forms to their local GS1 agent. The IP Policy was created by EPCglobal to ensure that any ideas or standards cultivated within the EPCglobal organization are available to all of its members and remain nonproprietary (http://www.epcglobalinc.org/join/subscribe_epc, 2006). Subscribers can be placed into two categories: end users and solution providers. End users are the companies that make use of the RFID technology such as manufacturing businesses or retail stores. Solution providers are the companies that build the software and hardware that allows end users to implement RFID solutions.

Once a company has subscribed to EPCglobal, it can access all of the EPCglobal resources and participate in the action groups. Hardware Action Groups (HAGs) are devoted to the creation of RFID hardware and standards associated with the hardware. This includes tags, readers, and any supporting hardware, such as specialized RFID routers, for example. Members of the HAGs are usually RFID hardware manufacturing companies. Most HAG members tend to be solution-provider-type subscribers.

Table 2-2 Submission Track

EPCglobal Standards Development Step Number/Name	Participant	Document/Status upon Completion
0. Working Group Formation	0	Working Group Charter
0.1. Co-Chair selection	0.1 Action Group	
0.2. Charter Creation	0.2 WG Co-Chairs	
0.3. Charter Approval	0.3 Action Group & Steering Committee	
0.4. Call for Participation	0.4 WG Co-Chairs & EPCglobal Staff	
1. Requirements Definition	1	Business/Technical Requirements Document
1.1. Use Case Development	1.1 Working Group	
1.2. Business Requirements Development	1.2 Working Group	
1.3. Technical Requirements Development	1.3 Working Group	
1.4. Working Group Consensus		
2. Architectural Assessment	2	Architectural Assessment Report
2.1. Supply Chain Impact	2.1 Architectural Review Committee (ARC)	
2.2. EPCglobal Reference Architecture Impact	2.2 ARC	
2.3. Standards Development Organizations Assessment	2.3 ARC	
2.4. Architectural Review Committee Consensus	2.4 ARC	
3. Standards Requirements and Plan	3	Standards Requirements
3.1. Identify Standardization Opportunity	3.1 ARC	Standards Development Plan
3.2. Standards Requirements	3.2 ARC	
3.3. Standards Development Plan	3.3 Action Group	

Source: Reprinted with permission of GS1 US.

Table 2-3 Standards Track

EPCglobal Standards Development Step Number/Name	Participant	Standard Status upon Completion
4. Working Group Formation	4	
4.1. Co-Chair selection	4.1 Action Group	
4.2. Charter Creation	4.2 WG Co-Chairs	
4.3. Charter Approval	4.3 Action Group & Technical Steering Committee	
4.4. Call for Participation	4.4 WG Co-Chairs & EPCglobal Staff	
5. Development of Specification	5	Last Call Working Draft
5.1. Development	5.1 Working Group	
5.2. Last Call Working Draft complete	5.2 Working Group	
5.3. Intellectual Property Review	5.3 Working Group	
6. Action Group Review	6	Candidate Specification
6.1. Review & Comments	6.1 Action Group	
6.2. Comment Resolution	6.2 Working Group	
6.3. Certification & Compliance requirements	6.3 Working Group	
6.4. Validation Test Plan	6.4 Working Group	
6.5. Prototype participants selection	6.5 Working Group	

7. Validation, Prototype & Test	7		Proposed Specification
7.1. Prototype facility setup	7.1 Working Group		
7.2. Prototype creation	7.2 Working Group		
7.3. Prototype execution	7.3 Working Group		
7.4. Prototype and test report	7.4 Working Group		
7.5. Decision to move to step 5 or 8	7.5 Action Group		
8. Committees Review (Business (BSC) & Technical (TSC))	8		Recommended Specification
8.1. Working group notification	8.1 EPCglobal Staff		
8.2. Board notification of "Necessary Claims"	8.2 Working Group Participants		
8.3. Specification review	8.3 BSC and TSC		
8.4. Decision to move to step 5 or 9	8.4 Action Group		
9. Board Ratification	9		EPCglobal Standard Specification
9.1. Due diligence	9.1 EPCglobal Inc. President		
9.2. Board presentation	9.2 EPCglobal Inc. President		
9.3. Board ratification	9.3 EPCglobal Inc. Board		
9.4. Presentation package for other standards bodies	9.4 Working Group		
9.5. Presentation of ratified standard to other standards bodies	9.5 EPCglobal Staff		

Source: Reprinted with permission of GS1 US.

Software Action Groups (SAGs) are concerned with the creation of RFID software and standards required to support both the RFID hardware and the overall EPCglobal Network architecture described earlier. SAGs develop the middleware and electronic data exchange pieces used to harvest data from RFID readers and then make that data available across the EPCglobal Network. Most SAG members tend to be solution-provider-type subscribers.

The last type of action group is the Business Action Group (BAG). BAGs analyze and propose solutions to common RFID business concerns. BAGs target individual industries. By targeting individual industries, a BAG can address implementation questions specific to that industry and also develop "use cases" that provide industry-wide models for RFID success. BAGs mold this information into standards and best practices for each industry and incorporate them into the EPCglobal Network architecture. Table 2-4 shows a list of the current action groups as of the writing of this book.

It is also important to note that there are several Auto-ID labs that are involved in ongoing research and are affiliated with EPCglobal, Inc. The MIT Auto-ID center, along with five other labs, continues to research automatic identification technologies from RFID to smart card technologies.

The EPCglobal Network technology is a collection of five different components. These components include the EPC data format, identification system (tags and readers), EPC middleware, Discovery Services, and the EPC Information Services (EPC IS). The components that make up the EPCglobal Network architecture facilitate the collection and distribution of real-time product information across an enterprise or an entire industry. The EPCglobal Network allows members of the network to track products through the entire supply chain.

The EPCglobal Network attempts to enhance three main areas of the supply chain. The first enhancement is product identification resolution. In legacy technologies, such as barcodes, the resolution of product identification is constrained to the type of product, but with the introduction of the globally unique EPC, products can be identified at an even higher, product-specific resolution. The second enhancement removed the requirement that

Table 2-4 EPCglobal Action Groups (January 2007)

Business Action Groups	Software Action Groups	Hardware Action Groups
• Fast Moving Consumer Goods • Healthcare & Life Sciences • Transportation and Logistics	• ONS • EPC IS • Filtering & Collection • Reader Protocol • Reader Management • Security • Tag Data Translation • Tag Data Standards	• UHF Class 2 • UHF Generation 2 Protocol Maintenance • Item Level Tagging and Joint Requirements • Testing and Certification

the product be physically visible in order for it to be scanned. As discussed earlier in the section on barcodes, RFID readers can read tags in other rooms or inside boxes. The third and final enhancement allows supply chain partners to receive real-time information about a specific product as it moves through the supply chain.

The flow of data through the EPCglobal Network first begins with the tagging of a product. The unique EPC identifier allows for the product to be monitored throughout its lifetime in the supply chain. When RFID tags are read by a strategically placed EPC tag reader, the data is routed through the facility's EPC middleware to the facility's EPC IS repository. Once the data is recorded in EPC IS, authorized partners in the supply chain can use the Discovery Services, such as the Object Naming Service, to request information unique to the product such as its current location or any other status information. (EPCglobal, 2004). The details of each of these systems are discussed in Chapters 7 and 8.

2.6 Global Data Synchronization

Global supply chains and trade partners separated by continents and oceans are commonplace in today's global economy. GS1 (EAN.UCC) has recognized that product information must be available to all trade partners on a global scale in order to reduce supply chain problems that arise from unreliable product information. GS1 is building the Global Data Synchronization Network (GDSN) to combat this problem. GDSN came online in August of 2004.

The GDSN presents manufacturers and retailers with a common data access point called the GS1 Global Registry. It also ensures that the product information found in the registry is up-to-date and accurate. The GDSN is composed of several source data pools and recipient data pools (Figure 2-6). Catalogs of product data are found in these data pools. Source data pools are hosted by manufactures that wish to present product information to retailers. Retailers host recipient data pools that hold data received from manufacturers. Retailers are able to retrieve a manufacturer's product information by first looking up the location of a manufacturer's source data pool. This is accomplished by accessing the GS1 Global Registry. Once a retailer has retrieved the location of the manufacturer's source data pool, the retailer can pull the product information into its own recipient data pool for later use. The retailer's recipient data pool acts as a local cache that can be used to quickly retrieve product information.

The most basic types of data found in the data pool are the Global Location Number (GLN) and the Global Trade Identification Number (GTIN) or Global Product Classification (GPC), which is mutually exclusive with respect to the GTIN. The first piece of information stored in the data pool is the GLN, which is used to identify legal entities such as manufacturing companies or retailers. As discussed earlier in this chapter, the GTIN iden-

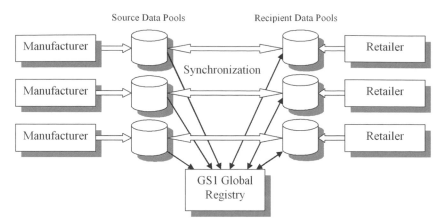

Figure 2-6 GDSN architecture.

tifies a specific product, while the GPC specifies a class or type of product. Any of these pieces of information can be used by the retailer to query information about a product or manufacturer.

Once the data relationship has been established between the source/ manufacturer and recipient/retailer data pools, data synchronization must occur to initially populate the recipient data pool. After the recipient data pool is initially populated, it must be updated whenever the manufacturer changes any product information in the source pool. This is the point where the Pub-Sub electronic data integration paradigm is implemented as discussed earlier in Section 2.3. The manufacturer is the publisher and the retailer is the subscriber. Once the retailer has subscribed to the manufacturer's source data pool, the retailer is sent a synchronization event when the manufacturer publishes any new data to its source data pool. Any number of retailers that have subscribed to that manufacturer can immediately update their data so that it will always be up-to-date in their own recipient data pool.

The standardized data formats and Global Registry ensure data quality as well, which is one of the primary goals of the GDSN. As mentioned earlier in the discussion on EDI, automated electronic data interchange is less prone to errors than manual data entry. Thus, data synchronization can occur quickly and flawlessly as long as the source data pool is populated with clean and up-to-date information.

To access the GDSN, an organization must meet a few basic qualifications. First, the organization must be GDSN compliant with EAN.UCC System standards. This means that they must be able to correctly register with the GS1 Global Registry and successfully implement either a source or recipient data pool depending on their role. Implementation of a data pool not only includes synchronization capabilities but also data format compliance. Some smaller organizations may choose not to host their own data pool. If an organization chooses not to host its own data pool, it must post its information to a third-party data pool and access product information from a certified recipient data pool. Second, the organization must have a valid GLN so that it can be recognized by the network. Next, the GS1 Global Registry Service Level Agreement must be signed and approved by GS1. Last, the GDSN membership fee must be paid. This fee has been waived in the past to help promote GDSN adoption.

The first question usually pondered when learning about the GDSN is "How does this relate to the EPCglobal Network?" The answer is that the two networks track different types of data but both share fairly similar system architectures. The GDSN data is much more static in nature than EPCglobal Network data. The product types (GPC) and organization information (GLN) rarely change when compared to information found in the EPCglobal Network, such as product location. The GDSN does share one common piece of data with the EPCglobal Network, the GTIN. Because of the flexibility of the EPC standard for each target industry, GS1-compliant organizations will format the EPC as a GTIN. The GTIN formatted EPC can then be used to relate EPCglobal Network data to GDSN data (EPCglobal, 2004).

The GDSN is fundamental to the success of the EPCglobal Network. Before dynamic data, such as location, can be useful, trade partners must understand what products are available, their characteristics, and how to identify them. This is the job of the GDSN. Once trade partners have a common catalog of product information, the RFID tracking data can be useful. There are internal enterprise solutions that have no need of GDSN because the objects being tracked will never be visible outside of the enterprise or a small, closed set of partners. For these implementations, the EPCglobal Network solution can stand on its own (Kearney, 2004).

2.7 Anticipated Future Impact

Radio frequency identification has already changed in many ways since its initial implementation in the radar IFF system developed during World War II. Changes have been related to both engineering and applications of the technology. As engineers developed a richer understanding of the principles of electromagnetic radiation, new RF devices were produced that could send and receive RF signals more reliably. At the same time, industries began to invent revolutionary ways to make use of the technology. The same changes are happening today with RFID. Engineers are refining how to properly implement RFID systems, and new business cases are being thought of every day.

RFID is going to change the way we interact with the world around us. In today's society, organization is a prized skill. Enough books have been written on the subject to fill entire libraries. RFID will turn conventional organization and logistical paradigms upside down. There is no reason to organize items when RFID can find them instantly, and there are situations when disorder may improve how fast an item can be retrieved.

For example, in warehouses around the world, products are packed neatly into their appropriate locations so they can be found easily when an order is filled. When a picker, a person who gathers items from around a warehouse, is sent to pick an order, some of the items may be on opposite sides of the warehouse. In this case, the picker must traverse the entire length of the warehouse in the name of organization. Granted, smart logistical algorithms can reduce the types of combinations that cause the pickers to travel large distances. It is theoretically possible that if the products were randomly placed around the warehouse, the products needed to fill an order would most likely be found in closer proximity to one another than in a conventionally organized warehouse. Using the location information available from the installed RFID real-time location system, a software application could easily find the fastest path for the picker to gather the products in question (Maney, 2004).

The world is waiting for proof that RFID is the next step in supply chain management. A University of Arkansas research project conducted in early 2005 based on the Wal-Mart RFID initiative showed that Wal-Mart stores equipped with RFID technology had 16 percent less out-of-stock incidents than those stores not equipped with the technology. The RFID-enabled stores have also reduced manual supply orders by 10 percent. These preliminary numbers looked very promising for the future of RFID (Hardgrave, 2005). In 2006, the University of Arkansas research team released new findings that further substantiate the benefits of RFID in the retail industry. Under tighter research controls, the research team found that the out-of-stock incidents were actually 30% less when RFID was used. This was a 14% decrease in the out of stock incidents when compared to the preliminary findings reported from the 2005 study (Hardgrave et al., 2006). An awakening is happening across the industrial world in which industries are beginning to understand that there is a new domain of data available to them. This new data will cause a paradigm shift in the practices of the industrial engineers and logisticians from the previous generation, and RFID is the mechanism through which this data will be collected.

In an interview with Kevin Ashton, former chairman for MIT's Auto-ID Center and now principal at ThingMagic Incorporated, it was suggested that technology has evolved through two eras in the past 200 years and is now entering "the Sensor Age." According to Ashton, the 1800s dealt with the automation of work, the 1900s dealt with automated knowledge, and today technology is embarking on the automation of perception. Today, an extremely high percentage of the data collected involves some sort of direct human action, be it typing in data through a computer keyboard or scanning a barcode. The Sensor Age is a change in the way data is collected. Ashton believes that RFID is one of the first steps in the direction of autonomous data collection.

Everyone agrees that the future of RFID is not set in stone. The dust from the initial hype has not yet settled. As of the writing of this book, some technology analysts are implying that RFID is getting in the way of technologies that provide real solutions to problems. The antithesis to this type of mentality are those who believe that RFID will solve every problem with 100 percent accuracy. As in most cases, the correct view lies somewhere in between the extremes. RFID realists understand that RFID cannot be couched as a 100 percent accurate solution. Perfect accuracy is only found in a laboratory. Future RFID hardware and software will compensate for the dynamic nature of real-world environments and become more and more fault-tolerant. RFID software packages today are already using sophisticated pattern recognition algorithms and fuzzy logic to present more accurate results when supplied with partial data. RFID can save time and money over conventional solutions. One thing is for sure, RFID is not going to disappear.

According to Kevin Ashton there are not many products that Wal-Mart does not sell, and there are not many products that the U.S. Department of Defense does not buy; therefore, the RFID mandate from both of these entities points to a healthy and long-lasting future for RFID. RFID is the next step in automatic identification and cannot be ignored. Ashton noted that there are many items that consumers purchase today in supermarkets that are amazing feats of logistics and manufacturing, but most consumers take them for granted. A can of Coca-Cola® is composed of approximately 360 different raw materials from the aluminum used to forge the can to the sugar in the syrup. It is a modern miracle that a consumer can purchase a can of Coca-Cola for less than US$1. If RFID can streamline industries beyond what is available today it could create a better life for everyone in the world. RFID could potentially be the tool that enables millions to be fed and brings health care and medicine to the sick around the globe.

At this writing, Gartner Inc. has classified RFID technology in the fourth stage of the Gartner "hype" cycle. The Gartner cycle has five distinct stages:

1. *The technology trigger.* The event that generates interest in a new technology or idea.
2. *Peak of inflated expectations.* The height of excitement about the future of a new technology, which is usually brought about by the overinflated expectations of the technology that have been kindled by technology dreamers and the press.
3. *Trough of disillusionment.* The disappointment of a technology that did not live up to its most extreme expectations.
4. *Slope of enlightenment.* Hard research and development efforts produce realistic expectations and methodologies required to implement the technology in a real-world solution.
5. *Plateau of productivity.* The technology becomes stable and the technology becomes beneficial to adopt and implement.

In order for RFID to break through to Stage 5, the technology must be simplified in both practice and understanding (Stage 4). Today, the installation of an RFID solution can seem to be very complex. Some books instruct users in the proper way to conduct "site surveys" in which radio frequency patterns are checked using tools such as RF spectrum analyzers, and time studies must be performed to understand how the RF spectrum changes throughout the day in an installation target environment. If this level of complexity continues, it will eventually kill the technology. Ashton's dream is for RFID to become a ubiquitous technology that is seen as a tool available to the industry and not as black magic. As the understanding of RFID and its applications evolve, students of the technology begin to realize that simplification is the key to a solid RFID solution. New software algorithms and revolutions in antenna and tag technology have created solutions that are tolerant to dynamic environments.

Ashton compares the adoption of RFID to that of e-mail. In the early 1990s, it was extremely hard to find anyone that had an e-mail account, and then, without notice, if you didn't have an e-mail account, everyone would look at you as if you were in the Stone Age. E-mail took over the world in a matter of a few years, and it was as if businesses were crippled overnight because they did not have e-mail. Ashton believes that RFID will sneak up on the world in much the same way.

Acronyms

3DES—Triple Data Encryption Standard

AES—Advanced Encryption Standard

ANSI—American National Standards Institute

ARC—Architecture Review Committee (as applied to EPCglobal)

ARPANET—Advanced Research Projects Agency Networks

ASC—Accredited Standards Committee

ASN—Advanced shipping notice

B2B—Business to business

BAG—Business Action Group (as applied to EPCglobal)

BBC—British Broadcasting Corporation

BSC—Business Steering Committee (as applied to EPCglobal)

CCD—Charge-coupled device

DES—Data Encryption Standard

DMZ—Demilitarized zone (as applied to networking)

DNS—Domain name server

DoD—Department of Defense

EAN—European Article Number

EAS—Electronic article surveillance

EDI—Electronic data interchange

EPC—Electronic Product Code

EPCIS—EPC Information Services (as applied to EPC Global)

FAQ—Frequently asked questions

FTP—File Transfer Protocol

GDSN—Global Data Synchronization Network

GLN—Global Location Number

GPC—Global Product Classification

GTIN—Global Trade Identification Number

HAG—Hardware Action Group (as applied to EPCglobal)

HTML—Hypertext Markup Language

HTTP—Hypertext Transfer Protocol

IAN—International Article Numbering System

IFF—Identification, friend or foe

IFX—Interactive Financial Exchange

IP—Internet Protocol (as applied to network protocols)

IP—Intellectual property (as applied to commercial ownership)

IS—Information services

ISO—International Organization for Standardization

IT—Information technology

LAN—Local area network

MIT—Massachusetts Institute of Technology

OFX—Open Financial Exchange

ONS—Object Name Service

OTA—Over-the-air

PML—Physical Markup Language

PSC—Policy Steering Committee (as applied to EPCglobal)

QR—Quick Response (as applied to barcodes)

RCA—Radio Corporation of America

RF—Radio frequency

RFID—Radio frequency identification

ROI—Return on investment

SAG—Software Action Group (as applied to EPCglobal)

SGML—Standard Generalized Markup Language

SGTIN—Serial Global Trade Identification Number

SOA—Service-oriented architecture

TSC—Technology Steering Committee (as applied to EPCGlobal)

UCC—Uniform Code Council

UPC—Universal Product Code

URI—Uniform Resource Identifier

W3C—World Wide Web Consortium

WAN—Wide area network

WBIMB—WebSphere Business Integration Messaging Broker

XML—Extensible Markup Language

References

Adam Communications. 2005. "Barcode History." Available online via www.adams1.com/pub/russadam/history.html (accessed October 11, 2005).

ASC X12. Home page. 2005. Available online via www.x12.org/ (accessed January 14, 2007).

Denso Wave Inc. "QR Code Features." 2003. Available online via www.denso-wave.com/qrcode/qrfeature-e.html (accessed January 14, 2007).

Eagle, Jim. 2002. "RFID: The Early Years." Available online via http://members.surfbest.net/eaglesnest/rfidhist.htm (accessed January 14, 2007).

EPCglobal, Inc. 2004. "The EPCglobal Network and The Global Data Synchronization Network (GDSN): Understanding the Information and the Information Networks.". Available online via http://www.epcglobalus.org/dnn_epcus/KnowledgeBase / Browse / tabid / 277 / DMXModule / 706 / Command / Core_Download/Default.aspx?EntryId=155 (accessed January 14, 2007).

EPCglobal, Inc. 2005a. "EPC Generation 1 Tag Data Standards Version 1.1 Revision 1.27: Standard Specification. May 10" Available online via www.epcglobalus.org/dnn_epcus/KnowledgeBase/Browse/tabid/277/DMXModule/706/Command/Core_Download/Default.aspx?EntryId=296 (accessed January 14, 2007).

EPCglobal, Inc. 2005b. "Object Naming Service (ONS) Version 1.0." Available online via http://www.epcglobalus.org/dnn_epcus/KnowledgeBase/Browse/tabid/277/DMXModule/706/Command/Core_Download/Default.aspx?EntryId=299 (accessed January 14, 2007).

EPCglobal, Inc. 2005c. "Standards Development Process." March 8. Available online via http://www.epcglobalinc.org/standards/sdp/SDP_March_2006_V1.2.pdf (accessed January 14, 2007).

Floerkemeier, Christian, Dipan Anarkat, Ted Osiski, and Mark Harrison. 2003. "PML Core Specification." September 15, 2003. Available online via www.autoidlabs.org/uploads/media/STG-AUTOID-WH005.pdf (accessed January 15, 2007).

Hardgrave, Bill C., Matthew Waller, and Robert Miller. 2005. "Does RFID Reduce Out of Stocks? A Preliminary Analysis." November. Available online via http://itrc.uark.edu/research/display.asp?article=ITRI-WP058-1105 (accessed January 15, 2007).

Hardgrave, Bill C., Matthew Waller, and Robert Miller. 2006. "RFID's Impact on Out of Stocks: A Sales Velocity Analysis" June, 2006. Available online via http://

itri.uark.edu/research/display.asp?article=ITRI-WP068-0606 (accessed January 15, 2007).

Kearney, A. T., Kurt Salmon Associates. 2004. "Connect the Dots: Harness Collaborative Technologies to Deliver Better Value to Customers." February. Available online via www.atkearney.com/shared_res/pdf/connect_dots_5.pdf (accessed January 15, 2007).

Krim, Jonathan. 2005. "U.S. Passports to Receive Electronic Identification Chips." *Washington Post*. October 26, 2005. Available online via www.washingtonpost.com/wp-dyn/content/article/2005/10/25/AR2005102501624.html (accessed January 15, 2007).

Landt, Jeremy and Barbara Catlin. 2001. "Shrouds of Time: The History of RFID." Available online via www.aimglobal.org/technologies/rfid/resources/shrouds_of_time.pdf (accessed January 14, 2007).

Maney, Kevin. 2004. "RFID: Robot for Infinite Decluttering?" October. Available online via www.usatoday.com/money/industries/technology/maney/2004-10-05-maney_x.htm (accessed January 15, 2007).

Penley, Bill. 2002. "Penley Radar Archives, Radar: Early Radar History—An Introduction.) Available online via www.penleyradararchives.org.uk/history/introduction.htm (accessed January 14, 2007).

Schneier, Bruce. "Wired News: Fatal Flaw Weakens RFID Passport." *Wired.* November 3. Available online via www.wired.com/news/privacy/0,1848,69453,00.html?tw=wn_tophead_2 (accessed January 15, 2007).

TechTarget. 2006. "Barcode Reader." Available online via http://searchcio.techtarget.com/sDefinition/0,,sid19_gci857995,00.html (accessed January 14, 2007).

Tracey, Paul. 2005. "Two Ways to Play the Growth in Radio Frequency Identification (RFID)." Available online via www.wallstreetsecretsplus.com/contributors/paul_tracy/art030405.aspx (accessed January 14, 2007).

University Corporation for Atmospheric Research. 2000. "Windows to the Universe: Radar History." Available online via www.windows.ucar.edu/tour/link=/earth/Atmosphere/tornado/radar_history.html (accessed January 15, 2007).

Weisstein, Eric W. 2005. "World of Science and Biography: Maxwell, James.", Available online via http://scienceworld.wolfram.com/biography/Maxwell.html (accessed January 15, 2007).

WGBH. 1998. "A Science Odyssey: People and Discoveries: Guglielmo Marconi." 1998. Available online via www.pbs.org/wgbh/aso/databank/entries/btmarc.html (accessed January 15, 2007).

Wikipedia, "CK722." 2005a. Available online via http://en.wikipedia.org/wiki/CK722 (accessed January 15, 2007).

Wikipedia. "Heinrich Rudolf Hertz." 2005b. Available online via http://en.wikipedia.org/wiki/Heinrich_Hertz (accessed January 14, 2007).

Wikipedia. "Identification Friend or Foe." 2005c. Available online via http://en.wikipedia.org/wiki/Identification_Friend_or_Foe (accessed January 14, 2007).

Wikipedia, "Transistor." 2005d. Available online via http://en.wikipedia.org/wiki/Transistor (accessed January 14, 2007).

Basics of RFID

Practitioners must understand the fundamentals of RFID technology before they can successfully build real world solutions that solve business needs. The RFID tool belt contains numerous components that can be leveraged to correctly build RFID solutions, but the practitioner must first understand which tools should be used for specific applications and why.

Those who are new to the physical laws of electromagnetism and the nuances encountered in dynamic RF environments will find this chapter extremely helpful. It not only presents practical information about the core components used in the construction of an RFID solution such as tags, readers, tag density, enhanced component durability, and active tag battery life, but it also covers some of the more scientific areas of RFID such as how electromagnetic radiation behaves at different frequencies and in different environments.

3.1 RFID Tags

RFID tags come in many different shapes, sizes, and capabilities. When an RFID solution is designed, the solution's architect must take into account both business and technology requirements before choosing the type of RFID tag to use. This section examines the different types of tags available and discusses how and when a certain type of tag should be used.

All RFID tags have the following essential components in common:

1. Antenna
2. Integrated circuit
3. Printed circuit board/substrate

3.1.1 Antenna

An RFID tag's antenna's chief responsibility is to transmit and receive radio waves for the purpose of communication. The antenna is also known as the coupling mechanism. In electronics, coupling refers to the transfer of energy from one medium to another (Wikipedia, 2007). In the case of RFID, the transfer of energy is in the form of electromagnetic radiation, which is the way the tag and reader communicate. Some antennas are also designed to collect energy from radio waves. In the correct environment and proximity to an RFID tag reader, these antennas can collect enough energy to power the tag's other components without a battery. Based on the type and intended use of the tag, the antenna may have many different shapes and sizes. The different types of antennas found on each type of tag are discussed later in this chapter.

3.1.2 Integrated Circuit

The integrated circuit (IC) is a packaged collection of discrete components that provide the brains for the tag. The IC in an RFID tag is much like a microprocessor found in any cellular phone or computer, but it is usually not very sophisticated, and for many RFID tags, the IC component has a single purpose. Its purpose is to transmit the tag's unique identifier. If the tag has any peripheral components, the IC is also the master controller that is responsible for gathering any extra information and transmitting it along with the tag's unique identifier.

To ensure that all tags do not transmit their information at one time, the IC is responsible for implementing the correct transmission algorithm. These algorithms either ensure that the tag transmits at the proper time slot or cause the tag to transmit at random intervals. These types of algorithms are discussed in more detail in Chapter 4.

3.1.3 Printed Circuit Board/Substrate

The printed circuit board (PCB) is the material that holds the tag together. The circuit board may be rigid or flexible and is composed of many different types of materials, depending on the type and purpose of the tag. For example, tags that are used for tracking components on an assembly line where extremely high temperatures may be encountered would tend to be much more rigid and are usually placed inside a protective enclosure. Flexible tags must be durable enough to withstand the stress of any normal barcode tag but also protect the internal IC. RFID tags used in document tracking solutions may be very flexible, so that they bend with the paper. Flexible tags use thin plastic films in which the tag's components and circuitry are embedded. Flexible PCBs are also known as inlays. Tags that may be applied to a part or subsystem in a manufacturing process may use inflexible tags that encase the tag's components and circuitry in a type of epoxy resin. Most rigid tags are also housed in some time of enclosure to further protect the PCB and components.

3.1.4 Active Tags

There are two major classifications of RFID tags: active and passive. The defining characteristic of an active tag is that it contains its own power source, usually in the form of a battery. In contrast, passive tags have no battery. The onboard power source allows active tags to be extremely flexible in terms of the functionality they can offer. The battery affords the tag a greater read range and allows the tag to be read through materials that are usually impenetrable to magnetic radiation broadcast by other types of tags; however, active tags do not get as much publicity today as the other types of tags found on the market. This is mainly because active tags are larger in size and cost more than passive tags.

The most basic active tag sends out a signal at a regularly scheduled rate. This is known as the *beacon rate* of the tag. Tags can be configured to have any beacon rate from subsecond to several minutes. The beacon rate chosen depends on the needs of the solution. Most active tags have a beacon rate between 1 and 15 seconds. Each beacon's signal is encoded with a tag's identifier in addition to any other telemetry the tag may gather.

The onboard power source also allows active tags to support different types of peripheral functionality such as temperature, humidity, and pressure sensors, as well as writable memory. The size of the tag grows as the number of extra components and as the size of the battery increases. Figure 3-1 shows an example of an active tag manufactured by RFCode Corporation. The metallic clip pictured on the front of the tag holds the tag's battery.

Active tags that use batteries as a power source have a limited life span. The tag's life span is usually measured in years of operation. Most active tags offer a replaceable battery for when the tag has depleted the energy stored in the battery. The life span of the battery is also bound by three variables: the beacon rate of the tag, the strength at which the tag transmits, and the maximum shelf life of the battery. If a tag transmits a beacon every two seconds, it will use all of its battery power before a tag with a beacon

Figure 3-1 RFCode Corporation, active tag and enclosure.

rate of five seconds, assuming that the two tags use the same amount of energy per beacon. Active tag manufacturers include the tag's battery life expectancies in their tags' data sheets. In addition, tags that have a read range of 1 kilometer will deplete their batteries earlier than tags that have a read range of 100 meters.

Companies that already manufacture wireless access points like Cisco Systems, Inc. have been leading the 802.11-based active tag market. Cisco's Aironet® product line offers businesses the ability to integrate RFID into their wireless network, which can reduce infrastructure and installation costs. Some of the criticisms of 802.11-based systems are their cost, the fact that each tag requires an IP address on the system, low location resolution, low tag density, and short battery life.

The active tag is the first choice in almost any solution where the cost, size, and battery life span of the tag are not issues. Active tags allow for more flexible architectures because of the tag's transmission strength. When RFID must be deployed in a harsh environment such as a construction site or assembly line with extreme manufacturing conditions, the delicate components of the tag must be protected. Figure 3-2 shows an example of enhanced durability enclosures offered by Lost Recovery Network, Inc. (LRNI).

For some solutions, the RFID tags must be able to withstand extreme temperatures, pressure, and humidity or full submersion in order to traverse an entire supply chain or assembly line. Using space-age materials and processes, LRNI developed tag enclosures that can withstand some of the worst conditions imaginable.

Active tags are commonly used in real-time location systems (RTLSs). RTLSs allow organizations to instantly know the location of a tag because the tag is constantly monitored by a network of antennas and readers. Tags are associated with assets such as laptops and other types of expensive or vital equipment. In most RTLSs, the tagged assets must be visible to the system at all times. If an asset disappears, the system will notify the proper

Figure 3-2 LRNI enhanced-durability tag enclosure for RFCode Corp. active tag.

users that an asset has disappeared in addition to the asset's last known location.

Process analysis is also a common use for active tags. Tags are placed on the various actors in a process such as people, tools, and products. The active RFID system collects data as the process is performed. This data can then be analyzed later by industrial engineers or quality assurance teams to refine the process in question.

3.1.4.1 Active Tag Antennas

The antennas found on an active tag are not as important as the antennas found on a passive tag (see Section 3.1.11). The antennas used on an active tag only have the responsibility of transmitting and receiving. They do not have the added burden of powering the tag as do the passive tag antennas. The most important antenna in an active RFID solution is the antenna attached to the reader. The antenna attached to the reader is the component that allows an RFID designer to define an area of coverage like a room or a table in a room.

Active reader antennas can be classified in several ways. First, it is important that the antenna can read a tag in close proximity consistently. Many antennas today fail to receive a large percentage of the tag beacons as the tag is placed closer and closer to the antenna. It is not feasible to deploy these types of antennas in solutions where the coverage area is very small such as a single room. In addition, antennas should report the signal strength of a tag on a linear scale as a function of distance. As the tag is moved farther away from the antenna, the signal strength should drop linearly, not randomly or exponentially. Lastly, antennas should be configurable. One type of antenna does not provide the diversity required to meet the needs of every installation. It is important that RFID practitioners have a wide selection of antennas with different characteristics so that any requirement can be met.

Today, most antennas are connected directly to the RFID reader. The reader controls the range at which the antenna receives tag transmissions. In this configuration a reader is installed at the location where the monitoring is to be performed. LRNI has developed a suite of patented antennas specifically designed to combat the problems found in legacy RFID installations. LRNI antennas can be installed in a remote or direct connection configuration with the reader. The remote configuration allows the reader to be placed in an inconspicuous location where power and network connectivity may be readily available. The LRNI antennas can then be connected to the reader through a run of coaxial cable that can be greater than 50 meters in length.

3.1.5 Semi-Active Tags

Semi-active tags are a cross between a passive and an active tag. They do contain an onboard battery like the active tag, but the battery is not used unless the tag is interrogated by a reader. A semi-active tag still has a short interrogation range when compared to an active tag because, as with a purely passive tag, it must travel fairly close to an antenna in order to activate the battery. Once the battery is activated, the tag can behave exactly like an active tag. If the tag has temperature or chemical sensors, the battery can power those peripherals exactly the same way that a pure active tag can. Also, the battery allows the tag to transmit at the same power level as an active tag, which gives the tag greater transmission distance. Semi-active tags may contain peripheral functionality on the same scale as an active tag. They also enjoy a longer battery life than a purely active tag because they do not transmit a beacon on a regular interval. It is important to keep in mind that both active and semi-active tags are bounded by the maximum lifespan of the onboard battery.

3.1.6 Passive Tags

When someone is talking about an RFID tag, he or she is usually referring to a passive tag. Passive tags are significantly cheaper; thus, they are the tag of choice for high-volume, supply chain solutions where thousands to millions of objects will be tagged. Passive tags do not contain an onboard power source. This equates to lower-cost and typically smaller tags when compared to most active tags. Passive tags may be up to several inches in length, but they can be paper-thin.

Passive tags derive their energy from an electromagnetic field supplied by a close-proximity antenna attached to a tag reader. The lack of an onboard power source limits the range at which passive tags can be powered and read. The distance at which a tag can be read is directly proportional to the amount of energy it can absorb from the electromagnetic field generated by an antenna connected to a reader. In addition, the amount of energy that can be absorbed is directly proportional to the length of the tag's antenna. The physics related to antennas and how antennas derive energy from electromagnetic fields is described in more detail in Chapter 4.

Passive tags are usually much smaller than active tags. Some passive tags, such as Hitachi's μ-Chip®, depicted in Figure 3-3, can be smaller than a grain of rice. The μ-Chip's read range is extremely limited because of the length of the tag's antenna, but it can achieve a read range up to 25 cm when an external antenna is used. This range would be reduced even farther if the tag was separated from the reader by a type of material that impaired the propagation of electromagnetic radiation between the tag and reader.

Passive tags transmit their information using an RF technique called "backscatter." A tag uses the backscattering technique when interrogated by a reader by transmitting the response data back along the reader's original interrogation carrier wave. Most passive tag antennas are engineered for energy collection and efficient backscattering, which creates an antenna

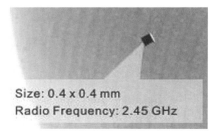
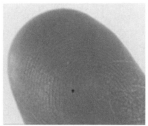

Figure 3-3 Figure 1. Hitachi μ-Chip on fingertip (*Source:* Reprinted with permission of Hitachi America, Ltd.).

that is not very good for transmitting. RFID tag readers must be very sensitive in order to recognize the small changes in the magnetic field around the reader's antenna created by the tag's backscattering.

Passive tags are packaged in several different forms. The two major forms are inlay and label. The inlay form is simply the "naked" tag. The tag is naked because it has no outer protection except for the tag substrate. Figure 3-4 is an example of an inlay manufactured by Alien Technology called the ALN-9440 Generation 2 Squiggle Tag.

The label form is a combination of an inlay, labeling paper, and adhesive backing. The labeling paper usually has the tag's information printed on it, along with a barcode encoded with the tag's unique identifier and adhesive backing, which makes it easy to attach to a box, paper, or any other object that needs to be tracked.

Special RFID tag label printers are used to create the tags. The tag label printer is loaded with a roll of inlays and a roll of paper. The RFID tag printer has a built-in tag reader that interrogates the next tag on the roll to determine what data is on the tag and then prints the tag's data on the paper, along with a barcode encoded with the tag's unique number. The paper and inlay are then married into one label, and they are both cut from their respective rolls to form a stand-alone RFID label. Some of the more advanced RFID tag readers can even write data to the tag before it is printed. These types of printers also perform a verification step to ensure that the data was written to the tag correctly. Avery Dennison Corporation, IBM Corporation, Intermec Corporation, Sato Corporation, and Zebra Technologies are just a few of the companies that sell RFID label printers.

In addition to the features listed, RFID label printers are classified by how fast they can program and print labels. Label printing speed becomes very important for high-volume assembly lines and shipping businesses.

Figure 3-4 ALN-9440 Gen2 squiggle from Alien Technology (Reprinted courtesy of Alien Technology Corporation).

The speed of a printer is measured in inches per second (IPS). A standard RFID label printer has a speed of 6 to 12 IPS (15.2 to 30.5 cm/sec). Extremely high-speed printers may achieve a speed of 24 IPS (61 cm/sec). Most RFID label printers use a thermal printing method to transfer the image or text onto the paper. Standard dots per inch (DPI) range from 100 to 300 DPI. The higher the DPI, the higher will be the resolution and quality of the image that will be on the label.

3.1.7 Semi-Passive Tags

Semi-passive tags are a subset of the passive tag classification even though they contain an onboard power source; however, the power source plays no role in the tag's RF transmission characteristics. The battery is only there to power the tag's internal circuitry and peripheral functionality. The tag benefits from the onboard power source because the tag can use all of the energy collected from the reader's antenna to transmit its data. This results in longer read ranges.

3.1.8 Radio Frequency Harmonic Tags

Radio frequency harmonic tags are a revolutionary new technology that has just begun to be developed. The leading pioneer in this arena is a company named Demodulation Inc. RF harmonic tags are similar to passive tags in that they do not have a battery, yet they are very different in that they also do not have an antenna or an integrated circuit. The RF harmonic tag has been dubbed μ-Fiber Microwire™ by Demodulation Inc., and it is part of their Microfiber Sensor Tracking system. This technology is discussed in more detail in Chapter 5.

3.1.9 EPC™Tag Classifications

EPCglobal, Inc. has defined six classifications for RFID tags (0 to 5). Table 3-1 is an overview of the classifications of tags based on their power characteristics, read ranges, memory capabilities, communication protocol, and peripheral systems. Passive tags are usually classified in the class 0 to 3 range. Class 4 describes active tags, and class 5 is reserved for tag readers and active tags that can read data from other tags.

3.1.10 Systems Operating at Various Frequencies

Electromagnetic waves have distinguishing characteristics that influence how they propagate through vacuums and through different types of materials. When related to RFID, the wave's frequency is the most important. Figure 3-5 depicts a standard radio wave pattern. The wavelength, λ, is the distance from one crest of the wave to the next crest in the wave, or from one trough to the next. The frequency of a wave is the count of the number of crests that pass a stationary point in a given period of time. For example,

Table 3-1 EPC Tag Classifications

Class	Power	Range	Memory	Communication	Peripherals	Cost
0	None	< 3 m	1 to 96 bits, Read Only	Backscatter	None	Low
1	None	< 3 m	1 to 96 bits, Read/Write Once	Backscatter	None	Low
2	None	< 3 m	1 to 96 bits, Read/Write	Backscatter	Security	Medium
3	Battery Assisted	< 100m	< 100 Kilobytes, Read/Write	Backscatter	Security, Sensors	High
4	Battery Assisted	< 300m	< 100 Kilobytes Read/Write	Active Transmission	Security, Sensor	High
5	Battery Assisted, AC/DC connection	Unlimited	Unlimited, Read/Write	Active Transmission	Security, sensors, can communicate with other tags	Very High

Source: Reprinted with permission of GS1 US.

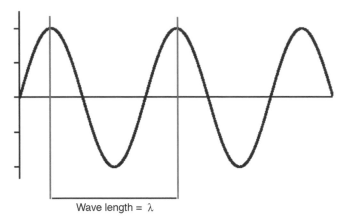

Wave length = λ

Figure 3-5 Radio wave (sine wave).

a wave with a frequency of 10 kHz would have 10,000 wave crests pass a point in one second. The wavelength can be calculated by dividing the speed of light, 299,792,458 meters per second, by the frequency of the wave. The equation is given by $\lambda = c/f$ where λ is the wavelength, c is the speed of light, and f is the frequency of the wave. Table 3-2 shows the common abbreviations used to quantify the frequencies related to RFID electromagnetic waves.

The frequency of a radio wave can be classified into standard categories as shown in Table 3-3. Frequencies from 1 GHz to 300 GHz are also referred to as *microwaves*. The majority of RFID tags fall into the LF (low frequency) to UHF (ultrahigh frequency) range, but there are a few RFID systems that operate in the microwave spectrum.

3.1.11 Passive Tag Antennas

There are two components to electromagnetic radiation: the magnetic component (H-field) and the electric component (E-field). Passive tag antennas are designed to power themselves off of one of these two components. If the tag is designed to operate in a spectrum less than VHF (see Table 3-2), it is designed with a coil type antenna. The Texas Instruments' Tag-It™

Table 3-2 Frequency Magnitude Abbreviations

Abbreviation	Cycles per Second
1 Hz (hertz)	1
1 kHz (kilohertz)	1,000
1 MHz (megahertz)	1,000,000
1 GHz (gigahertz)	1,000,000,000

Table 3-3 Frequency Classifications

	Designation	Frequency	Wavelength
ELF	Extremely low frequency	3 Hz to 29 Hz	100,000 km to 10,000 km
SLF	Super low frequency	30 Hz to 299 Hz	10,000 km to 1000 km
ULF	Ultralow frequency	300 Hz to 2999 Hz	1000 km to 100 km
VLF	Very low frequency	3 kHz to 29 kHz	100 km to 10 km
LF	Low frequency	30 kHz to 299 kHz	10 km to 1 km
MF	Medium frequency	300 kHz to 2999 kHz	1 km to 100 m
HF	High frequency	3 MHz to 29 MHz	100 m to 10 m
VHF	Very high frequency	30 MHz to 299 MHz	10 m to 1 m
UHF	Ultrahigh frequency	300 MHz to 2999 MHz	1 m to 10 cm
SHF	Super high frequency	3 GHz to 29 GHz	10 cm to 1 cm
EHF	Extremely high frequency	30 GHz to 299 GHz	1 cm to 1 mm

inlay, shown in Figure 3-6, is an example of a coil type antenna. Because of the longer wavelength of the 13.56 MHz high-frequency wave, the tag is designed to operate in the "near field." The near field is the area inside the distance of one wavelength. Based on the equation from the previous section, a 13.56 MHz wave has a wavelength of approximately 22 meters. Even though they are designed to work in the near field, it is still limited to a much closer read range than 22 meters because of the H-field strength, which is based on the frequency of the wave, the area of the antenna, and several other factors that are discussed in more detail in Chapter 4. Tags that derive energy from the near field are also called *inductive tags*. Coil type antennas are found on most tags that are to be used in applications that track or come in close contact with liquids. The reason for this is discussed later in this chapter. Inductive tags work well in applications in the clothing and laundry industries, as well as in pharmaceuticals. Texas Instruments Incorporated offers its Tag-It ™ inlay in a package that can be used for tagging clothing for dry cleaning and other laundry-type applications.

The second component is the electric component. This component is used by tags that operate at UHF and higher frequencies. Tags that derive power from the electric component have antennas that are based on a linear design in which the antenna leads are mostly straight. The electric field is also

Figure 3-6 13.56-MHz Tag-It inlay (*Source:* Reprinted by permission of Texas Instruments Incorporated).

known as the "far field," and these types of tags are also known as *radiative tags*. Table 3-4 shows an overview of the relationship to radio wave frequency and tag antenna types.

For the electric component of an electromagnetic wave to induce a current in an antenna, the wave must intersect the antenna at a right angle. The physics behind this phenomenon is explained in depth in Chapter 4. RFID tag antenna designers must always keep this in mind when they develop a new tag. "Squiggle" tags were created to present the antenna to the wave at all the angles possible. Squiggle tags are useful for solutions where the object being tracked may be set at different orientations. Figure 3-4 is an example of a squiggle tag.

For RFID solutions where the tag orientation can be controlled, a dipole antenna may be used. Dipole antennas are two (hence, di–) poles separated by a small gap in which the tag's IC is usually placed. The poles are placed on each side of the IC in a symmetric layout such that the energy collected by the poles is directed into the IC. Figure 3-7 is an example of a single dipole antenna manufactured by Symbol Technologies, Inc. This antenna is 15 cm long and 2.5 cm wide.

The dipole antenna is 15 cm long because it is tuned to receive a 915-MHz carrier wave. Dipole antennas should be approximately half as long as the carrier wave frequency for optimal coupling. Dipole antennas that are half the wavelength of the carrier wave will resonate at the correct frequency required to induce a current in the antenna.

RFID tags must absorb as much energy from the reader's high-gain antennas as they physically can. Not only does the orientation of the antenna help couple the tag's antenna with the reader's antenna, but the width of the antenna also matters. Figure 3-8 shows a tag manufactured by Alien Technology. The ALN-9354-R "M" tag is designed for difficult tagging locations. Its width allows it to absorb much more energy than a tag with a simple dipole antenna.

3.1.12 RF Characteristics

Radio waves exhibit different characteristics at different frequencies. These characteristics should be taken into account in the design of an RFID solution. For RFID solutions, there are three main characteristics to keep in mind:

Table 3-4 Overview of Tag Antenna Types

Frequency	Field	Tag Type	Antenna Type
LF	Near	Inductive	Coil
HF	Near	Inductive	Coil
UHF	Far	Radiative	Linear

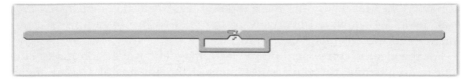

Figure 3-7 Single-dipole inlay (*Source:* Reprinted by permission of Symbol Technologies Inc.).

1. *Data rate.* The amount of data that can be encoded into an RF transmission
2. *Permittivity.* The types of materials through which a radio wave is able to propagate
3. *Distance.* The maximum distance that a tag can be powered

3.1.12.1 Data Rate

The first characteristic to keep in mind is the data rate that can be attained at a specific frequency. The amount of data that can be sent using a radio wave increases as the frequency increases. At higher frequencies, more wave crests will come in contact with the receiving antenna than would occur if the wave was at a lower frequency. A single piece of data can be encoded in each wavelength of the wave (see Figure 3-5). If the reader is able to "see" more wave crests in a shorter period of time, then it will be able to decode more data. Details on how data is encoded into and decoded from the wave are given in Chapter 4. For solutions in which the tags will be moving at a high velocity, such as a high-speed conveyor belt, the data rate must be sufficiently high enough to transmit all of the tag's data before the tag leaves the reader's interrogation range.

The available bandwidth in the radio frequency spectrum is also a contributor to the maximum attainable data rate. The maximum data rate increases with the bandwidth. A wider bandwidth allows more devices to communicate simultaneously. If all devices communicated at one frequency, it would be very hard for a large number of devices to effectively share the single frequency. The devices would be required to take turns transmitting

Figure 3-8 ALN-9354-R "M" tag (*Source:* Courtesy of Alien Technology Corporation).

which would reduce the data rate as the number of devices increased. Communication algorithms take advantage of the bandwidth to share the spectrum.

Ultra wideband (UWB) is a new form of RF communication where a very large frequency range is utilized, but the transmissions are so short and weak that there is no interference between devices. UWB can attain tremendous data rates. There are regulations regarding the ranges in the RF spectrum that can be utilized for RF communications. These regulations place limits on the data rates that can be obtained by certain types of devices. The reason for this regulation is discussed later in this chapter.

3.1.12.2 Permittivity

When designing an RFID solution, the designer must keep in mind the materials that will be in close proximity to the tags. Each type of material will absorb a certain frequency because of the atomic structure and density of the material, which results in a retardation of the wave's propagation through the material. A good example of this is a microwave oven. The waves that are emitted by the oven are in the microwave spectrum, which is a frequency greater than 1 GHz. As the microwaves contact water molecules in the item (food, soup, water, etc.) being heated, the microwaves transfer their energy into the water. As the water absorbs more and more energy, the water's temperature begins to rise. The microwaves may also transfer their energy into other composite materials of the food, but the microwave frequencies are tuned to efficiently transfer their energy into water molecules. As the temperature of the molecules rise, the item is heated and eventually cooked. The absorption of the energy on the borders of the item will heat the item from the outside to the inside.

RFID tags experience signal attenuation problems when placed near materials that absorb the RF energy that they require in order to power themselves and transmit data. RFID systems that operate at microwave frequencies should not be deployed into environments that operate in close proximity to liquids. For this reason, the pharmaceutical industry has decided to use HF tags, such as those that operate at 13.56 MHz, as opposed to UHF tags, because many pharmaceutical products contain a sufficient amount of water to attenuate radio waves in the higher frequency ranges.

3.1.12.3 Distance

The amount of energy that can be absorbed from an electromagnetic wave is directly proportional to its frequency; therefore, passive RFID systems that operate at higher frequencies have greater read ranges. Because of this, most passive RFID systems today operate in the UHF spectrum at 915 MHz.

3.1.13 Radio Frequency Regulation

The radio frequency spectrum that engineers today are capable of utilizing is not infinite. The finite RF spectrum can be a serious issue if multiple devices are attempting to send data at the same frequency and they are in close proximity to one another. The interference would effectively jam everyone's transmissions. Because of the fact that there exists only a finite amount of RF real estate available, it must be regulated to avoid confusion. RF spectrum regulation ensures that the endless numbers of RF-capable devices in the world are not all communicating at the same frequency or that they share the bandwidth in an organized manner.

Most countries around the world have a governmental organization that regulates the radio frequency spectrum in the country. The Federal Communications Commission (FCC) is the organization in the United States that is responsible for RF regulation, and the European Telecommunications Standards Institute (ETSI), headquartered in France, oversees the RF regulation for Europe. Table 3-5 lists a few of the many telecommunications regulatory agencies from around the world.

Even though the RF spectrum is regulated mostly on a country-by-country basis, there are frequency ranges that are widely adopted around the world. Part C presents RFID activities in 10 countries including regulation in those countries.

The spectrum is regulated by frequency ranges, and it is sliced into thousands of regulated frequencies with each slice having an intended purpose. For example, Citizen's band (CB) radio is assigned the HF range from 26.965 MHz to 27.405 MHz. This spectrum has been allocated for short-range communication radios as well as for remote controls for various devices such as toys. The allocated frequency range for RFID in the United States is 902 MHz to 928 MHz. It is customary to refer to this frequency range by its middle frequency, which, in this case, is 915 MHz. It is proper to say that RFID systems in the United States operate at 915 MHz even though they communicate across the allocated range of frequencies plus-or-minus 15 MHz from 915 MHz. The range of frequencies allocated is also known as the *bandwidth*. The majority of EPC-compliant RFID tags operate

Table 3-5 Telecommunications Regulatory Agencies

Country	Name
Australia	Australian Communication and Media Authority
China	National Radio Administration Bureau under the Federal Network Agency
Germany*	Federal Network Agency
Japan	Ministry of Internal Affairs and Communication
United Kingdom*	Office of Communications
United States	Federal Communications Commission and the National Telecommunications and Information Administration

*The Radio and Telecommunications Terminal Equipment Directive, known as the R&TTE directive or RTTE for short, is the main route to compliance for Radio and Telecoms equipment that is sold in Europe.

at 915 MHz, but other frequency ranges are available for RFID in the United States. These ranges include 13.56 MHz, 2.4 GHz, 303 MHz, and 433 MHz, to name a few.

The United States has allocated a fairly large range (30 MHz) for RFID, while countries in Europe have allocated much less, usually 865.6 MHz to 867.6 MHz (2 MHz). There are several methods for utilizing the allocated bandwidth efficiently. For a large bandwidth, as in the United States, a method known as Frequency Hopping Spread Spectrum (FHSS) is employed. Implementations that have less bandwidth use the method known as Listen Before Talk (LBT).

FHSS changes frequencies pseudorandomly through the allocated spectrum while broadcasting. Both the receiver and the transmitter must change to the same frequency at the same time. FHSS helps to minimize interference that may exist in some of the frequencies because only a very small slice of the communication is done on each frequency. If the transmitter and receiver were to communicate on one frequency and that frequency had some interference, then it may not be able to communicate at all. FHSS avoids this problem. FHSS also implements a very mild form of security. In order to eavesdrop on a conversation using FHSS, the eavesdropper would need to know the pseudorandom frequency hopping algorithm; otherwise, the eavesdropper would only receive a very small portion of the transmission.

Listen Before Talk is not as forgiving as FHSS, but it works well when there is limited bandwidth allocation. The LBT algorithm mandates that each transmitter must listen to the frequency it wishes to use prior to broadcasting. If something else is communicating on that frequency, the transmitter must either wait until the other user's transmission is finished or move to another frequency. This method is very slow when compared to FHSS because of the listening time required before the transmitter can safely broadcast its information. With both LBT and FHSS, there is a saturation point at which there is not enough bandwidth to service all transmitters. When bandwidth saturation occurs, devices may be denied service with LBT protocols, or all the frequencies may be used such that no transmitter can send an uninterrupted transmission with FHSS protocols.

When a range of frequencies is regulated, there is usually a restriction on who can broadcast in that range. Citizens band in the United States can be used by any U.S. citizen, but there are restrictions on how powerful the transmitter can be. Most regulated frequencies have rules regarding the maximum broadcasting power, expressed in watts, and the type and size of antenna that can be used to broadcast. The power ratings for broadcasting can be defined by two separate ratings. The first rating is the Effective Isotropic Radiated Power (EIRP). This measurement of the power is based on an isotropic antenna (a spherical emitter). An isotropic antenna broadcasts evenly in all directions to create a sphere around the antenna. The second rating is the Effective Radiated Power (ERP). This measurement is based on a dipole antenna. Dipole antennas do not broadcast in a spherical pattern. Dipole antennas cannot emit electromagnetic radiation from the ends of the dipole. The result is a donut-shaped area around the dipole antenna. ERP values can be converted to EIRP values by using the simple equation:

$$EIRP = ERP \times 1.64$$

EPCglobal maintains a living document that records the current RF regulation status for the UHF spectrum related to RFID entitled "Regulatory Status for Using RFID in the UHF Spectrum." Table 3-6 shows a small sampling of the information contained in the document. The document contains information for 98 countries, which encompasses a large percentage of the world's gross national income (Barthel, 2006). The "Status" column identifies the current state of RF regulation in the associated country. If the status is "Ok", the spectrum is available for RFID to use.

Table 3-6 Telecommunication Regulation Status for EPC-Compliant Tags

Country	Frequency	Power	Technique	Status
Australia	920–926 MHz	4W EIRP		Ok
Brazil	902–907.5 MHz	4W EIRP	FHSS	Ok
	915–928 MHz	4W EIRP	FHSS	Ok
Canada	902–928 MHz	4W EIRP	FHSS	Ok
China	917–922 MHz	2W ERP		In Progress: License Only
Egypt				In Progress
France	865.6–867.6 MHz	2W ERP	LBT	Ok
Germany	865.6–867.6 MHz	2W ERP	LBT	Ok
Italy	865.6–867.6 MHz	2W ERP	LBT	In Progress: Military Conflict, No Licensing
Japan	952–954MHz	4W EIRP	LBT	Ok
Russian Federation	865.6–867.6 MHz	2W ERP	LBT	In Progress: LBT License Only
South Africa	865.6–867.6 MHz	2W ERP	LBT	Ok
	917–921 MHz	4W EIRP	FHSS	Ok
United Kingdom	865.6–867.6 MHz	2W ERP	LBT	Ok
United States	902–928 MHz	4W EIRP	FHSS	Ok
Uruguay	902–928 MHz	4W EIRP	FHSS	Ok
Venezuela, RB	922–928 MHz			In Progress

3.2 RFID Readers

RFID readers are also referred to as interrogators because they query tags as the tags enter their read range. Readers are classified by EPC as a class 5 device. The reader is responsible for orchestrating the communication with any tags in its read range and then presenting the tags' data to an application that can make use of the data. The frequency ranges at which a system operates is defined by the reader because it is the reader's antennas that emit the energy used by the tags in a passive tag implementation. As discussed earlier, an antenna for a 915 MHz tag is tuned to resonate at the correct frequency so that it can easily couple with the reader's antennas. The reader's antennas must generate the carrier wave at the correct frequency so that the tag in its range will be able to absorb the RF energy.

Readers must be able to sense minute changes in the electromagnetic field that they generate through their antennas because this is the way in which the tags communicate with the reader. The communication between the reader and tag can be compared to a game of tug-of-war. The reader and the tag are the two players in the game. Once the tag has latched onto the rope, it can pull on the rope to send signals back to the reader, but the reader can always pull on the rope with a much stronger force than the tag. The reader must be able to sense these "pulls" in order to receive the tag's information. Each pull on the rope sends 1 bit of information. The tag strings together a series of these bits to form bytes (8 bits) of information. Bytes of information form messages such as EPC data or any other type of data that the tag needs to communicate.

The reader must also communicate with the tags. The reader orchestrates the communication between itself and all of the tags in its read range. Readers have a power source; therefore, in the RF tug-o-war, they can pull exponentially harder on the tag than the tag can on the reader. The reader's antennas must be supplied with enough power to emit sufficient electromagnetic radiation to power the tags, but the amount of electromagnetic radiation needed to power the tags creates an equivalent amount of RF noise. The net effect is that the reader is screaming while the tag is whispering.

3.2.1 Reader Components

RF Code Inc., Savi Technology, Inc., Intermec Technologies Corporation, IPICO, and Thing Magic are just a few of the companies that manufacture RFID reader hardware. Most of the readers produced by these and other RFID manufacturers are targeted for the EPC Gen 1 and Gen 2 specification.

3.2.1.1 Enterprise Management Console

Manufacturers differentiate themselves from each other with their software and enterprise deployment model. Companies that offer an enterprise-wide solution along with their hardware enable their customers to easily manage their reader installation from one central back-office console. Central management consoles enable enterprise solutions by adding real-time hardware failure alerts, remote reader interrogation, and software deployment and upgrade management.

3.2.1.2 Application-to-Reader Interface

Most RFID reader manufacturers provide a software starter kit in the form of a collection of software libraries or application programming interfaces (APIs). These software components can greatly decrease any custom application development time that a company must invest in a new RFID project where a custom application is being written.

If a custom application is not the goal, most RFID readers are bundled with generic out-of-the-box software that will aggregate RFID data across a set of RFID readers and deposit the data in a database. The database can then be queried using standard database reporting tools to generate reports from the collected data.

3.2.1.3 Hardware Interface

Readers are available with many different types of hardware interfaces. These interfaces range from RS232 (serial communications) to wireless 802.11B/G. The most common interfaces are RS232 for close-proximity connectivity, RS480 for industrial medium distance connectivity, and TCP/IP over Ethernet or 802.11B/G for enterprise-wide installations.

3.2.1.4 Enhanced Durability

The possible applications for RFID are infinite. With an extremely large number of applications for RFID comes a myriad of environments in which RFID readers will be deployed. Some environments are extremely harsh and require enhanced durability enclosures. Many readers that are built based on military specifications are able to operate, for example, in extreme temperatures and hostile environments. These types of readers also have enhanced connectors that withstand being jolted or dropped.

3.2.1.5 Tag Density

One of the most important reader characteristics is a metric that identifies the maximum number of tags that a reader can successfully read in one second. Today's standard is somewhere between 50 and 100 tags for passive tag systems and 50 to 900 tags per second for active tag systems. In warehouses where pallets are made up of several containers that in turn include several tags, tag density may be a real concern. One method to reduce tag density is to deploy more readers with smaller coverage areas. This method effectively reduces the number of tags each reader must process while still covering the required area.

3.2.1.6 Form Factor

Depending on the application, a stationary or handheld reader may be necessary. Mobile scanners come in two main form factors. The first is the fully integrated device. These devices are built just for reading RFID tags. Some come with barcode scanning capabilities as an added feature. The second option is a PCMCIA, SDIO, or CompactFlash cards. These interface cards can plug into most desktop PCs, laptops, and an ever-growing number of handheld devices.

3.3 Tag and Reader Communication

3.3.1 Passive Systems

Once a tag is powered and has established a physical link with a reader, a communication protocol must be followed in order for the tag and reader to communicate in a meaningful way. The protocol allows the reader to interrogate tags inside its read range using a basic set of commands and knowledge of how memory is organized on the tag. The EPC air interface protocol that defines the memory layout and interrogator-to-transponder communication is discussed in the following sections. The version 1.0.9 specification can be found at the EPCglobal Web site via http://www.epcglobalus.org / dnn_epcus / KnowledgeBase / Browse / tabid / 277 / DMXModule/706/Command/Core_Download/Default.aspx?EntryId=292 (EPCglobal, 2005). The EPC standard is not the only standard for passive communication, but as of the writing of this book, it is the most widely adopted. Chapter 7 provides a detailed discussion of RFID standards.

3.3.1.1 Passive Tag Memory Layout

Passive tags store information such as their unique identifier, current state, and user defined data. Figure 3-9 shows the layout of data as it is stored in a set of four memory banks on the tag. These are called the reserved, electronic product code, tag identification, and user memory banks. Each bank groups together related tag data.

The reserved memory bank, shown in Figure 3-10, contains the Kill and Access passwords. For tags that implement passwords, a reader is required to supply the appropriate password to successfully issue a Kill command or Lock Tag Memory. If a tag does not implement password protection, the tag must treat this memory location as zero values that are permanently locked to read and write operations.

The next memory bank is the Electronic Product Code (EPC) bank, as shown in Figure 3-11. The definition of EPC in this context does not refer

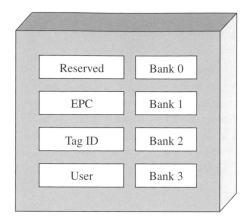

Figure 3-9 Tag memory layout.

to the Electronic Product Code as defined by EPCglobal, though this memory bank can contain an EPCglobal EPC if the tag manufacturer is complying with the EPC specification. The first piece of data found in the EPC bank is a 16-bit Cyclic Redundancy Check (CRC-16) field. The CRC-16 value is a computed quantity that is used to validate the integrity of the rest of the data found in the EPC memory bank. Located directly after the CRC-16 value is the Protocol Control (PC) field, followed by a code that uniquely identifies the tag. This code is what RFID is all about. For EPC compliant tags, this code is an EPC as defined by EPCglobal. Other types of codes can be placed in this field depending on the data format specification implemented by the tag manufacturer. The length of the code and the Numbering System Identifier (NSI) are encoded in the PC field mentioned earlier.

The Tag Identification (TID) memory bank contains an 8-bit ISO/IEC 15963 class identifier, as shown in Figure 3-12. This TID associates the tag

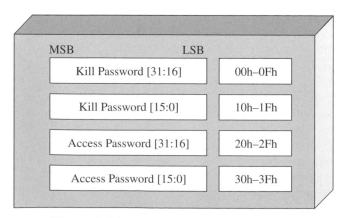

Figure 3-10 Reserved memory bank layout.

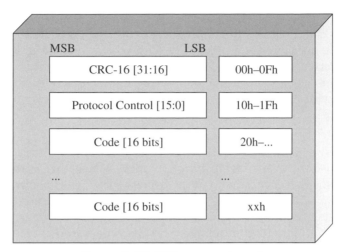

Figure 3-11 EPC memory layout.

with the type/manufacturer of the tag. The hexadecimal value of E2 identifies EPC tags. The memory located above the first 8 bits in the TID memory bank contains data that enumerates the class-specific capabilities of the tag.

The last memory bank is a user-defined data storage area. For tags that support user-defined data, this is where reads and writes will be targeted. The size of this bank is determined by the manufacturer and can be found in the tag data specification.

3.3.1.2 Tag Commands
The reader issues commands to tags in its read range in order to access the data found on the tag. Tags in the reader's range are also referred to as the

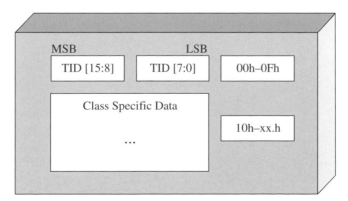

Figure 3-12 TID memory bank layout.

reader's tag population. Each tag has a set of commands coded in its IC that allows RFID readers to communicate with the tags. These commands allow the reader to select a set of tags with which to communicate, inventory the selected tags, and read and write data and status information from each tag. Some of these commands must be implemented by a tag in order to comply with ISO 18000-6 and EPC Air Interface specifications. All commands are issued from the reader.

3.3.1.2.1 Select Command The reader may not always want to retrieve information from every tag in its population. When this is the case, the reader has the Select command at its disposal. The Select command allows the reader to select a subset of the tag population based on data found on each tag using union, intersection, and negation of sets of tags.

The selection criteria are defined by a data mask and memory location on the tag. When a tag processes the Select command, it compares the data mask with the memory location specified by the select. If the mask matches the data at the specified location on the tag, the tag is "selected" into the active population. The selected state is also known as the *arbitrate* state.

If the reader wants to select all tags that are EPC tags, the reader would issue the Select command targeting the TID memory bank with an E2h mask for the data at offset 0 in the TID memory bank. This will select all EPC tags because the allocation class identifier is stored in the first 8 bits of the TID memory bank, and the EPC class identifier value is E2h.

3.3.1.2.2 Inventory Commands After the reader has selected a subset of the tag population, ranging from one tag to all the tags, the reader must determine which tags are in the selected population. The Air Interface protocol defines a set of inventory commands that allow reading the tag's unique identifier, CRC-16, and a random number generated by the tag. The random number helps decrease the number of tag transmission collisions, provides a simple cryptography key, and is used as a handle to identify the tag. The inventory commands are Query, QueryAdjust, QueryRep, ACK, and NAK.

3.3.1.2.2.1 Query The query is the first command issued to a selected tag population. One of the parameters to the query command is a Q value. The Q value is a seed number used to generate a random number. A reader can pass a Q value from 0 to 15. The tag generates a random number in the range of 0 to 2^Q-1, which is 0 to 7FFFh because the maximum value for Q is 15.

The tag stores this random number in a "slot" memory location. If the random value is 0, the tag immediately transmits its 16-bit random number; otherwise, it waits for another command from the reader.

A reader will send an ACK (acknowledge) (see Section 3.3.1.2.2.4) command back to the tag if it successfully receives the tag's information. Upon receipt of the ACK command, the tag transmits its PC, unique identifier, and CRC-16 value and switches to the acknowledged state. If more than one tag generates a zero, the reader may not be able to distinguish one tag's transmission from the other. In this case, the reader will not respond to the tag and the tag will immediately set its slot value to 7FFFh.

If a reader expects a large population of tags, a reader may use a large Q value for the query. A larger Q value will allow the tags to generate a larger range of random numbers. A larger range of random numbers ensures that fewer tags attempt to transmit at the same time. Smaller tag populations should be queries with a smaller Q value such that the chance of generating a random number of 0 is greater. If a tag does not generate a random number of 0 when the reader issues the Query command, it will usually get another chance to transmit when the reader issues one of the other inventory commands.

Every tag in the selected population can be inventoried if a Q value of 0 is used. However, this method really only works when the reader's tag population is one because if more than one tag transmits at the same time, the reader will only respond to one tag if possible. Most likely, the reader will not be able to get a fix on any of the tag transmissions and all of the tags will be ignored by the reader.

3.3.1.2.2.2 QueryAdjust The QueryAdjust command allows the reader to change the Q value used in the original Query command and force all tags to calculate a new random slot number. The reader may lower the Q value so that more tags will get an opportunity to transmit when they generate a random number of 0, or increase the Q value to reduce the number of tags that are attempting to transmit at the same time. The QueryAdjust command has a parameter that tells the tags to either increase, decrease, or do not change the Q value. If a tag already has a 0 or 7FFFh slot value, no change is made to the Q value for the tag. In either case, a new random number is generated.

3.3.1.2.2.3 QueryRep The QueryRep command instructs the tags to decrement their slot value. When a tag's slot value reaches 0, it transmits its 16-bit random number, which starts the process described in the Query command above. A tag slot value of 0 is the key to inventorying the reader's tag population. A reader may issue a Query command to set all the tag's initial slot values and the issue multiple QueryRep commands to inventory all tags as each tag's slot value reaches 0.

3.3.1.2.2.4 ACK and NAK The ACK command stands for "acknowledge." The ACK command is sent to a tag after it has transmitted its random number when its slot value is 0. A tag responds to an ACK by transmitting its PC, unique identifier, and CRC-16 value. The NAK command stands for "negative acknowledgement." The NAK command issued by the reader when the reader wants to reset a tag to the arbitrate state.

3.3.1.2.3 Access Commands These commands are used to access the user memory bank. The access commands include Req_RN (for request random number), Read, Write, Kill, Lock, Access, BlockWrite, and BlockErase. Req_RN can be executed by the tag once it is placed in the acknowledged state. Read, Write, and Access can be executed if the tag is in the open or secured state. Kill can be executed from either the open or secured state, while Lock can only be executed from the secured state.

3.3.1.2.3.1 Req_RN A reader can request a 16-bit random number from a tag using the Req_RN command. The reader must pass the 16-bit random number transmitted by the tag earlier along with a valid CRC-16 calculated using the random number and Req_RN command code. If the CRC-16 is validated by the tag, the tag will generate and store a new random number and transmit it back to the reader. The tag also transitions into the open state. If the tag is already in the open or secured state, the tag will generate a new random number, transmit it back to the reader, and remain in its current state. The new random number is used as a handle for future access commands.

3.3.1.2.3.2 Read To access user data, the reader can execute a Read command. The Read command allows the reader to read data from all four memory banks. The parameters for the Read command select a range of memory in a bank to return to the reader. The parameters include the memory bank identifier, the offset in the memory bank, and the number of words (16 bits each) to read. If the word count is 0, the read will return memory from the specified offset to the end of the selected memory bank. If the requested memory location is locked, an error will be returned to the reader.

3.3.1.2.3.3 Write A Write command is the opposite of a Read command but shares many of the same parameters. A Write command writes one word (16 bits) to the specified memory bank and offset on the tag. The data is exclusive OR'd (usually written as XOR) with the tag's handle value before being sent to the tag. The XOR of the data with the handle ensures that the data is not passed in cleartext. If the specified memory write location is locked, an error will be returned to the reader; otherwise, the data is written to the targeted location and can be read by subsequent Read commands. On a successful write, the tag must respond with a success message within 20 milliseconds.

3.3.1.2.3.4 Kill A tag can be sent the Kill command if the tag is to no longer respond to any commands ever again. Issuing a Kill command is a multicommand process. Once the process is started, any errors will return the tag to the arbitrate state. The multicommand process involves the Kill command and the Req_RN command. See Figure 3-13 for a complete overview of the Kill command sequence.

3.3.1.2.3.5 Access This command is the way to transition from the open state to the secured state. Tags with nonzero access passwords can make this transition by following the same basic process used by the Kill command. Once the transition has been made to the secured state, the Lock command can be issued. The Access command is an optional command and is not implemented by all tags. See Figure 3-14 for a complete overview of the Access command sequence.

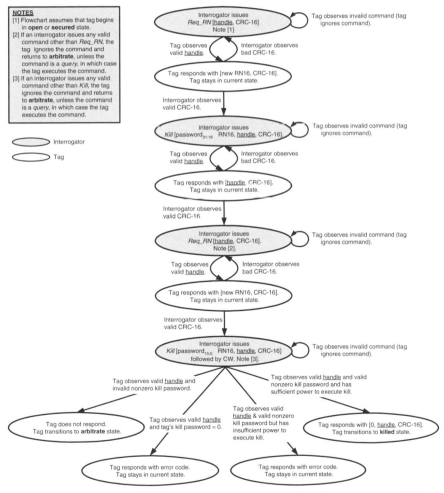

Figure 3-13 Kill command sequence (*Source:* Reprinted with permission of GS1 US).

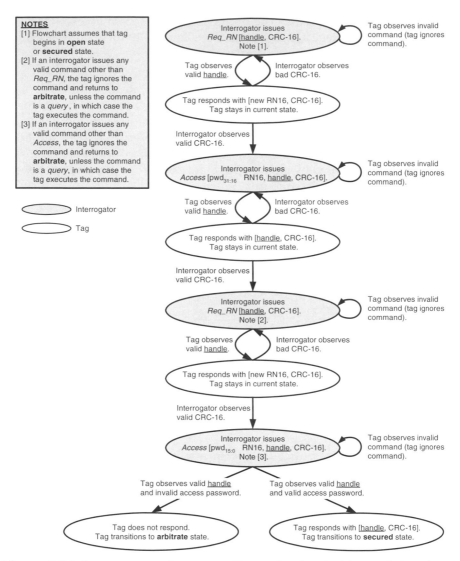

Figure 3-14 Access command sequence (*Source:* Reprinted with permission of GS1 US).

3.3.1.2.3.6 Lock This command is used to lock memory locations from being read or written. The Lock command has a special mode called *permalock*. The permalock functionality allows a reader to permanently lock a password or memory bank. A tag must first be in the secured state before this command can be executed.

3.3.1.2.3.7 BlockWrite and BlockErase The BlockWrite command works just like the Write command, but instead of writing one memory location at a time, it writes a block at a time. The data written through BlockWrite is passed as cleartext, unlike the Write command. Like the BlockWrite, the BlockErase operates across a range of memory locations on the tag. A BlockErase can erase 1 to x memory locations in a single command. Implementation of the BlockErase and BlockWrite commands by the tag are both optional.

3.3.1.3 Active Systems

Active tags do not have the same requirements or limitations as passive tags because of their onboard battery. The battery opens up a world of possibilities for the tag. Active tags can afford to have very advanced memory layout structures and access protocols. The diversity and specialization of active-tag-based systems has kept memory layout and communication standards at bay as of this writing. Most active tag manufacturers prefer to keep their methods of power management, anticollision algorithms, and memory layout under lock and key. Until the day when these corporations agree on an open standard, RFID practitioners must access the tags through each corporation's defined interface for their system. Active RFID systems that are not built on top of standardized protocols do have some advantages. Non-standardized systems usually allow for greater tag density, smaller tag size, and longer battery life. The tradeoff is that the infrastructure is proprietary and the tags will only work in facilities that have the same RFID hardware provider.

There is a hierarchy of tags that have their foundations built on existing technologies. Protocols such as Wi-Fi (802.11x), ZigBee (802.15.4), and Ultra Wideband are all platforms for RFID technology. The following sections will compare and contrast these technologies.

3.3.1.3.1 Wi-Fi Tags   Active tags that communicate over the 802.11x protocol are called Wi-Fi tags. In this type of system each tag has its own IP address that uniquely identifies the tag across the network and each wireless access point on the network functions as a reader. Using a Wi-Fi type active tag allows businesses to leverage their existing wireless infrastructure to quickly become RFID enabled. In most cases, any devices that already have Wi-Fi network adapters can be tracked. These are the top two advantages of Wi-Fi based RFID over other active tag platforms. Basically, any Wi-Fi enabled device becomes a Wi-Fi tag. Businesses find this very attractive because of the ease of becoming RFID enabled.

Wi-Fi tags do have some downsides. The tags are expensive, large in size, and have a relatively short battery life. Wi-Fi tags also consume IP addresses that can become a resource management problem for a business' IT department as the tag population grows. They also use network bandwidth. If the existing network is already saturated, the introduction of hundreds or thousands of tags could flood the network to the point where both RFID and business data communications become extremely impaired.

Many RFID engineers claim that Wi-Fi tags do not provide the resolution of coverage that most other RTLSs deliver today. As location algorithms become better, the resolution that can be attained using a Wi-Fi infrastructure will improve. Wi-Fi tags have their place in the RFID tool belt and should be used in the correct applications.

3.3.1.3.2 ZigBee Tags   ZigBee tags communicate over the 802.15.4 protocol. ZigBee got its name from the way that bees zigzag between flowers when they are collecting pollen. The analogy of bees pollinating flowers refers to the way in which this protocol transmits relatively small amounts of data between computers, appliances, and tags on the network. The 802.11 protocol has high data communication rates at up to 54 Mbps while ZigBee transmits at a maximum of 250 kbps. ZigBee is an ideal choice for certain types of applications where data throughput is not an issue. A remote control is an example of a good ZigBee application. ZigBee was initially targeted at home and industrial automation, but RFID has latched on to the technology as well.

ZigBee tags offer a longer battery life than Wi-Fi tags, and they do not require as much software embedded in the tag to implement the protocol. The protocol software is usually referred to as a "stack." A small stack equates to less memory and less CPU horsepower required. ZigBee tags are smaller than Wi-Fi tags and generally cost less.

ZigBee can operate at various frequencies. This is not to say that ZigBee tags can change between the frequencies dynamically, but there is an option to buy ZigBee tags with radios that target a specific frequency such as 303 MHz, 433 MHz, or 2.4 GHz. The selectable frequency allows ZigBee to be a player on the global RFID market.

The ZigBee infrastructure does require ZigBee access points to be installed just like conventional active tag infrastructures. However, once a ZigBee infrastructure is installed it can be used to communicate with any ZigBee enabled device as well as ZigBee tags. In a healthcare setting, ZigBee enabled telemetry devices such as intra-venous pumps or fetal heart monitors could take advantage of the existing ZigBee infrastructure.

3.3.1.3.3 Ultra Wideband Tags   Ultra Wideband (UWB) technology is a relatively new way of communication using RF. Classically, any protocol that has a bandwidth greater than 500 MHz or that is 20% of its center frequency is classified as UWB. Starting February 14, 2002, the United States FCC allocated a bandwidth of more that 7 GHz to UWB! The band begins at 3.1 GHz and ends at 10.6 GHz. UWB communicates by sending very short and low power signals throughout this wide spectrum at specific points in time based on the communication protocol implemented. This is vastly different from traditional RF communications where the bandwidth is narrow and the information is encoded onto an RF carrier wave. UWB is sometimes referred to as "zero carrier" radio due to this fact. The pulses range from 10 picoseconds to 1 nanosecond.

Along with the wide spectrum comes a tremendous transmission rate. UWB can transmit over 100 megabits per second. The data rate that is achievable is dependent on the distance between the communication endpoints. The highest data rates are achievable within the 10 meter range. As with ZigBee and Wi-Fi, an increase in distance decreases the data rate of the protocol. Even though the high data rates are not a real bonus for RFID there are several other reasons why UWB is a great fit for RFID.

As discussed earlier in this chapter, traditional RF communications are licensed by the government to ensure that devices do not drown each other out. UWB communications do not have this problem. UWB transmissions are not powerful enough to interfere with classic RF transmissions. In fact, the transmissions are weaker than the spurious signals that are emitted by most consumer electronic devices. Until recently, these types of transmissions were referred to as RF garbage. Even though UWB will not interfere with classic carrier wave transmissions, the FCC has defined what UWB is and how it should behave. UWB transmits at around 0.25 milliwatts when aggregated across the entire UWB spectrum. This is minute when compared to the 10 to 100 milliwatts for Wi-Fi. The low power requirements for UWB transmissions equates to longer battery life for RFID tags. UWB RFID tags have a standard battery life of up to one year.

All carrier wave based transmissions share a common problem called multipathing. Multipathing is the distortion of a signal that is caused when direct and reflected signals arrive at a reader's antenna. In indoor environments, multipathing can be an extremely difficult problem to solve because a signal has so many objects that can reflect the signal. Some of the RF waves may travel directly to the antenna while others may bounce around the room before they eventually make it to the antenna. The reader then has the tough job of determining which one of the signals is the best. UWB does not have this problem due to the extremely short pulses when transmitting. The accuracy of transmission creates new opportunities for RTLSs. UWB can pinpoint an object in a room to within 30 centimeters using triangulation and location algorithms like time distance on arrival (TDOA) and angle of arrival (AOA). This is vastly better than the other types of active tag systems that can at best give a resolution of 3 meters using triangulation.

The increased granularity comes at a price. The UWB readers, which are also known as sensors, are more expensive because of the high quality components that are required to differentiate signals at that resolution. Most off the shelf systems require four or more sensors in a single 10 by 10 meter room to achieve 30 centimeter resolution. There are applications in which this level of granularity is needed, but most RTLSs need at most room level granularity.

Classic RFID systems can achieve higher levels of granularity by using a zone based approach rather than triangulation in areas where increased granularity is a requirement. Zone based systems place attenuated antennas at the location where the restricted coverage is desired. If a tag enters the zone, it can be reported to that zone based on the antenna that is reading the tag. This type of approach can yield a granularity of less than 30 centimeters but is not feasible for entire rooms.

3.3.2 Summary

Building an RFID solution that will satisfy business needs requires knowledge of the RFID building blocks that are available. The two most basic building blocks are the tag and the reader. Tags and readers are also referred to as transponders and interrogators, respectively. There are several types of tags and readers that can be utilized based on a solution's need. Tags have different read ranges, life spans, durability, and costs. All of these factors must be weighed during the design of an RFID solution. Along with the multitude of tags available comes a wide selection of manufacturers. Some build only hardware components, while others build everything including hardware and a suite of software tools for reporting and sharing RFID data.

Today, EPC specifications are leading the way for passive RFID solutions. Companies such as IPICO are also defining standards in the international arena. As of the writing of this book, the standard of choice for most industries in the United States is the standard for EPC Class 1, Generation 2 tags. Companies are reducing infrastructure costs by creating new-edge devices that simplify and reduce the cost of installation and system management. Active RFID systems are beginning to blossom as more and more industries understand their capabilities and as the cost of hardware and installation drop.

RFID has already reached around the world. Governments and regulatory agencies are gearing up for the myriad of RFID-enabled devices that will soon flood the market. Because the world is becoming smaller every day, it is extremely important that RFID is standardized on a global scale. Goods from China may travel half way around the world and come in contact with tens if not hundreds of RFID systems along the supply chain. EPCglobal and ISO are leading the way toward this global standard, and it is important that all RFID practitioners foster the standardization effort.

Acronyms

ACK—Acknowledgment

AOA—Angle of arrival

API—Application programming interface

CB—Citizens' band

CPU—Central Processing Unit

CRC—Cyclic Redundancy Check

DPI—Dots per inch

EHF—Extremely high frequency

EIRP—Effective Isotropic Radiated Power

ELF—Extremely low frequency

ERP—Effective Radiated Power (as applied to RF)

ETSI—European Telecommunications Standards Institute

FCC—Federal Communications Commission

FHSS—Frequency Hopping Spread Spectrum

HF—High frequency

IC—Integrated circuit

IPS—Inches per second

LBT—Listen Before Talk

LF—Low frequency

MF—Medium frequency

NAK—Negative acknowledgement

NSI—Numbering System Identifier

PC—Personal computer

PC—Protocol Control (as applied to EPC Air Interface Standard)

PCB—Printed circuit board

PCMCIA—Personal Computer Memory Card International Association

RTLS—Real-time location system

SDIO—Secure Digital Input Output

SHF—Super high frequency

SLF—Super low frequency

TCP—Transmission Control Protocol

TDOA—Time Distance on Arrival

TID—Tag Identification

UHF—Ultrahigh frequency

ULF—Ultralow frequency

UWB—Ultra Wideband

VHF—Very high frequency

VLF—Very low frequency

XOR—Exclusive OR (as applied to Boolean logic)

References

Barthel, Henri. 2006. "Regulatory Status for Using RFID in the UHF Spectrum." December 7. Available online via http://www.epcglobalinc.org/tech/freq_req/ RFID_at_UHF_Regulations_20061124.pdf (accessed January 16, 2007).

EPCglobal, Inc. 2005. "EPC Radio-Frequency Identity Protocols Class-1 Generation-2 UHF RFID Protocol for Communications at 860 MHz–960 MHz Version 1.0.9" Available online via http://www.epcglobalus.org/dnn_epcus/KnowledgeBase/Browse/tabid/277/DMXModule/706/Command/Core_Download/Default.aspx?EntryId=292 (accessed January 17, 2007).

Wikipedia. 2007. Definition of "coupling." Available online via en.wikipedia.org/wiki/Coupling (accessed January 14, 2007).

4

Beyond the Basics

In this chapter the basics of RFID operations described in Chapter 3 are further explained. The physical principles that readers and transponders utilize to couple and exchange energy are discussed. Energetic interaction is not sufficient to allow communication; therefore, a description of the methods used to modulate the signal is necessary (modulation is the modification of certain characteristics in the transmitted signal such as amplitude, frequency, or phase to allow transmission of information). This is similar to defining a "vocabulary" between the reader and tags. After establishing a vocabulary, the "grammar" needs to be defined usually through particular encoding schemes defined in standards such as those provided by the ISO discussed extensively in Chapter 7.

The elementary modules existing in readers are described with an equation that sets the maximum read range between tags and readers and another equation that sets the maximum data transfer capacity. Finally, the whole communication scheme is related to the OSI (Open Systems Interconnection) model. An overview of the RFID fabrication process is presented so that a grasp of its costs and complexity can be appreciated. The SAW (surface acoustic wave) approach, a way of reducing manufacturing cost of tags by entirely omitting the tag itself, is then discussed.

4.1 Coupling Mechanisms

In order to understand each coupling mechanism, the differences in operation between passive/semi-active, and active tags, discussed in previous chapters, are introduced in this chapter. Passive tags obtain power from an interrogation pulse from the reader. They use this power to send an information message, a reply. Since the tags have no battery they essentially last forever, and they do not wear out. A passive RFID tag is little more than a loop of antenna with some basic circuitry. It has a read range up to about

10 m. Active tags have an onboard battery; hence, they are able to respond with a signal that can travel perhaps as much as 150 m or more to a remote reader. Semi-active tags contain batteries, but this internal power source is not used to power up the integrated circuit (IC). The microchip still obtains the power from the transmitter reader signal like the passive tags. The battery is only used to provide power for onboard electronics to perform specialized tasks (i.e., powering a sensor module). The reading distance of a semi-active tag can be up to 30 m.

Depending on the tag type (passive/active/semi-active), there are four types of coupling mechanisms between the tag (transponder) and the reader:

1. Inductive coupling
2. Modulated backscatter coupling
3. Transmitter (beacon) type
4. Transponder type

For passive and semi-active tags, the transfer of data is achieved using inductive or modulated backscatter coupling. Inductively coupled tags are almost always operated passively. This means that the reader provides all the energy needed for the operation of the microchip. The generation of the electromagnetic field from the reader's antenna coil penetrates the cross section of the coil area and the area around the coil. Since the signal's wavelength is several times greater than the distance between the reader's antenna and the transponder (for example, a signal of 135 kHz in the LF band has a wavelength of 2,222 m, and a signal of 13.56 MHz in the HF band has a wavelength of 22.1 m), the electromagnetic field behaves like a simple alternating magnetic field with regard to the distance between the transponder and the antenna. This is called "near-field coupling," as shown in Figure 4-1. In the near field, the electromagnetic energy lines are formed moving outward from the radiating element and then back into the radiating element as shown in the figure. Near-field coupling occurs within roughly one wavelength of a radiating element. Near-field coupling occurs for RFID applications operating in the LF and HF bands with relatively short reading distances well within the radian sphere, r, defined by $\lambda/2\pi$ (λ = wavelength in free space), because of the relationship $\lambda = 2\pi r$.

The occurrence of modulated backscatter coupling takes place in the "far-field coupling" region as displayed in Figure 4.2. Beyond the near-field region, where the far field starts, the electromagnetic energy simply propagates outward and the power drops off based on the inverse-square law. The power decreases by one-quarter as the distance doubles. Longer-read-range UHF and microwave RFID systems utilize far-field coupling.

4.1.1 Inductive Coupling

The partial penetration of the emitted field from the antenna coil of the transponder creates current on the coil of the reader. To fully explain this,

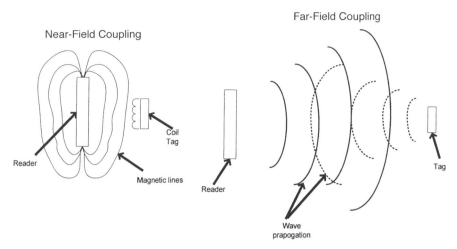

Figure 4-1 Near-field (LF and HF) and far-field (UHF) coupling mechanisms.

it is necessary to define the term electromagnetic induction. *Electromagnetic induction* is a phenomenon through which a change in the magnetic field of a source such as a transmitter creates a voltage level in a remote circuit such as a tag. A parallel circuit used to tune the tag's operating frequency to that of the reader is formed by a capacitor in parallel to the tag's antenna coil, which behaves as an inductor. At a certain frequency, the receiver's antenna interchanges energy at a particular rate, called *resonant frequency*, which depends on several design parameters such as size of the coil, number of turns, or distance between the capacitance plates, among others. At this time high currents are generated in the reader's antenna coil by the method known as *resonance step-up*. Resonance step-up occurs when the frequency of the transmitted signal becomes similar to the designed resonant frequency of the circuit. At this point a portion of the energy stored as magnetic form in the inductor is transferred into electrical form in the capacitor. Before achieving a stable state, a temporary adjustment in the energy levels at the tag's inductor and capacitor occurs; this whole process explains the before mentioned resonance step-up effect. After reaching the stable state at resonant frequency, the received energy is "stored" in the tag by transfer back and forth from the capacitance to the inductance, in accordance with the required field strengths for the operation of the remote transponder. A constant current is required for IC's operations; this can be achieved by using a rectifier, a built-in component that transforms the alternating energy arriving at the tag into a constant current. As a general principle, inductively coupled systems are based upon a *transformer-type coupling* between the primary coil in the reader and the secondary coil in the transponder. This is true when the distance between the coils does not

ENCODING MECHANISM	WAVEFORM	DESCRIPTION
	Data: 1 1 0 1 0 0 0 1 0	
	Clock signal.	Clock signal.
NRZ (Non-Return to Zero) Direct		'1' is represented by a logic high level. '0' is represented by a logic low level.
Manchester		A level change always occurs at the middle of a clock cycle. '1' is represented by a low to high transition. '0' is represented by a high to low transition.
Miller		'1' is represented by a transition (either low-to-high or high-to-low) in the middle of the clock cycle. '0' is represented by a continuation of the logic state of the '1' over the next clock cycle. A sequence of zeros is represented by a transition at the start of the clock cycle.

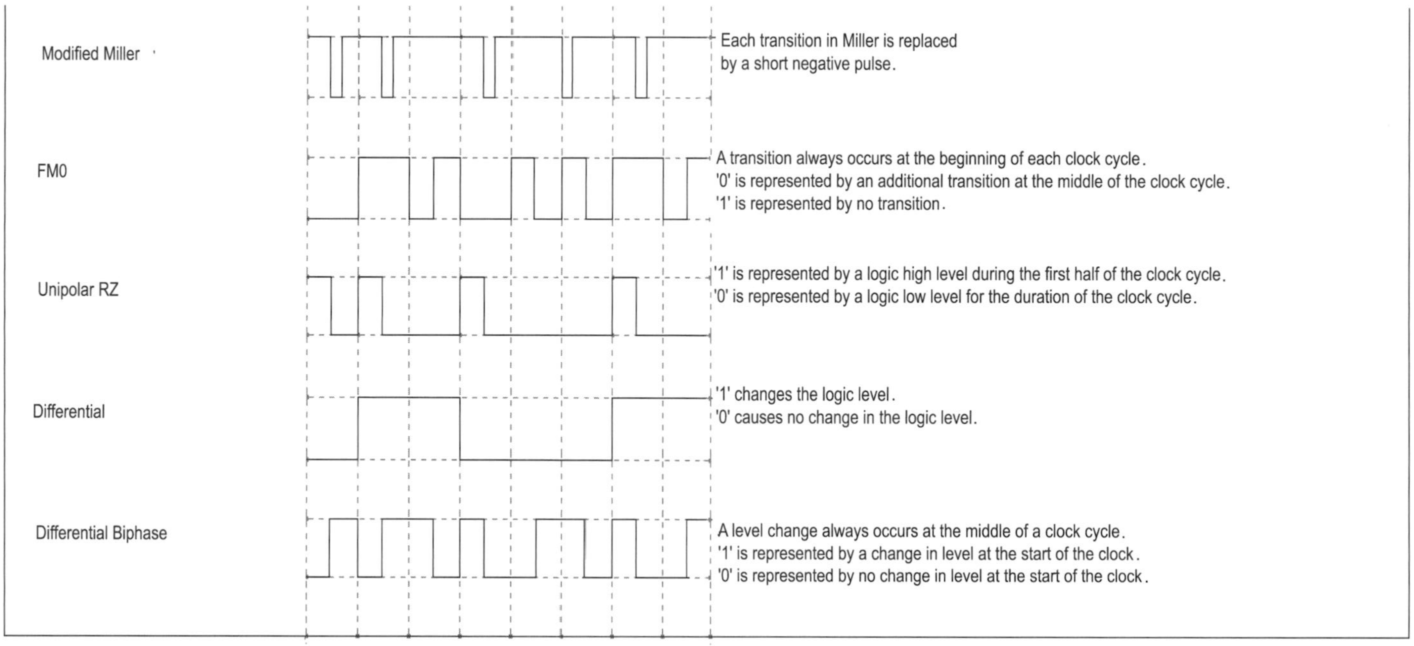

Modified Miller

Each transition in Miller is replaced
by a short negative pulse.

FM0

A transition always occurs at the beginning of each clock cycle.
'0' is represented by an additional transition at the middle of the clock cycle.
'1' is represented by no transition.

Unipolar RZ

'1' is represented by a logic high level during the first half of the clock cycle.
'0' is represented by a logic low level for the duration of the clock cycle.

Differential

'1' changes the logic level.
'0' causes no change in the logic level.

Differential Biphase

A level change always occurs at the middle of a clock cycle.
'1' is represented by a change in level at the start of the clock.
'0' is represented by no change in level at the start of the clock.

Figure 4-2 Encoding mechanisms.

exceed $\lambda/2\pi$ (~16 percent of the wavelength λ), which defines the near-field of the transmitter antenna.

4.1.2 Modulated Backscatter Coupling

The interrogation pulse generated from the reader propagates outside the near field of the reader antenna. As this RF signal travels outward, it may encounter the antenna element in the tag. According to radar technology, an electromagnetic wave bounces off an object with dimension greater than half the wavelength of the electromagnetic wave. The "reflection cross section" can then be defined as the parameter that determines the strength of the returned signal. An electromagnetic field propagates outward from the reader's antenna and a small proportion of that field (reduced by free space attenuation) reaches the transponder's antenna. Since the incoming signal is a sinusoidal continuous wave (CW), it needs to be converted from AC power to DC power by using a rectifier circuit with diodes. This power is then supplied to deactivate or activate the power-saving "power-down" mode

The antenna of the transponder captures a portion of the incoming RF energy, and this energy is then reflected by the antenna of the tag and reradiated outward. By changing the load connected to the antenna the *reflection characteristics* (i.e., reflection cross section) of the antenna can be manipulated. A load resistor (or capacitor) connected in parallel with the antenna is turned on and off synchronously with the data stream to be transmitted. This generates the transmission of data from the transponder to the reader. By varying the load of the transponder antenna, the strength of the signal reflected and reradiated from the transponder to the reader can be modulated. In electromagnetic terms, this is referred to as *modulated backscatter*. Once the modulated and encoded data stream in the IC reaches the reader, it is then decoded and subsequently demodulated allowing the user to retrieve the required information.

4.1.3 Beacon (Transmitter) Type

When the precise location of an asset needs to be tracked, beacons are used in most real-time location systems (RTLS). Active tags are used in this type of communication. In an RTLS, a beacon transmits a signal with its unique identification number at predefined intervals. The query time could be done at many different times and could be as frequent as, for instance, every two seconds or once a day, depending on how often it is needed to know the location of an asset. At least three reader antennas positioned around the perimeter of the area where assets are being tracked detect the beacon's signal. In this way, the exact location of the asset can be found. RTLSs are usually used in a large, open area; however, automakers use the systems in large manufacturing facilities to track parts.

4.1.4 Transponder Type

Upon receiving a signal from a reader, active transponders are awakened. Transponder-type active transponders are used, for instance, in toll payment collection, checkpoint control, and port security systems. In toll payment collection, a reader at the booth transmits a signal that activates the transponder mounted on the car's windshield. When a car with an active transponder comes in close proximity of the tollbooth, the transponder then sends out its unique ID to the reader. Battery life conservation can be achieved by having the tag communicate with the reader only when it is within the read range of that reader.

4.2 Data Encoding in RFID Systems

RFID tags operate as the heart of the RFID system. Data is stored, accessed, transmitted, and changed in RFID tags (depending on the type of the tag). *Data encoding* refers to the processing of the data from the time that the signal arrives at the RFID tag and travels back to the reader. Several data-encoding algorithms have been defined for RFID; the choice affects the implementation cost, data error recovery, and data reliability. In addition, several types of data encoding algorithms have been developed. A list of encoding synchronization capabilities and other aspects of RFID system design methods have been set by RFID standards such as ISO 14443, ISO 15693, ISO 18000-6, EM4102 from EM Microelectronics, and others, depending on frequency of operation and application (See Chapter 7 for more information on these standards). Following is a listing of encoding methods used for inductive and/or capacitive coupling RFID systems:

- *NRZ (nonreturn to zero) direct.* In this method a binary 1 is represented by one significant condition (logic high level) and a binary 0 is represented by another (logic low level).
- *Manchester encoding.* Also called split-phase encoding, this encoding mechanism does not require any additional information about the transmit clock (in other words, it is self-clocking). A level change always occurs at the middle of a clock cycle. A 0 is translated into a low to high transition (0 to 1), and a 1 is translated into a high to low transition (1 to 0).
- *Miller encoding.* Also referred to as "Miller subcarrier encoding," in this mechanism a binary 1 is represented by a transition (low to high or high to low) in the middle of the clock cycle. A binary 0 is represented by a continuation of the logic state of the 1 over the next clock cycle. If a sequence of binary zeros occurs, a transition takes place at the start of the clock cycle. Moreover, a Miller sequence might consist of two, four, or eight subcarrier cycles/bit.

- *Modified Miller encoding.* In this mechanism, each transition (in Miller) is replaced by a short negative pulse.
- *FM0 encoding.* Also known as biphase space encoding, here a transition occurs at the beginning of each clock cycle. A binary 0 is represented by an additional transition at the middle of the clock cycle, and a binary 1 is represented by no transition at the middle of the clock cycle.
- *Unipolar RZ encoding.* In this method a binary 1 is represented by a high logic level during the first half of the clock cycle and a binary 0 is represented by a low logic level for the duration of the clock cycle.
- *Differential encoding.* In differential encoding a binary 1 changes the logic level and a binary 0 causes no change in the logic level.
- *Differential biphase encoding.* In this mechanism a level change occurs at the middle of a clock cycle. A 1 is represented by a change in level at the start of the clock, and a 0 is represented by no change in level at the start of the clock.
- *Pulse-interval encoding* (*PIE*). Also called, pulse-pause encoding, here a binary 1 is represented by a pause of duration $2T$ prior to the following pulse and a binary 0 is represented by a pause of duration T prior to the following pulse. Other sources such as Finkenzeller (2003) have the binary 1 (T) and 0 ($2T$).

Figures 4-2 and 4-3 illustrate the encoding mechanisms in the list. These figures show waveforms representing data bits of logic 1s and 0s (shown at the top of the figures) for each encoding algorithm. A clock signal is also shown in Figure 4-2 for easier illustration of each algorithm.

As an example, ISO 15693 systems operate at 13.56 MHz; hence, utilizing magnetic pulses (or near-field coupling), Manchester encoding, modified Miller, differential biphase, NRZ, and PIE are being used in such systems. These encoding algorithms are being used in uplink (tag → reader) and/ or downlink (reader → tag) communications.

As for ultrahigh-band frequency (UHF) RFID systems operating at 902 to 928 MHz in North America, 865 to 868 MHz in Europe, and 952 to 954 MHz in Japan, and that use the electric field to transfer power, PIE is being used for downlink (reader → tag), and Miller subcarrier and the FM0 for uplink (tag → reader). These coding algorithms are set by ISO 18000-6 and are in use as of this writing.

4.3 Data Modulation

Data modulation refers to the process of changing a carrier wave so that it can contain information to be sent in a transmission medium. A *carrier wave* is defined as an unmodulated electromagnetic wave. The three main parameters to be modulated are power or amplitude (amplitude modulation, or AM), frequency (frequency modulation, or FM), and phase positioning

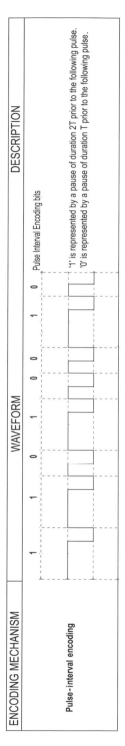

Figure 4-3 Pulse-nterval encoding.

(phase modulation, or PM). These parameters comprise the main characteristics of electromagnetic waves. All other forms of modulation are derived from these main modulation schemes (AM, FM, and PM), but a thorough explanation is beyond the scope of this book. See Proakis and Salehi (2004) for further information.

Different data modulation systems can provide different data rates (speed at which data transfers between reader and tag), and some are more vulnerable to noisy environments (undesired signals caused by neighboring electrical devices, equipment, machinery, etc.) than others. In RFID, digital modulation of binary 1s and 0s is accomplished using amplitude-shift keying (ASK); which is based on AM; frequency-shift keying (FSK), which is based on FM; and phase-shift keying (PSK), which is based on PM.

A brief description of each modulation scheme (including benefits and drawbacks) is as follows:

- *ASK.* In ASK two states (logic high and logic low) in the envelope (modulated signal) exist. A 1 represents logic high, and a 0 represents logic low. ASK can provide a high data rate but has low noise immunity.
- *FSK.* In FSK there are two different carrier frequencies, where the carrier frequency is defined to be the arithmetic mean of the two, are used. Logic levels 0 and 1 are defined by changes in the frequency of a signal. FSK has strong noise immunity but produces lower data rates.
- *PSK.* In PSK the phase of the signal is modulated to carry the data to be transmitted. There are two types of PSK phase changes: a change in phase at the binary 0, or a change in phase at any binary change 0 to 1 or 1 to 0. PSK allows for relatively good noise immunity, and it also has a faster data rate than FSK.

4.4 Anticollision

Many applications of RFID require the use of multiple tags simultaneously. For example, consider a shipping truck that contains hundreds of boxes, each with an RFID tag. When the truck enters a warehouse, it would be ideal for the tags on all the boxes to be read at the same time to avoid the time-consuming task of reading one box at a time. Without proper management, the multiple uses of tags could lead to a failure in communication between tag and reader called *collision.* There are two types of collision that can occur with the application of RFID: tag collision and reader collision. We will consider tag collision and methods of management.

Tag collision occurs when two or more RFID tags communicate with one reader at the same time. Since a reader can only communicate with one tag at a time, multiple tags communicating with the reader at the same moment can cause confusion to the reader. There are two ways to tackle this problem:

1. Reader anticollision algorithm
2. Tag anticollision algorithm

4.4.1 Reader Anticollision Algorithm

The reader adopts a singulation or an anticollision procedure to provide multiple accesses to simultaneous tags. With this protocol, a reader can communicate with several tags within a very short time frame such that communication appears simultaneous. This type of communication is referred to as multi-access. For multi-access communication to be realized, a variety of procedures have been developed to separate individual signals from one another and to prevent different tag data from colliding with one another. There are many basic multi-access procedures that are applicable to RFID systems. To mention a few Space Division Multiple Access (SDMA), Frequency Division Multiple Access (FDMA), and Time Division Multiple Access (TDMA).

4.4.1.1 Space Division Multiple Access

This procedure is accomplished by reusing the resources such as the channel capacity of devices that are spatially separated. For example, the use of a directional antenna on a reader will cause the reader to communicate only with a tag that lies directly in its read range. Therefore, tags communicating with a reader will be differentiated based on their angular orientation. The technical realization of this procedure is difficult because of the high cost of implementing such a complex antenna system. This restricts the use of SDMA as an anticollision procedure in many RFID applications.

4.4.1.2 Frequency Division Multiple Access

Frequency Division Multiple Access is a digital transmission procedure that allows a certain number of tags to simultaneously use a bandwidth for transmission. In FDMA, a given RF bandwidth is divided into smaller frequency bands, each with a unique carrier frequency. Therefore, tags simultaneously use several transmission channels with various carrier frequencies. In RFID systems, different and noncoinciding transmission frequencies are allocated to the tags. When a query is sent out to an RFID tag in the read range, the tag can respond on one of several available frequency channels in the frequency range. Since one distinct receiver must be available for every channel on the reader, the cost to produce readers to implement this procedure is relatively high. Therefore, like SDMA, FDMA has a restricted use for anticollision procedures.

4.4.1.3 Time Division Multiple Access

Time Division Multiple Access is a digital transmission procedure that allows a certain number of tags to use a RF channel without interference. This procedure is accomplished by dividing the available channel capacity into unique time slots that are allocated to each tag within each channel. TDMA is the most widely employed anticollision procedure for RFID systems. Since only a certain time period is allowed for each tag, there is also restriction on the amount of data that can be transmitted to the reader. TDMA is used for reader anticollision as well as two of the most common tag anticollision algorithms in RFID systems today: ALOHA and Tree Walking.

4.4.2 Tag Anticollision Algorithm

Like the reader in the reader anticollision algorithm, the tag could also adopt an anticollision or singulation protocol that will enable effective communication with the reader without colliding with other tags in the read range. There are two main types of tag anti-collision algorithms in use today:

1. ALOHA for high frequency systems typically 13.56 MHz
2. Tree Walking for ultrahigh-frequency systems, typically 860–915 MHz.

4.4.2.1 ALOHA and Variations of ALOHA for HF RFID Systems

Developed in the 1970s, ALOHA is a basic TDMA protocol in which a tag begins transmitting as soon as it has data to send without any form of synchronization. At the start of the communication between reader and tag, the tags in the read range automatically send their tag IDs to the reader upon entering the read range. If one tag has data to send during the same time interval as another tag, the interval during which the two tags transmit overlaps and this results in either a complete or partial collision. In the simplest form of a random back-off protocol used by the ALOHA algorithm, an occurrence of a collision forces the tags to stop transmitting. Then the colliding tags are assigned a randomly determined delay (waiting time). Each tag retransmits its data after its allocated delay has expired.

The main problem with the basic ALOHA protocol is the time period allocation for collision avoidance. Because of the continuity on the time axis, any tag in the read range that begins transmitting during the allocated time period will cause a collision. Furthermore, because of the increase in delay between transmissions, this basic ALOHA algorithm only has a low efficiency. For the purpose of tag anticollision, *offered load* refers to the total number of tags waiting to transmit data to the reader. In the basic ALOHA algorithm, for a small offered load, the channel capacity is not efficiently used because of large delay times. If the offered load is increased, the probability for collisions also increases. Therefore, for both small offered loads and large offered loads, this simple system is always inefficient. In a normal situation, ALOHA has been theoretically proven to have a maximum throughput (or channel utilization) of about 18 percent (Lahiri, 2005). The anti-collision protocols used in HF tags are usually a variation of the basic ALOHA protocol.

Slotted ALOHA is one of the algorithms developed to improve the efficiency of ALOHA. In the slotted ALOHA algorithm, a constraint is added to the basic ALOHA protocol discussed previously to boost transmission efficiency. The data packets from tags can only be transmitted at synchronized time intervals called *slots*. In this case, the reader employs a method of controlling when each tag begins to send or receive data. A tag is constrained to begin transmitting right after a slot delimiter, meaning that a tag can only transmit at the beginning of a slot. Because of this constraint, packets in transmission either have complete collision or no collision at all. Therefore, the problem of partial collisions is eliminated. In a normal situation, the Slotted ALOHA protocol doubles the channel utilization of ALOHA—that is, a maximum throughput (or channel utilization) of about 37 percent. Figure 4-4 illustrates the difference between basic ALOHA and the slotted ALOHA protocols.

4.4.2.2 Tree Walking for UHF RFID Systems

For UHF RFID tags, a more deterministic scheme is used to avoid collisions. The reader could sort through tags in its read range based on their tag ID. Singulation is generally the basic method used in this procedure. *Singulation* is a means by which an RFID reader identifies a tag with a specific serial tag ID from a number of tags in its field. This identification process is necessary in situations where multiple tags simultaneously communicate with the reader. If each tag is not uniquely identified, the transmission will be disrupted. There are different methods of singulation, but tree walking is the most common method adopted for RFID systems. In tree walking, the space of *k*-bit identifiers is viewed as the leaves in a tree of depth *k*. A reader traverses the tree, asking subsets of tags to broadcast a single bit at a time. For example, if a reader is seeking a tag with ID 1010, the reader sends out a query requesting that all tags with a serial number that starts with a 1 to respond. If more than one responds, the reader might ask for all tags with a serial number that starts with 10 to respond. Again, if more than one tag responds, the reader again sends out a query for tags with serial number that starts with 101. The reader repeats this querying until it finds the specific tag with serial number 1010. Because of the querying method adopted by this procedure, this protocol is very susceptible to eavesdropping. Any system that can get data from the reader can get all but the last bit of the tag's serial number. Because of this, more advanced tree-walking-based singulation classes have been developed to reduce the susceptibility to eavesdropping. These protocols are Class 0 UHF and Class 1 UHF.

4.4.2.3 Class 0 UHF

Class 0 UHF is a tree-walking algorithm that adopts certain changes to reduce the susceptibility to eavesdropping. The interface for class 0 is based

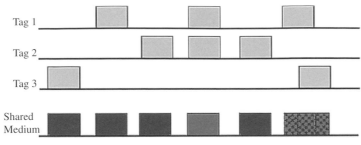

Simple ALOHA procedure

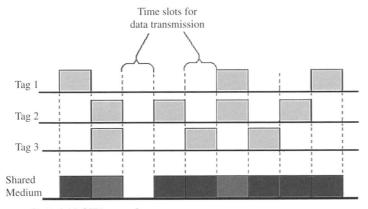

Slotted ALOHA procedure

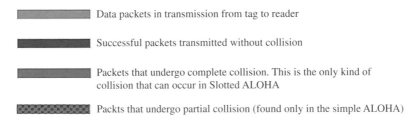

Data packets in transmission from tag to reader

Successful packets transmitted without collision

Packets that undergo complete collision. This is the only kind of collision that can occur in Slotted ALOHA

Packts that undergo partial collision (found only in the simple ALOHA)

* * * NOTE: For most ALOHA algorithms, the maximum tag saturation level ranges from 50 to 200 tags per second.

Figure 4-4 Basic ALOHA and slotted ALOHA.

on pulse-width modulation for the reader-to-tag link. The reader-to-tag link uses 100 percent amplitude modulation or 20 percent amplitude modulation of the carrier signal for transmission. There are three basic Class 0 reader-to-tag symbols: binary 0, binary 1, and Null. A binary 0 is transmitted by turning the reader off for a brief time, τ, after which the power is turned back on for the remainder of the symbol. A binary 1 is transmitted by turning the reader off for a longer period, for instance, 2τ. The null is a symbol used to inform the tags when to change their state. For the implementation of a Class 0 algorithm, a binary tree anticollision protocol is usually employed. Figure 4-5 illustrates the binary tree anticollision protocol for searching for tag with identifier 1010.

4.4.2.4 Class 1 UHF

A Class 1 tag has a unique identifier that is combined with an error detection/correction code applied. The error detection/correction code is usually a cyclic redundancy check (CRC). The Class 1 tag data (identifier and CRC) is stored in the identifier tag memory. Class 1 procedure is divided into two different generations for implementation. This is a more advanced technology that uses a filter capability that is built into reader commands

For the Class 1 Gen 1, the same modulation encoding technique as Class 0 is used. However, instead of a binary tree, a query tree walking technique is used. Here, the reader sends a Query command to the tags in its read range by using a group of bits that contain the filter bits and CRC plus identifying bits. The tag for which the query was intended replies with an 8-bit response in one of the eight time slots allocated.

For Class 1 Gen 2, the ASK, FSK, or PSK is the modulation scheme used in combination with the PIE for this procedure. In this algorithm, the reader picks the encoding format for the tag-to-reader link. Two distinct sets of tag symbols are used: FM0 encoding and Miller encoding. Variations of the ALOHA random algorithm are used for the anticollision process

4.5 Transmission Characteristics

The essential factors to be considered when designing an RFID system are as follows:

1. Maximum data rate
2. Transmission distance

Even with careful choice of the parameters influencing those factors, it is important to take into consideration what materials impede the transmission of the signal and the multipath effect, responsible of the reception of multiple signals initially originated in a single tag.

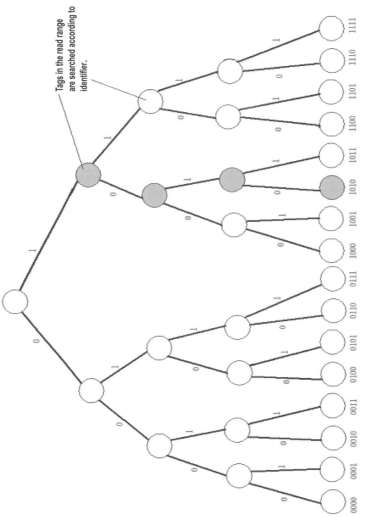

The Binary Search algorithm for tag with identifier 1010 adopted by Class 0 as a tree-walking scheme

NOTE: Algorithms based on binary trees are often O(log n). This is because a perfectly balanced binary search tree has log n layers and searching for any element in a binary search tree requires traversing a single node on each layer. So as the number of tags increase, the size of the search tree increases.

Figure 4-5 Binary tree anticollision protocol.

4.5.1 Maximum Data Rate

One of the main characteristics of the RFID link (reader → tag or tag → reader) is the rate at which data is being transmitted. Another term used in the literature is "throughput," and it is also a good estimate of the channel capacity of a communication link. The unit for data rate is normally bit per second (bps or bits/s). Often the usage is kilobits per second (Kbps or kilobits/s) or megabits per second (Mbps or megabits/s).

In RFID, the data rate is primarily determined by the bandwidth of operation, the carrier frequency (frequency of operation), or the field (electric or magnetic) that is used to transfer the data from the tag to the reader. According to the Nyquist formula, the channel capacity is determined by the bandwidth (and hence the frequency of operation).

The Nyquist bit rate formula is given by the following:

$$C = 2B \log_2 L$$

Here C represents the channel capacity (the rate at which bits may be transmitted through a system), B the bandwidth, and L the number of logic levels used to encode bits. For example, the theoretical capacity in bits per second of a transmission medium with a frequency spectrum of 50 MHz to 100 MHz (channel bandwidth of 50 MHz) and with $L - 2$ (logic levels of 1s and 0s) is 100 Mbps. Notice that with the same percentage bandwidth of another channel in a higher position of the electromagnetic spectrum a higher data rate is achieved. Also note that the Nyquist formula is theoretical and assumes a noise-free environment (i.e., no other interference from neighboring electrical devices, etc.).

However, Shannon's formula, which is derived from the Nyquist formula, considers undesired environmental effects caused by noise. The new component to the preceding formula is the signal-to-noise ratio (SNR) and is a measure of the power ratio between a desired signal and the background noise. Noise can be generated from several different sources; for example, a listing of noise sources in industrial environments includes ambient noise produced by motors and other machinery and radio transmitters.

Shannon's formula is given by the following:

$$C = 2B \log_2 (1 + \text{SNR})$$

where SNR is often specified on the logarithmic scale. In practical situations much lower channel capacities are achieved than the value given by Shannon's formula. Channel capacity is the maximum rate at which data can be transmitted over a given communication path, or channel, under given conditions (the upper bound for the bit rate that can be driven down a connection or maximum data rate for a channel). According to the Nyquist-Shannon theorem, the channel capacity C has to be less than or equal to 2B.

In general, the greater the bandwidth of a given path, the higher the data transfer rate. Increasing the bandwidth in a transmission path allows for an increased noise level and hence a reduction in SNR. It is also worthwhile to note that the higher the frequency of operation, the higher the bandwidth (assuming the same percentage bandwidth for most applications; here RFID) and the higher the data rate or throughput rate that can be achieved.

4.5.2 Transmission Distance

When determining the read range of an RFID tag, one must consider both the distance at which the reader will be able to detect the scattered signal and the distance at which the tag receives enough power to operate. Usually, the high sensitivity of the tag limits the operating range. Using the Friis free space formula, it is possible to derive the following maximum range:

$$r_{\max} = \frac{\lambda}{4\pi} \sqrt{\frac{P_t G_t G_r \tau}{P_{th}}}$$

where λ is the wavelength, P_t is the transmitted power from the reader, G_t is the gain of the transmitter antenna, G_r is the gain of the receiver tag antenna, P_{th} is the minimum threshold power at the reader, and τ is the power transmission coefficient (a design factor that takes into account the amount of energy transferred from the antenna to the reader chip).

4.5.3 Materials Impeding the Signal

RF-opaque objects and RF-absorbent objects impede the signal. This is especially true for high-frequency tags. Metal is an example of an RF-opaque object that impedes a signal. Liquids are RF-absorbent objects that pose a major obstacle in RFID operation by diminishing functionality. Specifically:

- *RF-opaque objects.* A metallic object creates reflection; therefore, metallic objects are considered to be RF-opaque. This situation prevents the tag from absorbing enough energy from the reader, since the metallic material holds most of it, therefore detuning the operating resonant frequency at which the tag was supposed to operate. Two possibilities of tagging such objects are the use of antennas with precise tuning or use of tags mounted on a foam platform, which avoids direct contact with the metal.
- *RF-absorbent objects.* Liquid materials such as soap, water, or salty solutions are RF-absorbent. These materials considerably absorb the radio

waves arriving to the transponder, thus reducing the available energy necessary to operate the tag. If we have severe absorption, the transponder will not be able to capture the necessary energy to operate and the reader will not detect its signal. It is important to note that not all liquids behave identically.

The impact of RF-absorbent or RF-opaque objects is not as strong in HF as in UHF. The explanation of this can be found in the ratio of the wavelength to the object size. Broadly speaking, it is possible to classify the object depending on its dimensions relative to the wavelength in the following categories:

- *Rayleigh range.* The wavelength is much larger than the object dimensions. For objects smaller than half the wavelength, reflection is minimal and metal would not interfere in the normal operation of a tag.
- *Optical range.* The wavelength is smaller than the object size. In this case a metal would appear "visible" to an RF signal.

4.5.4 Multipath Effect

One significant advantage of RFID is that it can operate in an environment in the absence of line of sight. For RF transparent material, the signal transmitted from the reader can travel through the obstacle and reach the tag. For instance, a reader set up in the proximity of a conveyor belt can detect a paper box with a tag stuck on its backside, without the necessity of turning the box over.

When a large amount of RF reflecting materials, such as metals, are presented in the operating environment, the reflection of the UHF signal on RF reflecting objects will cause a "multipath effect." For example, consider a warehouse filled with iron containers. RF signals from the reader installed in this environment may bounce several times off the surface of containers before arriving at the tag, resulting in multiple propagation paths. Through the different propagation paths, RF signals will also have varied phases. Interference among signals will happen because of these different phases. This phenomenon is depicted as fast fading. At some specific location, added signals can cancel each other. As a result, serious degradation of system performance might result. RFID tags could become unreadable even if they are within the range of the reader. In this case, a line of sight between the reader and the tags is highly preferred to achieve a good read accuracy. A directional reader antenna could also enhance the performance by suppressing the signal reflected from other directions (i.e., metal).

When a line of sight is not available, a technique called *diversity* accomplished by adding another reader some distance away from the original one is the best solution. The basic idea is that when one antenna is suffering from a weak received signal from the tag because of the multipath effect, another antenna at another location may have a stronger signal to compensate that. More readers can also be added to build up a constellation. In this way, high read accuracy can be easily achieved. Another solution is to use smart DSP algorithms, which have the ability to zero in on the best signal to mitigate the multipath effect. Such smart DSP algorithms should be deployed in the reader side because of the limitation of hardware sizes.

4.6 The Reader

Another important part in an RFID system is the reader subsystem. It is possible to divide an RFID reader system into two differentiated groups, namely, the high-frequency interface and the control system. These groups interact among each other and with an external host system, as shown in Figure 4-6.

The main functions performed by a reader are demodulating the data retrieved from the tag, decoding the received data, and energizing in the case of passive and semi-passive tags. A more detailed diagram of the reader is shown in Figure 4-7.

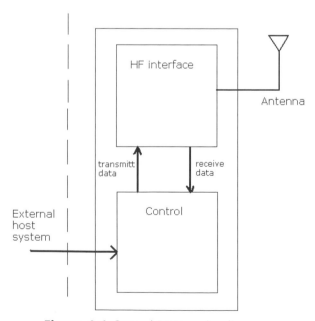

Figure 4-6 General RFID reader diagram.

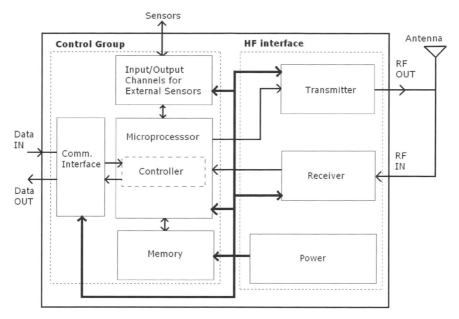

Figure 4-7 Subblock reader diagram.

4.6.1 The HF Interface

The HF interface performs the following basic functions:

- Demodulating and decoding the date retrieved from the tag
- Energizing, in the case of passive and semi-passive tags

Elements include the following:

- *Transmitter.* The main task of this element is to transmit power and the clock cycle to the tags. It is part of the transceiver module.
- *Receiver.* This component is responsible for receiving signals from the tag via the antenna. Afterward, it sends these signals to a microprocessor, where the digital information is extracted.
- *Power.* This module supplies adequate power to all components in the reader.

4.6.2 The Control Group

To allow the functions of decoding, error checking, and communication with an external system, the control unit makes use of a microprocessor, a controller, a communication interface, memory, and input/output channels:

- *Microprocessor.* In the microprocessor the reader protocol is implemented. The microprocessor interprets the received commands, and depending on the protocol required by the specific standard (i.e., ALOHA for HF frequencies, Tree Walking for UHF frequencies), the microprocessor searches the memory for the corresponding program code and executes it. It is here where error checking is performed.
- *Controller.* In order to allow joint operation with an external system, a system called the controller, responsible for converting external orders to understandable microprocessor binary code, is needed to enable communication. It is possible to have a controller in either a software or hardware form.
- *Communication interface.* By using the controller, the communication interface is able to interact with an external host system by transferring data, passing or responding to instructions. The communication interface can be a part of the controller or an independent entity depending on the integration level and speed requirements.
- *Memory.* The memory is responsible for storing the data retrieved from the tags. The data will be transmitted to the host system when demanded.
- *Input/output channels for external sensors.* When a reader is in operation, the tags might not be in its read range, making continuous operation a waste of energy. By using external sensors able to detect the presence of an item nearby—for instance, in a conveyor belt crossing in front of the reader—it is possible to efficiently operate the reader by activating it at the required times.

Additionally, it is possible to classify the readers by the communication interface in use or by its mobility. A brief description of each category follows.

Communication interface:

- *Serial reader.* This reader uses a RS-232 (Recommended Standard 232) serial port to communicate with the host system and transfer data or commands executed by the user or application. These readers have a lower data transfer rate compared with others, such as a wired network reader, and have a cable length limitation. On the other hand, serial port connections are more reliable
- *Network reader.* This reader can be connected wired or wirelessly to a computer; therefore, it appears as a network device. In this case, the cable length is not a limitation, but the connection is not as reliable as in serial readers.

Mobility of readers:

- *Stationary reader.* These readers are mounted on a wall, portal or suitable structure in the read zone. They can be mounted on moving objects such as trucks. These readers usually are connected to external antennas. *Agile readers* are able to operate in different frequencies and use different communications protocols. An *RFID printer* is a type of stationary reader able to print a bar code and write on its RFID tag
- *Handheld reader.* This type of reader has an integrated antenna on it and can operate as a handheld unit.

4.7 The OSI Model

To better understand the communication among the components of an RFID system, it is important to understand the open systems interconnection reference model, also called OSI model. The OSI model is a conceptual illustration for data communication. The module is hierarchical in structure and is constructed of layers that define the requirements of communication between two end users (i.e., reader and tag).

The OSI is not based on hardware or software models; instead, it is better to view the OSI as a logical description of the environment and network protocol design. The focus of the OSI model in this chapter is on RFID operations. The OSI consists of seven layers:

- *Layer 1.* Physical layer
- *Layer 2.* Data link layer
- *Layer 3.* Network layer
- *Layer 4.* Transport layer
- *Layer 5.* Session layer
- *Layer 6.* Presentation layer
- *Layer 7.* Application layer

The OSI model allows for the integration of all of the seven layers (in RFID, layers 1, 2, 6, and 7 are used) in an illustration as shown in Figure 4-8. Each layer depends on a previous layer. For instance, a data link establishing the transmission of data blocks, therefore, cannot be created without a physical interface such as RFID antennas (tag and reader). The network layer is not used, since communication in RFID is point to point and does not require an intermediate user. The transport layer is not used in RFID, since no complex links between the end users are involved (an example of such complex links is keeping track of packets transmitted). The session layer is responsible for procedures such as restart and termination of operation, and hence, there is no need for this layer in RFID. The pre-

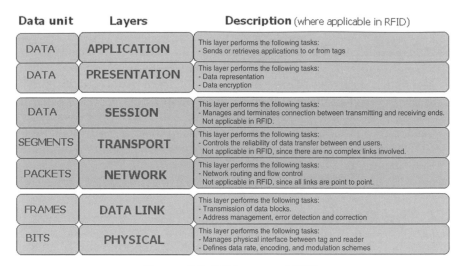

Data unit	Layers	Description (where applicable in RFID)
DATA	APPLICATION	This layer performs the following tasks: - Sends or retrieves applications to or from tags
DATA	PRESENTATION	This layer performs the following tasks: - Data representation - Data encryption
DATA	SESSION	This layer performs the following tasks: - Manages and terminates connection between transmitting and receiving ends. Not applicable in RFID.
SEGMENTS	TRANSPORT	This layer performs the following tasks: - Controls the reliability of data transfer between end users. Not applicable in RFID, since there are no complex links involved.
PACKETS	NETWORK	This layer performs the following tasks: - Network routing and flow control Not applicable in RFID, since all links are point to point.
FRAMES	DATA LINK	This layer performs the following tasks: - Transmission of data blocks. - Address management, error detection and correction
BITS	PHYSICAL	This layer performs the following tasks: - Manages physical interface between tag and reader - Defines data rate, encoding, and modulation schemes

Figure 4-8 OSI layers and RFID.

sentation layer encrypts data to certain standards to be used by the application layer (the function of this layer may also be embedded onboard integrated circuits). Finally, the application layer, which is the main interface to the user, is responsible for carrying the application done onboard the IC in the tag to and from the reader. The OSI layers used by RFID, along with a brief description, are illustrated in Figure 4-8.

4.8 Fabrication

The most common RFID manufacturing process involves a series of steps ranging from chip production to antenna creation and final encapsulation. Although the number of steps may vary from one manufacturer to another, the core manufacturing process include the following:

1. Production of chip die
2. Creation of antenna
3. Inlet assembly
4. Converting inlet into usable form

A brief description of the steps is as follows:

1. *Production of chip die.* Using silicon as a base element, it is possible to produce a high number of chips simultaneously. All microchips are fabricated in a thin silicon sheet called *wafer*. A well-known semiconductor process developed over the years in the chip manufacturing

industry is applied in sequence to create each of the layers forming the chip circuitry. The process involves doping, exposure, etching, and washing of the surface repeatedly; after which the chip die is ready for testing. The fabricated chip will include the RF components and memory elements necessary for regular operation of the tag. Once the tags are tested, encapsulation in an adequate module isolates the chip from external factors such as moisture, high temperatures, or chemicals.

2. *Creation of antenna.* In this step the fabrication process will significantly vary depending on the frequency of operation. For tags operating in the HF band, thin copper wires are used to manufacture the antenna, whereas for tags working in the UHF and microwave bands, metal etching (of copper or aluminum) is more commonly used.

3. *Inlet assembly.* In this phase the produced antenna and the chip die are connected usually using an automated robotic arm. An operational test is usually performed after this phase to validate the system operation.

4. *Converting inlet into usable form.* At this point the inlet is changed into a commercially usable form by using various packaging techniques such as encapsulation in glass, addition of some adhesive backing on the bottom, or use of some plastic molding process.

4.9 SAW RFID Devices: An Alternative to IC-Based RFID

Surface acoustic wave technology can be used in RFID tags for lower cost and easier fabrication, since there is no IC requirement. The main idea is to convert the RF wave from the reader into a nanoscale surface acoustic wave (other names used in literature are surface waves and Raleigh waves) on the SAW chip. This is done by an interdigital transducer (IDT) placed on a piezoelectric substrate such as lithium niobate or lithium tantalate. The IDT is connected to the antenna for direct receiving/transmitting to and from the antenna. Once the wave is transformed into an acoustic wave, it travels past a set of SAW reflectors (or a series of electrodes with a unique pattern, i.e., placed in a unique manner on the substrate) that are placed on the surface with a unique configuration, thus defining its "ID number."

Furthermore, these reflectors are placed in a manner that encodes the data by using time delay, amplitude delay, phase delay, pulse positioning, on/off pulse, encoding, or other variables. On/off pulse encoding and pulse position encoding mechanisms encode one data bit at each pulse positioning and achieve similar data density per unit time with one utilizing less reflectors (pulse positioning) and hence an improved insertion loss of the tag (better performance), since each reflector slightly decreases the amplitude of the backscattered signal. Another encoding mechanism used currently in SAW tags has spacing of allowed pulse positioning equal to the time width of the pulses (1/bandwidth).

Up-to-date SAW RFID devices can hold up to 256 bits of data on a single SAW RFID tag. A reflected wave is formed, passes back at the IDT, and travels to the reader. The reflected wave thus constitutes a unique pattern determined by the reflectors and is read by the RFID interrogator, which then decodes and extracts the tag data. For example, a number of slots (for the reflectors) are assigned (for example, 75) to each SAW tag; then according to the requirements of the data (for example, 16 bits), a number of reflectors are placed (four reflectors for 16 bits) and so forth.

Modulation methods utilize time overlapped pulse position modulation along with simultaneous phase offsets and with multiple pulses per data group. SAW RFID operates in the ISM band (Industrial, Scientific, and Medical) at 2.45 GHz. They do not require a DC power source for data transmission (fully passive tags). SAW RFID also utilizes operation at low power levels. An illustration of a SAW RFID tag showing RF/surface waves interface is given in Figure 4-9.

Some of the benefits of SAW over IC-based RFID tags are as follows:

- They use a lower-cost chip.
- They use low power and no DC source (battery).
- They have a longer read range (compared to microchip RFID tags at the microwave band 2.45 GHz).
- SAW RFID tags are extremely secure, since their ID number is programmed when manufactured. In addition, the data is stored in a secured network database.

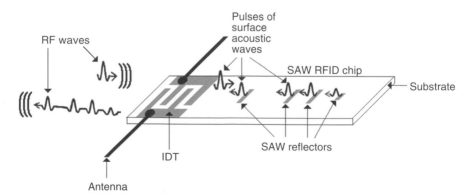

Figure 4-9 Typical SAW RFID tag showing data exchange between reader and tag.

4.10 Summary

RFID tags have the property to behav
depending on the frequency of oper
This difference in operation accounts
tances depending on the RFID workir
of the underlying physical principles
fundamental differences behind disti
design approach needs to be taken ir
with HF tags or UHF tags where diff
ductive coupling of HF vs. modulate
formance highly depends on the frec
existing in the ambient environment.
such as data transfer or read range, l
for the coupling transmission mect
quency.

Once the frequency of operation ha
ulation and encoding of the transferre
allowed by the transmission channel.
achievable noise immunity and data t
selecting a specific modulation schem
FM provide good noise immunity b
other hand, other schemes such as /
bad performance in noisy environme
of data transmission.

In addition to choosing a specific
application, understanding the probl
measures to reduce it is one of the n
of its nature, an RFID reader has to b
multiple tags at the same time whil
Selecting a specific communication sc
or Frequency Division Multiple Acce
formance; hence, making a choice th
ticular operating conditions become:
RFID system. Price also is to be cons
process complexity, and the associate
factors posing major drawbacks to a
novel approaches for tackling the cos
paper-based material or chipless tags

Acronyms

AC—Alternating current
AM—Amplitude modulation

verview. Upper Saddle River, NJ: Prentice

. Fundamentals of Communication Systems.

Inspection in RFID Assembly." Advanced
http://ap.pennnet.com/Articles/Article_
E_ID=245398&VERSION_NUM=2&p=

ntification: RFID 'Tagging' for Wireless
vailable online at www.connect802.com/

ag with Large Data Capacity." Proceedings

ddle River, New Jersey: Pearson Educa-

to RFID Technology and Its Use in the
online at www.printronix.co.uk/library/
hite-paper-english.pdf (accessed July 11,

e at www.rfidguardian.org (accessed July

ology." RFID Journal. Available at www.
37/1/129/ (accessed July 11, 2006).

Technical Approach to RFID." Available
20RFID%20Whitepaper.pdf

enbaum. 2006. "The Evolution of RFID
1): 62–69.

ntification. New York: McGraw-Hill.

ncyclopedia. Available online at http://
:essed July 16, 2006).

to Thwart Forgers." USA Today. August
y.com/travel/news/2005-08-08-electronic-

5

Recent Advances in the Technology

Radio frequency identification hardware and tag technology has come a long way since the late 1960s and early 1970s, as discussed in Chapter 2. Its uses are attracting a broad business audience that is continuously hunting for the next technical development that will give them a competitive advantage. The potential for individuals to live in a more highly automated world where mundane tasks are achieved with technology enables more time spent in areas of personal choice. Eliminating time waiting in a grocery store line or no longer losing luggage at the airport are ways that RFID can improve people's lives. Authenticating that medication matches the written prescription or improving automobile safety has a positive impact on our livelihood through radio frequency technologies. RFID is in an era of explosive interest in the business community. Though it has been available for many years, RFID technology is targeting a startling number of new uses and is just beginning to expose the tip of the iceberg of how and why it may change our world.

Like many technological advances, test lab results and experiments sprout into a business vision. At the root of new use cases are physicists, researchers, and creative thinkers who continue to be driven with innovative ideas to allow the sharing of information using radio waves. Through experimentation and lab work, these technology pioneers are validating many of their assumptions and discovering new concepts with wireless technology. Entrepreneurs are realizing the value that RFID can bring to the consumer. Further opportunities for business operational improvement are being identified in the logistics of the supply chain. This is creating momentum behind countless pilots and tests in the work place. As these programs are tuned and tweaked, they are proving their worth with regularity as they begin to impact and influence our everyday life in many ways.

5.1 RFID Hardware

The broad appeal and benefit of RFID is largely possible because radio waves can be sent and received across a wide spectrum of frequencies. New applications of RF are being discovered in part because of the varying characteristics associated with these open-air frequencies. In the world of radio frequency communication, not one size fits all. RFID tag technologies, which are sometimes called transponders, differ in purpose, frequency, size, and strength. Matching the best frequency to the application is as much an art as a science (for sample applications, see Table 5-1). For example, at the receiving dock at the Metro Store HF or UHF would be selected for use over a LF radio signal for logistical operations because of its ability to read multiple tags per second. By contrast, LF typically reads only one item at a time. A hospital room is more conducive to HF than UHF because UHF radio signals from a neighboring room can result in unwanted reads. The range for a UHF signal is greater than HF. When two companies collaborate

Table 5-1 Common Frequencies and Their Uses

Frequency Range	Common Frequency	Common Uses
LF—Low frequency	• 30 kHz • 125 kHz • 134.2 kHz • 300 kHz	• Access control • Animal identification • Lot identification • Chemical process use • Distribution
HF—High frequency	• 3 MHz • 13.56 MHz (ISO 15693) • 30 MHz	• Logistic warehouse management • Automotive manufacturing and tracking • Retail • Hospitals • Baggage check • Library management • Parcel tracking • Security • Smart cards
UHF—Ultrahigh frequency	• 300 MHz • 433 MHz • 866 MHz (Europe) • 915 MHz (United States)	• Retail • Toll roads • Logistics—Inside a factory and through the supply chain • Long-range applications • Item tracking
Microwave frequency	• 2.45 Gigahertz • 3.0 Gigahertz	• Long-range applications • Item tracking • Freight tracking

to share information using RF technology, a tight coordination is required to collectively determine the best frequency to use that allows both members of the partnership to realize value from the data.

One of the most significant advancements for RF tags in the last several years is the adoption of EPC™ (Electronic Product Code) compliant Gen 2 tags (discussed in more detail in Chapter 7). As early adoption of Gen 2 is being accepted and is forming the foundation and common reference point for future RF tag advancements. The EPC Gen 2 specification was initially targeted at UHF technologies. The most widespread use of passive RF tags has historically been with low frequency and high frequency. Usage in the passive UHF ranges is relatively new. The need for increased transmitting distance at a low cost is fueling much of the interest in UHF. This development is encouraging new applications where historically only a very inexpensive barcode could be utilized.

5.1.1 Tags

It is believed by many that we are at the commencement of what is expected to be an exponential growth rate in tag usage over the next several years. When considering Gen 2 UHF tags only, in its first full year of adoption (2006), the market absorbed nearly 1 billion RF tags. This number will climb over 2 billion the following year and is expected to skyrocket toward the 30 billion range by its fifth year. UHF tags are the least expensive RF tags. At this writing, the lowest cost passive RF tags are selling at US$0.05 in volumes of 100 million units (Smartcode, 2006). This is a significant milestone that has been the target for tag makers. This will, of course, spark added RF usage and new applications, which is factored into the stated growth rate.

Tags are built to comply with a categorization called a *class*. Classes progressively have greater capability. Following is a general description of functionality that each class is required to comply (Thorne, 2005). See Table 3-1 for specification information on tag classes.

- *Class 0/class 1*. These classes provide the basic RF passive capability. Class 0 is factory-programmed. Beyond class 0, including class 1, the tags are user-programmable.
- *Class 2*. Additional functionality is added, which includes encryption and read-write RF memory
- *Class 3*. Batteries are found on board that will power logic in the computer circuit. Class 3 provides longer range and broadband communications
- *Class 4*. Active tags are part of the definition of class 4 tags. Peer-to-peer communications and additional sensing are also included.
- *Class 5*. Class 5 tags contain enough power to activate other tags and could be effectively classified as a reader.

Reliability, when reading RF tags, is a most important factor for any successful RFID application. It is imperative that the readers and tags have an extremely high level of performance. When an error in reading occurs, it can have a negative impact for both the tag holder (i.e., the item that is tagged) and the tag reader. False information will lead to risky decision making. An RF-tagged aircraft that has a read failure (no read occurs) during its normal inspection routine will likely require manual intervention, which will hold up all passengers until the issue is resolved. This is a huge inconvenience for travelers and impacts airline customer satisfaction while increasing costs caused by missed flights and flight-handling delays. An incorrect RF read is potentially worse. Think of an invalid safety inspection where an incorrect tag read may allow an airline to continue the flight with an aircraft operating in an unknown condition. This type of safety concern dictates that the RFID technology be robust and reliable as it is put into day-to-day environments.

RF tag sizes vary greatly as they are applied in different industries. Selecting the correct size for the purpose is an important decision in an RFID initiative. BMW® uses a cylindrical-shaped tag that is 15 cm in length and 2 cm in diameter for tracking parts on the automobile (Buchmann, 2005). This industrial-strength tag will provide greater range at HF and is able to be read through difficult materials. At the other end of the spectrum, the smallest tags are in the microwave frequency. Even miniature-sized tags can maintain a reasonable read range. The semiconductor manufacturing industry uses a highly durable tag the size of an aspirin capsule, often referred to as a "pill." An example of a common UHF tag size in retail is 15 cm in length, 1 cm high, and is effectively flat.

Different shapes produce different physics properties and determine radio signal direction and strength. Research labs are developing very tiny transponders that could be placed in a very small object, such as the end of a pen. Pushing the envelope further are companies like Symbol Technologies, who claim the smallest RFID tag on the market at 550 microns square and an antenna that is as small as 12 mm in size. This tag is smaller than a grain of sand when the antenna is removed. German RFID maker KSW Microtec has created an RFID tag that is designed to be sewn into clothing and is durable enough to be washed. A plethora of RF tag size options can be found, as unique solutions require different capabilities.

A key force behind continued advancement of RF tags is the cost of the tag. Many RF tag designs and reengineering efforts are intended to drive lower-priced tags, allowing RFID users to achieve greater business benefit. As consumer packaged goods (CPG) companies introduce tracking at the item level, the added cost of the tag relative to the product must be low enough to make tracking financially viable. Placing a tag on a bicycle will have a nominal cost effect because the price of the RF tag is minimal compared to the overall bicycle cost. However, placing an RF tag on a can of Coca-Cola® may be cost-prohibitive. It will either drive up the cost of the soft drink or place a burden on the seller (unless the gains from having additional information outweigh the tag cost). The retail sector is most interested in using the ultrahigh-frequency bandwidth because it can read many tags simultaneously and it can read longer distances. RF tag costs have been slowly dropping and are expected to continue to fall over time. In the early days of the EPC definition, a target tag price aimed toward the US$0.05 range. The US$0.05 tag is believed to be the point at which a broad base of retailers will track at the item level and achieve a positive ROI, as discussed in Chapter 6. As with any technology, as lower-priced tags are available, the RF tag cost target will move downward and cost expectations will be reset. This will put in motion a new set of business applications and uses for RFID technology.

There are clear challenges ahead to take steps forward in tag cost reduction. Historically, RFID tags have been supplied by semiconductor companies. Texas Instruments™ and Philips® have been very active in the RFID market and are generally recognized as the leading providers in this arena. During manufacturing, each tag goes through an extensive fabrication process, which is a contributor to the price remaining relatively high. Raw materials, a highly automated environment, and the high-cost process equipment required in tag manufacturing are historic inhibitors to RFID tag price reductions. Whether the next wave of low-cost RFID tags will evolve from a silicon-based manufacturing process or a revolutionary more disruptive manufacturing process, the race is on and the reward at the finish line is sizeable.

Tag manufacturers and RFID reader companies are expending significant resources and energy striving to carve out their share of the market ahead. Discovery and prototyping is only the first step in RFID tag advancement. As new RF technologies are introduced, tags and readers must go through a rigorous process of standard compliance and validation. Maturity and measured reliability achievements must be earned over time. As the new tag technology proves it is robust in design and implementation, a mass-production environment must be developed to meet the market demand for the new tag. User acceptance in the court of consumer opinion must occur as the adoption of the technology hits the market. Volume buying caused by widespread usage of the new and improved RFID tag will enable its price to drop.

RF tags must be applied to the item or container that is being tracked. The operation of applying RF tags has an additional cost, further driving up a per-tagged-object cost. Since tags come in a variety of shapes and sizes and may be square, flat, round, cylindrical, and so forth, there are many different methods and requirements in applying a tag. Cost is a major issue in the decision on how to apply the tags. Consider that someone or something has to attach the tag to an item or container. This takes equipment and/or manpower. In electronic manufacturing, RF tags are commonly welded into a precast hard-plastic container. This allows the container to be tracked over a five- to seven-year life and withstand extreme heat and exposure to harmful chemicals, and operate where a process requires immersion in liquids as it continues to function in a normal fashion. By contrast, cattle are tagged manually because the animal's movement was not predictable enough to attach the tag properly otherwise. The scenario of applying RF tags manually to each DVD that is produced for a local music reseller would be far too expensive to justify labor costs of using the technology. Therefore, tagged DVDs are typically applied with automation as they move through the supply chain to the retail store. In RF tag application, new extensions to existing software is required whether the tag-to-asset relationship is manual (which increases the risk of error) or the tag application equipment is integrated to an existing software infrastructure. Using RFID data at the point of sale requires further electronic communication and integration. This requires an infrastructure that in turn is supported by an IT staff, which comes at a cost. These added costs should be weighed properly during evaluation of an ROI for an RFID solution (for more on ROI, see Chapter 6).

The burning need to apply tags automatically has lead to the RFID printer. These devices are very much like a barcode printer as they apply RF tags. With adhesive on one side and an embedded RF tag, application is typically in a predefined position on the container or item. For example, Kimberly-Clark applies tags to boxes of diapers as they move through the product line. As tags are applied, the tag ID is logically associated to the item or container in a software tracking system.

Improved tag performance and reliability will be driven by tag maturity and growing advancement in the physics of RF tags. Key topics in the evolution of RFID advancement include the following:

- *Battery life.* Longer battery life for active tags increases the life of the product in which they are embedded. RFID batteries for active tags are nonrechargeable. The batteries with the longest service life currently are based on a lithium/thionyl chloride cell (Jacobs, 2006). It has an operational life of 15 to 20 years and is excellent for applications like aircraft.
- *Encryption.* Encrypted data is key to the security of RF technology. Gen 2 specifications provide introductory encryption guidance for passive tags, yet significant work still needs to be done. A user must weigh the security risk with the data on the tag to determine if security is important. A can of Campbell's® soup, for example, will probably not contain too much sensitive data on the RF tag. More care and interest in privacy and data encryption are being used with active tags. A major reason for the added interest in active tag encryption is due to the longer distances that active tags can transmit (refer to Chapter 10 on privacy and security).
- *Power consumption.* Reducing the power consumption on passive transponders is an important element in effective RF tags. The lower the

power, the farther the distance a reader and tag can communicate. Greater distances can lead to more advanced usage per the selected frequency, though higher frequencies have greater challenges because of interference with metal or water. Lower tag power consumption will also contribute to improved reader reliability. Some microwave implementations can run on near zero power consumption.

- *Nonvolatile memory.* Writable nonvolatile memory (NVM) is a key component when data is allowed to be stored and reprogrammed on the tag. STMicroelectronics' RFID tag uses nonvolatile memory technology enabling 40-year data retention and more than 10,000 write/erase cycles to support the requirements of long-life applications (STMicroelectronics, 2005). For Impinj, Inc., NVM enables an increased writing range when the contents of a tag need to be reprogrammed (or rewritten). The company is claiming successful writes up to 25 m with its recent Self-Adaptive Silicon™ RF products (Colleran, 2005).

- *Circuitry.* New generations of tags are requiring more complex circuitry. One tag maker cites a recent class 0 RF tag that has just fewer than 42,000 transistors on board. The same maker states that its Gen 2 tag is populated with approximately 60,000 transistors (Colleran, 2005). Another maker contrasts a Gen 1 tag at 12,000 transistors and its Gen 2 tag at near 40,000 transistors. This illustrates the large difference in technology complexities with the advancement to Gen 2.

- *Antennas.* IBM® researchers have introduced what they call the "Clipped Tag." It enables a consumer to shorten the length of the antenna, thus attenuating the reading range. It effectively allows the tag to be disabled. The concept would enable the tag to still be read at a reduced range providing much greater opportunity to protect the client's privacy yet enabling the tag to read at extremely close ranges if necessary. Tests have shown the range dropped from 2 m to near 5 cm (O'Connor, 2005a). Multiple methods of shortening the length of the antenna were explored, such as scratching off a portion of the antenna at a midpoint, a built-in perforated line to tear the antenna, or a pull tab that is removable. Each of these methods achieves the same end goal of reducing the RF range of the tag for the consumer (IFTF, 2006).

The smart card, which is based on radio frequency, is a much touted and somewhat controversial topic. Making personal and sensitive data available on an RFID chip will likely have its place and time and become more openly accepted in the not-so-distant future. But today in many countries there is heavy resistance to the use of the smart card. This is due to RFID's ability to read at distances where historically magnetic strips or barcodes required line of site or direct contact. Usage of the smart card is expected to provide fast transactions, more convenience, reduced fraud, and allow quicker transactions for its card holder. A working example of the smart card is one supplied by ExxonMobil. The business case is based on a higher speed at the point of sale believed to lead to increased purchases. ExxonMobil, has more than six million customers who use its Speedpass™ contactless card (based on RF technology), briefly discussed in Chapter 1, as a preferred option of payment (RFID Journal, 2003). The company discovered that Speedpass users spent 15 percent more on merchandise, which increased total sales by 4 percent. Another compelling use of the smart card is the Hong Kong Octopus Card, which is used by more than 95 percent of the population in Hong Kong. It is accepted at over 160 retailers and convenience stores. Pay phones, parking garages, and photo booths, among a host of others, also readily accept the card. Convincing business cases are propelling the smart card into business prominence.

Financial transactions with RF are in use today and will be rolling out to consumers with greater regularity. A look back in history shows that banking introduced the plastic credit card in 1959. Electronic payments with magnetic strips on the card came into the mainstream in 1981. One-third of consumer transactions in the United States in 2005 were card-based, while the remaining two-thirds of transacations are completed with cash or check. By the year 2010 this number is expected to flip, where RF card-based purchases and payments will be two-thirds of spending and one-third of the transactions are with cash or check (Mullagh, 2005). Fast-food chain giant McDonald's® has successfully run RF trials at over 400 of its restaurants in the Chicago area. This has lead to wider adoption, as they have installed 55,000 RFID readers in approximately 13,500 different sites (Mullagh, 2005). The readers increase the speed at the checkout counters and drive-up windows. This benefits both the consumer as well as McDonald's. Supporting the trend are credit card leaders Visa®, MasterCard®, and American Express®, who are all deploying RF technologies as a form of payment.

Another example is found at the point of currency withdrawal. Consider a unique usage where an ATM (automated teller machine) without a keypad at the terminal. The user's card contains a keypad which has RF technology embedded into one normal-sized bank card. The cardholder places the bank card near the ATM, and the ATM reader recognizes the card and its owner. The user then enters the PIN (personal identification number) on the card's keypad, which is then transmitted to the ATM via radio waves to initiate and complete the transaction. Because the keypad is distributed to the user's credit card, greater security measures are realized. The European Central Bank is looking one step beyond credit cards with RFID, as they are embedding RF tags into euro bank notes in an effort to deter counterfeiting throughout the region.

RF solutions can be integrated with other sensors, tracking and combining the data of varying sources with related properties and characteristics in the given environment. Temperature, for example, is an important measure to track for foods or chemicals, that may be disposed because of overaging. At the NASA Dryden Flight Research Center at Edwards Air Force Base in California, RFID tags are used together with temperature sensors and motion detectors to help improve the safety in areas with hazardous materials. The objective is to be able to manage an extreme situation, such as a terrorist attack, from an external environment. Tracking includes location, chemical condition, and the handling of the chemicals (Wasserman, 2005). Milk, cheese, or other perishable products have been in the proper chilled environment through the distribution and shipping process to meet the required FDA freshness standards. Other sensory data may also be written to a tag as it flows through the supply chain that may answer questions about its contents such as "Where have I been?" "When was I there?" "What is my current state?" "What is my pressure reading?" and so on. Answering these types of questions at the item level will enable real-time decisions anytime the tag is read.

RF tag life expectancies will differ with usage. A tag on a container of cream cheese has a useful life from the date that the tag is applied until it is consumed or spoils and the box discarded. Using an inexpensive printable UHF label will work well for cream cheese and is conducive to an open-loop environment where the tag will be disposed when its container is discarded. Tires on your automobile, which are tagged to comply with the United States' Transportation Recall Enhancement, Accountability, and Documentation act, will have an expected life of three to five years. This more durable tag, which can properly function with vibration and motion, is necessary for automobile usage. The airline industry is in the process of adopting RFID to track parts on planes in an effort to improve safety inspections. An aircraft is expected to be in service for 30 to 50 years after assembly. As parts are tagged on an aircraft, manufacturers must use RF tags that are acceptable by the FAA and will withstand harsh environments (temperature, pressure, moisture, etc.) for a very long time.

RF tag creators such as Demodulation Inc. are pushing the envelope for the future with the use of harmonic tags (introduced in Chapter 3, "Basics of RFID"). These tags, called Microwire, are the size of a human hair, less than 50 microns in diameter, and less than 2.4 cm in length. The basic structure of the tag is an amorphous alloy coated in glass, much like fiber optics, that respond to the frequency of a carrier wave emitted by a reader. The alloy can be encoded with bits of information that are reflected back to the reader when excited by a carrier wave. Demodulation's research team has created a tag that can withstand $\pm 400°$ F ($\pm$ 220°C) temperatures, responds at multiple frequency ranges, and has an amazing cost of less than US$0.01 per tag. The tag can even power itself off of the beat of a human heart if held close enough to the chest. Demodulation Inc. reported that Microwire tags can be read at up to 25 m, but as the technology is refined, the distance will increase. The first application for this technology will be an article surveillance system. Other applications such as electronic pedigree (e-pedigree) and anticounterfeiting are future possibilities for Microwire. Demodulation Inc. researchers believe that the Microwire tag may be integrated into traditional tags to boost read distance and decrease tag sizes. This technology may represent a new era in RFID. Only time will tell, whether RF harmonic tags will help achieve the goals set for RFID applications today.

5.1.2 Readers

RFID readers communicate with RF tags, interrogating the data on the tag. A reader has a power supply that allows it to transmit and receive information with an RFID tag. Readers for passive RF tags initiate radio transmission, usually when a signal (such as an optical sensor or a pressure sensor) is triggered and sends a message to the RF tag indicating the beginning of communication. Passive tags rely on the readers to provide enough energy to transmit data on the tag back to the reader. Conversely, active RF tags have an onboard battery that allows the active tag to asynchronously initiate RF interaction. Tags with onboard batteries use their own energy to communicate with a reader. This allows greater transmission distance for active tags compared to passive tags. Though commonly called "readers," many of these devices also have the capability to write to the RF tag. Historically, readers have been custom-built to match unique physics properties that best suit the environment where they are being used. Readers have an attached antenna to transmit radio signals back and forth with an RF tag of a matching frequency. These basic capabilities lay the groundwork for advancements in RFID readers.

RFID reader shapes and sizes can be as diverse as the application of use. Facility layout and purposes will help dictate what reader and antenna is best for a particular RF deployment (see samples in Figures 5-1 and 5-2). Antenna shapes will dictate direction and intensity of the signal being transmitted. An oblong-shaped antenna has different directional capabilities than a round antenna (see Chapter 3 for more about the basics of RFID antennas). The United States Department of Defense, one of the largest users of RF technology, uses handheld readers with active RF tags to track assets in the military theater (field of combat). These readers are not much bigger than a remote control for a television and include a small LCD screen as part of the mobile reader. Reader manufacturer SkyeTek, Inc. touts the smallest RFID reader on the market, the SkyeModule M0™ (see Figure 5-3). At approximately 18 mm square it complies with RF industry standards and will read a variety of manufacturers' tags. Its predecessor, the tiny SkyeTek M1™ mini, less than 3 mm thick and approximately 25 mm in diameter, is used to confirm whether or not accurate medication is administered to the correct patient (Quinn, 2004). If the wrong medication is identified, a reader will either send a warning signal or stop the operation of the medical equipment applying the dose. At the Marks & Spencer® foods division, extremely large vertical standing readers have been created that are roughly 2 m by 1 m. This uniquely sized reader with antenna transmits the RF signal horizontally to a series of totes. Large stacks of totes carrying

Figure 5-1 Vertical antenna (*Source:* With friendly approval of Harald Buchmann. Brooks Automation. 2006).

Figure 5-2 HF reader (*Source:* With friendly approval of Harald Buchmann. Brooks Automation. 2006).

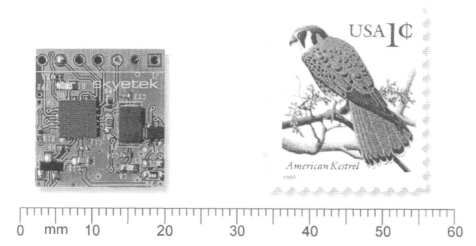

Figure 5-3 SkyeTek SkyeModule M0 versus a standard postage stamp. (*Source:* Courtesy of SkyeTek, Inc., 2006).

food are placed at the side of these massive readers as the contents of the totes are written to multiple 13.56 MHz RF tags. By performing a batch write, Marks & Spencer has achieved a savings of 400 percent in the operational time spent at this step of its food-handling process as compared to working with barcodes (Stafford, 2005). Shapes and forms of readers will forge ahead as emerging RFID uses are discovered.

When a company prepares to deploy RFID in a business operation, the cost of readers is one of the more important items to evaluate. However, in many industries the cost of readers no longer has the overall impact it once did. This is due to multiple factors. First, the technology is improving at a rapid rate. RFID reader suppliers have sprung up over the last several years, marking a competitive landscape that is much fiercer than before. With more offerings on the market, the increased pace of RF research is hastening RFID adoption. Second, solutions are sliding up the frequency scale, enabling greater read distances than they would have experienced in the past. This movement allows RFID users to run processes with fewer readers on the operating floor. At the receiving dock of a Wal-Mart® distribution center, readers are placed in a portal. When pallets or goods are transported past the readers, each individual tag is automatically read. UHF readers are used to provide the distance necessary to read each item or carton on the pallet. A final factor is the growing interest in using RFID for open-loop applications. (As mentioned, an open-loop application only uses the RF tag once through a product lifecycle; the tag becomes disposable and isn't recycled). Consequently, each tag must be negligible in price compared to the merchandise to which it is attached. Individual tag costs should dwarf the cost of readers in an open-loop environment.

As with tags, RFID reader advancements are headed toward smaller size and lower cost. Many reader manufacturers are developing a new generation of readers that can be pushed to a computer chipset. The first chipsets of readers started to hit the market in the 2007 time frame. Texas Instruments introduced one of these early chipset readers which is of the size 5 mm by 5 mm and supports multiple protocols (*RFID Update,* 2007). RF readers are trending toward becoming more commoditized and less customized for specific RFID applications. These chipsets of readers will not only shrink reader sizes, but reader units will drop in price by more than half over the earlier generation of readers. Work is also under way toward the creation of a reader residing on a single chip. This signifies that the entire reader functionality will be local to a single chip rather than requiring a set of computer chips that assemble into a reader unit. It is expected that readers-on-a-chip will trail chipset readers by approximately one year, with a target of 2008 for market rollout. When this becomes a reality, readers-on-a-chip will further drive down the reader prices to levels of about 25 percent of chipset readers, which is about 10 percent of assembled units (Colleran, 2005). Pushing further is a concept where more generic chipsets are using onboard software or firmware to perform reader functions. This software reader could be configured with different properties and be easily upgraded in the field in a real-time manner.

Many readers have the ability to write data to RF transponders. The function of openly writing new contents to an RFID tag provides a degree of flexibility and reusability not found in read-only tags. However, concern has been raised about the security risks of the data that resides on the tag. Reusable containers or totes with RFID tags attached can be used over and over in an application. The tag may be updated to contain data about the contents of the container and other relevant attributes to the process or operation of the tagged object. Pharmaceutical manufacturers in a high-throughput facility, for example, face a more difficult task because they are performing a write function. If a read error occurs to a tagged bottle of medication, the tag can simply be reread at another location where a decision is made whether to allow the bottle to proceed through the process flow or not. If an RF write failure takes place, the drug may never be readable or the tag may be nonsensical. A worse condition could occur if the tag is then readable and the contents of the bottle don't match the RF tag data. In this situation, the bottle must be locatable and a rewrite of the correct data must occur. To ensure accuracy, the RF tag must correspond to the contents of the bottle as originally intended. This is a difficult task in some business processes.

Higher-capacity tags are able to have data written and appended onto the existing tag data. This will provide a knowledge base that allows complex decisions to be made on the item tagged once it is read. The EPC Gen 2 standard has declared that to be performance-compliant, an RFID device must be able to write a minimum of five writes per second. The standard has defined a target of 30 writes per second, which give reader buyers a target criterion.

With tags that can be reprogrammed in circulation, the potential exists for a breech of security with tag data. Write-locking algorithms, passwords, encryption, and other technology advancements are available to diminish the potential for RF write misuses. Business processes must be put into place with proper security measures to help reduce the risk of unintended reprogramming of RF tags. When planning to write to an RF transponder it is important to recognize that typically the range to perform a tag write is smaller than performing a read (commonly two-thirds the range of a read). Thus, reader positioning and facility layouts need to be engineered for the proper use of the RF reader-writer.

A great deal of the excitement surrounding RFID is the opportunity to collaborate with trading partners. Sharing information up and down the supply chain enables information flow that hasn't existed before. As companies roll out RFID initiatives, they must make many decisions. One of the more important choices is which frequency to use. Companies who join forces for a common business purpose may face the risk of incompatible frequencies for their respective RF initiatives. Standard frequencies have been adopted in the LF and HF ranges. Within the range of the UHF band there is less of an agreement on which frequency to use. As industry standards are maturing, they aid in solving this problem, but standards can only do so much. Multifrequency or combo readers are becoming necessary to solve some of these problems and are readily available on the market.

Multifrequency readers simply are RF devices that are able to read radio signals using two or more frequencies. A common use for a multifrequency reader would be interrogating item-level tagged objects with mismatched frequencies that come from a different source. One vision where this could be applied in the home is to have a reader in a refrigerator that can collect RF data, monitor the refrigerator contents, and notify the owner which groceries remain. This will allow the owner to detect items that should be on the next grocery shopping list. It can also aid in identifying products that may be near spoilage. In this example, it is unlikely that all tagged items in the refrigerator will have the same RF tag frequency. Multifrequency readers will read a broader range of tags, providing a more accurate inventory. Many reader experts believe that there is a long way to progress with multifrequency readers, but once resolved, there isn't likely to be much added cost for a multifrequency reader compared to a single-frequency reader. The greater cost is expected in the infrastructure and setup.

While RFID adoption more broadly grows, readers will more rapidly become integrated into different everyday devices. Common household appliances such as a washing machine is envisioned to come equipped with RF reader technology. When one does the laundry, decisions are made about the cycle, which detergent should be used, and whether or not the batch of laundry is compatible (colors, materials, etc.) for the scheduled washing. Integrating readers into the washing unit and negotiating decisions with tagged clothing enables a new level of automation in a household environment.

Though at times RF applications may seem extreme, over time RF device costs are expected to come into alignment with RFID usage as it institutes change in day-to-day activities. Examples include keyless locks based on RF technology. These have been provided by automobile makers for several years. The radio signal allows the driver to lock and unlock the car remotely. Amal Graafstra took his automobile security to new heights by implanting an RF transponder into his hand (see Figure 5-4). Similar to using a wireless key, when he waves his hand near his automobile, his car unlocks and he is endowed with a built-in password for entry. Amal also uses his implanted hand transponder for entry to his home as well and as a login password to his computer (Torrone, 2005). Amal has enjoyed his RFID implant so much that he had a second one implanted in his other hand for additional purposes.

Shrinking reader sizes will further facilitate RFID into daily living. Consider mobile cellular phones and how more useful they have become over recent years. Cell phones exploit active RFID technology. Navigating the Internet, text messaging, and playing games on cell phones are commonplace activities for many. Photos can be taken and sent using a cell phone and RF technology. Leading cell phone providers, such as Nokia®, are now providing cell phones with HF readers built in. This flips the reader-tag paradigm and enables the reader to be mobile and the tag to be placed at a fixed location. Airbus® plans to use readers embedded in cell phones to

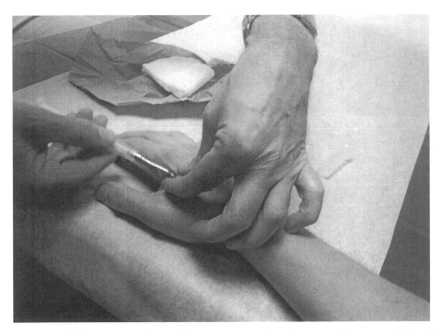

Figure 5-4 RFID implant into a hand (*Source:* With permission Courtesy of Amal Graafstra. 2006).

improve their inspection procedures (Heitmann, 2005). Maintenance engineers will place their cell phones near tagged parts as they begin performing an inspection, which will easily associate the engineer with the inspection process. Nokia is using this technological advancement in industrial asset management such as gathering data from gas pipelines. The RF read is initiated from the phone, associated data is then keyed in from the phone keypad (like a text message), and the information is quickly uploaded to a central data system. Nokia sees many uses in security management via RFID readers embedded into cell phones. One such scenario involves a security guard who quickly reads an RF tag and validates that doors are still locked in the surveillance of a protected area. Predefined numbers are called under certain tag read conditions, allowing immediate notification if a problem arises (Romen, 2004). The addition of RFID to everyday devices that many people already carry such as a cell phones brings convenience to users and presents the potential for a new breed of business applications.

While most RF reader technology includes components that are fabricated on a computer chip, some less traditional work is under way around the globe:

- Conductive Inkjet Technology has introduced an inline printer that produces a printable antenna. At high speed, copper is laid down on a substrate in a two-layer process: a metal-conductive layer and a water-soluble layer, which is later dissolved. Printable antennas are generally considered to be more environmentally friendly. They offer a new level of flexibility and quick customization for RFID solutions (Johnson, 2005).
- New Zealand innovator Sandtracker is patenting RF equipment where the tag is constructed with a quartz crystal diode rather than a silicon chip. This enables a stronger signal that has shown the ability to read 4,000 simultaneous tags at ranges up to 18 m in the lab. The cost of such a chip is just under the magical $0.05 (Collins, 2004). The company is also developing RF technology that works well with metal rather than against it. These tags actually have proven to enhance read performance when attached to metal (Hilder, 2005).
- In Stockholm, Cypak AB has developed an RF technology called the "paperboard computer." The high-frequency conductive circuitry is graphite which is printed onto paper. The paperboard computer has a finite number of individual uses with limited computing capabilities, low power consumption, and low cost. An example cited is tracking the access into a secured box such as a courier package. When the circuit is broken, a read is triggered and data is automatically recorded to the tag, providing tamper detection. Multiple occurrences of the disconnected circuits are recorded, offering added information about the security of the box. The Nordic Bank is performing tests with the paperboard computer by using a keypad on a credit card and commu-

nicating with RF tags (Ehrensvard, 2005). As paper usage of RFID becomes more accepted, it may open the door to many potential low-cost RFID solutions.

5.2 Software

Software will breathe life into an RFID solution. While heavy RFID focus is on the frequencies, transponder technologies, printer devices, and readers that send and receive radio waves, by themselves they are not much more than an intriguing discovery of a physics phenomenon. Attaching these devices to software will bring to life the circumstances and environment where RFID activity results in value. The most basic form of software provides essential connectivity converting data from the physical world to a logical world. It enables a real-world event to be recognized and captured as one of a series of happenings that may provide personal convenience or business value. The science of RFID hardware is the first building block to a greater RFID opportunity. The manner in which RFID data is used when integrated with software can transform an RFID implementation to new heights by advancing the user's process.

When comparing RFID software to RFID hardware advancements, one needs to consider some differences. Using a reader can be pretty straightforward and generally can be acquired and tested at a low out-of-pocket cost. When integrating RFID software, a greater level of awareness of its usage environment is necessary. As the data becomes integrated with other people and processes in a scenario, the software design may need to become tailored to its use. The same type of readers in the same facility may be used in a different manner. With software integration, a major part of the investment is paid up front. Careful definition, design, and planning are necessary for an effective RFID deployment.

Pumping RFID data into software requires the data to be stored in a common location. The RF data and its associated attributes are then retrievable for future use. Information such as physical location of the items, associated item properties, or its container provide dynamic data for real-time decisions to be made. Software allows an operation to garner results that are both repeatable and predictable compared to manual processes. RF software decisions are based on predictability. As an RFID-tagged pacemaker flows through a medical device manufacturing line, the process path it follows is recorded and stored for future retrieval. The specific path or route can be retraced and re-created if needed. If a defect is identified in the pacemaker, subsequent pacemakers that followed the same steps can be identified for further testing in search of a trending manufacturing problem. This is the normal case scenario. Software becomes even more effective when abnormal activity occurs during a process. An anomaly may be as simple as an RF read or write failure. It could be an RF-tagged container or item arriving at an unexpected reader or a more complex unexpected condition that is recognized by a software system.

As an example of anomaly resolution, consider the above-mentioned RFID-enabled pacemaker becoming misplaced during its assembly. The first time this error occurs, an operator is forced to set the device aside (risking loss or contamination) while determining the next course of action to take. Predictable anomaly-handling conditions evolve into best practices and policies in this type of manufacturing environment. Upon the occurrence of future incidents, the operator will know exactly what to do each time the situation is encountered. RFID can assist with the ability to self-identify the pacemaker when it is placed before a reader. As automation becomes more complex, the policy for error handling described above may be designed and written in software to automatically handle the situation based on the RFID data validation. The predictability in the manufacturing process as each pacemaker is identified with RFID allows this level of automation. This will in turn lead to greater repeatability of throughput and productivity in a manufacturing line. Looking ahead, medical and pharmaceutical manufacturers will require electronic signatures by those authorized. RFID is equipped to support this type of initiative.

A chief objective of RFID systems is to replace or reduce human actions and enable the user to enjoy the fruits of a minimized workload. To perform this goal, software is attached to RFID equipment to capture data and/or automate a process where the results of the process can be trusted. Key elements of an RFID implementation can be categorized as data capture or process automation:

- *Data capture.* Software directly connects and communicates to RF devices reading, writing, and printing labels. This provides a centrally located reservoir of data associated with RF activity. Using a spreadsheet to keep track of mathematical data, such as a personal financial account, provides a convenient method for data input and enables easy future data changes for quick review of the current status of the account. The spreadsheet provides automatic recalculation as the data changes, giving real-time feedback to a decision-making audience. Ease in attaining data is also experienced with RFID. For example, a clothing purchase in an RFID-enabled clothing store allows the convenience of a much simpler checkout process. The customer simply moves through the checkout station by pushing a cart through the reader portal. A receipt is then created and a credit card automatically transfers payment from the buyer to the seller. The clothing retailer now automatically has up-to-date inventory data to replenish stock. They also have a micro-glimpse into the buying patterns of customers without conducting an expensive labor-intensive inventory procedure (i.e., a physical inventory).
- *Process automation.* Software provides an opportunity to undertake new levels of automation when multiple interactive sources communicate

with each other. Software can bridge the gap between human and machine, make judgments or decisions on a state of affairs, and cause an action to execute that allows a process to continue. Playing a game of solitaire on a personal computer is an example of software that executes in an everyday setting. The player selects which card to move and the location to place the card. In response, the software takes action on the player's decision and paints the new view of the game on the computer display. RFID is treated as a source of mechanized input with a greater automation objective. RFID activity on the battlefront of a military operation will provide necessary indicators of military-related movement and updated progress during the operation. The connected software can then provide updated status, which leads to making decisions relative to the situation. It can force action to be taken such as the initiation of a warning protocol to notify troops of increased risk in a particular situation.

RFID advancements using software need to maintain focus around finding the real business value or user advantage. The application stacks (refer to Chapter 8, "System Components") and integrated solutions that are successful with RFID data are growing at a rapid pace. Integration of systems that act on RFID data is a challenge. This is fostering a growing community of awareness for standards that will help align these different and diverse software applications. Many companies use a software package called ERP (enterprise resource planning; not to be confused with effective radiated power in Chapter 3) in their daily operations to aid tracking actions and fulfill customer demands. Manufacturing, assembly, warehousing, and other enterprises can gain growing value as they include RFID data in the decision-making methodology. For example, leading ERP provider SAP® promotes the ISA (the Instrumentation, System, and Automation Society) S95 (an ERP interfacing standard) interface in their NetWeaver® exchange architecture to promote plug-and-play components in their ERP. The initiative is intended to bring together global end users, thought leaders, and application providers striving for a standard way for their applications to interact. Software packages that are compliant to the S95 standard will be more easily integrated into many business environments. The adoption of XML (Extensible Markup Language) over the recent past also aids in a quicker standards-based method of communication between software packages. Such standards will speed up the time to integrate RFID with existing and new software packages.

Software applications that will have the greatest staying power in the market are those that have a high degree of reliability. Achieving high reliability is easier said than done. What happens to the business operation if the RF application fails? Is an RFID user prevented from completing a transaction? Is the business process that drives income halted? If such a scenario adversely impacts business, then a higher level of software reliability is necessary. As with RF hardware, software that fails or crashes is of diminishing value. As applications are made available to control RF devices and perform inventive new tasks, it is natural to have a heavy focus on features and functions. Application software must be designed and developed with stability in mind; however, a strong validation of performance is not achievable in a pilot or proof of concept. Paramount Farms™ is the largest almond and pistachio producer in California. They have realized a significant reduction in setup time and reduced costs of leased storage trailers with their RFID system. Dave Szeflin, Paramount Farms vice president of operations states, "The big challenge with a pistachio harvest is that once it starts, there's no way to stop it." Within a six-week peak period Paramount processes over 500 million pounds of incoming product. The process is temperature-sensitive and some loads arrive with temperatures over 38° C or 100° F (Intermec, 2005). If the RF system were to fail or the tracking software plugged into the system fails for even a short period of time, a portion of the crop is wasted. This creates output problems and cuts directly into successful order fulfillment and customer satisfaction.

When RF systems are integrated with other software systems and a failure occurs, the systems it interfaces may be adversely impacted. As the failed systems are restored, data resynchronization with other systems is necessary. Failure during a transaction that was in midstream can be a problem as well. Many business environments require a round the clock (24×7) continuation of business. Simon Palinkas, the Tesco RFID Program Manager, an early adopter of RFID in the retail sector states, "a 24×7 environment at a distribution center is a must for Tesco" (Palinkas, 2005).

Many such implementations require highly available computing nodes that are clustered together for greater uptime. In these cases, typically separate power sources are accessed such that if the power were to fail from one source, the other nodes are able to continue running the operation. The running software automatically fails over to an alternate computing node and starts the application on the node with power to allow processing to continue with minimal or no recognizably adverse impact. Uptime percentages are often called "five 9s," which is measured uptime against a common goal of 99.999 percent uptime. Years of maturity of a software product are typically required to achieve this level of measured success.

RFID systems installed and used today may not have the same purpose a year from now. The ability for software to scale and change without shutting a facility down is a significant advancement in the use of some RFID software in manufacturing. The demand in the cell phone market is an example of a product that is driven by styles and add-on technical features and services. The consumer's fluctuating interests and needs drive regular change in the design of a cell phone. Cell phone manufacturers must walk a tightrope of providing proper supply to the market without overproducing goods that struggle to get launched. Fashion trends and technology advancements are pushing more products to the market at a faster pace than ever before. This is forcing manufacturers and suppliers to shorten cycles of production for products in the supply chain. They must manage and produce more products than ever before to compete. Often this requires change in the process of manufacturing, assembly, test, and warehouse management.

Life cycles of cell phones range from four to eight weeks as demand changes (Bellini, 2006). Manufacturing and assembly must be nimble and implement process change to respond to the market in a timely manner. This type of change often requires facility expansion, compression, or reconfiguration to effectively build the next cell phone for the market. As RF data is gathered through the process and decisions are made for execution and logistical purposes, the data must be stored ultimately in a central location. If the tracking software requires significant time to reconfigure new RF devices, then the operation must be halted. To the cell phone business, this means money lost. Scalability and reconfigurability of the RF solution is becoming more and more essential in today's world. Time wasted because of productivity loss will cost all interested parties money.

Data integrity is critical in using RFID in any day-to-day operation. Decisions are made based on data that is associated with the RF tag. These are becoming a factor in the productivity of an operation. RFID permits greater data sampling than has been realized with the barcode or most other methods of identification. A process that once required a human (reading or scanning each entity) allows information about an item to be captured without human intervention, where an identifier is readable through many materials. More data can be gathered with RF technology than in the past, which drives the need to store more data than previously existed. Data storage requirements play a major role in the software system design and impact the performance of the RFID system. It is important to know what to store. It is equally important to determine what not to store. Data must be properly managed and discarded. Storing more information than is practically useful will cause performance degradation while the data is examined. As events and activities occur at the edge of the RF system (or near the readers), data filtering is important.

With the implementation of an RF solution, time to implementation and ease of software support are critical in the decision-making process. RFID will impact the flow of normal business processes. As software advancements surrounding RF technologies become more complex and advanced, building software solutions on a solid foundation and using supportable tools is an important factor to consider. There is no need for an RFID adopter to reinvent the wheel if RFID is not a core competency. This would introduce latency, cost, and instability to the adopting user. Portions of the software stack will become a commodity and can be purchased on the open market. Other elements will incorporate key logic that is proprietary to the company's intellectual property and, perhaps, should be specifically developed for a target application.

Evaluation of RFID software is easily confusing. Software isn't material like a physical reader, but the results can be positive or negative. It is less tangible than hardware, causing more doubt and uncertainty during an evaluation. A perceived software product may not always equate to the expected result. This drives corporations to work more closely with those they trust. Mature software companies are often a good bet for becoming RF partners. Similar to the dot-com boom of the late 1990s, software vendors for RFID are coming out of the woodwork with many hopes and promises of getting a slice of the RFID action. Suppliers will likely evolve toward consolidation as the vendor population settles over the next several years.

RFID value in software is more realized as the information moves past the middleware and gets integrated into a higher level of decision making. Automating processes using radio frequency technology and RF-enabled software integrated with existing software will facilitate a path of operational optimization. To better consider the opportunities, refer to Figure 5-5, which breaks down the software packages by purpose, as follows:

a. *Gather and consolidate RF data.* The function of gathering information into a centrally located place is fundamental to RFID usage. Initially there is a great amount of focus on this portion of an RF initiative— and rightfully so, as obtaining the RF read data and interfacing to RF devices is the foundation for business applications. Once devices are controlled and tags residing on items, cartons, or pallets can be placed and read, many mandates can be met. Added benefits can be derived in the area of reduced data entry error and knowing where assets or

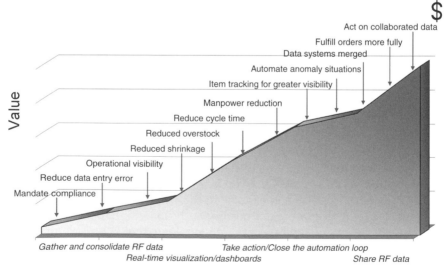

Figure 5-5 RFID user value opportunities.

product reside in the facility at a given point in time. Data gathering and consolidation provides a solid beginning to RFID deployment.

b. *Compare indicators with real-time visualization/dashboards.* The benefit of an RF deployment is enhanced by being able to automatically sense movement in the process and by comparing the operational activity to the key performance indicators (KPIs) of the business. Visual dashboards and reports generated in real time supply data that enable a new level of decision making. This operational visibility assists in pinpointing problem areas such as shrinkage (loss caused by waste or theft), overstock items, or out-of-stock inventory.

c. *Take action/close the automation loop.* As knowledge of the business is better revealed with the use of RF technologies enabling better knowledge of the business situation, an opportunity is provided to take firm action. Whether the action is manual or automated, it is important to respond to the situation as quickly as possible and to close the loop of automation by taking advantage of the new knowledge gained. Execution software is quick and allows immediate action to a situation if the scenario is definable. Some circumstances may be too difficult to define a resolution process or may be so inexpensive to solve manually that software automation isn't necessary. On the other hand, some environments may be such that human intervention isn't possible or human latency is too slow to take advantage of the state of affairs. Acting on the situation will create opportunities such as manpower reduction, shorter cycle time on a key process or manufacturing, or automation of anomalies to maintain process flow.

d. *Share RF data.* Moving the RF data from one user to another has driven much of the recent excitement with RF technologies. Exchanging information more openly and immediately from system to system is enabling opportunity for business advancement that may not have been possible in the past. Some of the entities that share RF data include the following:

   i. Working with a customer—Sending RF-tagged objects to a customer provides the ability to validate shipment, verify proper process protocol, and arm the customer with data to take action upon receipt.

   ii. Working with a supplier—Receiving RF-tagged objects from a vendor removes the burden of tagging and allows a user full traceability from receipt to shipment of the item. It provides the opportunity to receive data or have process collaboration for collective business advancement.

   iii. Intracompany operations—Companies are able to pass information back and forth within complementary corporate operations using RFID. Some manufacturers are more effective by passing materials between facilities for product creation. Data control and ownership is more transparent when RFID is used. This sharing of information will help integrate complementary facilities that have historically operated in a stovepipe fashion.

iv. *Enterprise integration*—Integrating RF reads and coordinating the low-level RF activity up to the enterprise level provides the promise of better coordination between order fulfillment and actual operations. Scheduling intelligence of an execution system at the automation layer can manage the "bill of material" as it optimizes assets. However, this level of information isn't always exposed to the enterprise level. Therefore, the ability to shift away from the plan of record to meet a high-priority order from a key customer is difficult. Making data available to an ERP of material levels, for example, can assist in a quick change of operations. Only 4 percent of manufacturers use point-of-sale data to predict demand (Roberti, 2005). This integration is a necessary advancement to further realize the vision of demand-driven execution through the supply chain. (For more granularity, see Chapter 8, "System Components.")

Businesses that are ready to adopt RFID or extend their RFID initiatives will attain best results when they identify and visualize their long-term operational objectives. Each should lay the foundation and bite off as much as can be economically consumed at a particular point in time. With RFID, the question of adoption may be a matter of when, rather than if. Jumping into RFID to obtain a specific internal optimization measure without considering trading partners may become risky. For example, rushing to integrate an RF system to achieve operational visibility could be good, but if a customer you supply then creates a mandate requiring RF-tagged goods, you may be in a situation of incompatibility with RF deployments. Conversely, running out to slap and ship tags (applying tags as they leave the facility) to meet mandated requirements may not provide the flexibility or a system that will allow an integration strategy into existing systems (refer to Chapter 6, "The Business Case for RFID" for additional examples). With RFID, it is first important to develop a vision of the business problems that are to be solved.

For years, simulating work and business flow has been used to best predict the impact of new technologies and modifications in a process. As the use of RF data is adopted, it is important to measure the results that it can provide. As companies contemplate the affect that RFID could yield and the daily impacts that are placed on the operations, deploying RFID could be viewed as a risk and an expensive proposition. Business process change can have a heavy influence on productivity and cause loss of products or goods if not properly managed. To assist, various RFID test centers have sprouted up to help prove RFID concepts. The use of simulation is a very effective tool to help predict the effectiveness of an RFID rollout. Simulation models will help determine where best to put RF readers and/or how best to optimize the process with integrated readers for maximum productivity. Models are changeable, allowing "what if" scenarios to be run to validate possible results regarding product mix changes, relocating equipment, and reassigning people tasks. When simulating, it is important to be as accurate as possible with the assumptions that are built into the model. The closer to real-life the model is, the more predictive the simulation can become. Simulation will allow a user to quantify impact and investment prior to popping the big money for a facility-wide rollout (Trebilcock, 2004).

5.3 Data Collection and Exchange

At a young age children often learn to draw simple lines with two end-points. Joining these lines allows a shape to begin to form. A dot-to-dot picture allows a child to connect unrelated points on a piece of paper that together build a simple picture with visual meaning. This simple drawing has similarities to the data that is gathered with RFID readers. Each RFID read produces a single data reference point that depicts the momentary state of the tagged object at a specific point in time. Individual RF reads may have little meaning or minimal stand-alone value. However, as these data points are read and assembled into a common data storage place, they can be interpreted with a greater degree of sophistication. The drawing that is created by attaching points is an early step in the natural growth of a child's artistic skills. Likewise, finding new ways to exploit the information and connect the dots with an RF deployment can become an evolving opportunity and challenge for continuous improvement. Passing RF records on to other RF users enable them to exploit the data that has already been captured.

A key catalyst of the recent RFID exuberance is a direct result of the dot-com era of the late 1990s. When the bubble burst, it signaled a new day where Web technology could allow both the business community and the consumer an opportunity for growth by coming to realize the tremendous value of sharing electronic information. The early dot-com movement supplied many businesses an artificial benefit from a diverse range of electronic dealings. Most of these transactions were driven by humans. Simple interaction such as sending a message instantaneously to a specific location connected people to other people across an easy-to-use new medium. Making an electronic purchase coupled people to business in a way not previously comprehended.

Information trading hands has become a fact of life, as data exchange may just be at the tip of new growth. How often is an e-mail to a loved one sent in replacement of a handwritten letter, a phone call, or a personal visit? Consider how many times e-mail was sent just this week compared to written letters. Though less personal, and some would argue socially degenerate, it is widely used and accepted because it is faster than postal mail and less expensive than using a traditional telephone. Software driven by humans is now replacing interpersonal transactions.

RFID offers new ways of passing information to others. It introduces and enables another step in a communication paradigm shift. Many types of transactions can now be automated, where inanimate objects with RFID tags and/or readers communicate one with another. Whether at the local checkout counter or a nearby ATM, merchandise can be read or bank cards recognized using RFID. These devices are integrated into billing systems, providing data to the seller and convenience to the public. And RFID is doing it by providing these services faster and cheaper.

There are several advantages reached from a formalized data-sharing strategy. Almost any transaction requires information or records to be kept. Whether the transaction involves a shipping manifest, the record of a bank deposit, or passage through international borders, interested parties nearly always track their activity. Turning a page back in time, these types of bookkeeping entries have been conducted manually and recorded on paper. Following is a description of the data- capturing and -sharing progression of recent years:

- Manual processes are time-consuming, labor-intensive, and error-prone. It wasn't too many years ago when any purchase at the local RadioShack™ was accompanied by the clerk manually handwriting the name and address of the buyer along with each merchandise line item. This was a painful and tedious process for both the buyer and the store clerk. Counting inventory was laborious, typically requiring the entire staff to work during the night into the wee hours of the morning to manually identify each and every sellable good that existed in the store (yes, including every tiny resistor and capacitor). This exercise cultivates an environment where employees are prone to generate mistakes, as fatigue impacts accuracy. Manual practices of this sort are quite inefficient in today's marketplace. The majority of companies that continue to gather, exchange, and retrieve data in a manual fashion will struggle to be competitive.

- Electronic storage was introduced allowing easier management of the data. Once raw data is gathered, data entry was necessary to place information into the electronic media to maintain the information captured. This allowed data to be examined visually, providing a positive step in sharing information. Data entry required a manual translation process and keystrokes, which create a new source of potential data error.

- The advent and acceptance of reading a UPC on a barcode solved a number of data entry problems. Scanning was mostly done manually using handheld devices. Data entry errors were greatly reduced, as the ID was automatically transferred into a data warehouse, enabling the user to take advantage of the new information. As discovered by barcode users, time largely consumed to interpret and transform paper data was saved.

- RFID launched a new level of benefit in data gathering and exchange because of its technical advantages over the barcode. Basic RFID capabilities include the ability to read without line of sight (in most cases), conduct multiple reads per second, rely on a more durable tag, access information from longer reading distances, reprogram (or write) the tag, and benefit from the opportunity for hands-free processes. Data now automatically loaded into a system was the driver for systems to talk one to another to share the information automatically.

- Data communication between software systems represents a variety of new obstacles. The records must be readable by both systems. Formatting mismatches from system to system created a major obstacle to overcome. The easiest and most common method of transferring this data was to export the data to a file or dump it to an Excel® spreadsheet. After the file of exported data was sent to the receiving application, the data had to be imported into that system. Removing human translation from the process was a major step forward as the wheels of automation progressed. A measure of data security could be utilized by means of an electronic method. Though a progressive step, it is fraught with elements of potential problems. Over time, software extensions become necessary and data misalignment between applications arises (new data elements or attributes are created or changed).

- To correct this dilemma, translators on both sides of the data transfer had to be altered. Tight and regular management was necessary to preserve data integrity. Mid- to long-term support is expensive. Furthermore, as data is loaded into the receiving system, it often has intelligence or logic that validates the correctness of the information as it passes through the interface. When effectively using RFID data, the RF technology allows a greater volume of information to be captured during a process. High transaction volumes will amplify any weakness of a communication channel.

- This led to the development of an integrated solution between two or more software applications. In an integrated solution, both software applications effectively communicate in real time. This further decreased latency and allows each application to act on situations that may arise during an RFID automated process. This provides more usability than downloading and uploading data. Yet these integrated solutions are commonly quite custom and don't lend themselves to easy extension/integration to other software packages. Custom applications can be relatively expensive to create, maintain, and upgrade.

- As data of the same type began to be exchanged in varying and diverse ways, common users of applications often form action groups to define standards to enable application interoperability. Standards are not trivial to create and maintain. The broader the user base for a standard, the more widely accepted it can become. A well-known standard of this sort is the electronic data interchange (EDI), which is a widely accepted method of transferring information between partners as well as intracompany. Many leading companies in the United States have adopted EDI. One of the major difficulties with standards is the flexibility to adapt it to business needs. Some EDI users have reverted back to using mail, e-mail, fax, and telephone to communicate because EDI is built for serial interaction rather than parallel interaction. EDI then becomes less conducive to use in a real-time automated environment that pushes data through the supply chain (Bellini and Fingar, 2004). Flexibility and opportunity for growth and change is critical to successful standards. RFID standards bodies such as EPCglobal are working to describe a common model for communication. In many cases, standards also help describe common functionality in the various applications. This can drive an amount of consistency for the buyers of these applications. It also lends itself to the commoditization of various packages, where competitors' offerings are more similar and less laden with intellectual property.

- Standardized and open format such as HTML (Hypertext Markup Language), XML, and EPC's PML (Physical Markup Language) are self-describing interfaces that promote more open electronic communication minimizing up-front interfacing work. It is helping to drive a more open communication layer for applications.

The primary RFID data interactions and data sharing that are typically performed can be categorized into three types of data communication: (1) data exchange between software interacting with a human, (2) data exchange between software systems, and (3) RF data and RF-tagged objects exchanged by business partners.

5.3.1 RF Data Exchange with Humans

The use of RF data becomes valuable when there are decisions made about the surrounding activities and environment as the tagged object is used. The initial and most common form of exchange is interacting with humans. Asynchronous scenarios arise and decisions must be made about what to do next based on new information. RF data has self-describing attributes about the contents of the item that has been tagged. These attributes may natively reside on the RF transponder or in a data system that connects to the RF transponder. Humans visualize the situation via a display device of some sort. Keypad input can be replaced by automatic RF reads, where the RF activity may or may not be known to the interacting human. Examples where this provides value are given in the following paragraphs.

A physician's office or hospital is a location where often time saved is essential. Precision in taking appropriate action with the correct tools or medication is critical. It is estimated that between 44,000 and 98,000 preventable deaths occur each year in hospitals (Mun, 2005). Additionally, there are 770,000 known injuries as a result of medication errors annually. Hospital administrator Dr. I. Mun reports that on average approximately US$1 million of assets disappears in a hospital on an annual basis. Equipment, devices, medicine, and so on necessary to perform medical procedures must be easy to find and accessible at a moment's notice as decisions are made. Failure in any critical area can create catastrophic problems during an emergency. The medical community is in the early process of adopting RF technologies to assist in tracking these critical assets. Hospital workers ensure these RF-tagged devices are properly stored, and that their tracking system allows them to be tracked as they move from room to room. In the operating room it is critical for the surgeon to have full access to a sterilized tray of surgical instruments. As preparation is made, RF-tagged instruments can be read as the tray passes through an RF-enabled portal, allowing surgical personnel a hands-free process. Immediate knowledge of the surgical instruments is known, thereby facilitating a more rapid preparation for surgery.

In 2004 there were more automobiles recalled in the United States than sold (Bellini, 2006). Recalls are a huge expense to the auto dealer, and the expense ultimately will be passed on to the consumer. Data gathered makes information available to an auto dealer regarding a vehicle, which facilitates a more effective and rapid recall process. A visit to one of the German automaker BMW assembly plants reveals how RFID captures information about the automobile manufacturing process. RF-tagged parts are tracked through the line. Shop floor operators make decisions based on which part arrives at a predetermined location. As transponders are identified, tagged parts are associated with the chassis and tracked. Information is passed from the low-level reader into a coordinated data warehouse as integrated systems share RF data. Data corresponding to a specific vehicle is then available for retrieval at a later date.

5.3.2 RF Data Exchange between Software Systems

Automated systems are gradually replacing human-driven processes. As these systems expand in capability, there is a growing need for them to communicate. At the outset this seems like a daunting task. To illustrate a potential set of steps, consider a pilot project in the food packing industry and the basic steps followed as an RFID system was implemented.

Headquartered in Wisconsin, leading U.S. meat snack manufacturer Jack Link's Beef Jerky implemented a four-phased approach to their RFID implementation (Strub, 2005). A growing portfolio of meat snack products has made the processing steps at Jack Link's Beef Jerky more and more complex. Differing spices, varying smoking processes, and different meat cuts all contribute to the complexity. Each of the successive phases gathered and exchanged data to a greater degree.

- Phase 1 was conducted over a three-week period during which the company ran a pilot program using RFID technology. RFID-enabled labels were printed and applied to the packaging as the ERP assigned the RF identity to the label. The cartons were then read and further validated. Individual EPC tagged objects were read and test data gathered to validate that the RFID technologies could be used in the processing environment.
- Phase 2 included a broader verification and use of middleware to push the RF data into the ERP system. The data had to be filtered to a usable granularity. This provides the foundation for data retrieval, as data may now be exchanged with other factory areas. This also gave the company greater opportunity to determine future reader locations, locate environmental obstacles, and validate RF usage in the manufacturing process.
- Next, in phase 3, tagged objects were associated with totes. Historically, paper had been used to track the raw material through the facility. Real operational data was ready to be gathered. Product lots were tracked at key locations as they moved through the facility and attributes associated with each lot (tracked with an RF tag). This provides operational visibility of the meat and its progress that wasn't possible with paper.
- In phase 4, tags are being applied to all cases of product. Information about the contents of each product case is associated with an RF tag attached to the case. Inventory is tracked and managed to the point of receipt at the distribution center (DC). The foundation is now laid to be able to enhance the logistics and reengineer processes of the business. At the DC many manual processes may now be automated as goods are received and data is exchanged from manufacturing through the supply chain (Strub, 2005).

The Jack Link's Beef Jerky case shows how expanding the integration of an RFID implementation progressively enables more data to be shared both within the four walls of an operation and then extending to the distribution chain. Automated data sharing is an enabler to streamline local operations at each point of the supply chain. This data exchange infrastructure positions the company to incorporate additional phases of improvement as they gain incremental value from their RFID investment.

5.3.3 RF Data Exchange with Business Partners

Trading information and sharing processes with partners opens a new opportunity for value with an RFID system. For those who can find value, they will be able to compete at a higher level in the marketplace than was possible while trying to solve many challenges within their own four walls. Questions need to be addresses such as, "Is the company's IP exposed?"

and "Does the collaboration support the business strategy?" RFID will open the door to enable new collaborative opportunities that have not previously existed.

Best Buy is implementing RFID systems to track electronics goods from the back room to the sales floor through the point of sale. Best Buy is one of the early adoptors of item level tagging. This is more easily achieved for them because approximately 70 percent of Best Buy's inventory has only one item in a carton. As they use the information to improve the sales floor process and backroom operations, they are proactive in providing RF activity and data back to their electronics suppliers. Good RF data to their supplier will allow Best Buy to better meet consumer demand and improve visibility of the ready-to-sell inventory. "We need to move the product more efficiently and faster to reduce the forecast windows, which benefits everyone," states Best Buy RFID lead Paul Freeman. This data can ultimately enable suppliers to streamline their processes to reduce the cost of the item. Best Buy also intends to work with suppliers to determine which RF data is valuable and collectively establish what RF data makes sense to share for the benefit of both (Freeman, 2005).

There are a variety of factors that may inhibit RFID collaboration between two or more complementary companies. In addition to the technical challenges, coordination requires cooperation akin to a joint venture with multiple management teams that have differing objectives. A publicly traded company has obligations to its shareholders to show profitable results and report this on a quarterly basis. Within any given corporation, this can create internal conflict when short-term goals with long term strategies are compared. Managing evolving strategy changes, growing market share, improving product quality, reducing prices, and maintaining short-term profitability is an immensely challenging task for any management team. RFID is a technology that can assist in a tighter collaboration of multiple companies.

To join forces with supplier or customer using RFID would typically extend to the process level of each company. Driving compatible processes is no trivial matter. Geographical separation (despite phones, e-mail, Web communication, etc.) can be an obstacle in successful collective deployment. Senior management turnover will lead to changing operational philosophies and goals that may bring into question the validity of a relationship with a particular partner. Language and culture differences are no small obstacle in many cases. A U.S. company is typically focused on profitability of the current and upcoming quarter with a one- or two- year strategic plan. To a Japanese company short-term profitability is interpreted in a three- to five- year window. Famous for long term planning some Japanese companies are sometimes even able to provide the name of the person who is expected to run the company 50 years from now.

Ensuring safety at international ports in today's heightened security environment is an important example of collaboration and data exchange that may involve governments and logistics providers to cooperate. RFID plays a key role in the ease of integration for this type of implementation. Validating the contents of large containers without visual inspection is achieved by attaching active RFID tags with an electronic seal. The information is read at exit and entry ports as the containers are transported. The WhereNet Corporation in collaboration with E.J. Brooks supplies this type of RF technology using microwaves (at 2.4 GHz) in marine terminals at various sites along the U.S. coasts and in Europe (O'Connor, 2005). This is increasing the speed of processes for shipping companies and doing it at a reduced cost.

The new Boeing™ 7E7 Dreamliner is due to be ready for shipment in 2008. This new generation of aircraft boasts state-of-the-art capabilities and efficiency, providing an enhanced flying experience for the traveler. Historically, an airplane is assembled over a time span of 18 to 30 days at the Boeing manufacturing plant. Precision in supply chain coordination is necessary to meet the on-time delivery demands of their customers. Boeing has embarked on a new assembly paradigm that is focused on the use of RFID plus collaborative processes for the 787 (formerly that 7E7 Dreamliner) targeted to reduce time to assemble an aircraft to 72 hours (Gillette and Porad, 2004). Boeing partners are assisting in portions of the subassembly and providing RF-enabled parts and components on the aircraft. RFID is part of the increased quality activities with their suppliers. Boeing is providing thought leadership in the area of RFID integration with their trading partners.

5.4 Summary

Advances in RFID are being accelerated because of a growth in discovering applications that can use the technology. Businesses have a wide range of opinions about RFID's use and how it should be implemented. Suppliers are anxious to provide improved solutions. Investment is growing on both the supplier and buyer side. Others are simply worried about being left behind. Research and development workshops continue to bring new ideas to light. Adoption will provide the capital spending to further fuel technological advances in RFID. The widespread adoption of RFID and continued technological advancement will be tied closely with the cost of deploying applications that incorporate business value and consumer benefit.

Acronyms

ATM—Automatic teller machine

DC—Distribution center

EPC—Electronic Product Code

ERP—Enterprise resource planning

FDA—Food and Drug Administration

ISO—International Organization for Standardization

LCD—Liquid crystal display

NASA—National Aeronautics and Space Administration

NVM—Non-volatile memory

PIN—Personal identification number

XML—Extended Markup Language

References

Bellini, Joe. 2006. Brooks Software. Various presentations and speeches.

Bellini, Joe, and Peter Fingar. 2004. "The Real-Time Enterprise." Meghan-Kiffer Press

Buchmann, Harald. 2005. Hermos Division of Brooks Automation. "RFID Frequency Ranges and Uses."

Colleran, Bill. 2005. Impinj Inc. Presentation at RFID Journal Live! October 10.

Collins, Jonathan. 2004. "New Tags Use Diodes, Not Chips." *RFID Journal.* December 1.

Ehrensvard, Stina. 2005. Cypak. Presentation at RFID Journal Live! October 12.

Freeman, Paul. 2005. Best Buy. Presentation at RFID Journal Live! April.

Gillette, Walt. 2004. Boeing. Presentation at the Aerospace & Defense Summit. November.

Heitmann, Jens 2005. Airbus. Presentation at RFID Journal Live! October 12.

Hilder, Jan. 2005. Sandtracker. Presentation at RFID Journal Live! October 12.

IFTF. 2006. "Clip That RFID Tag." May. http://future.iftf.org/2006/05/clip_that_rfid_ (accessed January 17, 2007).

Intermec. "Paramount Nuts: Nut Grower Paramount Farms Speeds Load Processing Time by 60 Percent with Intermec RFID." www.intermec.com/eprise/main/Intermec/Content/About/getCaseStudy?ArticleID=1184 (accessed January 17, 2007).

Jacobs, Sol. 2006. *Battery Technology Choices for RFID Tags.* http://rapidttp.com/transponder/tadiran.html (accessed August 7, 2006).

Johnson, Mike. 2005. "Conductive Inkjet Technology." Presentation at RFID Journal Live! October 12.

Mullagh, Michael. 2005. VIVOtech. Presentation at RFID Journal Live! October 10.

Mun, I. 2005. Adventa Hospital and Medical Center. Presentation at RFID Journal Live! May.

O'Connor, Mary Catherine. 2005a. "IBM Proposes Privacy-Protecting Tag." *RFID Journal.* November 7.

O'Connor, Mary Catherine. 2005b. "WhereNet Tests Electronic Container Seals." *RFID Journal.* October 14.

Palinkas, Simon. 2005. Tesco. Presentation at RFID Journal Live! October 12.

Porad, Ken. 2004. Boeing. Presentation at EPCglobal conference, September.

Quinn, Paul. 2004. "The World's Smallest RFID Reader." March 1. http://www.scs-mag.com/index.php?option=com_content&task=view&id=18&Itemid=88 (accessed Nov 14, 2006)

RFID Journal. 2003. "RFID Smart Cards Gain Ground." *RFID Journal.* April 9. http://www.rfidjournal.com/article/articleview/374/1/1/ (accessed January 17, 2007)

RFID Update. 2007 "TI releases tiny multiprotocol HF RFID reader chip." January 11, 2007.

Roberti, Mark. 2005. At RFID Journal Live! Speaking of an AMR report. Communicated October 11.

Romen, Gerhard. 2004. :Nokia Unveils RFID Phone Reader." *Nokia & RFID Journal.* March 17.

Smartcode. 2006. "Smartcode™ Corp Announces the World's firt 5 cent RFID Tag." www.smartcodecorp.com/newsroom/01-05-06.asp (accessed January 17, 2007). May 1.

Stafford, James. 2005. Marks & Spencer. Presentation at RFID Journal Live! October 11.

STMicroelectronics. 2005., "New EPC Gen2 RFID Chips from STMicroelectronics Ready to Facilitate Supply Chain Management." Technical press release. September 13.

Strub, Joseph J. 2005. "Jack Link's Beef Jerky Case Study: 'Wal-Mart Didn't Make Me Do It." http://www.ism.co.at/analyses/RFID/SME.html (accessed January 17, 2007). March 8–10.

Thorne, Alan. RFID Journal Live! 2005. "RFID Basics." Presentation at RFID Journal Live! October 10.

Torrone, Phillip. 2005. "Interview with RFID Implanter." April 15. http://www.makezine.com/blog/archive/2005/04/interview_with_2.html (accessed January 17, 2007).

Trebilcock, Bob. 2004. "Simulating RFID." *Modern Materials Handling.* December 15.

Wasserman, Elizabeth. 2005. *"A Chemical Solution: Sensors and RFID."* *RFID Journal.* September/October.

6

The Business Case for RFID

Ever since the Industrial Revolution, businesses have relied on economic tools and methodologies to make short-, medium-, and long-term decisions. One of these methodologies is the *business case*, which makes use of analytical tools such as *return on investment* (ROI), *internal rate of return* (IRR), and *present value* (PV) analysis tools. These tools provide a relatively standardized methodology to compare projects that compete for limited resources, such as capital, personnel, and time—three of the major factors affecting business decisions. Because these three factors are interrelated (sometimes directly, sometimes inversely), it is necessary to use such tools to help businesses understand what will be the expected economic impact from different projects. Figure 6-1 shows the interrelation among these three factors and their direct relationship to projects.

RFID projects are usually considered to be medium- to long-term projects. In other words, these are projects that have a life expectancy of years, not months or weeks (*Note:* Although these terms are subjective, it is generally accepted that short-term projects have a life expectancy of less that one year, medium-term projects have a life expectancy of anywhere between one and three to five years, and long-term projects have a life expectancy that is longer. Figure 6-2 provides a graphical depiction of these terms.) This is especially true since RFID projects are normally considered to be IT projects, an area where investment timeframes have a relatively well-defined time horizon given the technology evolution.

When one considers all the factors that must be included in an RFID project, such as hardware, software, business process reengineering, and information management, it is easy to see that these projects will require nontrivial amounts of capital, personnel, and time. This is important to understand because the methodology and effort required when considering medium-term or long-term projects may differ quite drastically from the methodology and effort involved when evaluating short-term projects. The

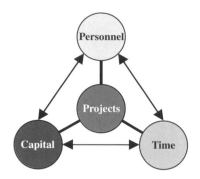

Figure 6-1 Project competing resources.

main difference is in the effort required at the initial stage of the analysis. This effort normally begs for thorough data research, multifaceted skill set teams, good understanding of the current as well as future business trends, and clear commitment from a high-level executive (or set of executives) in the organization.

Even though tools such as ROI rely on economic data, there are times when nonquantifiable factors must be considered when projects are analyzed. Because of their qualitative nature, these factors do not sit well in a numerically driven analysis. Examples of these factors are as follows:

- Customer goodwill
- Quality of service
- Quality of work environment
- Corporate image
- Market position
- Market share

These factors have an indirect impact on business but are very hard to quantify. This is why a business case analysis is broader than an ROI anal-

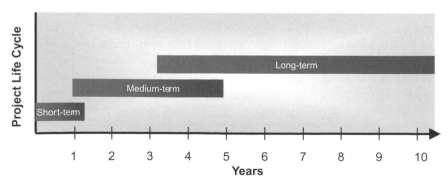

Figure 6-2 Project life cycles.

ysis; it can incorporate quantitative as well as qualitative data into the analysis. In fact, a business case will commonly incorporate an ROI analysis as part of the study.

In this chapter we provide some background on these important tools and illustrate how and why they can be used for measuring and justifying RFID projects.

6.1 Financial Primer

Companies have for a long time used a set of financial statements to help business executives as well as investors and creditors understand the financial situation of a company. Although this is not an engineering economy book, it is necessary to relate RFID projects to their impact on the economics of the company's financial picture. For this purpose we present a limited description of some key financial concepts and terms.

6.1.1 Key Business Drivers

The key business drivers for a project are the factors that compel a company to consider the project in the first place. These can be categorized into quantitative drivers and qualitative drivers. ROI analysis methodology calls for quantitative data to be input into the formula. But since qualitative data may be nonnumeric, there is a risk that not all of the costs and benefits may be included in the ROI analysis. Project managers have devised very creative methods to convert qualitative data into quantitative data. Probability theory is one such method.

For instance, a way to measure the "value" of the corporate image is to assign a probability to the act of a customer purchasing a product from the company based on the level of consumer confidence in the corporation. It is logical to assume that a good corporate image makes people feel positive about the company and its products, thus increasing their likelihood to purchase. The actual probability value to assign based on the "level" of corporate image is more of an art form than a mathematical procedure, but nevertheless, it can be done.

Figure 6-3 shows an example of how the function relating corporate image to a probability measure might appear. From this figure, one can see how a perceived corporate value can influence the probability of buying a product from that corporation—for instance, if the perceived level of the corporate image is 7 out of 10, then the probability of buying products from this corporation is about 55 percent. This methodology allows project managers to calculate expected benefits given a certain set of assumptions.

Arriving at the actual correlation between the qualitative data (i.e., the perceived level of corporate image) and the quantitative data (i.e., the probability of buying a product from the corporation) is an explorative, iterative, and sometimes subjective process. It may require focus group analysis, mar-

Corporate Image Value

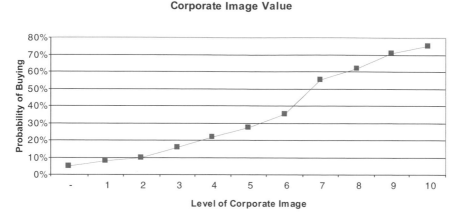

Figure 6-3 Converting qualitative data into quantitative data.

ket research, historical information, and other techniques to create a theory of how the variables are interrelated. However, once this correlation has been agreed upon, the expected benefits, which happen to be quantitative data, can be used in standard ROI analysis.

Furthermore, even when all the factors have been converted to quantitative data, there is another classification that is important to consider in understanding the effect of the key business drivers on the business case: *hard* costs/benefits and *soft* cost/benefits. We will expand on these after we review the financial statements.

6.1.2 Financial Statements

As mentioned, projects may have an effect on a company's financial statements. Financial statements are reports generated from the operations of a company that record the company's financial flows and levels. The financial statements are typically made up of the following:

- The *income statement* (also known as the *profit and loss statement*)
- The *balance sheet*
- The *cash flow statement*
- The statement of retained earnings (not relevant for our purposes)

We will only present a brief description of each of these statements for purposes of this book.

6.1.2.1 Income Statement

As defined in Wikipedia (accessed January 20, 2007), the income statement

indicates how Net Revenue (money received from the sale of products and services before expenses are taken out, also known as the "top line") is transformed into Net

Income (the result after all revenues and expenses have been accounted for, also known as the "bottom line").

In layperson's terms, the income statement helps investors and creditors understand how much money a company made or lost (before and after taxes) over a specific period of time. Table 6-1 shows an example of an income statement. Note that although this is a basic income statement, it captures the essence of how it can be affected by RFID projects.

For example, assume that Company A believes that it is not fully charging its clients for its rental equipment because it cannot reliably track when the equipment is in use and which client is using it. Company A decides to implement an RFID project that allows it to track rental equipment utilization by recording information of when the equipment is in use and to which client it is assigned. Company A can argue that the benefit of this project, after performing a before-and-after comparison, is that the RFID project increased the captured revenue by some percentage. This amount will directly impact the income statement under the "Rent revenue" line.

6.1.2.2 Balance Sheet

As defined in Wikipedia (accessed January 18, 2007), the balance sheet

is a statement of the book value of a business at a particular date, often at the end of its "fiscal year," as distinct from an income statement, which records revenue and expenses over a specified period of time.

Table 6-1 Sample Income Statement

Income Statement		
Revenues		
Net sales	$	3,400,000
Rent revenue	$	40,000
Interest revenue	$	12,000
Total revenue	$	3,452,000
Expenses (usually sorted by amount)		
Cost of goods sold	$	2,000,000
Selling expenses	$	450,000
Administrative expenses	$	350,000
Interest expense	$	45,000
Total expense	$	2,850,000
Income before taxes	$	602,000
Income taxes	$	180,600
Net income	$	421,400
Earnings Per Share	$	4.21

In other words, the balance sheet describes the financial condition of the company at specific point in time by describing all of the company's assets and liabilities. Table 6-2 shows a sample balance sheet for a company as of December 31, 2006:

To illustrate how an RFID project can directly affect the balance sheet, assume that Company B, which makes large engine components, carries a large amount of inventory because of its inability to find the right part at the right time in the manufacturing process. Because these parts are big and expensive, the vice president of production decided to implement an RFID project where parts costing more than $5,000 are tagged with an active RFID chip that can tell production personnel where the part is within their 25 hectare (62 acre) plant. After successful implementation, the number of parts in inventory is reduced by 35 percent because of the effective tracking RFID system. This will directly reduce the "Inventory" line and increase the "Cash and cash equivalents" line in the balance sheet—a most favorable change in this statement.

6.1.2.3 Cash Flow Statements

As defined in Wikipedia (accessed January 18, 2007), the cash flow statement

is a financial report that shows incoming and outgoing money during a particular period (often monthly or quarterly). The statement shows how changes in balance sheet and income accounts affected cash and cash equivalents and breaks the analysis down according to operating, investing, and financing activities. As an analytical tool the statement of cash flows is useful in determining the short-term viability of a company, particularly its ability to pay bills.

Table 6-2 Sample Balance Sheet

Balance Sheet			
as of Dec 31, 2006			
ASSETS		**LIABILITIES AND SHAREHOLDERS' EQUITY**	
Current Assets		Liabilities	
Cash and cash equivalents	$ 10,000	Accounts payable	$ 20,000
		Taxes payable	$ 5,000
Accounts receivable	$ 35,000	Long-term bonds issued	$ 15,000
Inventory	$ 25,000	TOTAL LIABILIT IES	$ 40,000
Total Current Assets	$ 70,000		
		SHAREHOLDERS' EQUITY	
Fixed Assets		Common stock	$ 40,000
Plant and machinery	$ 20,000	Retained earnings	$ 8,000
Less depreciation	$ (12,000)	TOTAL SHAREHOLD ERS' EQUITY	$ 48,000
Land	$ 8,000		
Intangible Assets	$ 2,000		
TOTAL ASSETS	**$ 88,000**	**LIABILITIES & SHAREHOLDERS' EQUITY**	**$ 88,000**

Anyone who has to pay bills on a monthly basis (think about a house mortgage or a car payment) should be very familiar with the cash flow statement. It is a way to monitor whether the next payment can be made or not. Table 6-3 is an example of a cash flow statement.

To illustrate how an RFID project could affect the cash flow statement, consider the following example. Company C, which provides hospital equipment management, has determined that it must carry an unusually large number of employees to keep track of the equipment managed by the company for its client hospital. The equipment is highly specialized and must be maintained frequently. But because the equipment could be anywhere in the 10-story hospital, the company's employees must make walking rounds to find the equipment and bring it to the maintenance room. After studying the problem, the vice president of operations decided to implement an RFID asset-tracking system. This system tells the company's employees, in real time, where every piece of equipment is located. After successfully implementing the RFID solution, Company C determined that it can reduce by 25 percent the number of employees required to find the equipment. This solution would directly impact the "Payroll" line of the cash flow statement.

Table 6-3 Sample Cash Flow Statement

Cash Flow Statement				
	April	May	June	TOTALS
Beginning Cash Balance	$ 1,075,000	$ 2,722,000	$ 3,225,900	
Cash Inflows (Income):				
Cash Collections	$ 2,150,000	$ 1,715,785	$ 1,302,297	$ 5,168,082
Credit Collections	$ 375,000	$ 398,613	$ 245,702	$ 1,019,315
Investment Income	$ 125,000	$ 175,922	$ 182,207	$ 483,128
Other:	$ 150,000	$ 183,160	$ 243,011	$ 576,172
				$ -
Total Cash Inflows	$ 2,800,000	$ 2,473,480	$ 1,973,216	$ 7,246,697
Available Cash Balance	$ 4,675,000	$ 5,195,480	$ 5,199,116	
Cash Outflows (Expenses):				
Advertising	$ 50,000	$ 49,015	$ 35,894	$ 134,909
Inventory Purchases	$ 985,000	$ 872,949	$ 875,062	$ 2,733,011
Maintenance & Repairs	$ 12,000	$ 14,246	$ 7,779	$ 34,025
Operating Supplies	$ 125,000	$ 148,423	$ 75,065	$ 348,488
Payroll	$ 350,000	$ 425,856	$ 311,120	$ 1,086,976
Office Related	$ 15,000	$ 20,214	$ 25,134	$ 60,348
Taxes	$ 45,000	$ 40,908	$ 45,707	$ 131,615
Other:	$ 75,000	$ 87,580	$ 48,376	$ 210,956
				$ -
Subtotal	$ 1,657,000	$ 1,659,192	$ 1,424,136	$ 4,740,328
Other Cash Out Flows:				
Capital Purchases	$ 185,000	$ 171,462	$ 89,004	$ 445,466
Loan Principal	$ 75,000	$ 93,807	$ 81,778	$ 250,585
Owner's Draw	$ -	$ -	$ -	
Other:	$ 36,000	$ 45,120	$ 56,569	$ 137,689
				$ -
Subtotal	$ 296,000	$ 310,389	$ 227,351	$ 833,740
Total Cash Outflows	$ 1,953,000	$ 1,969,580	$ 1,651,487	$ 5,574,067
Ending Cash Balance	$ 2,722,000	$ 3,225,900	$ 3,547,629	

6.1.3 Hard and Soft Costs and Benefits

Hard cost/benefits directly affect one or more of the financial statements. Soft cost/benefits indirectly may affect one or more of the financial statements. In other words, hard cost or benefits can easily and directly be shown to affect the financials of the company because their impact can be measured by traditional financial methods. On the other hand, soft cost or benefits may still affect the financials of the company, but their impact cannot directly be reflected by traditional financial methods and oftentimes represent a shift of hard costs or benefits. To clarify these concepts, Table 6-4 categorizes commonly known costs and benefits of IT projects:

Consider the following example where a hospital implements an RFID equipment-tracking system. After successful deployment of the RFID solution, the hospital is able to remove 250 of their 1,000 intravenous (IV) pumps because of increased utilization of the equipment. This was enabled by providing real-time location information on the IV pumps and therefore required less time to find the units and put them to use, thus yielding higher utilization. If the used market value for these IV pumps is US$3,500, the hospital could sell them and reclaim US$875,000 of capital expenditure. Assuming that the cost of the project was US$350,000, the hospital would save roughly US$525,000. This would be considered *hard* savings, since these amounts would hit the balance sheet. The hospital also realized that before the solution was deployed, nurses were spending on average 25

Table 6-4 Hard and Soft Costs and Benefits

Hard	Soft
Typically hard costs and benefits can be easily quantified and directly tied to specific financial statements.	Typically hard costs and benefits cannot be easily quantified and directly tied to specific financial statements. Instead, they indirectly cause costs or benefits that could be easily quantified and directly tied to financial statements.
Examples: • Capital expenditure • Equipment maintenance • Equipment rentals • Equipment or parts shrinkage • Inventory levels	Examples: • Staff productivity • Improved processes • Improved communications • Reassignment of work • Corporate image

percent of their time looking for equipment. After the RFID solution was put in place, the amount of time spent by nurses looking for equipment was only 5 percent, a 20 percent difference. This would be considered a *soft* savings: The hospital would still have to fully pay the nurses for the work hours, but the nurses' time would be realigned to more patient-care-related tasks, allowing them to provide better service to the patients. Also, because the hospital required fewer pumps, it would have to service fewer pumps and replace fewer pumps in the future, yielding further *soft* savings.

6.1.4 What Is ROI and Why Is It So Important?

Let's start with a formal definition. As defined in Wikipedia (accessed January 18, 2007) ROI

> *is a calculation used to determine whether a proposed investment is wise and how well it will repay the investor. It is calculated as the ratio of the amount gained (taken as positive) or lost (taken as negative), relative to the basis.*

In its simplest form, the mathematical formula to calculate ROI is as follows:

$$\text{ROI} = \frac{V_f - V_i}{V_i} = \frac{V_f}{V_i} - 1$$

where:

V_i is the investment required by the project

V_f is the final monetary yield of the project

Note that ROI should be expressed as a percentage value and it can be either positive, for a profitable project, or negative, for an unprofitable project. So, for example, if you had a project whose initial investment was US$10,000 and the final benefit was US$12,500, according to the formula, this project would generate a 25 percent ROI, as shown by the following calculation:

$$\text{ROI} = \frac{12,500}{10,000} - 1 = 0.25 = 25\%$$

This simplistic formula, however, does not provide ROI visibility into projects that should be measured over multiple time periods, say, months or years, thus negating the time value of money. Consider the following two examples:

Project A: It requires an initial investment of US$25,000. It is estimated that this project will have a life span of four years. The benefits resulting from this project have been calculated to be as follows:

US$12,000 in year 1

US$11,000 in year 2

US$10,000 in year 3

US$9,000 in year 4

Project B: It requires an initial investment of US$25,000. It is estimated that this project will have a life span of four years. The benefits resulting from this project have been calculated to be as follows:

US$9,000 in year 1

US$10,000 in year 2

US$11,000 in year 3

US$12,000 in year 4

It is clear that if we use the above formula, both projects would result in an aggregated final monetary amount of US$42,000, thus yielding a 68 percent ROI:

$$\text{ROI} = \frac{42,000}{25,000} - 1 = 0.68 = 68\%$$

However, if we take into consideration the time value of money, we must modify the formula to account for its effect on the yield. The following formula takes this into consideration:

$$\text{ROI} = \frac{\sum_{t=1}^{n} \frac{V_t}{(1 + D)^t}}{V_i} - 1$$

where:

V_i is the investment required by the project.

V_t is the monetary yield of the project at the end of time period t.

n is the number of periods in the analysis.

t is the iterative time period.

D is the discount rate for the time value of money.

If we performed the math for the preceding examples and assuming an equal discount rate of 5 for both projects, the new formula would yield, for Project A:

$$
\text{ROI}_A = \cfrac{\dfrac{12,000}{(1 + 0.05)^1} + \dfrac{11,000}{(1 + 0.05)^2} + \dfrac{10,000}{(1 + 0.05)^3} + \dfrac{9,000}{(1 + 0.05)^4}}{25,000}
$$

$$
- 1 = 0.50 = 50\%
$$

and for Project B:

$$
\text{ROI}_B = \cfrac{\dfrac{9,000}{(1 + 0.05)^1} + \dfrac{10,000}{(1 + 0.05)^2} + \dfrac{11,000}{(1 + 0.05)^3} + \dfrac{12,000}{(1 + 0.05)^4}}{25,000}
$$

$$
- 1 = 0.48 = 48\%
$$

In summary, there is a 50 percent ROI for Project A and a 48 percent ROI for Project B. Since Project A's ROI is higher than Project B's, the company would find Project A is more attractive than Project B.

There are a few points to note from these examples. First, the ROI yielded by the simple formula is much higher than the ROI yielded by the formula adjusted for the time value of money. This is because the present worth of money (purchasing power of today's dollar) is typically higher than the future worth of money (purchasing power of tomorrow's dollar) because of inflation (or discount rate). Second, the ROI yielded by Project A is higher than the ROI yielded by Project B. This is because Project A recuperates more money earlier than Project B and the time value of money dictates that money temporarily closer to the present is worth more than money temporarily further from the present. Third, it is entirely possible to have a negative ROI. This would indicate that the project is anticipated to yield a loss as opposed to a profit.

Companies usually equate the *discount rate* based on their *cost of capital*. One way to estimate the cost of capital is the interest rate that banks pay the company for money deposited. The rationale is that if a company has cash and it does not put it to work in the business, it could deposit that cash in a bank that would pay interest on that money. That is the lowest cost of capital that the company would expect. However, companies believe that they can get a better return on their money by putting it to work in their business, and thus the actual cost of capital used by most companies is higher than the interest rate paid by the banks. Essentially, this can be computed using the *net present value* formula.

6.1.4.1 Net Present Value

The net present value, or NPV, is a mechanism to understand the value of money (or a cash flow series) in terms of the present purchasing power of money. As defined in Wikipedia (accessed January 18, 2007), NPV

is a valuation method based on discounted cash flows. NPV is calculated by discounting of a series of future cash flows and summing the discounted amounts and the initial investment (a negative amount).

The formula for NPV is as follows:

$$NPV = \sum_{t=0}^{n} \frac{V_t}{(1 + D)^t}$$

where:

V_t is the cash flow series at time period t.

n is the number of periods in the analysis.

t is the iterative time period.

D is the discount rate for the time value of money.

To illustrate the dramatic effect that time has on money, consider the previous example in which we were comparing Project A and Project B. The NPV would tell us what would be the worth of the project if we could bring all of its future benefit to the present:

$$NPV_A = \frac{-25,000}{(1 + 0.05)^0} + \frac{12,000}{(1 + 0.05)^1} + \frac{11,000}{(1 + 0.05)^2}$$
$$+ \frac{10,000}{(1 + 0.05)^3} + \frac{9,000}{(1 + 0.05)^4} = \$12,450$$

and:

$$NPV_A = \frac{-25,000}{(1 + 0.05)^0} + \frac{9,000}{(1 + 0.05)^1} + \frac{10,000}{(1 + 0.05)^2}$$
$$+ \frac{11,000}{(1 + 0.05)^3} + \frac{12,000}{(1 + 0.05)^4} = \$12,020$$

From the results we can observe that Project A's NPV is higher than Project B's. Therefore, Project A looks more attractive than Project B on the basis of NPV.

Note that for this calculation, t starts at 0. This means that the initial investment is part of the calculation. This formula happens to be embedded in the ROI calculation, demonstrating that the ROI formula basically brings the value of the benefits to the present. This allows apples-to-apples comparison of projects.

6.1.4.2 Internal Rate of Return

This brings us to another interesting and interrelated metric used by companies to evaluate projects. The *internal rate of return,* or IRR. Wikipedia (accessed January 17, 2007) defines the IRR as:

> *the discount rate that gives a net present value (NPV) of zero. The NPV is calculated from an annualized cash flow by discounting all future amounts to the present.*
> The formula is as follows:

$$\sum_{t=0}^{n} \frac{V_t}{(1 + IRR)^t} = NPV = 0$$

where:

V_t is the monetary yield of the project at the end of time period t.

n is the number of periods in the analysis.

t is the iterative time period.

IRR is the internal rate of return that forces NPV to be zero.

Note that for this calculation, t starts at 0. This means that the initial investment is part of the calculation. It is interesting to note that there is no closed-form methodology (i.e., apply a formula once) for calculating the IRR. It must be done iteratively over multiple values until the proper value is found. IRR would be the number that makes the value of the formula yield zero. Figures 6-4 and 6-5 show the IRR for the example projects above. Note that the IRR for Project A (26.03 percent) is higher than the IRR for

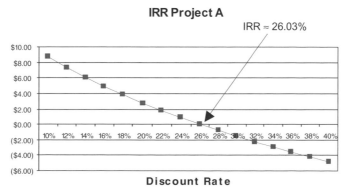

Figure 6-4 IRR for Project A.

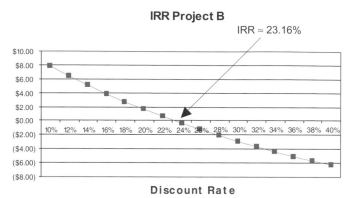

Figure 6-5 IRR for Project B.

Project B (23.16 percent). This is consistent with the results of the ROI analysis, making Project A more attractive (higher IRR) than Project B.

IRR represents the discount rate below which an investment results in a positive NPV (and therefore should be made) and above which an investment results in a negative NPV (and therefore should be avoided). So if two projects are compared using the IRR method, the project that yields the highest IRR is more desirable.

Technically speaking, IRR and NPV provide the same information, but many managers prefer to speak in terms of percentages as opposed to net values and therefore favor the IRR method over the NPV method for comparison purposes.

6.1.5 How It All Ties Together

As we have seen, ROI, IRR, and NPV are very much interrelated. The usage of these measurements will depend on the preferences of the people analyzing the projects. This book focuses primarily on the ROI method, although we may include the IRR and NPV methods for some examples.

RFID projects typically fall under medium- to long-term projects within IT departments. The reason is that a big component of an RFID solution is technology, although business process reengineering and components (training, etc.) should also be considered. As such, when one considers an RFID project in which an ROI is to be calculated, all the cost components of the solution must be included. The next section presents a rational approach for performing ROI analysis on RFID projects.

6.2 RFID ROI

As we have seen in this chapter, ROI analysis is a component of the business case tool used by companies to justify resource-consuming projects or to compare different projects to determine which one is more attractive to a company. ROI analysis on RFID projects has proven to be a difficult, if not daunting, task because of the current stage of the RFID industry. Although every day, new professionals embark in the journey of RFID implementations, there are relatively few people with actual RFID implementation experience, and most of the companies that have successfully implemented RFID solutions on a large scale tend to keep their process well guarded, as they consider that information part of their competitive advantage.

A good analogy to the difficulty associated with calculating ROI for RFID projects is the early 1990s, when the World Wide Web was beginning to become popular. Just like RFID, the Internet had been around for a few years prior to becoming the hot topic about which everyone wanted to talk. To use the old paradigm, it was like teenage sex: Everyone talked about it but few actually did it. There was an immense pressure for companies to put up a Web site and make their presence in the WWW. However, traditional finance departments had a very difficult time justifying the great expense (at the time) associated with creating and maintaining a Web site. Many thought that the WWW was just a fad that would come and go like many other technologies, and therefore, such an expense on noncore business, with hard-to-quantify returns, would not be worth the diversion of resources toward such a project. Many finance departments focused too much on the pure analytical issues of Web sites:

- Would revenue increase?
- Would cost decrease?

But there was not enough on the qualitative issues concerning Web sites:

- Would corporate image improve?
- Would employee productivity increase?
- Would customer service improve?
- Would business processes be more streamlined?
- Would partner collaboration improve?

Although these questions seem very obvious and simple questions to answer, they were not at the time. Finance departments needed quantifiable data to justify the expenses, but this data was not easy to obtain. Early adopters of the technology used Web sites as a mechanism to show their technical prowess and futuristic vision to impress the technologically savvy computer users. Few people actually understood how to build and maintain Web sites, and even fewer knew how to make Web sites generate income or reduce expense.

As time went by and the technology became more widely accepted, an exponential growth in the number of Web sites occurred. Suddenly, developing and hosting a Web site was not a project that needed to be justified by a positive ROI; it had become an everyday necessity without which a company could not properly function.

However, executives demanded that project proponents conduct ROI analysis for these types of projects, just like executives today demand the same from proposed RFID projects. Since, just like Web site development and hosting, RFID ROI is very closely related to general IT ROI analysis, how does one go about creating an ROI analysis for an RFID project? As explained above, the ROI analysis requires an understanding of the required investment for the project and a projection of benefits that will be derived from the project. To do this, one must understand the key drivers in an RFID project.

6.2.1 RFID Key Drivers

As shown, key drivers can be qualitative or quantitative. For purposes of illustration, Table 6-5 shows a list of typical quantitative and qualitative key factors for RFID projects.

6.2.2 RFID Key Cost Components

RFID implementations are made up of a variety of components. At a high level, these components can be divided into six categories:

Table 6-5 Key RFID Drivers

Quantitative	Qualitative
Major Categories: • Cost reduction (CR) • Revenue increase (RI)	Major Categories: • Service improvement • Customer service increase
Cost Reduction: • Reduce labor force required • Reduce quality issues • Decrease shrinkage • Reduce labor time required • Increase asset productivity • Increase supply chain visibility • Provide location visibility	Service Improvement: • Customer goodwill • Quality of service • Quality of work environment • Corporate image • Market position • Market share
Revenue Increase: • Increase revenue-capture rate	Customer Service Increase: • Increase repeat customers

- Hardware cost components
- Software cost components
- System integration cost components
- Personnel
- Installation services
- Business process reengineering

It is important to truly understand all the cost components (obvious and hidden, direct and indirect) in order to properly analyze the ROI of the project.

6.2.2.1 Hardware Cost Components

Hardware cost components are all tangible, physical assets required for the deployment of the RFID solution. These typically include the following:

- RFID readers
- RFID tags
- RFID antennas
- Support brackets
- Cabling and connectors
- Computers
  - Servers
  - Clients
- Network switches
- Wireless access points and repeaters
- Barcodes
- Barcode printers and readers
- Handheld units
- Uninterruptible power supplies (UPSs)
- Electrical outlets and electrical wiring

Depending on the specific solution, not all these costs may apply. For example, some RFID applications may not use any wireless infrastructure, so there is no need to consider wireless access points or repeaters. At other times, however, physical building construction must take place to accommodate the RFID infrastructure. For instance, with outdoor RFID solutions, rigid brackets or towers may have to be built to house the RFID equipment. This should be considered as part of the hardware components.

It is important to note that, according to generally accepted accounting principles (GAAP), some hardware components may have to be depreciated over time, whereas others may be taken as an expense. These considerations are important when calculating ROI over time. For example, assume the case where Company A decides to implement the RFID infrastructure by purchasing the equipment, whereas Company B decides to outsource the

RFID solution to a third-party provider who charges a monthly fee for the use of the infrastructure. In the former case, Company A will create a capital expenditure and most likely will have to depreciate the cost of the equipment over the expected life of the infrastructure. Company B, on the other hand, can show a monthly operational expense equal to the monthly fee charged by the third-party provider.

6.2.2.2 Software Cost Components

Every RFID implementation requires a software component that is responsible for collecting the electronic data and translating RFID events into meaningful business events that can be used in decision-making processes. The software components can be divided into the following categories:

- Middleware system
  - Hardware controlling system
  - Event translation and processing
  - Event reporting
- Database system
- Interface system
  - Other information systems
  - Users
  - Reporting system
  - Business process systems
- Maintenance fees (usually annual fees as a percentage of software cost)

Commonly, RFID vendors bundle all software necessary for the operation of the RFID infrastructure.

6.2.2.3 Integration

One aspect often overlooked in RFID implementations is the cost associated with integrating the data resultant from the RFID infrastructure into the other general business applications running at the company. Because of the huge amounts of data generated by an RFID infrastructure, it is usually a major task to incorporate this information into existing business applications in a way that makes sense and provides useful insight into the operations.

Integration costs are typically high because older business applications must be changed in a way to support the real-time data. Often this is a major challenge because of lack of support for the business application or because customization requirements in the business application. Two main aspects must be considered for integration purposes:

- Amount of customization done in the business application. Generally, the more customized the application, the more effort is required to make changes to it. Therefore, a highly customized business application that must interact with real-time RFID data will take significantly more time, effort, and resources than a more standard application.

- Availability of internal or external resources to work on the business applications. Many times, software companies either stop maintaining specific versions of their applications or stop supporting the application at all. If this is the case, the program manager must perform a gap assessment to determine the feasibility of accommodating the changes with resources that may be unfamiliar with the business application. This is often a red flag that should be discovered and raised early in the project to avoid potentially terminal problems in the implementation of the RFID project.

Assuming that these two aspects are manageable, only qualified personnel should provide the proper time and cost resources required to incorporate the RFID information into the business applications.

6.2.2.4 Personnel

Normally, external personnel costs are easy to estimate because the third-party provider will estimate the cost associated with the people involved in the deployment and operation of the RFID infrastructure as part of the cost proposal. Internal personnel are, however, another matter. Because RFID is a relatively new type of application in most industries, there is a lot of confusion in terms of how many people will be needed for how long to implement and operate an RFID infrastructure.

Internal personnel are normally reassigned from other tasks to be involved in RFID projects. Therefore, when considering the cost associated with internal personnel, you must not only consider the direct cost associated with their time but also consider the opportunity cost of pulling personnel from their customary job assignments. In addition, the productivity of personnel will, at least initially, be lower than expected because of the learning curve associated with this technology. Business people tend to use their historical knowledge to make estimates of cost and effort. Because there is little history of RFID implementations, practitioners should use caution when making these estimates.

6.2.2.5 Installation Services

Installation services refer to all activities associated with actually deploying the RFID infrastructure. A good analogy is that of a local area network (LAN) or wide area network (WAN) deployment process. This includes the following:

- Setting up the electric power network grid (if nonexistent)
  - Wiring and power outlets

- Setting up the network environment (if non existent)
  - Cabling and network drops
  - Setting up the appropriate servers
  - Installing the appropriate operating systems, databases, and applications in the network
- Field-assessing the location and topology of the RFID infrastructure, including:
  - Readers
  - Signposts
- Field-testing antennas for proper shape and orientation
- Field-testing the environment to ensure reliable RFID reads

This process will probably be the most foreign aspect of an RFID implementation to business practitioners. It is said that setting up an RFIR infrastructure is part science and part art. There are basic physics principles behind the RFID infrastructure, but the interaction and interference from the environment in which it is deployed really make deployment an art form mastered by a small number of individuals.

6.2.2.6 Business Process Reengineering

RFID solutions often require business process reengineering in order to maximize the results of the solution. Because of its very nature, RFID solutions require a new way of looking and interacting with real-time events. Most systems deployed today are not designed to cope with the high demands of real-time data. In extensive deployments of RFID infrastructures, the costs associated with this reengineering may be comparable to the costs associated with the deployment of enterprise resource planning (ERP) systems. It requires involvement from many organizations of the enterprise to ensure maximum yield.

6.3 A Sample RFID Business Case Analysis

To illustrate all of the concepts laid in this chapter, we will use the following example. Assume that Bienêtre, a 2,000-bed hospital in the heart of Paris, has decided to improve its biomedical operations in order to look for cost-saving opportunities. Biomedical operations are all the processes concerned with servicing and maintaining the hospital's medical equipment, for instance, X-ray machines, IV pumps, ultrasound machines, and so on.

Bienêtre's owns roughly €200 million worth of movable biomedical equipment (MBE), which represent about 50,000 MBEs. Bienêtre has experienced about a 10 percent yearly turnover on its biomedical equipment over the last 10 years, since most of the equipment has a 10-year life cycle. This means that, on average, they need to purchase about €20 million worth of new biomedical equipment on a yearly basis to replace equipment that is inoperable, lost, or stolen. Additionally, Bienêtre estimates a 5 percent turnover because of unaccounted equipment, either lost or stolen. This equates to roughly €10 million (5 percent of €200 million).

The biomedical department employs about 80 biomedical technicians that are responsible for locating, transporting, and servicing the equipment based on scheduled intervals or whenever there is a problem reported with the equipment. Management has estimated that, on average, biomedical technicians spend 35 percent of their work time just locating the equipment that needs to be serviced. Bienêtre employs roughly 80 biomedical technicians. Besides biomedical staff, management has also noticed that nurses and clinical staff spend roughly 20 percent of their time locating equipment for use on patients. Bienêtre employs roughly 5,000 nurses and assistants.

Management has also estimated that because of low equipment utilization rates, which they believe is in the low 30 to 40 percent range. Bienêtre rents about €10 million worth of biomedical equipment. This is primarily due to their inability to find the right equipment at the right time, since the equipment gets hoarded by nurses and staff and therefore is not available for general use when needed (this is common practice in many hospitals throughout the world).

Management believes that an RFID solution can enable significant savings by tracking the biomedical equipment throughout the hospital and providing near-real-time information about its location. In turn, Bienêtre's management recruited Jacques Tranchant, an industrial engineering professor at Ecole Normale Supérieure, to provide his expertise on this subject and rationalize the RFID project—in other words, determine if an RFID solution could indeed provide a positive ROI and if so, determine the approximate payback period of such an RFID solution.

After proper scope definition of the project, Jacques researches the available RFID technologies and determines what he considers to be the best solution for Bienêtre. Using the information provided by Bienêtre as well as his previous experience, Jacques creates an ROI model that clearly identifies all the costs involved and the expected benefits from the RFID solution.

As a way of comparison and to make sure that the costs estimated by Jacques are reasonable, management asked Jacques to solicit a bid from a firm that specializes in RFID deployment solutions. After some research, management decides to invite SolTraquer, a solutions firm that has been in business for the last five years providing RFID solutions to different industries.

As a result of Jacques' work, Bienêtre will consider two proposals. Proposal A is to be deployed by Jacques and Bienêtre's team. Proposal B is to be deployed by SolTraquer. Management is interested in performing a business case analysis comparison to determine if any of these two proposals make sense and if so, which one is more attractive. One important assumption to keep in mind is that management demanded both proposals to provide the exact same solution (and therefore the exact same benefits).

6.3.1 Proposal A: Internal Project Deployment

Table 6-6 shows the costs associated with the hardware (H/W) necessary for the installation of the RFID and WiFi infrastructure. Note that Jacques included every piece necessary to operate an RFID infrastructure via wires or wireless.

The costs associated with the network and applications hardware and software (S/W) is shown in Table 6-7. These costs include the necessary computer network and application systems for the operation of the RFID infrastructure.

Most RFID implementations require some form of integration to other computer systems. For Bienêtre it was determined that the RFID application would have to interface to the Patient Admission System, many of the online instruction manuals for biomedical (original equipment manufacturer, or OEM) equipment, the call center system, and the facility security system to control gate access based on RFID events. Table 6-8 shows the integration costs related to the RFID infrastructure in Bienêtre.

Jacques determined that there would be some indirect costs incurred by the hospital's employees associated with the RFID solution. These costs include both the amount of work done by hospital employees in the actual deployment of the RFID solution and the amount of time required for the training of hospital users on the RFID solution. These costs are captured in Table 6-9.

Finally, Jacques tabulated the professional service's cost associated with the deployment of the RFID solution. These include the actual installation

Table 6-6 RFID and WiFi H/W costs

#	RFID and WiFi Hardware Description	Unit Cost	Qty	Cost
1	Tags	10	60,000	600,000
2	Tags Installation HW	2	60,000	120,000
3	Readers	2,000	200	400,000
4	Reader Installation HW	50	200	10,000
5	Antenna	500	500	250,000
6	Antenna Installation HW	20	500	10,000
7	Barcode Labels	0.10	100,000	10,000
8	Handhelds	1,000	100	100,000
9	Power and Cabling Infrastructure	50,000	2	100,000
10	WiFi Access Point	1,000	15	15,000
11	WiFi Repeaters	200	120	24,000
	Subtotal			**1,639,000**

Table 6-7 Network and Application H/W and S/W costs

#	Network and Application H/W and S/W Description	Unit Cost	Qty	Cost
1	Web Server	5,000	8	40,000
2	App Server	10,000	8	80,000
3	Database Server	15,000	8	120,000
4	UPS	1,000	24	24,000
5	Network Switch	2,500	4	10,000
6	Database System	50,000	1	50,000
7	Web Server Software	20,000	1	20,000
8	App Server Software	20,000	2	40,000
9	Middleware Application	100,000	1	100,000
10	Tracking Application (per year)	150,000	1	150,000
	Subtotal			**634,000**

work done to deploy the RFID H/W and S/W, the computer network, the outsourced centralized help desk, and the training classes. Table 6-10 shows the amount associated with these.

The sum of all these component costs add up to the total project cost, as shown in Table 6-11.

However, it is important to note that under this proposal some of the costs are one-time costs and others are annual costs. Specifically, item 10 of Table 6-7 and item 3 of Table 6-10 are annual costs. All other items in the tables shown are one-time costs. As the project is to have a five-year life, the total cost of the project in Proposal A is shown in Table 6-12:

The total estimated cost for the project approaches €5 million. Bienêtre hopes that the benefits from the implementation and operation of the RFID solution yield a much higher number than the cost of its deployment, so Jacques' ROI analysis must provide convincing evidence that the benefits will indeed surpass the costs. To do this, Jacques quantified every thinkable benefit and included it in the business case and ROI analysis. Jacques started by making a set of assumptions that would be signed off by Bienêtre upper management. The accuracy of these assumptions is absolutely critical for a level of confidence that the ROI analysis will demand.

Table 6-8 Integration costs

#	Integration and Interfacing Description	Unit Cost	Qty	Cost
1	Integration to Patient Admissions System	85,000	1	85,000
2	Integration to OEM Instructions Manuals	50,000	1	50,000
3	Integration to Call Center System	75,000	1	75,000
4	Integration to Facility Security System	75,000	1	75,000
	Subtotal			**285,000**

Table 6-9 Personnel Associated costs

#	Personnel Description	Unit Cost	Qty	Cost
1	Training of Personn el	25,000	1	25,000
2	Tem poral Reassignment of Personnel (work)	500,000	1	500,000
	Subtotal			**525,000**

6.3.2 Proposal B: SolTraquer Project Deployment

SolTraquer took a different approach to cost the RFID solution. It proposed to deploy the entire RFID infrastructure, including hardware and software, all the integration work and professional services for a monthly fee that would start six months after the project began. There would be a five-year commitment from the hospital to pay the €100,000 monthly fees while it operated the solution. The cost structure is relatively simple, as shown by Table 6-13.

6.3.3 Estimated Benefits

Table 6-14 shows the set of parameters collected by Jacques from the hospital's operation and presented to management. This table represents actual operational data that has been compiled by the different hospital's information systems.

From these collected parameters, a set of calculated or derived parameters are then presented. Table 6-15 shows a list of relevant information that will be used in the business case. These numbers are deduced from the defined parameters and help management understand many of the cost factors in the current operation.

In the next step of the business case analysis, Jacques made some assumptions as to how the RFID solution would impact the operations at Bienêtre. Jacques made these assumptions based on the results of many interviews with the hospital's personnel, which allowed him to diagram the business processes affected by the RFID infrastructure. Table 6-16 shows the set of assumptions that Jacques presented to management.

Jacques rationalized that by using the RFID infrastructure, the average utilization of the MBEs would increase from the current 45 percent to an

Table 6-10 Professional Services costs

#	Professional Services Description	Unit Cost	Qty	Cost
1	RFID Installation Services	75,000	1	75,000
2	Network Installation Services	40,000	1	40,000
3	Centralized Help Desk/Maintenance (per year)	200,000	1	200,000
4	Training Department	50,000	1	50,000
	Subtotal			**365,000**

Table 6-11 RFID Solution cost—1st Year

	Totals - 1st Year	
#	Description	Cost
1	RFID and WiFi Hardware	1,639,000
2	Network and Application H/W and S/W	634,000
3	Integration and Interfacing	285,000
4	Personnel	525,000
5	Professional Services	365,000
	Total for RFID Solution Implementation	**3,448,000**

estimated 65 percent. He also rationalized that because there was better utilization of the MBEs, not only would Bienêtre require less MBEs but also the rate at which Bienêtre needed to rent equipment to satisfy demand would decrease (from 5 percent to 4 percent)—a double win. After talking to the medical staff, Jacques concluded that nurses and assistants would spend about half the time of what they currently spend searching for equipment. This meant that they would spend only 5 percent of their time looking for MBEs, as opposed to the current 10 percent of their time. Likewise, biomedical technicians believed that their search time would drastically decrease (from 45 percent to 25 percent). Finally, Jacques argued that because of better visibility as to the location of the assets, the RFID infrastructure would serve as a deterrent to thieves and reduce the shrinkage rate from 5 percent to 3 percent. Management agreed with the assumptions and in fact thought that they were conservative.

Given such information and assumptions, Jacques calculated the benefits that the hospital realized if everything went according to plan. Table 6-17 shows a list of quantified benefits.

Let's take a moment to understand how Jacques estimated these benefits. Item 1 in Table 6-17 refers to the average number of MBEs per bed used in the hospital. Currently, Bienêtre carries 50,000 MBEs. Given that it services 2,000 beds, this number is, on average, 25 MBEs per bed:

$$\frac{\text{Number of MBEs}}{\text{Number of beds}} = \frac{50,000 \text{ MBEs}}{2,000 \text{ beds}} = 25 \text{ MBEs/bed}$$

Given that the current average utilization of 45 percent yields 25 MBEs/

Table 6-12 Proposal A Total Cost

	Totals - Life of Project			
#	Description		Cost	
1	One-Time Costs	3,098,000	1	3,098,000
2	Yearly Costs	350,000	5	1,750,000
	Total for RFID Solution Implementation			**4,848,000**

Table 6-13 Proposal B Total Cost

RFID and WiFi Hardware		Cost
Contract Term—5 years		–
Monthly Fee	100,000	6,000,000
Total Project Cost		**6,000,000**

bed (current state), an estimated 50 percent utilization would yield 22.5 MBEs/bed:

$$\frac{\text{Current utilization}}{\text{Estimated utilization}} * \text{MBEs/bed} = \frac{45\%}{50\%} * 25 \text{ MBEs/bed}$$

$$= 22.5 \text{ MBEs/bed}$$

This means that with the higher utilization rate, Bienêtre would only have to carry 45,000 MBEs (item 2 in Table 6-17) to do the same job that it is doing today:

$$\text{Number of beds} * \text{MBEs/bed} = 2,000 \text{ beds} * 22.5 \text{ MBEs/bed}$$

$$= 45,000 \text{ MBEs}$$

Thus, Bienêtre would reduce the necessary equipment by 5,000 MBEs, which has an estimated value of €12.5 million (item 3 in Table 6-17). This would show as a reduction of capital assets in future balance sheets—a substantial amount.

The rental expenditure also decreases, since rental is a function of current inventory and current utilization rates. This lowers the required amount of

Table 6-14 Defined Parameters

Defined General Parameters			
#	Parameter	Value	Description
1	Project Life (Years)	5	This is the length of the RFID project.
2	Number of Beds	2,000	Hospitals are meassured by the number of beds in them.
3	Number of Nurses	4,500	Bienêtre employees 4,500 nurses and assistants.
4	Nurses Salary	65,000	Average salary for nurses and assistants.
5	Total number of MBEs	50,000	Total number of Moveable Biomedical Equipment (MBE) pieces.
6	Average cost of a MBE	2,500	Average cost of a MBE.
7	Average MBE Life (Yrs)	10	Averege life span of a MBE.
8	Rental Percent	5%	Rental percent of the toal number of MBEs.
9	Inventory Auditing Cost per MBE	70	Average cost to audit a MBE.
10	Maintenance Cost	10%	Maintenance is estimated to be a percent of the cost of a MBE.
11	Number of Biomedical Technicians	83	Bienêtre employees 83 biomedical technicians.
12	BioMed Technician Salary	45,000	Average salary for a biomedical technician.
13	MBE Average Utilization	45%	Average utilization of MBEs.
14	Shrinkage Rate	7.5%	Average shrinkage (loss or stolen) rate.
15	Nurses Hours/Year	2,000	Hours worked in a year by a nurse or assistant.
16	Biomedical Technicians Hours/Year	2,000	Hours worked in a year by a biomedical technician.
17	Nurses' MBE Search Time	10%	Average amount of time spent by nurses and assitants searching for MBEs.
18	Biomedical Techinician MBE Search Time	45%	Average amount of time spent by biomedical technicians searching for MBEs.
19	Bienêtre Cost of Capital	18%	Bienêtre cost of capital.
20	MBE Recovery Value	750	Average recovery (salvage) value for a MBE.

Table 6-15 Derived Parameters

Calculated General Paramters		
# Parameter	Value	Description
1 MBE's Value (capital in inventory)	125,000,000	This is the total value of the MBEs.
2 MBE Value per Bed	62,500	Amount of capital carried by each bed.
3 MBEs per Bed	25	Number of MBEs assigned to each bed.
4 MBE Yearly Replenishment	12,500,000	Yearly capital required to replenish MBEs due to life cycle.
5 Nurses per Bed	2.25	Average nurses and assistants per bed.
6 Value of Nurses' MBE Search Time	29,250,000	Cost of nurses and assistants' time when searching for MBEs.
7 MBEs per BioMed Technician	602	Number of MBEs that a biomedical technician can service in a year.
8 Value of Biomedical Technician MBE Search Time	1,680,750	Cost of biomedical technicians' time when searching for MBEs.
9 Yearly Number of Rental MBEs	2,500	Number of rental MBEs per year.
10 Annual Rental Value	6,250,000	Value of annual rentals.
11 Annual Shrinkage Value	9,375,000	Yearly cost of lost or stolen MBEs.

MBEs while increasing the MBE utilization, yielding an annual savings of roughly €1,750,000. This is expressed in items 4 and 5 of Table 6-17:

Current rental requirement:

Number of MBEs * Rental rate = 50,000 MBEs * 5% = 2,500 MBEs

Estimated rental requirement:

Number of MBEs * Rental rate = 45,000 MBEs * 4% = 1,800 MBEs

Saving in rentals:

Current rentals − Estimated rentals = 2,500 MBEs

− 1,800 MBEs = 700 MBEs

Number of rentals * ValueI of MBE = 700 MBEs * €2,500/MBE

= €1,750,000

Items 6 though 8 of Table 6-17 deal with the benefits associated with reducing the time required by biomedical technicians to search for MBEs. In the case of biomedical technicians, Jaques assumed that the number of MBEs that a technician could service was directly related to the amount of time technicians spent searching for the MBEs. Since it is estimated that the amount of search time would decrease from the current 45 percent of the

Table 6-16 Improvement Assumptions

Improvement Assumptions		
# Assumption	Current	Estimated
1 MBE Average Utilization	45%	50%
2 Rental Percent	5%	4%
3 Nurses Time Searching for MBEs	10%	5%
4 Biomedical Technician Time Searching for MBEs	45%	25%
5 Shrinkage Rate	5%	3%
6 Inventory Auditing Cost per MBE	70	5

Table 6-17 Estimated Benefits

Estimated Benefits	Current	Estimated	Difference
# Due to Increased Utilization and Decrease Rental Rate			
1 MBEs per Bed	25.00	22.50	2.50
2 Number of MBEs	50,000	45,000	5,000
3 Value of MBEs	125,000,000	112,500,000	12,500,000
4 Number of Rentals	2,500	1,800	700
5 Value of Rentals	6,250,000	4,500,000	1,750,000
# Due to Better Tracking and Decreased Search Time			
6 MBEs Per BioMed Technician	602	821	219
7 Number of Biomedical Technicians Required	83	55	28
8 Salary of Biomedical Technicians	3,735,000	2,475,000	1,260,000
9 Nurses' Time Searching for MBEs (hrs)	900,000	450,000	450,000
10 Value of Nurses' Time Searching for MBEs	29,250,000	14,625,000	14,625,000
11 Value of MBE Shrinkage	6,250,000	3,375,000	2,875,000
# Due to Less MBEs			
12 MBEs That Could Be Sold for Recovery	-	5,000	5,000
13 Value of MBEs That Could Be Sold for Recovery	-	3,750,000	3,750,000
14 Maintenance Related Expenses	12,500,000	11,250,000	1,250,000
15 Inventory Auditing Cost	3,500,000	225,000	3,275,000
16 MBE Replenishment	12,500,000	11,250,000	1,250,000

technicians' time to an estimated 25 percent of their time, the number of MBEs that could be serviced by a technician went up from 602 to 821:

$$\text{Number MBEs per tech} * \left(\frac{1 - \text{Estimated search time}}{1 - \text{Current search time}} \right)$$

$$= 602 \text{ MBEs} * \left(\frac{1 - 25\%}{1 - 45\%} \right) = 821 \text{ MBEs}$$

This means that the number of biomedical technicians required could be reduced from 83 to 55, and therefore their salary, estimated at €1,260,000, could be reallocated to other functions:

Current number of biomedical technicians requirement:

Number of MBEs/MBEs per tech = 50,000 MBEs/602 MBEs per tech

$$= 83 \text{ techs}$$

Estimated number of biomedical technicians requirement:

Number of MBEs/MBEs per tech = 45,000 MBEs/821 MBEs per tech

$$= 55 \text{ techs}$$

Savings in biomedical technicians:

Current techs − Estimated techs = 83 techs − 55 techs = 28 techs

Number of techs * Average salary/Tech = 28 techs

* €45,000 per tech = €1,260,000

The case for nurses, as shown in items 9 and 10 of Table 6-17, is similar but not exactly the same. Jacques assumed that the total number of MBEs in the hospital did not really have an effect on the time that nurses spent searching for equipment because nurses tend to work in small areas of the hospital. Instead, the search time would decrease as a function of the improved visibility of the location of the equipment nurses needed. With this in mind, Jacques estimated a whopping €14,625,000 that could be used more effectively:

Current nurses' hours spent searching for MBEs:

Hours per year * Average search time * Number of nurses

= 2,000 hours/year * 10% * 4,500 nurses

= 900,000 nurse-hours per year

Estimated nurses' hours spent searching for MBEs:

Nurses hours per year * Average search time * Number of nurses

= 2,000 hours/year * 5% * 4,500 nurses

= 450,000 nurse-hours/year

Saving in nurses' time:

Current nurse-hours per year − Estimated nurse-hours per year

= 900,000 − 450,000

= 450,000 nurse-hours per year

$$\Rightarrow \left(\frac{\text{nurse-hours per year}}{\text{hours per year}} \right) * \text{Average nurse salary}$$

$$= \left(\frac{450,000 \text{ nurse-hours per year}}{2,000 \text{ hours per year}} \right) * €65,000$$

= €14,650,000

MBE shrinkage is also reduced given the fact there are fewer MBEs and the visibility of where MBEs are and how they move allows hospital se-

curity personnel to provide more effective protection against theft and mis-placing. Item 11 of Table 6-17 shows that Jacques has estimated a reduction of €2,875,000:
Current shrinkage value:

Number of MBEs * Average value per MBE * Shrinkage rate

$$= 50,000 \text{ MBEs} * €/2,500 \text{ per MBE} * 5\% = €6,250,000$$

Estimated shrinkage value:

Number of MBEs * Average Value per MBE * Shrinkage rate

$$= 45,000 \text{ MBEs} * €2,500 \text{ per MBE} * 3\% = €3,375,000$$

Savings because of estimated reduction in shrinkage:

Current shrinkage − Estimated shrinkage = €6,250,000

$$- €3,375,000 = €2,875,000$$

Items 12 and 13 of Table 6-17 show the potential recovery value of the equipment that Bienêtre would no longer require as a result of the RFID solution. The hospital could sell its used equipment and recover roughly €3,750,000:
MBEs not required that could be sold:

(Current number of MBEs − Estimated number of MBEs)

* Average recovery value per MBE

$$= (50,000 \text{ MBEs} - 45,000 \text{ MBEs})$$

$$* €750 \text{ per MBE} = €3,750,000$$

Item 14 of Table 6-17 refers to the maintenance cost associated with the active MBEs. Since the assumption is that the RFID solution would allow Bienêtre to operate with fewer MBEs, it is logical to expect that there would be a savings related to the maintenance of MBEs. Jacques has estimated that Bienêtre would save roughly €1,250,000 in maintenance costs, as shown by this straight formula:
Current maintenance costs:

Number of MBEs * Average value per MBE * Maintenance rate

$$= 50,000 \text{ MBEs} * €2,500 \text{ per MBE} * 10\% = €12,500,000$$

Estimated maintenance costs:

Number of MBEs * Average value per MBE * Maintenance rate

$$= 45,000 \text{ MBEs} * €2,500 \text{ per MBE} * 10\% = €11,250,000$$

Savings because of estimated reduction in shrinkage:

$$\text{Current maintenance} - \text{Estimated maintenance} = €12,500,000$$
$$- €11,250,000 = €1,250,000$$

Inventory auditing costs, as shown by item 15 of Table 6-17, refers to the cost associated with auditing the inventory carried by Bienêtre. This is how much it currently costs the hospital, on a per MBE basis, every time it must conduct a physical inventory of its assets—a task that must be performed at least once a year. Jacques has estimated that because the RFID solution provides real-time information as to the location of the MBEs, the reduction in cost because of inventory auditing would be €3,275,000, as shown by the following calculation:
Current inventorying auditing costs:

$$\text{Number of MBEs} * \text{Auditing cost per MBE} = 50,000 \text{ MBEs}$$
$$* €70/\text{MBE} = €3,500,000$$

Estimated inventorying auditing costs:

$$\text{Number of MBEs} * \text{Auditing cost per MBE} = 45,000 \text{ MBEs}$$
$$* €5 \text{ per MBE} = €225,000€$$

Savings because of estimated reduction in inventorying auditing costs:

$$\text{Current inventory auditing costs} - \text{Estimated inventory auditing costs}$$
$$= €3,500,000 - €225,000 = €3,275,000$$

Inventory replenishment is based on the life cycle of the MBE as well as on the number of MBEs in use. Given that the average life of an MBE is 10 years, reducing the number of MBEs by 5,000 would yield roughly €1,250,000 in savings, as shown in the following:

$$\text{Replenishment rate} = \frac{1}{\text{Average life of MBEs}} = \frac{1}{10} = 10\%$$

Current inventorying replenishment costs:

Number of MBEs * Auditing cost per MBE * Replenishment rate

$$= 50{,}000 \text{ MBEs} * €2{,}500 \text{ per MBE} * 10\% = €12{,}500{,}000$$

Estimated inventorying replenishment costs:

Number of MBEs * Average value per MBE * Replenishment rate

$$= 45{,}000 \text{ MBEs} * €2{,}500 \text{ per MBE} * 10\% = €11{,}250{,}000$$

Savings because of estimated reduction in inventorying replenishment costs:

Current replenishment − Estimated replenishment

$$= €12{,}500{,}000 − €11{,}250{,}000 = €1{,}250{,}000$$

Lastly, notice that not all benefits are direct savings for the hospital. In fact, some of these benefits are not real monetary savings, but instead better use of the money spent—in other words, a soft savings. An example of this is item 10 in Table 6-17, the value of the nurses' time used to search for MBEs. The €14,625,000 does not refer to money that the hospital would save because of the RFID solution—in fact, the hospital will not reduce the number of nurses. Instead, it refers to the reallocation of the nurses' time to provide better patient care by spending more time dedicated to that function as opposed to searching for equipment.

Items 7 and 8 related to the number of biomedical technicians, however, is not as straightforward. Given that the current number of biotech technicians is directly related to the work throughput capacity, it is reasonable to expect that if the technicians' effectiveness is increased by allowing them to work on more equipment in the same amount of time (a direct result of the RFID solution), then Bienêtre could reduce the number of technicians it employs. However, management made a strategic decision at the beginning of the project that the implementation of the RFID solution would not prompt any layoffs; instead, the hospital would reallocate that personnel to other areas. As a result of this decision, these two items were categorized in the same way that item 10 was categorized, a soft savings. In essence, Bienêtre will still spend the €1,260,000 in that personnel category, but it does not have to spend another €1,260,000 hiring other personnel that would be needed to do the job of the reallocated personnel.

Another point to note in Table 6-17 is that some of the benefits are annual benefits, while Item 13, for example, is a one-time benefit. Table 6-18 shows a different categorization of the same benefits, this time however, broken into recurring savings (hard and soft) and one-time savings.

Note how Jacques grouped items 6 and 7 into annual soft savings, reflecting management's decision to not lay off any personnel as a result of the RFID solution.

Table 6-18 Estimated Savings

Estimated Savings		Current	Estimated	Difference
#	Annual Savings - Hard			
1	Value of Rentals	6,250,000	4,500,000	1,750,000
2	Value of MBE Shrinkage	6,250,000	3,375,000	2,875,000
3	Maintenance Related Expenses	12,500,000	11,250,000	1,250,000
4	Inventory Auditing Cost	3,500,000	225,000	3,275,000
5	MBE Replenishment	12,500,000	11,250,000	1,250,000
	Total			**10,400,000**
#	Annual Savings - Soft			
6	Value of Nurses' Time Searching for MBEs	29,250,000	14,625,000	14,625,000
7	Salary of Biomedical Technicians	3,735,000	2,475,000	1,260,000
	Total			**15,885,000**
#	One-Time Savings - Hard			
8	Value of MBEs That Could Be Sold for Recovery	–	3,750,000	3,750,000
	Total			**3,750,000**

Summary	
Annual Savings—Hard	10,400,000
Annual Savings—Soft	15,885,000
One-Time Savings—Hard	3,750,000

Summary - Project Life	Amount	Years	Total
Annual Savings—Hard	10,400,000	5	52,000,000
Annual Savings—Soft	15,885,000	5	79,425,000
One-Time Savings—Hard	3,750,000	1	3,750,000
Total Project Savings over Life of Project			**135,175,000**

As with most IT projects, Jacques realized that not all the benefits would be attained starting in the first year. He assumed that benefits would start gradually and continue to accrue gradually until the RFID solutions was totally deployed in the operations of the hospital. Table 6-19 shows how Jacques assumed the benefits would accrue.

This means that, for instance, in year 2, Jacques expects to realize only 50 percent of the estimated benefits. Table 6-19 reflects the time that it takes to fully deploy the solution at Bienêtre, taking into account the time required to perform the business process reengineering demanded by the RFID solution. Note that Jacques makes reference to year 0 in Table 6-19. This is to reflect the six months of work required to install the RFID infra-

Table 6-19 Benefit Schedule

Benefits Schedule	Percent of Estimated Benefits
Year 0	0%
Year 1	25%
Year 2	50%
Year 3	75%
Year 4	100%
Year 5	100%

structure (the same for both proposals). Jacques expects no benefits while the infrastructure is being put into place.

6.3.4 Comparison

Although the estimated benefits of both proposals are exactly the same from the operations point of view within the hospital, the cash flow of each proposal is quite different. This will have an effect on the ROI analysis, as we will see in this section.

Let's start with the benefits cash flow series that Jacques assumed for this project, as shown by Table 6-20. Remember that Jacques estimated a six-month period (year 0) to set up the RFID infrastructure. During this period, there is no expectation of any benefits as systems are being put into place. The NPV column in the table reflects the net present value using the cash flow series shown and the predefined cost of capital (item 19 in Table 6-14).

Next let's examine the cash outlay for proposal A. Table 6-21 shows the project lifetime in terms of how the hospital will spend money over time to implement the RFID project. Remember that Jacques estimated a six-month period (year 0) to set up the RFID infrastructure. During this period, according to proposal A, the hospital would buy all the components necessary and reassign all the people necessary for the implementation of the RFID:

Proposal B has a much simpler cash flow series, as shown by Table 6-22.

By comparing items 8 of Table 6-21 and item 3 of Table 6-22, Jacques decided that a net present value analysis (which is equivalent to an ROI analysis, as we saw before) is more pertinent to demonstrate that the RFID solution, under both proposals, is a very attractive project for Bienêtre and furthermore that proposal B, although seemingly more expensive than proposal A, is more attractive when considering the time value of money. For completion, however, Jacques calculated the ROIs for both proposals, fur-

Table 6-20 Benefits Cash Flow Series

#	Estimated Savings Schedule	NPV	Y0	Y1	Y2	Y3	Y4	Y5	Total Project
#	Annual Savings—Hard								
1	Value of Rentals		0	437,500	875,000	1,312,500	1,750,000	1,750,000	6,125,000
2	Value of MBE Shrinkage		0	718,750	1,437,500	2,156,250	2,875,000	2,875,000	10,062,500
3	Maintenance Related Expenses		0	312,500	625,000	937,500	1,250,000	1,250,000	4,375,000
4	Inventory Auditing Cost		0	818,750	1,637,500	2,456,250	3,275,000	3,275,000	11,462,500
5	MBE Replenishment		0	312,500	625,000	937,500	1,250,000	1,250,000	4,375,000
6	Subtotal	17,453,737	0	2,600,000	5,200,000	7,800,000	10,400,000	10,400,000	36,400,000
#	Annual Savings—Soft								
7	Value of Nurses' Time Searching for MBEs		0	3,656,250	7,312,500	10,968,750	14,625,000	14,625,000	51,187,500
8	Salary of Biomedical Technicians		0	315,000	630,000	945,000	1,260,000	1,260,000	4,410,000
9	Subtotal	26,658,905	0	3,971,250	7,942,500	11,913,750	15,885,000	15,885,000	55,597,500
#	One-Time Savings—Hard								
10	Value of MBEs that could be sold for Recovery		0	937,500	937,500	937,500	937,500	0	3,750,000
11	Subtotal	2,137,231	0	937,500	937,500	937,500	937,500	0	3,750,000
12	*Total Hard Benefits*	19,590,968	0	3,537,500	6,137,500	8,737,500	11,337,500	10,400,000	40,150,000

Table 6-21 Proposal A Cash Flow Series

#	Proposal A—Cash Out	NPV	Y0	Y1	Y2	Y3	Y4	Y5	Total Project
1	RFID and WiFi Hardware		-1,639,000	0	0	0	0	0	-1,639,000
2	Network and Application H/W and S/W		-484,000	-150,000	-150,000	-150,000	-150,000	-150,000	-1,234,000
3	Integration and Interfacing		-285,000	0	0	0	0	0	-285,000
4	Personnel		-525,000	0	0	0	0	0	-525,000
5	Professional Services		-165,000	-200,000	-200,000	-200,000	-200,000	-200,000	-1,165,000
6	Total for RFID Solution Implementation	-3,552,974	-3,098,000	-350,000	-350,000	-350,000	-350,000	-350,000	-4,848,000
7	Total Estimated Hard Benefit	19,590,968	0	3,537,500	6,137,500	8,737,500	11,337,500	10,400,000	40,150,000
8	*Net Hard Benefit*	*16,037,994*							
	ROI		451%						

Table 6-22 Proposal B Cash Flow Series

#	Proposal B—Cash Out	NPV	Y0	Y1	Y2	Y3	Y4	Y5	Total Project
1	Cash Out	-3,180,174	0	-1,200,000	-1,200,000	-1,200,000	-1,200,000	-1,200,000	-6,000,000
2	Total Estimated Hard Benefit	19,590,968	0	3,537,500	6,137,500	8,737,500	11,337,500	10,400,000	40,150,000
3	*Net Hard Benefit*	*16,410,795*	*0*	*2,337,500*	*4,937,500*	*7,537,500*	*10,137,500*	*9,200,000*	*34,150,000*
	ROI		516%						

ther demonstrating that both proposals have a positive ROI and that proposal B is more attractive than proposal A:

$$\text{ROI}_{\text{PropA}} = \frac{19,590,968}{3,552,974} - 1 = 366\%$$

and

$$\text{ROI}_{\text{PropB}} = \frac{19,590,968}{3,180,174} - 1 = 421\%$$

6.3.5 Summary

As we have seen, the financial analysis required to compare the two projects dovetail into quite a bit of detail. Utilizing financial metrics, such as ROI and NPV, yield good insight into the financial expectations of projects. As we discussed earlier, these statistics represent the same information but in different form. Depending on the financial background of management, one form may be given preference over the other one, but ultimately they convey the same information. In our example, we showed how, by means of ROI and NPV analysis, that proposal B has a financial edge over proposal A. It is now left to management to make the final decision, but Jacques can feel good that he provided the necessary information for management to make an educated decision.

Acronyms

ERP—Enterprise resource panning

GAAP—Generally accepted accounting principles

HW or H/W—Hardware

IRR—Internal rate of return

IV-Pump—Intra-venous pump

LAN—Local area network

MBE—Moveable biomedical equipment

NPV—Net present value

OEM—Original equipment manufacturer

PV—Present value

ROI—Return on investment

SW or S/W—Software

WAN—Wide area network

Industry

arriers): Communication between

ata syntax): Format of data in the

ensuring that products meet the

D for item management): Use of ion areas.

plications are TC 104/SC 4/WG 2 /G). TC 104/SC 4/WG 2 develops (i.e. ISO 18185) while TC 122/104 supply chain applications of RFID re 7-2 shows relevant standards for he figure, ISO/IEC 15961 addresses pplication systems. ISO/IEC 15962 at application data into a structure EC 18000 series provides parameter ls within a common framework for RFID. This series was developed to ls for most of the widely used fre- uch that the problems of migrating

Regulatory standards are useful to all for government. Standards can ensure acteristics such as quality, interoperabil community. Currently there are many ward standardization of RFID. In this application standards developed by shows standards organization related capture (AIDC). The standards of one of another body, or, perhaps, to the st of the connecting lines in Figure 7-1 (obal, which is a joint venture between in a number of ISO groups (especially focused on AIDC). The secretariat for GS1 US (through the American Nati member organizations take part in t EPCglobal and its standard process we in Figure 7-1, each country has its ow which is the Korea Agency for Techno is the American National Standards I laborate with international standards utes to international standards in vari

RF TAG

18000-3

18000-4

AIR INTERFACE   13.56 MHz   2.45 GHz

18000-6   18000-7

Tag Driver and Mapping Rules   COMMANDS   RESPONSES   ~ 900 MHz   433 MHz

18000-2

Future Standard

<135 KHz   Air Interface Protocol

PHYSICAL INTERROGATOR

/IEC 15962   ISO/IEC 18000
Annexes

7.1 International Orga[nization for] Standardization

ISO (International Organization for St Electrotechnical Commission) jointly (JTC 1) to address subjects of interes SC 31, a subcommittee of ISO/IEC JT Currently, SC 31 consists of four w follows:

m component (Source: P. Chartier, "A data of ISO/IEC 15961 and 15962," reprinted

7.1.1 ISO/IEC 18000 SERIES

Among working groups in SC 31, WG 4 is mainly responsible for RFID air-interface standards for the item identification world within the ISO/IEC 18000 series. The series includes six published parts (originally there were seven parts, but ISO/IEC 18000-5: 5.8 GHz was withdrawn). These parts are as follows:

- ISO/IEC 18000-1: Generic Parameters for the Air Interface for Globally Accepted Frequencies
- ISO/IEC 18000-2: Parameters for Air Interface Communications below 135 KHz
- ISO/IEC 18000-3: Parameters for Air Interface Communications at 13.56 MHz
- ISO/IEC 18000-4: Parameters for Air Interface Communications at 2.45 GHz
- ISO/IEC 18000-6: Parameters for Air Interface Communications at 860 to 960 MHz
- ISO/IEC 18000-7: Parameters for Air Interface Communications at 433 MHz.

As shown, each part deals with different frequencies and has different performance because of different operating parameters. This standard only provides a framework for developers to select options suitable for their application requirement. It is important for users to understand the contents of each part and to develop suitable application requirements considering the performance characteristics. Among those standards, in this section we only focus on ISO/IEC 18000-6, which is widely used for supply chain management where medium-range, multiread, high-speed item identification is required.

7.1.1.1 ISO/IEC 18000-6 (Type A and Type B)

This standard describes a passive backscatter RFID system that identifies and communicates with multiple tags, operating in the 860- to 960-MHz range. The interrogator emits energy to communicate with the tags. The Type A standard was supported by companies including Supertag and EM Microelectronics; the Type B standard was supported by companies including Intermec and Philips. Type A uses pulse-interval encoding (PIE) in the forward link (i.e., reader to tag) and an adaptive ALOHA collision-arbitration algorithm. (These encoding algorithms, and others mentioned in this chapter were discussed in Chapter 4.) Type B uses Manchester in the forward link and an adaptive binary-tree collision-arbitration algorithm. Figures 7-3 through 7-6 show interrogators and tag architecture of each type, respectively (ISO/IEC 18000-6, 2004/2006). In the figures, amplitude-shift keying (ASK) is a form of modulation that represents digital data as

Figure 7-3 Type A interrogator architecture (*Source:* ISO/IEC 18000-6:2004/ Amd1: 2006; Reprinted by permission of ISO).

variations in the amplitude of a carrier wave (DSB indicates double side-band, and SSB indicates single sideband). The ALOHA protocol was originally developed at the University of Hawaii for use with satellite communication systems. In ALOHA, each transmitter in a network sends data whenever there is a frame to send. If the frame successfully reaches the receiver, the next frame is sent. If the frame fails to be received at the destination, it is sent again. Binary tree protocol requires a tag to remember the previous inquiry results (thus reducing the average inquiry time) and requires a tag to finish inquiry processing completely before responding to the next reader. If more than one reader works near the tag, the task of coordinating the readers becomes complicated (Zhou et al., 2005). Manchester code (also known as phase encoding) is a form of data communications line code in which each bit of data is signified by at least one voltage level transition (each bit is transmitted over a predefined time period). FM0 (biphase space) encoding inverts the base band phase at every symbol boundary; a data-0 has an additional mid-symbol phase inversion. In PIE, data is passed to the tag by pulsing the carrier wave at different time intervals to indicate the 1 and 0 bits.

In this standard, tags receive data as amplitude modulation of the power/data signal from the interrogator. During the time that the tag responds to the interrogator, the interrogator transmits at a constant radio frequency power level, while the tag modulates the impedance of its radio frequency load attached to the tag antenna terminals (ISO/IEC 18000-6, 2004/2006). The interrogator then receives the data back from the tag as a variation in a reflection of its transmitted power.

The scope of this standard is as follows:

- Error detection in interrogator-to-tag and tag-to-interrogator communications link
- Reading data from tag (individual tag or multiple tags); writing data to tag; rewriting data to tag are addressed
- Optional commands for the user to lock user memory permanently
- Both passive backscatter tags with or without batteries are supported

Figure 7-4 Type B interrogator architecture (*Source:* ISO/IEC 18000-6:2004/ Amd1: 2006; reprinted by permission of ISO).

Figure 7-5 Type A tag architecture (*Source:* ISO/IEC 18000-6:2004/Amd1: 2006; reprinted by permission of ISO).

7.1.1.2 Gen 2 and ISO/IEC 18000-6 (Type C)

Gen 2 was developed by the Hardware Action Group (HAG) of EPCglobal to address issues from old protocols such as Class 0 and Class 1 Gen 1. Class 0 (a factory-programmable tag) and Class 1 Gen 1 (an end user can write the serial number to it) specifications were open standards, but they were not interoperable. (i.e., a reader can't read both tags). To address issues of Class 0 and Class 1, Gen 2 was designed to meet most of the regulatory standards while maintaining high performance, to control memory access and to provide interoperability, which was not available in old protocols. (The main difference between Class 1 Gen 2 and Type C is the Application Family Identifier. Gen 2 is a subset of Type C.) EPCglobal submitted the Gen 2 air-interface protocol to ISO in early 2005 for inclusion as an amendment to ISO/IEC 18000-6 (Type C), and it was approved by ISO. Having the Gen 2 standard recognized as part of a global standard is extremely important for many companies operating outside the United States, particularly in Asia. The World Trade Organization (WTO) has guidelines about following standards endorsed by ISO and other global standards bodies (O'Connor, 2006a).

Gen 2 allows readable Electronic Product Code (EPC) Tag Identifier (TID) and user memories, but write access is controlled. Also, compared to Gen 1 tags, Gen 2 tags are expected to have almost four times faster reading speed and three times faster writing speed. Gen 2 also supports dense reader mode, which means that the number of simultaneously active readers can be almost the same as the number of available channels (e.g., 50 readers operating on 50 channels). This feature is necessary to prevent interrogators from interfering with each other. A general comparison of Gen 2 and the other EPC protocols is shown in Table 7-1.

As in the table, Gen 2 satisfies worldwide regulatory compliance, is able to read more than 500 tags/second, and has an industry certification plan prepared by EPCglobal, Inc. (EPCglobal, 2006).

Gen 2 (Type C) Protocol: Physical Layer
Figure 7-7 and Figure 7-8 show Type C interrogator architecture and Type C tag architecture, respectively (ISO/IEC 18000-6, 2004/2006).

Figure 7-6 Type B tag architecture (*Source:* ISO/IEC 18000-6:2004/Amd1: 2006; reprinted by permission of ISO).

Table 7-1 Comparison of Gen 2 with Class 0+ and Class 1

Feature	Class 0+	Class 1 Gen 1	Gen 2
World Wide regulatory compliance		●	●
Field rewritable memory	●		●
Optional user memory	●		●
Read speed > 500 tags/second	●		●
Dense-reader operation			●
Kill security	●		●
Industry certification plan			●

In Figure 7-7, an interrogator sends information to one or more tags by modulating an RF carrier using double-sideband amplitude-shift keying (DSB-ASK), single-sideband amplitude-shift keying (SSB-ASK), or phase-reversal amplitude-shift keying (PR-ASK) using a PIE format. Tags receive their operating energy from this same modulated RF carrier (ISO/IEC 18000-6, 2005).

An interrogator receives information from a tag by transmitting an un-modulated RF carrier and listening for a backscattered reply. As in Figure 7-8, tags communicate information by backscatter-modulating the amplitude and/or phase of the RF carrier. The encoding format, selected in response to interrogator commands, is either FM0 or Miller-modulated subcarrier. The communications link between interrogators and tags is half-duplex.

Gen 2 (Type C) Protocol: Tag Identification Layer

An interrogator manages tag populations using three basic operations (ISO/IEC 18000-6, 2004/2006):

- *Select.* The operation of choosing a tag population for inventory and access. A Select command may be applied successively to select a particular tag population based on user-specified criteria. This operation is analogous to selecting records from a database.
- *Inventory.* The operation of identifying tags. An interrogator begins an *inventory* round by transmitting a query command in one of four ses-

Figure 7-7 Type C interrogator architecture (*Source:* ISO/IEC 18000-6:2004/ Amd1: 2006; reprinted by permission of ISO).

Figure 7-8 Type C tag architecture (*Source:* ISO/IEC 18000-6:2004/Amd1: 2006; reprinted by permission of ISO).

sions. One or more tags may reply. The interrogator detects a single tag reply and requests the PC, EPC, and Cyclic Redundancy Check (CRC)-16 from the tag. Inventory comprises multiple commands. An inventory round operates in one and only one session at a time.

- *Access.* The operation of communicating with a tag (i.e., reading from a tag. writing to a tag). An individual tag must be uniquely identified prior to *access*.

7.1.2 ISO/IEC 15691 to ISO/IEC 15693: Data Protocol

Because multiple code structures are used in many organizations, there is a need to support each organization's data structure and any format of data and language. The purpose of ISO/IEC 15961, ISO/IEC 15962 and ISO/IEC 15963 is to provide a common data protocol that has no restrictions on frequencies used in applications and air-interface protocols and to describe numbering systems for the unique identification of RF tags

7.1.2.1 ISO/IEC 15961: (Data Protocol) Application Interface

This standard addresses information interfaces with the application system. It focuses on the interface between the application and the data protocol process (ISO/IEC 15961, 2004). It is intended to be a companion standard to ISO/IEC 15962 and includes functional commands and syntax for item management using RFID (see Figure 7-9). ISO/IEC 15961 commands are higher abstract levels than those of the ISO/IEC 18000 series.

As in Figure 7-9, ISO/IEC 15961 provides a protocol level management method (data level method is covered in ISO/IEC 15962) for the interface between application and RF tag. The RFID data protocol is as follows:

- Defines application commands and responses (e.g., application programs can specify what data to transfer to and from an RF tag).
- Defines error messages as response to the application.
- Specifies how data is presented as objects, each uniquely identified with object identifier, which can be encoded on the RF Tag (see Figure 7-10).

The object identifier in Figure 7-10 (ISO/IEC 15961, 2004) means ISO standard 15434. (If the first digit is 0,' it means ITU-T; 2 means joint ISO/ITU-T).

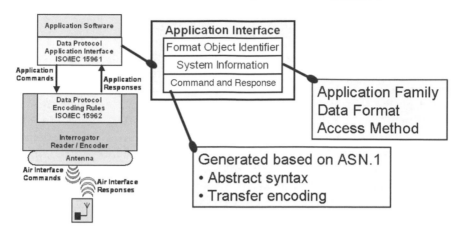

Figure 7-9 RFID data protocol ISO/IEC 15961 application interface (*Source:* P. Chartier, "A data protocol for RFID systems: An overview of ISO/IEC 15961 and 15962," reprinted by permission of P. Chartier).

The application interface of this RF data protocol is based on ASN.1 (Abstract Syntax Notation 1). ASN.1 is an international standard whose main purpose is the specification of data used in communication protocols, which provides the *abstract syntax* for defining the commands and responses and provides the *transfer syntax* that defines byte streams transferred between this standards and those of ISO/IEC 15962 (as in Figure 7-9).

7.1.2.2 ISO/IEC 15962: (Data Protocol) Data Encoding Rules and Logical Memory Functions

The RFID data protocol specifies how data is encoded, compacted, and formatted on the RF tag and how this data is retrieved from the RF tag in order to be meaningful to the application (ISO/IEC 15962, 2004). This protocol may be implemented as follows:

- On the same platform as an application
- On a separate platform linked to an application platform (e.g., linked serially, by LAN, or by Internet connection)
- On an embedded platform (e.g., in a barcode printer/RFID scanner or dedicated RFID interrogator)

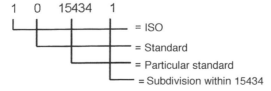

Figure 7-10 Object identifier (*Source:* ISO/IEC 15961, 2004, reprinted by permission of ISO).

As shown in Figure 7-11, the data protocol processor consists of the data compactor, the data formatter, and the logical memory. The data compactor performs all of the processes necessary to compact a data object and to determine the compaction type. The data formatter performs all the processes necessary to convert the input from the data compactor into bytes stored on the logical memory. It defines the access method, truncates the object identifier, and determines the type and length of the object identifier (i.e., it identifies whether a root object ID can be used to carry out defined processes to reduce the encoding space required for each object ID). It also maps the bytes in the logical memory to support either a directory or non-directory structure. Logical memory is a software representation of RF tag memory. It is structured by extracting system information from the RF tag. ISO/IEC 15962 provides a basis of interoperability for current and legacy systems and a migration path to future systems.

7.1.2.3 ISO/IEC 15963: Unique Identification of RF Tags

This standard describes numbering systems for the unique identification of RF tags. In particular, the standard addresses those cases when a unique ID is required as a part of read (or write) operations (ISO/IEC 15963, 2004). A unique ID does not need to be a permanent unique identifier in all situations. A virtual ID tag is sometimes sufficient in the case of identifying a tag unambiguously by data contents, physical position, or reply timing. When a unique tag ID is required, it can be done either by *virtual ID* (also known as logical ID or a session ID) or by *permanent unique ID*.

Virtual ID
This is a temporary ID based on tag parameters that may vary over the life of the tag. Several tags could have the same virtual ID at different times,

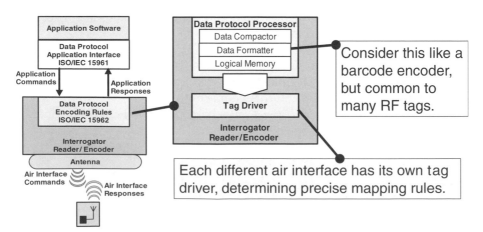

Figure 7-11 RFID Data protocol ISO/IEC 15962 data encoding rules (*Source:* "A data protocol for RFID systems: An overview of ISO/IEC 15961 and 15962," reprinted by permission of P. Chartier).

but at the same time all tags for the same interrogator should have a different virtual ID in order to provide an exact identification of each tag. The advantage of a virtual (session) ID is the reduced number of identification bits required; however, the virtual ID is unique only at a specific time and location.

Permanent Unique ID
When a globally unique ID is required, it is programmed into the tag. It guarantees a single ID independent of applications, spaces, and times.

7.1.3 ISO/IEC TR 18046: RFID Tag and Interrogator Performance Test Methods

The performance characteristics of RFID devices vary by application factors and particular RF air interfaces. This technical report (TR) provides a definition of performance, test methods, and parameters considering general supply chain applications. Table 7-2 shows short- and long-range test conditions, respectively (ISO/IEC TR18046, 2005). Among the conditions, *Distance* is between the antenna of the reader and the tag undergoing the test. *Tag population* means the number of tags being read in the test. *Tag geometry* is the arrangement of the tags in a population. The spacing of the tags within the defined geometry should be uniform (tag spacing is the minimum distance between the geometric centroid of each tag). *Tag orientation* means that tags within a population may have specified polarization relative to the interrogator antenna (e.g., relative to the z-axis). It includes angular rotation in three dimensions (ψ, θ, and φ). The *RF environment* is documented as part of the collected test data. Such documentation relates to the conditions of the test (i.e., anechoic chamber, open-air test site, etc.).

Table 7-2 Short and Long Range Test Condition

Condition	Range	Comment
Distance	0–10 meters (for short range), 10–100meters (for long range)	3 D (x, y, z)
Tag population	1, 10, 20, 50 , 100 (tags)	
Tag geometry	Linear, array, volume	
Tag orientation	0, 30, 60, 90, degree, random	3-D (ψ, θ, φ)
Tag volume	0. 016, 0.015, 1m^3	
Tag speed	0, 1, 2, 5, 10 m/sec	
Tag mounting material	Paper, wood, glass, plastic, metal	
RF environment	Benign, moderate, congested	WLAN, machinery, etc
Data transaction	1, 8, 16, 32 bytes	Read and write
Interrogator antenna height	0.5, 1, 2, 3 meters	Distance above ground plane

Source: ISO/IEC TR 18046, 2005, reprinted by permission of ISO.

Tag volume is related to the tag geometry. The volume should be cubic (having equal dimensions in all three directions), bounding the tag population. The *tag population* should be uniformly distributed within this bounding geometry for the reading test (see Figure 7-12). The structural material for establishing the bounding volume should be transparent to the RF frequency of the interrogator.

As in Table 7-3, the results of performance tests performed according to the test methods in ISO/IEC TC 18046 (or modified to reflect specific user-based applications) could be presented in a tabular format (e.g., matrix) in relation to the evaluated performance parameters. The RF environment and environmental conditions (such as temperature and humidity) should also be reported.

7.1.4 E-Seal: ISO 18185 Series

This standard specifies a read-only, nonreusable freight container seal identification system (based on a radio-communication interface) that provides a unique identification of the container seal, its status, and related information (ISO/DIS 18185-1, 2005). The standard specifies a system with the following:

- A seal status identification system
- A battery status indicator

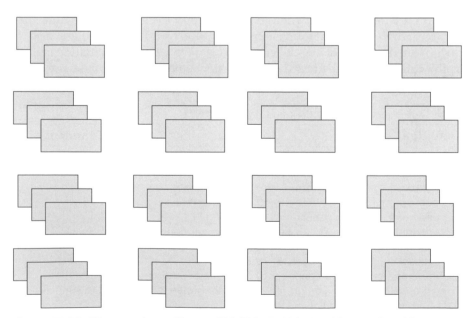

Figure 7-12 3D tag volume (*Source:* ISO/IEC TR 18046, 2005, reprinted by permission of ISO).

Table 7-3 Test Result

| Performance Parameter | | Extent (x) | Tag Mounting Material | | | | | |
			Corrugate Paper	Plywood	Plexiglas®	Aluminum	Glass	Comment
Identification	Range	Extent (y)						
		Minimum (z)						
		Maximum (z)						
	Rate							
Read	Range	Extent (x)						
		Extent (y)						
		Minimum (z)						
		Maximum (z)						
	Rate							
Write	Range	Extent (x)						
		Extent (y)						
		Minimum (z)						
		Maximum (z)						
	Rate							

Source: ISO/IEC TR 18046, 2005, reprinted by permission of ISO.

- A unique seal identifier, including the identification of the manufacture
- Seal (tag) type

Common Requirements

The seal should be uniquely identified by the tag manufacturer's ID and the tag ID (serial number) combination. This combination is called a *seal ID* and should be used in all point-to-point communication to uniquely identify a source (seal to interrogator) and destination address (interrogator to seal). The seal ID is permanently programmed into the seal during its manufacture and cannot be modified. However, the interrogator ID is a user-configurable parameter, and its assignment is not regulated by this standard (ISO/DIS 18185-1, 2005).

Seal Data

The electronic seal mandatory data includes a *seal tag ID* and a *manufacturer ID, date/time* for sealing and opening, *seal status, low-battery status, protocol ID, model ID, product version,* and *protocol version* (ISO/DIS 18185-1, 2005). The seal status occupies two bits and describes status such as that shown in Figure 7-13 as follows:

- *Open and unsealed.* The initial state of the seal, when the container is open and the seal is still unsealed.
- *Closed and sealed.* Physically closed and sealed (cable connected, bolt inserted, etc.)

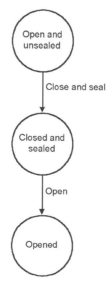

Figure 7-13 Seal status (*Source:* ISO/FDIS 18185-1, 2006, reprinted by permission of ISO).

- *Opened.* Physically open and the seal is broken (cable disconnected, bolt removed)

Figure 7-14 shows application of an example procedure for e-seal solution. The processes consist of eight steps: Create manifest and transmit it, use, e-seal, check (in-gate), read by hand-held reader, move to container terminal, use Web-based solution to store information and to track status, check before boarding, board secure container.

Currently, the ISO/IEC 18185 series consists of six parts (note that Part 5 was withdrawn), as follows:

- Part 1: Communication protocol
- Part 2: Application requirements
- Part 3: Environmental characteristics
- Part 4: Data protection
- Part 5 Sensor interface requirements (withdrawn)
- Part 6: Message sets for transfer between seal reader and host computer
- Part 7: Physical layer

7.1.5 Supply Chain Application of RFID

The ISO/IEC 17363 through ISO/IEC17367 series was prepared by the JWG of ISO TC 122 and ISO TC 104. These standards pertain to supply chain applications of RFID (ISO/IEC DIS 17364, 2005). The series includes the following:

- ISO/IEC 17363, Supply Chain Applications of RFID—Freight containers
- ISO/IEC 17364, Supply Chain Applications of RFID—Returnable Transport Items
- ISO/IEC 17365, Supply Chain Applications of RFID—Transport Units
- ISO/IEC 17366, Supply Chain Applications of RFID—Product Packaging
- ISO/IEC 17367, Supply Chain Applications of RFID—Product Tagging

The standards define the technical aspects and data hierarchy of supply chain management information required at each layer of the supply chain, as shown in Figure 7-15 (Harmon, 2003). Figure 7-15 provides a graphical representation of a hypothetical supply chain. Layers 0 through 4 are addressed in these standards (layer 5 is addressed by another working group or standard body). A *supply chain* is a multilevel concept that covers all aspects from raw material to a final product. In terms of life cycle, it is from shipping to a point of sale, followed by use/maintenance, and then followed potentially by disposal/or returned goods. Air-interface and communication protocol standards supported within these standards are given

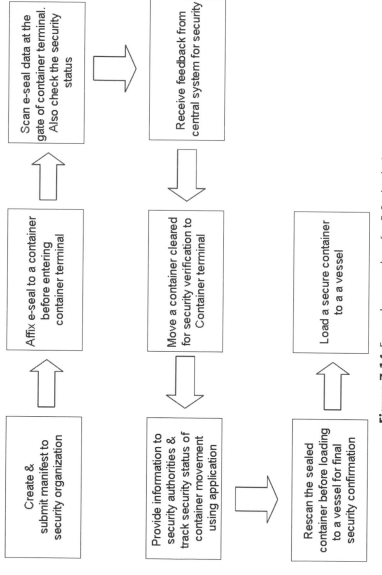

Figure 7-14 Example procedure for E-Seal solution.

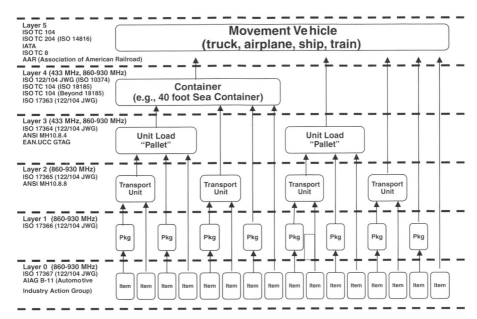

Figure 7-15 Supply chain application of RFID with relevant standards (*Source:* ISO/DIS 17364, 2005, reprinted by permission of ISO).

in ISO/IEC 18000. Commands and messages are supported by ISO/IEC 15961 and ISO/IEC 15962.

Minimum Performance Requirements (Range and Rate)

The performance of tags can be measured in accordance with ISO/IEC TR 18046. Minimum performance requirements vary for different functional applications of RFID. Table 7-4 shows the performance requirements for passive tags operating in supply chain with their usage. Even though minimum read distance is set as one meter, generally the user requires three meters for supply chain management. Another parameter frequently considered is the life of the battery for a handheld reader. Table 7-4 can be used as a reference for choosing an RFID hardware vendor.

7.2 Other Global Activities

Even though some activities are not started by ISO or standard bodies, the result of such activities could bring standardization to the user community and a wider adoption of RFID technology. In this section, we introduce some of these activities.

Table 7-4 Minimum Requirement for Passive Tag Performance

	Passive Technology		
Parameter	High-Speed Sortation	Handheld	Portal or Dock Door
How far—Minimum read distance	1 meter	0.5 meter	3 meters
How fast—Maximum item speed when read	16 kph	<2 kph	15 kph
How much—Amount of data per tag	256 bits	256 bits	256 bits
How many—Effective measure of tag data transfer rate and ability to do anticollision	200 tags/second	50 tags/second	500 tags/second

Source: ISO/DIS 17364, 2006, reprinted by permission of ISO.

7.2.1 Hibiki Project

In 2004, METI (Ministry of Economy, Trade and Industry), Japan launched the Hibiki Project to support the development of a low-cost IC tag (Shirai and Johnson, 2006). The goal was to develop RFID tags and reader chips selling at ¥5 (approximately US$0.05). They wanted to develop systems that are compatible with current EPC Class 1 Gen 2 spec (Gen 2 was approved by ISO as ISO/IEC 18000-6 C).

The target specification for the hardware is as follows:

- Operating frequency is 860 to 960 MHz.
- One meter write range (rewritable)
- 512 bit memory
- Read rate is 300 tags/second
- Reader has Frequency Hopping Spread Spectrum (FHSS) and carrier-sense functions for channel sharing.

Because the Hibiki project aims to minimize chip cost, the Hibiki protocol eliminated some functions so long as the user requirements are satisfied (O'Connor, 2005). For example, the team eliminated the Miller subcarrier, described in Chapter 4, from the analog block and eliminated the CRC 16 calculation function from the digital block. By doing so, the Hibiki chip die is about 40 percent smaller than the Gen 2 die. The project has been led by Hitachi with allied companies such as Dai Nippon Printing Company Lim-

ited (DNP), Toppan Printing Company Limited, and Nippon Electric Company (NEC).

7.2.2 Mandate of Some Organizations: Wal-Mart and DoD

Several mandates have boosted the adoption of RFID for some industries/organizations. Among them, DoD's and Wal-Mart's mandates have significantly impacted the fast adoption of RFID. They believe that tagging products will not only benefit them but will have value for their vendors as well. RFID system can help to share data on the movement of products between vendor and customer (and this kind of data will give vendors knowledge of their inventory and sales status).

7.2.2.1 Wal-Mart Mandate

In early 2006, around 100 Wal-Mart suppliers used RFID tags. However, this number should increase to 300 by the end of 2006. Wal-Mart has initially used Class 0 and Class 1 tags. Now there is an ongoing movement to use Class 1 Gen 2 (O'Connor, 2006b).

The Wal-Mart mandate was widely referenced by other retailers (VDC, 2003) and thus became a guideline for RFID specification for retailers:

- *Transponders*. Durable, temporary, or permanent read-only 96-bit Class 0 (factory-programmed), Class 0+ (read-write version of Class 0), or Class 1 version 1 (write once-read many). Now, Wal-Mart is driving toward Class 1 Gen 2.
- *Antennas*. One antenna required on each side of dock door/portal, one antenna above the dock door, and one antenna on each side or underneath a conveyor moving up to 1,000 m/min for case tagging (cases have to be read 100 percent of the time at 900 m/min).
- *Readers*. Should be agile (considering migration to Class 1 Gen 2 transponders), be Ethernet-based, have flexible output options, and have some security features.

7.2.2.2 United States Department of Defense

On October 2, 2003, the office of the under secretary of defense issued its first memorandum outlining the U.S. DoD's RFID policy, which was followed with an update on February 20, 2004, and the final update on July 30, 2004 (DoD, 2004). The policy directed the continuance of active tags, pallets and individual items requiring a unique identifier (UID). The deadline was later revised to early 2005.

Active RFID Business Rule
Active RFID tags used in DoD are data-rich and allow low-level RF signals to be received by the tag. The tag can generate high-level signals back to

the reader/interrogator (DoD, 2004). All returnable shipments (e.g., half- or full-size sea containers, large engine containers) of DoD cargo being shipped outside the United States must have active, data-rich RFID tags written at the point of origin for all activities (including vendors) stuffing containers or building air pallets. Content level detail is to be provided in accordance with current DoD RFID tag data specifications (DoD, 2004). Containers and pallets reconfigured during transit must have the RFID tag data updated by the organization making the change to accurately reflect current contents. Content-level detail comprises two components: asset-level detail (i.e., data elements that describe the asset) and content-level detail (i.e., data elements that minimally identify each level of a complete shipment entity).

Passive RFID Business Rule

Passive RFID requires strong RF signals from the reader/interrogator, while the RF signal strength returned from the tag is constrained to low levels by the limited energy. This low signal strength brings a shorter range for passive tags than for active tags. The DoD approved frequency range for passive RFID implementation is UHF 860 to 960 MHz. DoD has embraced the use of EPC tag data constructs, as well as DoD tag data constructs, in a supporting DoD data environment. As the available EPC technology matures, DoD is expanding the use of passive RFID applications for individual item tagging (DoD, 2004).

7.2.3 Global In-Transit Visibility (GITV)

The U.S. DoD has developed and implemented an in-transit visibility (ITV) system, which provides visibility of military assets from origin to destination. This system was validated through extensive use during Operation Iraqi Freedom (OIF). During OIF, ITV reduced inventories of supplies at both the origin and destination by tracking and managing supplies during transit. The United States initiated a project to share its in-transit visibility architecture with other nations in order to create a Global ITV Network in 2005. The vision of this project is to build a globally enabled capability/system to route ITV data between partners in order to increase the synergy between ITV systems. The Global ITV Network will utilize NATO and ISO standards. It will interface at the server level and will share only "license plate" information, not information about the contents of the shipment, and will utilize various automatic identification technologies (AIT) such as passive RFID, active RFID, and barcodes. Sharing ITV capabilities among nations will reduce costs and unnecessary redundancy and will provide a greater capacity than any nation can achieve on its own.

As in Figure 7-16, tag data is written by the docking station (TDS in the figure), and shipment tracking information is collected (or updated) by the mobile read-write reader (MR in the figure) or fixed reader (Reader in the

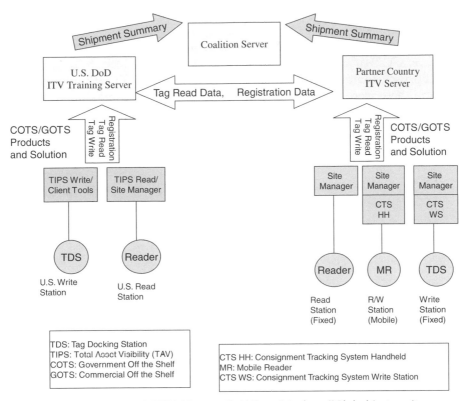

Figure 7-16 Concept of GITV (*Source:* G. Wilson-Mackey, "Global-in-transit project." 2006, reprinted by permission of G. Wilson-Mackey).

figure). Information such as "government off-the-shelf, "commercial off-the-shelf," and tag data are registered and stored at the United States ITV server or partner country's ITV server, depending on the ownership of shipment. If the shipment is moved to partner country's region (or vice versa, to the U.S. region), the updated shipment information is collected by the partner country's ITV system (or by the U.S. ITV system) and can be provided to the U.S. ITV server (or to the partner country's ITV server) through the coalition server. Information to be captured and subsequently passed to the owning nation is as follows:

- Consignment identifier
- Location identifier (where the consignment is)
- Owner nation (where to send the information)
- Date/time (date and time consignment was detected/scanned)

7.4 Conclusion

In this chapter, we introduced application standards that have been developed by ISO. We also introduced some of activities that result in standards for the user community and a wide adoption of RFID technology, even though these were not started by ISO or other standard-making bodies.

Acronyms

AIDC—Automatic identification and data capture

AIT—Automatic identification technology

ASK—Amplitude shift keying

ASN—Abstract syntax notation

CRC—Cyclic Redundancy Check

DNP—Dai Nippon Printing Company Limited

DoD—Department of Defense

DSB—Double sideband

DSB-ASK—Double side band amplitude shift keying

EPC—Electronic Product Code

HAG—Hardware Action Group

ISO—International Organization for Standardization

ITV—In-transit visibility

JTC—Joint Technical Committee

JWG—Joint Working Group

METI—Ministry of Economy, Trade and Industry

NEC—Nippon Electric Company Limited

OIF—Operation Iraqi Freedom

PIE—Pulse interval encoding

PR-ASK—Pulse reversal amplitude shift keying

SSB—Single sideband

SSB-ASK—Single side band amplitude shift keying

TID—Tag identifier

TR—Technical report

UID—Unique identifier

WG—Work Group

WTO—World Trade Organization

References

Autoid.org. 2005. "TC 104 SC 4 WG 2, sc4wg2n0216_DIS18185-1_20050428.doc." Available online via www.autoid.org/tc104_sc4_wg2.htm/ (last accessed January 22, 2007).

Chartier, Paul, 2005. "A Data Protocol for RFID Systems: An Overview of ISO/IEC 15961 and 15962." Available online via www.autoid.org/metatraffic2/ track.asp?mtr= / sc31 / wg4sg1 / nov05 / SG1 _ 200511 _ 004 _ ISO _ RFID _ Data _ Protocol_20051102.ppt (last accessed January 22, 2007).

DoD. 2004. "Memorandum for Radio Frequency Identification (RFID) Policy." July 30. Available online via www.acq.osd.mil/log/rfid/Policy/ RFID%20Policy%2007-30-2004.pdf (last accessed January 22, 2007).

ECPglobal, inc. 2006. "EPCglobal Global Certification and Accreditation Program." Available at www.epcglobalinc.org/certification (last accessed January 22, 2007).

Harmon, Craig, 2001, "RFID Standards." Available online via www.autoid.org/ 2002_Documents/TC%20122_WG%207/N026_RFIDStds_Updt_20010123.ppt (last accessed January 22, 2007).

Harmon, Craig, 2003, "Radio Frequency Identification What it is and how it works. Available online via "www.dodait.com/rfid/06-DoD_RFID_101-2_Dec_2003.ppt (last accessed January 22, 2007).

ISO/IEC DIS 17364." Available online at www.iso.org_.

ISO. 2004. "ISO 18046 TR." Available online at www.iso.org.

ISO. 2004. "ISO/IEC 15961." Available online at www.iso.org.

ISO. 2004. "ISO/IEC 15962." Available online at www.iso.org.

ISO. 2004. "ISO/IEC 15963." Available online at www.iso.org.

ISO. 2006. "ISO/IEC 18000-6:2004/Amd 1:2006." Available at www.iso.org.

O'Connor, Mary Catherine. 2006a. "Gen 2 EPC Protocol Approved as ISO 18000-6C." *RFID Journal.* Available online via www.rfidjournal.com/article/article-print/2481/-1/1/ (last accessed January 22, 2007).

O'Connor, Mary Catherine. 2006b. "Wal-Mart Specifies Gen 1 Sunset, Forklift Pilot." *RFID Journal.* Available online via www.rfidjournal.com/article/articleprint/ 2271/-1/1/ (last accessed January 22, 2007).

O'Connor, Mary Catherine. 2005. "Japan Offers ISO a Gen 2 Alternative." RFID Journal. Available online via http://www.rfidjournal.com/article/articleprint/ 1396/-1/1 (last accessed January 22, 2007).

Shirai Tadashi and Johnson, Paul, 2006, "Radio Frequency Identification (RFID), in Japan" , British Embassy, Tokyo, 2006.

VDC. 2003. RFID in the Supply Chain: The Wal-Mart Factor." 2003. Available online via www.vdc-corp.com/_Documents/pressrelease/03_rfid_walmart_pr1.pdf (last accessed January 22, 2007).

Wilson-Mackey, Gia. "Global In-Transit Visibility Project." 2006. Available online via www.pasols.org/multinat/gtiv.pdf (last accessed January 22, 2007).

Zhou, Feng, Chunhong Chen, Dawei Jin, Chenling Huang, and Hao Min. 2005. "Evaluating and Optimizing Power Consumption of Anti-Collision Protocols for Applications in RFID Systems." Auto-ID LABS-WP-SWNET-014. September. Available online via www.autoidlab.fudan.edu.cn/file/wp/AUTOIDLABS-WP-SWNET-014.pdf (last accessed January 22, 2007).

System Components

RFID implementations are becoming popular and interesting because they offer an expected benefit over the present way of doing things. Used in the proper situation, RFID can provide a better way of doing business or enable a much more convenient procedure for the consumer or user of the system. In many cases users of software systems may be unaware that they are using RFID. Because RFID is being integrated into the way we operate both individually and collectively, there are fewer clear boundaries around what constitutes the components of RFID. RF system elements may be as unique and different as the purpose to which they are being applied. For example, the set of RFID system components that benefit from data gathered by Airbus during its assembly process will be different than the RF data processing needs at Carrefour's retail operations. This chapter explores the typical elements that make up RFID components. It also addresses other areas where RFID is having a positive impact outside of what is typically considered fundamental RFID components.

Implementing an RFID system is in reality an attempt to integrate physical point activity in a distinct process with existing software elements. This defined relationship is needed to create a manageable physical representative environment for conducting business. As activity occurs in an operation, RF technology senses the situation. Data is aggregated and made available for better decision making. Information that can be extracted electronically in real time is more valuable than data gathered and maintained manually. Taking action on this RF data at various component levels allows repetitive actions to be completed with greater speed and with added accuracy. An RFID system plan should enable the value sum of the integration to exceed the value of the sum of the individual parts. Integrating scenarios with the ability to process real situations automatically will open new doors to cost savings through process improvement.

The functional purpose and characteristics of an RFID system are described to understand the components. Labels that are used throughout the RFID industry are then discussed. It is important to learn what functions are necessary based on the end objectives in a given RF system to maintain focus on the deployment. When a team is researching and evaluating differing properties of radio frequencies, reader shapes, tag properties, and middleware standards, sometimes it becomes difficult to tie the technical research back to the real purposes of the evaluation. Losing sight of end objectives can occur during the investigation cycle. Investing R&D monies in cool technology for technology sake without a real business driver is usually a poor investment decision. Technology upgrades to RFID must enable the user to be more effective in the day-to-day job.

Almost every business has interest in increasing sales, differentiating its product portfolio in the marketplace, running effective internal operations, and managing customers and suppliers. Integrating these objectives into the planning process is not always a trivial task. Recognizing market shifts and consumer buying patterns earlier in the planning cycle will facilitate a more accurate and a closer-to-real-time planning cycle. RFID is an enabling technology for this type of business objective in many instances. To meet such operational objectives, one must understand a general application stack that meets a business need. Figure 8-1 shows a ground-up view of many application needs.

The RFID application stack is broken into three major groups: RFID hardware, RFID middleware, and application software. Each of these groups will use RFID data. The lines of delineation aren't always identical in every usage; however, this general picture is a good starting point for discussion.

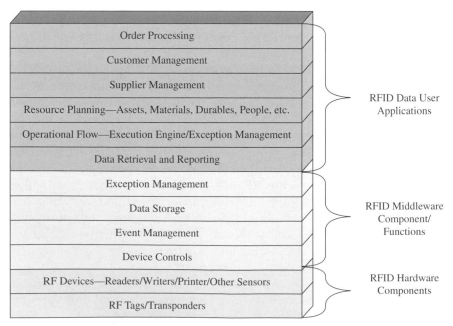

Figure 8-1 RFID component application stack.

RFID users will go through a period of discovery as they grow to understand how the technology will impact components in their software system. While many users don't want their initial RFID technology investments to be throwaway, many feel it is inevitable. After testing and experimenting with pilots, some may consider the end objective more achievable by starting over fresh (Gaughan and Meunier, 2005). Depending on each operational scenario, RF data has the possibility of bringing greater or lesser distinct value to each differing component.

8.1 Fundamental Components

8.1.1 RFID Hardware Components

This book has already provided a detailed description of the RFID hardware. This section is a review of earlier chapters. The most atomic element of RFID is the tag. The communication protocol between the antennas on the tag and on the reader allows the two entities to pass data back and forth. Power may be provided from the reader (passive tags) or from a battery activated tag (active tags) that initiates the communication, as shown in Figure 8.2.

The reader will broker the data and manage the physics of the hardware solution set. In some cases it may filter anomalous activity that may occur. Typically, reader properties are configurable, giving the reader different operational characteristics in varying environments. The reader normally manages a level of data smoothing, so that near-instant read retries that result from a physical bouncing motion of the tag in relation to the reader are minimized. Readers typically have firmware or software on board that

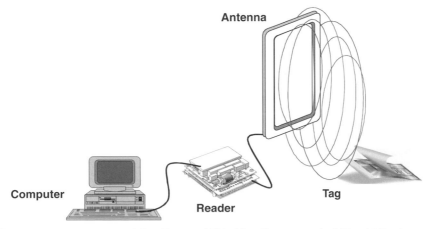

Figure 8-2 RFID connectivity (*Source:* With friendly approval of Harald Buchmann. Brooks Automation. 2006).

have varying degrees of configurability. However, it is the middleware that is typically considered the layer where software begins.

RFID readers interface upwardly to a software package typically called middleware. Even though it is usually referred to as a reader, many of these devices also can write or reprogram the tag (active and/or passive). Some reader providers offer a controller (or hub) to allow multiple readers to connect through a common port to the middleware. This is particularly popular where lower frequencies are used. This is because these systems often have a high number of readers because of its short reading range. Multiplexing at a low volume of reads won't overrun the controller with too much transactional activity.

Tags must be applied to the object that will be tracked. This occurs either manually or through an RFID printer device, as shown in Figure 8.3. Printers are necessary in some environments to rapidly apply the RF tag. It is very common for a printer to apply a tag that includes an RF code, a bar-

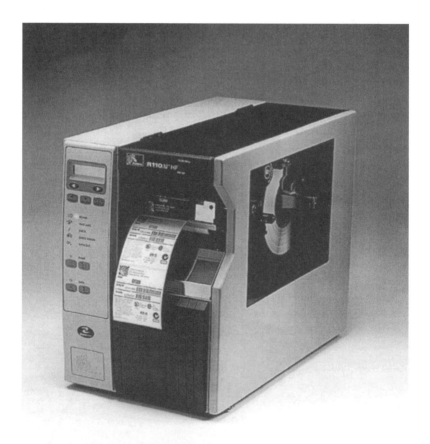

Figure 8-3 RFID printer (*Source:* Image courtesy of Zebra Technologies Corp. 2006).

code, and written text allowing the user to validate the contents in multiple ways.

8.1.2 Middleware Component

RFID equipment must get its information into a data system for usage. Middleware is the link between RFID devices and existing system software. The needed use of middleware will vary based on the specific implementation. As asynchronous actions occur during a particular scenario, each event must be managed. Middleware has the responsibility to make known when a particular event occurs. Often, related data that is associated with the captured event needs to be gathered and made available to the RFID user for processing. For example, as an RF-tagged box is read, the associated items may need to be reported together for external software to continue processing properly. A quick review of the *RFID Technology Guide* published by the Auto-ID Center (which later helped spawn the EPCglobal organization) describes an application stack that includes middleware as a necessary component (Auto-ID Center, 2003).

The pendulum of middleware capabilities swings from a dumb interface where as-is data is simply passed upward to systems that have a very specific need for process logic near the reader. The more intelligent implementations make complex decisions based on the RFID data prior to notifying external software systems. It then provides only the RFID-related information that is necessary for that particular system (filtering out unwanted data). There are pros and cons for each.

A dumb interface is easy to implement and provides value to fill up data systems with information. The quickest path to mandate compliance or data aggregation may be the business strategy for users of a dumb interface. A common disadvantage of these simple message passers is that data may not be effectively weeded out, making data storage near unmanageable in a mid- to high-volume environment. Architecturally, the dumb interface is an effective software add-on module that existing intelligent application suppliers add to their product portfolio. They consider RF devices as merely a souped-up form of a barcode. They are able to maximize customer value with the RFID add-on. The alternative is a highly intelligent middleware component that makes decisions and filters RFID related information. GlobeRanger® has attained a competitive position in the RFID market with what some refer to as Edgeware™. Edgeware is generally considered to be a subset of middleware and is referred to as a generic entity in this book. It provides business rules such that business-wise decisions can be made prior to an influx of data to a centralized integrated system. Data filtering based on a tag attribute is a simple version of logic that may exist in the middleware.

One of the most successful deployments of intelligent middleware exists in the semiconductor manufacturing world, where the RF device is treated like one of many sensors on an equipment controller of the device. As transponders are read, the process equipment software conducts a variety of verification steps that consider which item arrived and the changing states and availability of the equipment. Should the set of tagged items be at this process step? Are there other items that are required prior to the tool beginning? Several additional validations will occur prior to proceeding with the process step.

The edgeware then makes certain that the proper tool recipe is available to continue processing and commences operation by moving the product through a specific tool. It provides the RF data with other pertinent attributes to a manufacturing execution system (MES) for storage. One disadvantage of edgeware is that each device or device type will usually have different logic for a specific scenario and operation step. Thus, several different variations are necessary in the facility. Performing software development and a support life cycle for this type solution is no trivial task in a complex environment.

Storing the data in an organized manner is an important function regarding an RF implementation. Data storage is necessary for information retrieval at the proper moment in processing. Assembling a group of events enables the RF user to review sets of related activity on demand. Trend information can be very important to improving an operational scenario's effectiveness in the future. Users of the RF data are often interested in the association of RF tag-related information when a read occurs. Examples of associated data include time stamps of tag placement or tag removal, a contents list, a group ID, the last known location, a temperature, the next destination, and so forth. Persistent data should be kept for information that needs to be retrieved at a later time. Storage schemes may vary according to the operational use of the information. A data warehouse can provide this storage capability. Additionally, the stored data will assist in re-creating the operating environment in the case of a system crash.

Features and functions of middleware will vary from deployment to deployment, but many of the concepts are common to most successful RFID implementations. Three major functional segments are addressed in middleware capabilities: device controls, event management, and tagged object tracking (refer to Figure 8.1). Following is a more detailed list of other common middleware features and functions:

- Interface directly to a reader and pass information back and forth between the reader and the software layers. This, of course, is required to accumulate RFID data.
- Support asynchronous events at a high throughput rate in a public or production environment. As value using automation (including RFID) is discovered on a small scale, it will be amplified as it is rolled out more broadly.
- Initiate actions at the RFID device level when directed. This could be a read, a write, or to display RF data on a screen. This is a synchronized action that would be initiated typically by an intelligent software component such as a warehouse management system (WMS) or MES.

- Keep track of the current location of the tagged objects as they are stored or are moving through a predefined or a random path.
- Keep track of where the tagged object came from prior to its arrival at the current reader.
- Support multiple tagged object types (containers, items, pallets, devices, etc.) in most environments. As RFID becomes more prevalent, expanding of the use of the technology by tagging new objects will offer synergistic value from initial RFID investments.
- Maintain the relationship between tagged entities, such as a tagged carton to a palette or a tagged item to a carton.
- Provide the ability to group tagged objects that are alike as a logical group. This may entail mapping multiple tagged objects to a single container or having several grouped items span multiple tagged containers
- Execute a data write to a tag. This reprogrammable ability becomes valuable for tag reuse in a closed-loop environment. It is also used for tagged items that need to be identified in the open loop with an expected long–life, such as an airplane component.
- Maintain EPC numbering. This function will have a growing importance as EPC standards are adopted. The retail world is taking a lead to develop and promote these standards, which have impact back through the supply chain. Software that doesn't support this crucial capability will be greatly hampered in the marketplace.
- Interface with external software systems to coordinate business benefits. This critical element is often a key challenge for middleware, since this level of software standard is very difficult to both define and receive adoption. This interfacing has commonly been specific to the user.
- Support the receipt of queries for specific tracking information that is related to an RFID tag or group of tagged objects.
- Provide the user an interface that allows the setup and reconfiguration of the RFID devices. Being nimble at changing the operational environments will be vital in allowing users to continue business operations while altering a process that involves an RFID device.
- Organize data for statistical analysis. This functionality is necessary in many settings. This represents the activity of an RFID system. Value can be drawn through RFID analytics that can lead to greater operational visibility. This allows continuous improvement of the operation and an understanding of trending RFID-related activity.
- Provide visual notification of reader activity and operational display of activities. In some systems this is a useful feature, though it may not be a hardcore requirement.
- In some countries, to display RFID user interfaces in multiple languages is useful.
- Provide software security levels for user interfaces. This is a requirement in many applications and allows a broader use of an existing RFID middleware for varying roles and users.

- Deliver the ability to view logs and events in real time to learn of anomalous activity.
- Support RFID device interoperability enabling a user to pick and choose the best available hardware. This will be more easily achieved as standards mature but is achievable with noncompliant devices as well.
- Handle RF device anomaly situations as they occur. Automatically dealing with physical problems of hardware will enable continuation of operations even though the hardware may fail in many situations.
- Supply utilization information about the readers to assist in identifying bottlenecks or constraints to the processes using RFID data.

The functional descriptions could go on, but this is a relatively complete list of what most are using in lower-level software in RF deployments. Persistent data (storage) is typically considered part of middleware, but there may be cases where it isn't necessary in the middleware.

Middleware in its current form and definition may have a relatively short-lived existence in those industries that more rapidly embrace RFID. New solution architectures with embedded readers and generalized RFID capabilities will be introduced. In the short run RFID middleware specialists are the choice of early adopters. However, over time it is likely that the connectivity will be absorbed into IT infrastructure (Gaughan and Meunier, 2005). RFID pilots and early users don't have the advantage of mature standards either for the RFID hardware or the RFID software. Initially readers need to be physically attached onto existing devices or equipment, since its area of use is typically already in operation. With market maturity, devices will come with embedded RFID readers. With this evolution, device suppliers will offer integrated software controls for the readers.

This will help drive the need and maturity for software standards in these working environments. As standards mature, the need for traditional middleware will likely diminish as data is provided directly from the device controller. This is precisely the evolution that occurred in the semiconductor industry once it introduced RFID into the manufacturing process. In the mid-1990s, 200-millimeter wafer manufacturers found value using RFID. Readers were fastened to equipment in a variety of locations and orientations to achieve successful RF reading. This created learning, and as RF adoption grew, standards-making bodies integrated reader devices into industry architectures. Once the industry advanced to 300-millimeter wafer sizes, ID devices were to be managed by the equipment controllers (a form of edgeware described previously). It is the expectation of many that this will continue to happen in adopting industries that progress through an RFID maturity cycle.

8.1.3 Open-Loop Components

As enterprises have a growing need for developing a supply chain management strategy, EPCglobal has introduced an open-loop architecture that has support from some of the world's most influential organizations and companies. These efforts are intended to assist in supply chain initiatives. The EPCglobal vision that is shown in Figure 8.4 illustrates that suppliers of goods will host a data warehouse with information about the products they provide to their customers. This data warehouse is accessed across the Internet where data is stored in a format called the Physical Markup Language (PML). This is a derivative of the XML format. Arriving tagged objects are individually identified using RFID readers by their customers. Once identified, the customer may connect to an Object Name Service (ONS), which acts like a router and will direct the customer to the internet address of the data. The ONS is similar to the Domain Name Service that is used to look up an IP address for Web sites. Data related to the tagged object is then available across the internet. This provides an ability to operate in an open loop fashion. When a tag is read, the receiver can retrieve current data about the tagged object from the supplier. The supplier can regularly update the information related to the data as necessary. For example, the RFID tagged product may have an expiration date, some knowledge of specific properties of the contents shipped, or other information that is necessary for the receiver of the product.

This ONS/PML architecture is far beyond the conceptual phase and is operational. The set of highly available ONS servers has been implemented by VeriSign and is available to EPCglobal members. Information about finished goods, parts, containers, and so forth is more easily shared and more readily available than ever before.

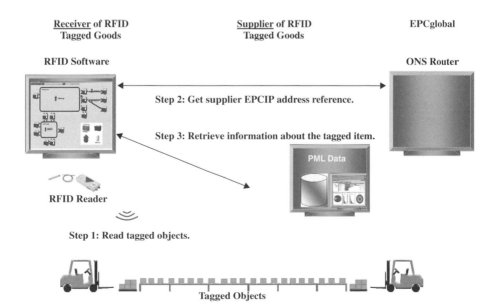

Figure 8-4 EPCglobal Vision for open-loop data (*Source:* Images courtesy of Brooks Software. 2006).

8.2 Extended Business Components

Data unused is opportunity lost in the business world. Meaningless data can be a burden in an operation. This is also true with RFID activity and stored events. RFID is an enabling technology that can allow business software components to operate at a greater degree of efficiency. To review some of the extended RFID components, we must first examine what some of these systems are and what they do. As we consider the various control systems that make decisions that are commonly used by a corporation, it is easy to become confused by all the acronyms. Connectivity between middleware and these decision-making engines can be complex and is described in more detail in Chapter 9 on integration to middleware and business application architecture. The components listed below are one or more software layers above the RFID middleware. To help sort out the alphabet soup, see Table 8.1.

8.2.1 Acme Manufacturing

Acme Manufacturing is a fictitious company created for the purpose of an example of how to use RFID components for business value. Acme has many of the same intricate operational challenges as many of today's manufacturing companies. Acme manufactures and assembles avionics products that are sold to aircraft makers. Acme has a lean initiative, and its major operating concerns encompass the following:

- Overproducing its avionic products to meet peak demands and being burdened with inventory it can't sell during slower business cycles.
- The need to support an expanding portfolio of products simultaneously (i.e., higher product mix). This creates more setup time, causing less productive manufacturing time. WIP (work in process) planning decisions are also more complex.
- Customer orders that are managed in their ERP are not comprehended in real time in the workflow system's bill of materials, asset planning, or supplier orders.
- The growing product mix is causing a reduced quality. Acme doesn't maintain a history or genealogy of the avionics products sold.

The Acme business processes track activities with its customers and suppliers. Internally this involves effective planning with various groups that include marketing, sales, logistics, plant floor planning, quality management, engineering, incoming inspection, outbound certification, and assembly.

Let's examine how Acme manages its data. Acme has been using a CRM (customer relationship management) system for three years to transact business with current customers and create new opportunities. Corporate goals and ongoing strategic decisions are data driven but are evaluated using

Table 8-1 Definitions for Extended Business Components

Acronym	Full Name	Description/Basic Functions
ERP	Enterprise resource planning	A computer system that is intended to integrate different departments within a business. This encompasses planning, manufacturing, and sales. More recent ERP systems include marketing, human resources, order tracking, accounting, inventory control, and customer service.
CRM	Customer relationship management	This software package is to manage information and data about customers in an organized manner. This includes contact information, customer service and support, sales activities, marketing campaigns, project management, and other outbound customer communication.
SRM	Supplier relationship management	An SRM package is viewed as a system that will set the stage for outward collaboration with suppliers. It analyzes global spending by various criteria (volume, supplier, category), assists in supplier selection and contract negotiations, helps leverage volume purchases, eliminate duplicate contracts from the same supplier, and measures a supplier's on-time-delivery.
PLM	Product life cycle management	This software system provides data sharing about a specific product spanning business functions and partners through the life of a product. This software tracks the product through its life cycle, from manufacturing through obsolescence. It knows historical information regarding who affected the product and how and when it was affected. It assists in the definition and execution of workflow in many environments. PLM also aids in several industries to meet quality requirements.
SCM	Supply chain management	SCM is a plan or a strategy to work with trading partners to bring greater value to the subsequent customer or consumer for the least possible supply cost. This includes streamlined procurement (such as online with e-signatures), connection between receiving and accounts payable, consideration of on-hand inventory during the purchasing process, and further automation of the shipping transaction and tracking process. SCM thought leaders are now performing collaborative strategic planning with their partners.
MES	Manufacturing execution system	An MES tracks inventory through a facility and can recall the activities on the shop floor. It is a collection of business rules and logic that drives workflow and coordinates assets and materials. It manages work in process (WIP), schedules product to be built, routes the product through a predefined set of steps, and manages the bill of materials. The MES is commonly integrated to equipment controllers. Product traceability, genealogy, and data collections are also characteristics of an MES system. An MES helps drive predictable results and flow through moderately complex to very complex manufacturing environments.

Excel® spreadsheets. An MES controls the shop floor activity, manages the workflow, and provides information on manufacturing yield. Capacity planning is a challenge and is also managed through multiple yet disconnected Excel spreadsheets. Acme recently went live with an ERP system. However, at the present it only houses CRM activity, although it provides the infrastructure for future expansion. With the growing burden on the mounting number of products manufactured simultaneously they are currently preparing to pilot test a product life cycle management (PLM) component to its ERP. Acme expects this to assist in product planning as new offerings are introduced to the market. The ERP has never been integrated with the MES, so the actual orders are not connected to the day-to-day planning and operations on the shop floor. Since the data is disparate, many of the groups unintentionally work in competition with one another. Each employee's goals and objectives aren't always consistent with the business goals either. Nonintegrated data systems drive a wedge into operations, as metrics are not in total alignment. The production manager is focused on output, while shop floor operators may be driven by tool utilization. An operator may keep any product moving through a production area to keep utilization rates high, but then these same products wait at a following operational step because it isn't a high priority for the facility. This causes an increase in cycle time, which drives up material costs. This is not an uncommon or an out-of-the-ordinary situation in many industries.

What does Acme's situation have to do with RFID? Let's examine some of the possibilities. We will assume that Acme is going to proceed with an RFID system that will track products as they move through the facility. Acme will tag containers that hold materials as they flow through production and assembly and then tag the container that ships to the customer. We assume that Acme's aircraft-assembling customers are interested in the same kind of initiative (common avionics among airlines is the norm).

Acme Problem	What Acme Can Do
Stale avionic products	Acme will now be providing RF-tagged products to their customers. This helps the accuracy of distribution and opens the collaborative nature of their relationship. The major aircraft builders are using the RFID data obtained from the Acme tagged products to their benefit. Automated tracking and order fulfillment accuracy is using RFID to execute supply chain initiatives. In return aircraft manufacturers provide earlier signals to its suppliers regarding demand for new aircraft and parts. This allows Acme to act quicker on its customer's feedback to streamline inventories. This data is a critical part of their planning process and lays the groundwork for real-time planning based on customer demand. This enables Acme to reduce overstock as well as prevent product shortages.

Acme Problem	What Acme Can Do
Increase product mix	The RFID tag is read at different process start points during manufacturing. Acme is able to sense the operational activity in the plant. This provides instant and accurate visibility of where each tagged product is at any given time. The RFID activity is fundamental to more accurate material consumption and replenishment. Acme's PLM implantation can now maintain tighter management as it pushes more product types through the manufacturing line. Data fed into the MES can provide real-time electronic reports regarding the status of individual product runs. Business rules in the MES can then act on these reports to manage the growing plethora of products that are produced by Acme.
No production feedback known about orders in process	As RFID activity populates the MES, the MES interprets the data relative to its comprehension of the product manufacturing and assembly process. Integrating the MES to the ERP allows a link between order fulfillment and shop floor automation that didn't exist previously. This step is not trivial. Product run data (using RFID events) is made available that will enable better order fulfillment decisions in the ERP layer. Likewise, the MES can inform the ERP of key production signals of material consumption or bottleneck steps that will assist in setting order priorities that allow that an MES to push forward a higher-priority product. High-priority orders can be pushed faster through the production line, as the MES senses all floor activity through RFID events. Additional benefits include providing sales better visibility into the actual product that will be available to sell and when it will be available. Customers can be updated of the status of orders that are in progress as desired.
Can't recall history of a product steps executed	RFID data stored in the MES contains time-stamped information for each product and groups or lots of product. This data is then offloaded to Acme's long-term storage warehouse for future retrieval when necessary. Each product's manufacturing data and process can be retrieved at a future time for evaluation based on RFID time stamps. If a particular product is defective and is recalled, this RFID data assists in Acme's root cause analysis and earlier recall of other potentially defective members of the same manufacturing run. This enables Acme to reduce recall costs. Process tracking is a growing need for Acme quality initiatives. It will also maintain the necessary records to be a long-term supplier in the aviation industry.

This still doesn't solve the problem of disparate data systems. The Auto-ID Center's application stack describes a software level on the subject of the temporal storage. The thinking behind temporal storage is to provide a high-speed data repository of disconnected systems into a centrally organized set of data. Data is stored as a time-stamped event with relevant data associated with the event. It is able to be captured based on the native data schemas from the source of the information. This means that data translation to a common format for disparate systems isn't required. The data becomes integrated in the repository and is available for high-speed retrieval. Reports (electronic and/or visual) can be created that tie the activity of the separate systems together. This reveals holes in the manufacturing process at Acme that were not realized previously. One industry that has embraced temporal technology is the semiconductor manufacturing industry. It is used heavily to reprioritize dispatch lists in real time and has resulted in significant cycle time reductions. The applicability of temporal technology built with RFID may be broad, but is a key component in the Auto-ID Center's *RFID Technology Guide* and vision (Auto-ID Center, 2003).

Don't take away from the Acme example that RFID can do everything for everyone and solve all problems. It can't. Further, implementing RFID without reengineering processes will limit the opportunity for improvement. The need to redesign operational procedures and processes is a key factor in maximizing an RFID return on investment. There are lessons to be learned about how RFID can positively affect various components of the business directly. How does this example relate to retail, asset management, or others looking to implement RFID? The extended business components may differ, but the underlying principles apply and value can be weighed and measured. RFID doesn't solve problems itself; it is only part of a bigger solution. This is why so many executives are paying attention to the RFID movement. RFID can provide real-time data, enabling improvement in an operation that can and will bring business benefit.

8.2.2 RFID Components Help Business

As RFID components become integrated into other business applications, they have the opportunity to contribute to the added value of the operation. Like many technologies, there is yet much to be discovered about exploiting RFID data. Some of the uses may be less traditional than one may consider (see Appendix A of this book for some unique uses of RFID). Following is a list of some additional ways that some are expecting to use RFID components in their enterprise:

- Using RFID data to assist in improving the levels of inventory to match the market demand. Empty shelves at the local clothing retail store costs the retailer in lost opportunity and customer satisfaction while costing the supplier brand loyalty. Highly advertised new products that can't be found by the customer will amplify a negative sentiment toward a company.

- The time-stamping of activity that is associated with RFID reads lends itself very well to a higher degree of understanding of where tagged objects are located at any given time. This increased understanding of the activity in the business operation can enhance the ability to comprehend where process changes may be necessary. This can lead to reduced cycle time in many RF deployments.
- Planning is an inherently difficult business problem. Operating plans are commonly incorrect as quickly as they are agreed upon. RFID data integrated into a real-time planning system can better facilitate the latency of manual decisions. It also may enable more frequent planning updates, leading to better prioritization in efforts to meet consumer/customer demand.
- Lean initiatives are the currently popular way of describing waste elimination. RFID provides more knowledge about day-to-day operations, enabling a greater opportunity to mitigate risks and thus assisting the reduction of waste.
- In some companies tools and assets are very expensive. Asset utilization can be tracked with RFID readers and tagged items flowing through the asset. Keeping high-priced assets productive is crucial in driving value to the bottom line.
- Striving to make certain that equipment stays operational is an important criterion for a successful business. Equipment requires maintenance and spare parts replacement. The aggregation of RFID activity at a particular piece of equipment (such as an ATM) can greatly assist in predicting when service of the equipment is required. Preventive maintenance strategies and spare parts management plans can be developed from this RFID data. This can drive a more predictable maintenance process, improving the ability across the enterprise to meet customer pressure.
- Nonconformance to customer requirements can be reduced with intelligent use of RFID data. Historical RFID data gathered at each production step can provide information that helps reduce risk and liability of goods that have the same source and have similar characteristics.
- Freed-up cash can also be realized through proper management and improved usage of commodities and durables. Analysis can be generated based on RFID activity that can assist in managing commodities and durables simultaneously. Matching elements that are alike allow optimization of these entities that directly influence order fulfillment.
- Warranty costs and the process of going through a return or recall is becoming a greater monetary burden. Putting quality processes in place to minimize returned merchandise is important. Further, having the

historical information allows an ability to pinpoint which products need to be recalled or reworked at an earlier time. This can result in a huge savings. RFID is a catalyst for tracking this type of information.

• Providing RF-tagged products to customers enable them to use the technology for better operational visibility. Ultimately, as companies have better intelligence on how a product is consumed, information can be fed back from customers. This permits an operation to be more effective in planning and integrate assumptions at an earlier point in time.

• Providing automatic notification or escalation of a specifically important incident or situation allows quick response and earlier proactive steps to be taken. As events or activities occur in an operation, RFID provides these important signals.

• Intelligent routing of materials or tagged objects is an important part of order fulfillment and on-time delivery. In complex environments RFID events can assist in the movement of a tagged object (manual or automated material movement).

• As inventory is received, immediate reconciliation may be achieved (rather than having to uncrate and open every box to verify an order). Likewise, confirmation of delivery to a customer is more easily attained. This means faster time to payment received in several industries.

8.3 RFID Component Characteristics

In addition to the varying array of features and functions necessary for successful long-term deployments, there are a number of general characteristics that should apply to all the components that use or are integrated with RFID. As the RFID-integrated components become buried in the day-to-day operations, it becomes a potential single point of failure for the business. If the systems breaks down, operations may be in jeopardy. Thus, the following compilation of characteristics is significant to consider in any long-term RFID deployment plan:

• The ability to scale an RFID implementation is crucial, as users will need to be expanding and changing the scope of RFID devices physical layout.

• A highly flexible system will be necessary that is architected for operational change, reconfiguring readers, printers, and other RFID devices.

• Highly available systems will be necessary in some environments that are required to operate round the clock.

• An open architecture where the data is quickly accessible and easily shared with other entities (people, software, hardware, etc.) supplies greater opportunity for value.

- Becoming compliant with standards will unlock opportunities to work more closely with suppliers and customers. Learning and knowing standards in a target industry as well as RFID standards is a prudent exercise. This will assist in rapid deployment and the opportunity to mix and match RFID components in a solution architecture. Interfaces that are adaptable will provide added value and will be essential for a long-term deployment.
- Controlling multiple RFID vendor devices simultaneously provides the ability to optimize processes with differing RF technologies.
- In many cases it is necessary to continue operations and reconfigure the system at run time. This would allow change while minimizing the impact on business operations.
- A secure system will be something that users will need. This is particularly important, as products and cases of products with RF tags are part of an open-loop supply chain initiative (such as in retail).
- Reporting or exporting data from the RF system into a format that can be messaged for decision making (whether automated or manual) is essential.
- Cost of ownership of RF technologies can be reduced with an RF solution that is easy to support. Those that match the company's technology direction are favorable.
- The quicker the benefits can be realized the better the impact on the bottom line. Time to market with the RFID deployment is a key element in many systems.

8.4 Summary

RFID components and their extended set of business components will vary from user to user. A guiding business vision is important to develop as RFID technology becomes understood and deployed. Integrating RFID into business processes and reevaluating these processes is important to achieve maximum benefit from RFID. Tying RFID data to existing software components and then taking action on the situation can provide added value and benefit to an enterprise.

Acronyms

ATM—Automatic teller machine

CRM—Customer relations management

EPC—Electronic Product Code

ERP—Enterprise resource planning

IP—Internet protocol

MES—Manufacturing execution system

ONS—Object Name Service

PLM—Product lifecycle management

PML—Physical Markup Language

SCM—Supply chain management

SRM—Supplier relationship management

WIP—Work in process

WMS—Warehouse management system

XML—Extended Markup Language

References

Auto-ID Center. 2003. *RFID Technology Guide*.

Gaughan, Dennis, and Marc-A Meunier. 2005. "Making RFID Middleware Decisions in a Changing Marketplace." April.

9

Integration

Many parts of an RFID system must be connected so that RFID data flows to a useful end. All data should have a destination, or the collection of that data would be meaningless. This chapter moves past the intricacies of RF and into the realm of data routing and data analysis. Providing useful data to the business so that it can move faster and make more informed decisions is where the real benefits of RFID are revealed.

9.1 Network Layer Integration

An RFID-enabled network is an assortment of appliances and computers that collect, route, store, share, and interpret RFID data. The following sections indicate the most important parts of the system, explain why they are important, and present examples of how they are used in real-world applications.

9.1.1 RFID Devices

As discussed in previous chapters, RFID devices include passive and active tags along with their associated readers. Transponders communicate with the readers using an air interface protocol. The following sections discuss the networking of components from the reader back to the data-processing servers and databases, rather than the network interface between tags and readers. The tag to reader interface is discussed in Chapters 3 and 4.

9.1.1.1 RFID Readers

Most RFID readers today connect to a business network over an Ethernet or 801.llx wireless interface. Ethernet is the most widely used standard for wired data transmission, and 802.11x is the most widely used standard for wireless data transmission for RFID networks today. The x in 802.11x is a variable letter that identifies the exact protocol. Today, the most common 802.11 types are A, B, and G.

Other interfaces exist such as USB (universal serial bus), RS232, and RS480. These interfaces usually require that the RFID reader be connected directly to a computer. The connected computer is responsible for collecting the data from its associated RFID reader and passing it on to the network. Readers connected directly to a computer instead of to the network are only accessible via their attached computer. This can sometimes add an extra level of complexity when software or firmware upgrades must be made to the reader. If software updates are pushed out to all the readers from a central server, the computers that the readers are connected to must first receive the update and then pass it on to reader. If the readers were connected directly to the network, the updated could be sent directly to the reader.

9.1.1.2 Edge Devices

Edge devices are those network appliances that provide a layer of services between the RFID readers and the business network. The edge devices offer services that include data collation, filtering, buffering, and event processing. Edge devices act as a buffer between the RFID specific part of a company's network and the network's backbone. IT departments attempt to insulate applications from each other on the network to increase network stability and maintainability. The edge device helps to make this possible. The edge device has the ability to inspect and filter any data before it is transmitted onto the company's network backbone. In Figure 9-1, there are three edge devices depicted. Each edge device is configured to service a group of three RFID readers. Figure 9-1 is a logical, more than a physical,

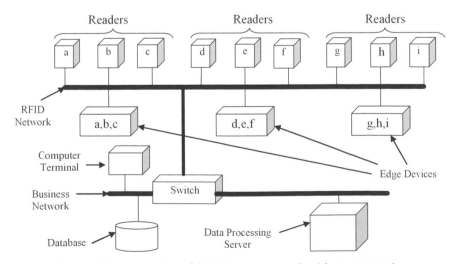

Figure 9-1 Integration of RFID into a network with segmentation.

representation of how RFID hardware can be integrated into an existing business network.

9.1.1.2.1 Data Filtering The scalability of an RFID solution greatly depends on the amount of extraneous data that can be removed at the edge of the network. There is no reason for hundreds or thousands of beacons from a tag to flood a company's network unless the beacons are meaningful. In most cases, the network is being pushed to its limits even before the addition of an RFID application. Most traffic on a network can be attributed to normal network traffic generated by everyday activities such as Web browsing, database queries, and file sharing. In real-time location systems (RTLSs), filtering can be a very important. Real-time monitoring usually equates to 100 percent coverage, 100 percent of the time, which generates a large amount of network traffic and data. Systems that use choke points or portals may not require this level of filtering because of the fact that data is only retrieved when the tag passes by the reader.

"Meaningful data" is the information that can be deemed significant by the intended application. In most cases, a beacon from a tag is only significant if it is the first beacon received or if the beacon contains information about changes in the tag's state such as signal strength, movement, or temperature changes. All other beacons are seen by most RFID applications as extra data that simply tells the system that the tag is still located near the same reader. An edge device can report the first beacon, filter all other beacons, and then report only when the tag is no longer seen by the reader. The device effectively distills a multitude of beacons into a few meaningful pieces of data: (1) the tag is in range, (2) the tag is out of range, or (3) the tag has changed state in some way.

It is important to note that not all applications allow edge devices to filter the data. In applications where data is used for forensic purposes, each beacon of the tag may be significant. In this case, an edge device should not be used for data filtering but may be used for data buffering and logging. When an application does require visibility of every tag beacon received, it is highly advisable to segment the network so that network traffic generated by the RFID system does not reach the core business network.

Network segmentation is a standard practice used by network engineers and IT groups. Using basic network appliances called "switches," the network administrator can route data so that it does not affect the core business network (see Figure 9-1). There are exceptions when dealing with a wireless network such as an 802.11B-based wireless network. Wireless networks cannot be segmented because of the fact that all data transmissions must share the designated frequency range and bandwidth. Network segmentation is advisable whenever it is possible. Segmentation also provides a level of data and infrastructure security. Computer viruses can only jump across networks at the points where they intersect. All networks must intersect at some point in order for data to be shared, but minimizing these points also minimizes the threat and provides clear choke points for security measures to be applied.

9.1.1.2.2 Data Buffering In mission-critical RFID systems, it is important that no data is lost once it is received by the reader and before it is stored in a data repository. In a very large network, it is not implausible that sections, or subnets, of the network will fail even in the most robust network possible. In these, hopefully rare, cases, an edge device can act as a data-buffering mechanism. Data buffering allows the edge device to store the data locally when it cannot be sent through the network because of a network outage or an unreachable destination computer. The buffered data can then be sent automatically when the problem is resolved to ensure that no data is lost. In this scenario, there is still a point of failure between the reader and the edge device, but the data loss is greatly decreased with buffering. It is preferable to store the data, when it is collected, on a non-volatile medium such as a hard drive or flash memory rather than requiring it to propagate all the way to the data store. If data is stored in volatile memory, such as RAM (random access memory), a power failure would cause the data to be lost.

Systems that continuously send small pieces of data across a network are said to be "chatty." Systems that buffer all of the little pieces of data into a larger data message use less network bandwidth than chatty systems. The difference can be found in the way in which a network sends and receives data. Every piece of data that is sent across the network has contextual information that is sent along with it. The combination of the contextual data and the data to be transmitted makes up a transmission packet (see Figure 9-2). For example, a 1-byte transmission requires hundreds of bytes of overhead. These extra bytes in the packet contain the "from" and "to" address of the data, and the extra bytes also contain data that ensures integrity as the data travels across the network. Each end of the communication involves some processing overhead for establishing and "tearing down" a connection between the endpoints. A chatty system can easily use more network bandwidth than a system that communicates using larger chunks of buffered data.

9.1.1.2.3 Data Logging Data logging is a standard tool used in almost every system to some degree. A system that supports data logging simply records the data and contextual information about the data as the system executes. This information may prove valuable in certain circumstances. Logging offers several advantages that may not be apparent when the system is running smoothly, but the advantages quickly reveal themselves when the system is having problems.

In mission-critical systems, data logging is a fundamental requirement. If the system becomes unstable at any time, the logged information pro-

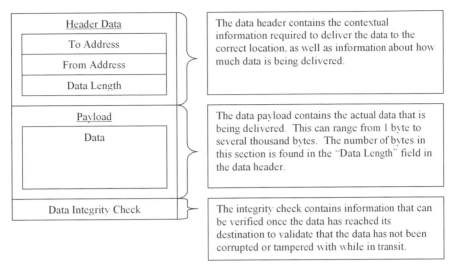

Figure 9-2 Basic data packet structure.

vides history about what was going on in the system when it became unstable and also provides clues into how a current problem can be resolved or how to avoid future problems. When data logging is implemented in an edge device, the device can provide a more detailed history than is possible at the root of the system. In a robust system, data logging should be implemented at each level so that the details associated with each level are logged.

Data logging must be configurable. There are situations when the system should record the minutest details, and there are other situations when very high-level logging is all that is required. Logging can be classified into several levels: fatal, error, warning, information, and debug. Fatal, error, and warning messages should always be logged. These pieces of data are critical to the system because they report problems or potential problems in the system. Information-level logging provides status information, while debug-level logging provides information that may only be useful to the developer of the system.

In the purchase of an RFID system, it is important to understand the logging capabilities of the system. Without this type of data, a simple 10-minute outage may become an aggravation that lasts for days. Logging information should be easily retrievable and searchable.

9.1.1.3 Data-Processing Servers

In most RFID systems, the data is processed before it is stored. This processing applies location algorithms and business rules to the data that may result in data transformation, routing, event notification, or all of the above. Depending on the complexity of the system, data-processing servers may be networked to share information or may work autonomously. After the data is processed, it may be stored in a database. In systems where there are no edge devices deployed, data-processing servers may also perform some of the same tasks as an edge device—for instance, filtering and logging as discussed in Sections 9.1.1.2.1 and 9.1.1.2.3.

9.1.1.4 Database Servers

Database servers usually represent the end of the journey for most RFID data until it is accessed by a system user. The data is stored in the database for history and reporting services. The databases available today allow some level of data processing by the database itself and also provide a suite of reporting and notification services.

Not only do databases store the data collected from the RFID system; they also may contain the configuration data for the system. When edge devices or readers boot up, they require some direction as to how they should function. In most cases, a reader runs with its current configuration, but sometimes a change needs to be made. In this case, RFID systems will push the new configuration to the reader or edge device. This topic is covered in more detail in Section 9.1.5.

9.1.2 Middleware

The concept of middleware is somewhat nebulous. Some computer system architects believe that middleware is the backbone of a robust system, and others see it as nothing more than a necessary evil. As with most debates, reality lies somewhere in the middle. A great deal of these varying views come from the fact that middleware does not have a clean and distinct definition. What is undisputed is that middleware is software and/or hardware, and its purpose is to facilitate communication between two or more components. Some standard middleware components include the following:

- Hardware abstraction layers (HALs)
- Application programming interfaces (APIs)
- Message routing engines
- Message transformation engines
- Synchronization engines
- Web services
- Code libraries
- Rules engines
- Load balancing
- Data abstraction layers (DALs)

In almost all enterprise-level RFID implementations, all of the types of middleware listed above are used. The edge device described in the previous section is a type of middleware. Figure 9-3 is an example of the most basic RFID architecture. The middleware in this architecture enables the communication between the RFID hardware and the applications. The middleware could implement several different components such as a HAL and an API.

When middleware is used to communicate between two or more components, the components do not have to span long distances. They can reside on the same computer or even in the same computer process. In most cases, data is shared between at least three components before middleware is needed. These types of architectures are called n-tier architectures, where n is the number of layers in the architecture. Some of these layers are labeled as middleware. Most systems architects today agree that a componentized design provides more flexibility in the system and decreases maintenance costs. They also agree that the interfaces between these components should be as loosely coupled as possible to reduce dependencies between the layers. The loosely coupled interface is described later in this section.

Classic three-tier architecture is made up of the client, data server, and data abstraction layer (DAL). The DAL in this example is the middleware. For the DAL to be effective, the client must always access the data server via the DAL. Not only does the DAL move data from the data server to the client, but it also provides a layer of abstraction between the client and server. The abstraction layer provides a standard interface to a component; in this case the data server. If the data server component ever needs to be changed or completely replaced, the DAL will insulate the client from these changes. The client does not need to know that the data server has changed. The following sections go into more detail about each of the reasons for middleware and how it is used in RFID solutions.

9.1.2.1 Rules Engine
Middleware is a logical place to inspect data and make decisions based on that data. When middleware acts as a rules engine, it can process data and take the appropriate actions. For example, a rules engine for a financial institution may inspect a loan request that originated through an online application. Before the application is authorized, the appropriate rules are

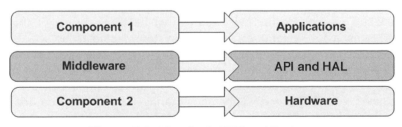

Figure 9-3 Most basic RFID architecture.

applied to the request to check the credit score for the applicant. Applicants with a high credit score may be instantly approved, while those with credit scores lower than a predefined minimum may have their application routed to a bank representative for further inspection.

A key point to note in the previous example is that there are several data points that influence the outcome of the application. These points include the credit score of the user, the minimum credit score that can be authorized online, and the list of representatives that can securely authorize the application. The credit score could even be calculated from several other data points. The middleware must be able to access this information and allow the system to be configured based on the business's wants and needs. During some quarters of a year, a financial institution may not want to take as much risk, so the minimum credit score should be able to be easily raised by the business. The rules engine allows the business to make these tweaks as needed.

The same logic can be applied to an RFID system. As tagged assets move through the system, certain rules may trigger various actions. If a package does not arrive by a specified time, for example, the middleware may alert the appropriate parties or start any type of task that is appropriate. It is easy to see that the definition of the rules and how they are implemented is completely dependent on the application.

There are several standardized rule definition languages. Most of them are built on top of the Extensible Markup Language (XML). Some examples are Rule Markup Language (RuleML) and Business Rules Markup Language (BRML). Both of these languages allow rules to be defined and then plugged into a rules engine that will use the rules to manage data.

9.1.3 Middleware Basics

9.1.3.1 Message Routing

Moving data from one point to another is one of the most basic functions of middleware. As discussed earlier, this transport can be around the globe or completely contained inside one computer. Sometimes data must be routed to different components in the system based on the type of data or the current state of the system. The routing can also be determined by a rules engine as discussed in the previous section. Whenever data must be routed, middleware usually gets the job.

There are several reasons why data must be routed. One of the most basic reasons is for system scalability. A system is said to be scalable if it can gracefully perform as the load on the system increases. One way to "scale" a system is to add more computing power to the system by distributing the processing across multiple computers. This is called *load balancing* (see Figure 9-4). Load balancing is managed by a type of middleware. The middleware monitors how much work each component is doing and

Source Components   Middleware   Distributed Components
(Routing)

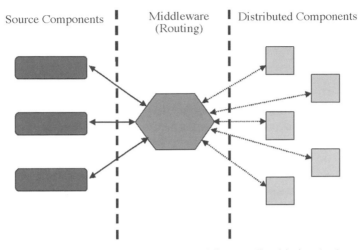

Figure 9-4 Basic data routing middleware (load balancing).

routes the incoming work so that it is evenly distributed across those components. In extremely high-load environments, the middleware may be a combination of software and hardware.

In an RFID system, as the number of tags being monitored increases, so does the amount of load balancing required. RTLSs sometimes require complex algorithms to pinpoint the location of a tag. Distributing this work across multiple computers (data-processing servers) is one way to perform these calculations for a large number of tags.

An e-mail server can also be viewed as a piece of middleware that helps make up the entire e-mail system. The endpoints are the e-mail clients (Outlook, Eudora, Elm). The e-mail server routes the messages to their appropriate destination. There are several other standardized systems that route messages including Network News Transfer Protocol/Usenet (NNTP), Internet Relay Chat (IRC), and AOL Instant Messenger (AIM).

9.1.3.2 Synchronization

In large corporations, data may need to be reported to several locations. If a company has several manufacturing facilities that are in different geographical locations, the data from these facilities may be reported to a central location in order for the data to be viewable and accessible on an enterprise-wide scale. Middleware is the component that is responsible for collecting the data from all for the disparate data sources and cataloging the data into a central data repository.

In the EPCglobal framework, the Global Data Synchronization Network (GDSN) provides synchronization between the source and recipient data pools. As data is changed, added, or removed from the source pools, the recipient pools are updated to ensure that the retailers have the most up-to-date information possible about the manufacturer's advertised products. A type of middleware performs this synchronization task.

9.1.3.3 Transformation

As data is routed from one component to another, it must be transformed to meet the data format requirements of the new component. The transformation can happen before the data is moved, in the middle by a third component, or by the receiving component itself. The data may be transformed into a completely new format or it may be filtered in some way.

Chapter 2 introduced the concept of Electronic Data Interchange (EDI), which is another form of middleware. EDI facilitates the transformation of data from one system's format to another. As discussed in Chapter 2, EDI is often used by different companies to share information.

9.1.3.4 Event Notification

Events are one of the core mechanisms used to drive a real-time system. In a computer, every click of a mouse button or key press fires an event. These events are caught by programs that wish to take action on these events. Middleware event notification is analogous to the previous example. In most cases, events are generated by the middleware based on its input, and any "listening" component can act on these events as necessary. Some events may be routed to a rules engine that is driven by the event notifications. Other events may be consumed directly.

In the case of an RFID system, a tag is read by a reader when it gets close enough to the reader's associated antenna. This action could occur at any time. The reader provides the data about the tag to the middleware, and the middleware fires the appropriate event, such as a "Tag Read" event. This event could be consumed by a security or logistics system. In the security system example, a tag being read by that reader may indicate that a product is being stolen. The security system would call security, start video surveillance, or lock the doors to the building. In the case of a logistics system, the tag could signify the arrival of a shipment. The arrival may cause an e-mail to be sent to the recipient informing him or her that a package has arrived. The events could be interpreted in many different ways depending on the RFID system's purpose.

It is important to note that the middleware that is generating the events does not need to have any special processing for a security system versus a logistics system. The middleware is only concerned with consuming the input and generating the appropriate events to the registered consumers. The consumers provide the business logic required to implement the appropriate solution.

9.1.3.5 *Standardized Interface*

A socket wrench is a great example of a type of middleware that exposes a standardized interface. Many times, middleware is also referred to as an *adapter*. The ratchet-to-bolt adapter allows the ratchet to be used to loosen or tighten any type of bolt, no matter the size, as long as the appropriate adapter is available. Most mechanics call this adapter a *socket*. In the ratchet example shown in Figure 9-5, every adapter has the same interface. This interface is the square hole on the top of the adapter. The ratchet can be attached to any adapter if the interface socket is of the correct dimensions.

Middleware adapters, analogous to the socket wrench example, are found throughout RFID software development. One of the most common adapter interfaces is the interface that allows an application to read data from many different readers even though they are all made by different manufacturers and may all have different interfaces themselves. The application developers do not need to worry about writing specialized code to read from each of the readers because the middleware will handle that. The application developers need only to write code to interface with the middleware. The middleware reduces the work that must be performed by the application developers from building multiple interfaces to just one. The standardized interface of the adapter allows one application, the ratchet, to interface with many different types of RFID readers, the bolts.

The interface can be viewed as working both ways. Once the interface becomes a standard, many applications may want to support that one interface because it is used in many RFID implementations. For example, businesses that host their information technology environment on the IBM WebSphere® environment will most likely install IBM's WebSphere RFID Device Infrastructure™ (WRDI) when they decide to venture into the RFID world. It could be a smart decision for those companies developing RFID applications to support the WRDI interface. If a company is looking for an RFID application, it will most likely choose an application that can be easily plugged into their existing environment.

Figure 9-5 Socket and ratchet interface.

9.1.3.6 Security

Potential security holes are created when another layer of software or hardware is introduced into a system. It is important that middleware components provide security mechanisms just as any application or database would be expected to implement. Hackers will always target the weakest link, and many times, it is found in the middleware. The user interface for the application is usually guarded with at least username and password validation, but insecure middleware components may not require any type of authentication or authorization before allowing other programs to interface with them. It is important to recognize that a user of a system is not limited to a human being, but a user can also be another component, software or hardware that uses the system. A capable hacker can develop software that interfaces with an unsecured middleware layer and thus completely bypass the security found at the front of the system. It is important to recognize that not all types of middleware require security because some are already protected by their environment. Those types of middleware that provide an open interface should implement some level of security.

Middleware developers should require credentials before allowing other applications to interface with them if they expose data that should be secured. These credentials can be passed with each access of the middleware, or the middleware can validate the credentials when it is first accessed by the application. The latter option sets up a secured session key that must be passed with each subsequent call to the middleware. The session key becomes the credential used to validate the user of the middleware.

Not only does the user have to be validated, but the data that is sent between the user and the middleware should be secured as well. A hacker may be able to capture the data as it is transferred between the two parties if it is not encrypted. There are several standards for securing the data. Some of the most commonly used mechanisms are IPSec (Internet Protocol Security) and various implementations of public key infrastructures (PKIs). Both of these methods ensure that no one can perform a "man in the middle" attack in which data is covertly captured. IPSec secures the data at the Internet Protocol layer of the communication stack of the Open Standards Interconnect (OSI) model. This ensures that no one can access the data as it is transmitted across a public or private network. Chapter 4 discusses the different layers of the OSI model in more detail. PKI allows the various components in a system to share encrypted data by enabling the exchange of encryption keys. PKI uses asymmetric encryption algorithms to share keys and encrypt data. Asymmetric cryptography is beyond the scope of this book, but it is a fundamental component in secure communications found in most computer systems. In fact, asymmetric cryptography is used when Web browsers transfer information such as credit card numbers across the Internet.

Some middleware solutions have been created to handle all of the security needs of an enterprise and provide solutions to many of the problems mentioned above. Security-type middleware allows applications and other middleware components to authenticate and authorize users, store encryption keys, and perform other various security related tasks. Developers who are building enterprise-scale RFID solutions will have to interface often with this type of middleware.

Many security models today are built on top of a technology called Lightweight Directory Access Protocol (LDAP). LDAP was originally designed as a lookup protocol to easily access resources such as printers, files, computers, or any other type of resource. A user profile is a type of resource that may be accessed via LDAP. The user profile can contain user authentication credentials and a list of programs that the user is able to access. Many security middleware providers interface with LDAP and other various security models.

9.1.4 Database Systems as Middleware

Most database systems provide data management services that perform some of the same functions as traditional middleware. These services include stored procedures, notification services, reporting services, and task management. Accomplished database administrators and developers can take full advantage of these existing services to provide much of the functionality offered by a middleware component, such as a standardized interface, security, event notification, transformation, and routing.

9.1.4.1 Stored Procedures

Database stored procedures allow developers to add custom code to their databases. This code can perform basic to advanced database queries. Some databases allow software developers to run customized code outside of the database. One example is Microsoft SQL Server 2005. SQL Server 2005 can run traditional stored procedures written in the T-SQL scripting language or execute .NET code written in any .NET-compatible language.

Stored procedures can be used to provide a standardized interface for manipulating data, and many times stored procedures execute faster than performing the same transactions using standard SQL text queries. Stored procedures are somewhat different from the DAL discussed earlier in that the abstraction is handled directly by the database and the procedures are limited by the scripting language and interfaces offered by the database. A database abstraction layer is much more flexible and customizable than a stored procedure. Remember that not all databases offer stored procedures, and the scripting language used to write a stored procedure may not be portable to another database.

9.1.4.2 Notification Services

Notification services are analogous to the event notification functionality offered by many middleware implementations. The notification services are usually configured and managed directly through the database. These services use standard interfaces to notify the consumers of the service that an event has occurred. These interfaces include queues, Web services, stored procedures, and many others. Most databases allow for custom modules to be plugged into the notification services framework. These modules may implement business logic or simply pass the information on to another system. It is up to the developer of the plug-in as to what the notification does.

9.1.5 System Management

As with any other enterprise-ready system, RFID systems must be manageable. RFID installations can include several physical locations, spread across hundreds or even thousands of miles. Each location may have tens of readers, with each reader reporting thousands of tags a day. There are hardware and software layers to this infrastructure that must be managed and data that must be stored and archived. It would not be very cost-effective if software updates were installed manually on each reader or server in the system, or if errors were not reported to a central location so that they could be recognized and resolved immediately. The larger the RFID implementation, the more a complete management system is needed.

Many middleware development companies have built performance-monitoring, error-reporting, and software deployment frameworks. These components, when integrated into an RFID system, provide another level of assurance to the availability and maintenance of the RFID system. System management middleware is sometimes overlooked in the evaluation of an RFID system because the value of a solid system management middleware is not realized until the system has problems. Many sales demos gloss over the real-world implications of administering and managing an enterprise-wide RFID system.

9.1.5.1 Centralized Management

An agile RFID system should be controllable from a central location. This location is called the *management console* or *management dashboard*. Robust systems allow the system administrator to do the following:

- Change system configuration settings.
- Deploy software updates or fixes to hardware and servers on the network.
- Review error logs and system performance metrics.
- Administer system security for users, hardware, and middleware components.

It is important to note that not all of the items listed may be part of one all-encompassing program. Each item could be implemented in separate programs, but the data controlled and presented by these components should all roll up to one point of control such as a system administration hub. In most large corporations, not all of these components are administered by one person. It would most likely be the responsibility of an entire information technology support group.

9.1.5.2 Error Detection

RFID middleware should be able to report errors in an effective way. If errors disappear once they happen, troubleshooting a problematic system could be much harder than it needs to be. One of the key components to centralized management discussed in the previous section was the ability to review error logs and performance metrics. When an error occurs at one of the farthest edge devices, it must be reported to the management console so that it can be identified and resolved. Depending on how large the organization is, this error may notify local administrators as well as corporate administrators. Many systems have the ability to send out notifications, such as e-mails, to system administrators if a certain type or level of error occurs in the system. An error is only useful if it contains the following pieces of information:

- What was the error?
- Where did it occur (what device, software module, physical location)?
- What was the state of the system when the error occurred?

Provided with the answers to these questions, a system administrator will have the data and tools required to resolve the problem correctly and efficiently.

Performance metrics allow administrator to predict problems before they occur. For example, if the load on the processing servers has been steadily increasing over the past three months because the business is making and selling more products, the administrator of the system can predict when more processing power is needed. The IT group may add another server into the cluster of data-processing servers, or the existing server may require an upgrade to its processor, memory, or storage capabilities. These types of predictive metrics help ensure the level of system availability required by the business.

9.2 Business Process Integration

Business process integration (BPI) is a huge topic on its own. There are several schools of thought on the proper way to implement BPI, as well as many companies with solutions to help facilitate it. With this large array of possibilities comes a new vocabulary with new acronyms and jargon. BPI is almost self-defining. It is the way in which a business integrates its business processes with its supporting technologies. In the case of this book, BPI is discussed in terms of how a business integrates an RFID system with its business processes.

Business models and process are different from industry to industry, so this section will not target any one industry. It will, however, address why BPI is important and the generalized framework and software necessary to integrate an RFID system into any business process. BPI builds a great deal on top the middleware components discussed in the previous section.

9.2.1 Frameworks

Many companies like SAP, IBM, Microsoft, and PeopleSoft, to name a few, provide "out of the box" frameworks for standard BPI needs. These frameworks provide standardized methods that include the following:

- Data collection
- Definition of business rules
- Integration with other business processes
- Integration with other businesses

In 99.99 percent of all BPI framework installations, the framework must be customized to the company's network layout, business processes, and overall business model. BPI frameworks provide hooks into which custom modules can be added to meet the company's specific needs. Most large companies must provide extensive customization to these frameworks to satisfy their business requirements and to accurately reflect their company's business model. Following are some of the most common frameworks:

- Enterprise resource planning (ERP)
- Business information warehouse (BIW)
- Customer relationship management (CRM)
- Human resources management system (HRMS)
- Product life cycle management (PLM)
- Supply chain management (SCM)

Each of these frameworks provide BPI for a specific business need. In the case of RFID, supply chain management is the most directly applicable framework, although RFID can be used to enhance many of the other frameworks listed as well. Today, most BPI framework companies provide RFID modules that plug into their core frameworks. It is important to understand that the RFID modules are not magic. They do not provide everything required for a business to make use of an RFID system. The RFID modules require configuration and customization in order to be useful to the business. Figure 9-6 depicts a basic RFID architecture which utilizes the BPI layer.

9.2.2 Data Collection

It has already been stated numerous times in this book that an RFID system's primary purpose is to collect data about real-world objects. Until the data is collected, the business has nothing on which to base any of its decisions. The data input can originate from many different sources such as being keyed in by an employee, manual barcode scans, or electronic data from another computer system.

A key function of BPI is to store the data input in a repository that models how the business works. The layout of an RFID system data model and example business models will be covered in more detail later in this chapter. Most BPI frameworks provide a data abstraction layer through which the underlying technology can access the BPI data model.

9.2.3 Definition of Business Rules

Most BPI frameworks allow the business to customize how the system performs as data is collected from the underlying technology. The customization of the base BPI framework allows a real-world application to be built. For example, if a BPI framework is analyzing data collected from employee time cards, a business rule may be set up that automatically changes the employee work schedule when an employee is approaching the maximum approved number of work hours. The business rules are part of the middleware discussed earlier called the rules engine. The rules engine is responsible for applying the business's rules to the collected data. These rules allow the business to customize the BPI framework to perform based on the business's processes and requirements.

In the previous example there were two main components to the business rule. The first component of the business rule is the condition(s) that must be met in order for the rule to be applied. The second part is the action

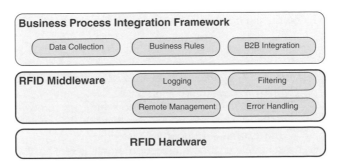

Figure 9-6 Basic BPI architecture.

that should be taken when this condition is met. Table 9-1 shows an example business rule broken into its two components.

Standard actions like sending e-mails are usually built into the basic BPI framework, but modifying the employee work schedules is a bit more complex. Most likely, a custom module was developed and referenced by the business rule, and the module was built so that it understood how to interface with the business's employee time-tracking system.

Not only do business rules interface with custom modules or send e-mails, but they may also send very simple messages called *events* when a condition is met. Events are usually not as complex as the tasks performed by the custom modules. Events simply notify another system of a change. Sometimes these events carry contextual information about the event, but they can also be very simple.

Other systems that are listening for these events can respond in any way necessary. For instance, if an employee is no longer affiliated with a company, the company's HRMS may fire an event notifying all other systems that the employee has been deleted from its system. These other systems may perform tasks such as deleting the employee's e-mail account or disabling his or her computer login credentials. Events tend to be asynchronous and provide a less tightly coupled mechanism for communication than other types of notification methods. In most systems, components register with each other, requesting notification of specific events. When the event occurs, only those registered are notified.

9.2.4 Data-Processing Models

There are three basic processing models that BPI frameworks use to govern when data is processed and actions are taken based on the data. Legacy systems tend to operate using the *batch processing model*. All collected data is processed on a regular schedule. This type of processing is regularly implemented by mainframe systems. Events are not generated until the data is processed, and business-to-business communication happens during the batch processing. The advantage of batch data processing is realized in the vast amounts of data that can be processed. When data is transferred to another system or business, the data is usually sent in one monolithic file or a group of files. These files are then processed by the receiving sys-

Table 9-1 Example Business Rule Components

Condition 1	Employee is an hourly employee.
Condition 2	Employee has worked 32 or more hours in three work days.
Action 1	Employee work schedule is modified so that the employee does not exceed a 40-hour workweek.
Action 2	A schedule change notification e-mail is sent to the employee's manager and the employee.

tem. These files may contain event notifications, data synchronization information, remote task invocation, or any other type of message.

The second type of processing model is the *buffered model*. This model is different from the batch model in that it executes based on the amount of data collected, not based on a schedule. The harvested data is stored until a certain high-water mark is reached. A standard data processing term related to buffering data, a *high-water mark* is the amount of data that is to be collected before it is processed. When this condition is met, data is processed, events are fired, and any communication with other businesses or processes is performed.

The final type is *real-time data processing*, also called online processing in the mainframe environment. In this model, the data is processed as it is collected, events are fired, and tasks are executed as business rule conditions are met. Communications between systems and businesses are brief, and the data transferred in the communication references only one operation—in contrast to batch data transfers, where a transfer may include millions of operations.

The ultimate goal of RFID systems is true real-time data processing and notification. Today, most systems operate based on the buffered model and in some special cases offer real time notification. Most business-to-business communication still occurs in batch mode, and it usually occurs during a relatively nonbusy period, like in the middle of the night. Keep in mind that the definition of real time is dependent on the environment. An operation is said to be real time if it is guaranteed to execute within a defined time period. This time period can be defined as one nanosecond or one week. If the requirements of the system are to process the RFID data once a day, then the system could be classified as a real-time system. Most RFID users expect that an RFID system that is labeled as real time must provide an almost instantaneous notification to users and other processes of an RFID tag's change in location. Real time is very subjective and is based on the processing model and the requirements of the system. As of the writing of this book the American National Standards Institute (ANSI) is developing a formal definition for real-time as it applies to RFID. ANSI is expected to define time restrictions of less than one minute that an RFID system must meet for it to be considered ANSI RFID real-time compliant. What really matters when evaluating an RFID system is that it processes the data within the time period defined by the business.

The leading BPI framework companies have been developing batch systems for decades, mostly targeted at mainframes. Transitioning from batch to real time is not an easy task. The core architecture of a batch framework is much different than a real-time framework, and the software development process for a distributed environment is also different. Despite the core architectural changes that had to be made, many of these companies now provide pseudo real-time systems that meet the needs of almost any business.

9.2.5 Business-to-Business Integration

As discussed in Chapter 2 Electronic Data Interchange is at the heart of how businesses exchange data and interact with each other. Business-to-business (B2B) communication is also one of the key facets of a BPI framework. The events and tasks described in the previous sections are not restricted to the confines of one computer, one network, or even one business. These methods of communication can span any number of organizations. For more details on how businesses share data, refer to Section 2.3. Note that the BPI framework governs when, how, and what data is communicated between businesses.

9.3 Information Layer

9.3.1 Storage

As data is collected from the RFID system, it is stored in some form of nonvolatile media. In most cases, the storage medium is a hard disk or array of hard disks. Organization and layout of data on the storage medium is very important when system performance and availability is a requirement. The organization of the data can be examined from both the hardware and software viewpoint. There are several hardware and software solutions to this problem depending on the targeted environment.

9.3.1.1 RAID

RAID is a hardware-based technology used to ensure data access performance and integrity. RAID stands for redundant array of independent (originally inexpensive) disks. The purpose of RAID is to spread information across multiple disks so that data is not lost should one of the disk drives fail and also to ensure that data is not corrupted. RAID is implemented by a piece of controller hardware found in a computer. The controller can be integrated into the motherboard or can be added as a daughterboard. A daughterboard extends the functionality of the motherboard through a standardized hardware interface. RAID controller cards are daughterboards that are not commonly found on the average personal computer, but they are found in workstations and servers.

There are eight levels of RAID and various combinations of the levels. Not all of the levels are not covered in detail in this book. Some of the RAID levels are not commercially viable because of their cost. The most commonly implemented levels are 0, 1, 5, and 0+1 (see Table 9-2). RAID level 0+1 is very expensive, as it is a combination of level 0 and 1, but it provides both data redundancy and performance gains.

The various RAID levels offer differing levels of data access speed, integrity, redundancy, and recovery. All or combinations of these attributes can be achieved depending on the RAID level(s) chosen. If enhanced data

Table 9-2 RAID Levels

Level	Data Parity	Data Redundancy	Increased Performance	Number of Drives
0	No	Striped	Yes	2+
1	Same disk	Mirrored	No	2+
5	Distributed	Striped	Yes	3+
0+1	No	Mirrored and striped	Yes	4+

integrity is one of the storage requirements, then a RAID level that supports data parity should be chosen. Parity is a mechanism used to check that data has not been corrupted or changed inadvertently. The parity information can be stored on an individual disk or spread across several disks. RAID levels that offer data mirroring or striping enhance data access speeds. Data mirroring simply creates copies of data across multiple drives, while data striping divides information across multiple drives such that each drive has part but not all of the data. Mirroring and striping techniques enhance data access because there are multiple drives that can access the data. If one drive is busy reading data, another drive that contains the same data can be accessed. Mirrored RAID levels increase the amount of time it takes to write data because multiple hard disks must be touched when data is written.

The RAID controller is responsible for ensuring that all disks contain up-to-date information when mirroring is used. The RAID controller interfaces with the hard drive controllers to act as a traffic cop as requests for reads, writes, and updates are executed. The RAID controller also makes the array of disk drives appear as one to the system. The fastest RAID systems pair one hard drive controller with each hard drive. This type of dedicated control is expensive but may sometimes be necessary to meet the system requirements. A RAID-type configuration is not always required. Sometimes periodic, software-initiated data backups are all that is required by the application. As mentioned previously, RAID can be very expensive, and the benefits must be weighed against the costs. For mission-critical systems, RAID is always a requirement.

9.3.1.2 Database Storage Configuration

Databases add another level of configuration and capabilities into the design of a storage architecture. Databases are usually composed of two types of files: data files and transaction log files. These files should never be stored on the same hard disk. The transaction log files allow the database to be re-created should the data file become corrupt or the hard disk fail. Specifying the location of these files is a standard database configuration option.

In addition to separating the data and log files across multiple hard disks, databases allow database tables to also be separated across multiple hard disks. The data model chosen should dictate how the tables are divided across the hard disks. All of the tables can reside on one disk if performance is not a factor. Tables that are accessed frequently are good candidates for being placed on separate disks.

9.3.2 Data Model

The data model is the heart and soul of an RFID system, as it is with most solutions. No matter how complex an RFID system becomes, there is a commonality that is shared across all implementations. This section presents a basic RFID data model that could serve as a starting point for any RFID information layer. The following examples define the relational database schema required to model a basic RFID system. In the following section, database tables are defined that represent key RFID data components. The definitions of these tables utilize basic relational database design concepts, and example queries utilize the Structured Query Language (SQL). An understanding of these concepts is beneficial but is not required.

For those readers who are not familiar with database design, there are a few things to keep in mind when reading through the rest of this section. Some of the example tables, like Table 9-3, present a database table's schema. Their layout may seem a bit confusing at first because of the way in which a database table's schema is represented in a printed table. Please keep in mind that the example schema is defining the columns of the database table. The rows in the printed schema represent columns in the table being designed. Table 9-4 is an example of the data found in a table in the database. Table 9-3 is the definition that determines what data can be inserted into the rows of Table 9-4. This method is followed throughout this section. First, the database table's schema is presented and then an example of the data in the table is presented.

A good place to start when designing the data model for an RFID system is with the RFID tag (see Table 9-3). The most fundamental attribute of a tag is its unique identification number (*TagID*). The *TagID* can be an EPC-compliant number or any other unique numbering system. For this example, the number is simply a 50-character value that can be a number or a combination of numbers and characters.

The *ID* attribute is a standard column that is recognized by those that have experience with relational database design. The *ID* column provides a unique identifier for a row of information in the database. This is different

Table 9-3 Example Tag Table Schema

TABLE: Tag	
Name	**Type**
ID	GUID
TagID	nvarchar(50)
Enabled	bit

than the unique identifier for the tag. The *ID* value can be used by other tables in the database to reference this specific row of information, which provides a reference to a specific tag in the database. A data type GUID (globally unique identifier) is often used in databases as keys to provide links between data in different tables.

The final column is the *Enabled* column. There are situations when RFID tags' beacon information should be ignored. For example, if a tag happens to fall into a hole in the ground and cannot be retrieved, it is important that the lost tag not continue cluttering up the system with worthless data. In addition, batches of tags may be loaded into the system before they are associated with an asset. These tags are not being used; therefore, they should not clutter up the system with useless information. The bit data type is a Boolean value that can represent true or false. The value is set to true when the tag is enabled or false otherwise. All of the enabled tags can be retrieved from the database with the simple SQL query found in Figure 9-7.

Database designers use a standard syntax for referencing unique fields in a database when describing a schema. The combination of the table name and the column name provide this unique reference. For example, *Tag.Enabled* is a reference to the *Enabled* column in the Tag table, shown in Table 9-3. If there was a table named *House* and it had a column named *Color*, it could be referenced by *House.Color*. This syntax will be used through the rest of this section. Table 9-4 shows sample data that may be found in the *Tag* table.

The next type of data found in an RFID system is the asset that is to be tracked. The asset is the real world object such as a chair or a bottle of pills. In some systems, the assets would be placed in categories that may be defined in another database table. The schema for the *Asset* table is defined in Table 9-5. The *ID* column is used in the same way as in the *Tag* schema. It is a key that uniquely identifies an asset row in the table.

The *AssetID* column may seem somewhat redundant when an asset has an RFID tag to identify it, but many times the asset has a secondary identifier such as a barcode or inventory control number. The *AssetID* holds this information and can be a key into a third-party database or system that does not understand RFID tags. Some solutions may take advantage of this column, while others may not. The *TagID* in the asset table is not the unique identifier of the RFID tag but is the key value used to reference a row in the *Tag* table described previously. Using the syntax defined earlier, this is a reference to *Tag.ID*. By setting *Asset.TagID* to the value of the *Tag.ID* field for a specific *Tag* row, the *Asset* row can be associated with a *Tag* row. This

```
SELECT * FROM Tag WHERE Enabled = 1
```

Figure 9-7 Enabled tag SQL query.

Table 9-4 Sample Tag Data

ID	TagID	Enabled
03B0AC5C-2CA1-4997-8882-A9584EBB1D4D	123456789	True
8A39F3D5-7F58-4de1-BCAE-946A0877EEA0	987654321	False
EFF14B06-E956-422e-B414-A8E287CFEBD3	567894123	True

is knows as a foreign key relationship. The *Description* column provides a short description of the asset, and the *Enabled* column serves the same purpose as it did for the *Tag* table.

In Table 9-6 the *TagID* column contains values found in the *Tag.ID* fields in the *Tag* table (Table 9-4). The last asset does not have any value in the *TagID* field. This means that no tag has been assigned to this asset.

The location of the asset is important to most RFID systems. A location can be a dock door, a floor of a hospital, or table in the corner of a lab. The schema of the *Location* table is described in Table 9-7. The location in this example is very basic. It only contains a unique identifier (*ID*) and a description (*Description*). The data found in Table 9-8 defines two unique locations. There may be hundreds of locations depending on the purpose of the system. For instance, real-time location systems may define a location for every room in a building.

To this point, all of the discrete data elements have been defined, but the system cannot really accomplish anything. The final type of table in this example enables the system to store useful data. Table 9-9 is the table that records the locations of the assets as they move through the system. This is the *History* table. It is important to note that the assets are being tracked and not the tags. An asset may have many tags associated with it throughout its lifetime; however, the asset is constant.

As shown in Table 9-9, the *History* table has three columns. The first is the *TimeStamp* column. It records the date and time of when an asset was at a location. The *AssetID* column references an asset defined in the *Asset* table by *Asset.ID*, and the *LocationID* column references a location defined in the *Location* table by *Location.ID*. The location of an asset at a specific

Table 9-5 Example Asset Table Schema

TABLE: Asset	
Name	**Type**
ID	GUID
AssetID	nvarchar(50)
TagID	GUID
Description	nvarchar(128)
Enabled	bit

Table 9-6 Example Asset Data

ID	AssetID	TagID	Description	Enabled
9E1A0E9C-2C8A-4d8e-910B-49D84BF89925	ABC123	03B0AC5C-2CA1-4997-8882-A9584EBB1D4D	Wheelchair	True
9860B8CB-2DE6-4fac-B7E8-4E71BFD55A61	123JEB	EFF14B06-E956-422e-B414-A8E287CFEBD3	Aspirin	True
6B610371-996D-498e-AB9F-E1FCF63E9374	SER2D-A		Laptop	False

Table 9-7 Example Location Table Schema

TABLE: Location	
Name	**Type**
ID	GUID
Description	nvarchar(50)

point in time can be determined when all three of these columns are populated. There may be thousands of entries in the *History* table for one asset. Table 9-10 is a small sample of data that may be found in the *History* table. Table 9-10 could contain millions of entries for millions of different assets. Table 9-10 provides information about the aspirin asset (highlighted), while all the other rows provide history for the wheelchair asset.

Together, the collection of entries for a particular asset provides the history for the asset. By using the relationships defined between the *Asset*, *Location*, and *History* tables, a simple SQL query can reveal when an asset changed location and where it went. The SQL query in Figure 9-8 joins all three tables and provides the assets history.

The query in Figure 9-8 retrieves information for the wheelchair defined in Table 9-6. The history for the wheelchair requested spans the entire year of 2005. The result set in Table 9-11 shows that the wheelchair was read at three different locations in 2005. In a real-world solution, an asset may move hundreds or thousands of times over the course of an entire year.

The data in the previous example was divided into four separate tables for a reason. All of the information could have been stored in one table, but each row would then require redundant information. Database designers break data into discrete tables to "normalize" the data model. Normalized data models are easier to maintain because of the reduction of the amount of redundant data in the database. Table 9-12 is an example of a nonnormalized table with redundant data. The *Enabled* column cannot be added to this model because there is no way to uniquely identify a tag as a whole. All that is stored here is history information, not system configuration information.

The previous example provides a basic understanding of the data required by a basic RFID system. Enterprise viable data models include many other tables such as asset categories, configuration information about the RFID readers, logging and event information, and much more.

Table 9-8 Example Location Data

ID	Description
35F05F8E-7E64-473c-8F79-5B449337EE06	Room 207
BA565749-0329-4882-8242-7C876884F203	Basement

Table 9-9 Example Asset History Table Schema

TABLE: History	
Name	**Type**
TimeStamp	datetime
AssetID	GUID
LocationID	GUID

9.3.3 Interface

The information layer must have an interface through which data can be read, added, deleted, and updated. The interface could be a traditional DAL, or it may be implemented as stored procedures in the database itself. Whatever the means, it is important to provide an interface that enforces certain business rules. The details of the database configuration and data model should be abstracted such that the developer does not need to know the details of how the database model is designed.

A software developer that is building an application on top of a data framework would rather have an interface that allowed them to ask questions about tags, assets, locations, and history than tables, rows, and columns. An example of a useful information layer interface would be one that defined a function to get the current location of an asset. The function defined in Table 9-13 shows the input and output parameters and sample values to retrieve the current location of an asset.

9.3.4 Reporting

Reporting on the data collected provides an overall view into the status of a system. Reporting enables trend analysis and provides the data required for identifying areas for process improvement. When data is stored in an open database, off-the-shelf products such as Crystal Reports® or Chart-FX™ can be used to generate almost any report required. In many cases, RFID systems are bundled with canned reports that are specific to logistics and supply chain management.

Some real-time location systems require data processing before a report can be generated. The data processing executes data smoothing and reporting algorithms that increase asset location reporting accuracy. These types of systems may also preprocess the data and place the processed data in a processed data table or in another database for third-party reporting components to digest.

Reports can be generated as needed. Some businesses may require anything from hourly reports up to yearly reports. The schedule is defined based on the business need, as well as the amount of time it takes to generate the report. If the report is very processing intensive to generate, it may only be run at a time when the server is not as active.

Table 9-10 Sample History Table Data

TimeStamp	AssetID	LocationID
12/8/2004 7:56 AM	9E1A0E9C-2C8A-4d8e-910B-49D84BF89925	35F05F8E-7E64-473c-8F79-5B449337EE06
5/16/2005 4:56 AM	9E1A0E9C-2C8A-4d8e-910B-49D84BF89925	BA565749-0329-4882-8242-7C876884F203
7/18/2005 5:12 PM	9E1A0E9C-2C8A-4d8e-910B-49D84BF89925	35F05F8E-7E64-473c-8F79-5B449337EE06
7/19/2005 9:00 AM	9860B8CB-2DE6-4fac-B7E8-4E71BFD55A61	35F05F8E-7E64-473c-8F79-5B449337EE06
8/25/2005 2:34 PM	9E1A0E9C-2C8A-4d8e-910B-49D84BF89925	BA565749-0329-4882-8242-7C876884F203
2/12/2006 2:34 PM	9E1A0E9C-2C8A-4d8e-910B-49D84BF89925	35F05F8E-7E64-473c-8F79-5B449337EE06
. . .	. . .	. . .

```
SELECT History.TimeStamp, Location.Description AS Location
    FROM History
    JOIN Location
       ON History.LocationID = Location.ID
    JOIN Asset
       ON History.AssetID = Asset.ID
    WHERE Asset.ID = `9E1A0E9C-2C8A-4d8e-910B-49D84BF89925' AND
       History.TimeStamp >= `1/1/2005 12:00 AM' AND
       History.TimeStamp < `1/1/2006 12:00 AM'
    ORDER BY History.TimeStamp ASC
```

Figure 9-8 History query for an asset.

9.3.5 Management

Long-running systems can become unstable as the amount of data they must manage increases. The information layer should be able to gracefully handle large amounts of data through archiving or purging. Archiving is the process by which relatively old data is copied to another storage site. The reduction in the amount of data in the primary storage site increases data access speeds. The archived data may be stored in an online or offline state depending on the needs of the system. Many systems archive old data to tape media. Access to online data that is archived to tape has a significantly slower data access rate because the tape is a sequential data access device. If the archived data will be accessed on a fairly regular basis, archiving to another table in the database would be preferable.

Data should be purged from the system only when it is absolutely necessary. Today, raw memory storage space is very economical for both disk and tape media. Businesses should define a set of requirements that data must meet in order to be purged.

9.3.6 Security

Security is an important part of every layer. The information layer is no different. All commercial databases today implement a robust security model. There are three different levels to the model. The first layer controls who can access the data. When a user logs into a database, a username and password must be sent. Some databases can use integrated security so

Table 9-11 History for Wheel Chair Asset

TimeStamp	Location
5/16/2005 4:56 AM	Basement
7/18/2005 5:12 PM	Room 207
8/25/2005 2:34 PM	Basement

Table 9-12 Nonnormalized Sample Data

TimeStamp	AssetID	Asset Description	Tag ID	Location Description
12/8/2004 7:56 AM	ABC123	Wheel Chair	123456789	Room 207
5/16/2005 4:56 AM	ABC123	Wheel Chair	123456789	Basement
7/18/2005 5:12 PM	ABC123	Wheel Chair	123456789	Room 207
7/19/2005 9:00 AM	123JEB	Aspirin	567894123	Room 207
8/25/2005 2:34 PM	ABC123	Wheel Chair	123456789	Basement
2/12/2006 2:34 PM	ABC123	Wheel Chair	123456789	Room 207
. . .	. . .			. . .

that the operating system simply passes the user's credentials behind the scene. Next, it is important that data is transmitted securely. In the case of a database connection, it is most often the job of the network and middleware to secure the data as it is communicated. Last, each user may have specific operations that he or she can perform on the database. Some users may be able to only read data, and others may be able also to write and delete data. The database management system will allow the administrator to control these permissions.

9.4 Summary

Building a system that can scale to an enterprise level, provide high system availability and be flexible enough to adapt to new business needs is not an easy task. Each level of the network, hardware, and software stack is crucial, and the interfaces between these layers are no less important. A layered middleware with well-defined communication interfaces provide scalability and flexibility. Today's architects advocate that interfaces between layers should be loosely coupled to remove hard dependencies between each layer.

Reliable system management tools and hooks into the system ensure that the system is available and healthy, and a well-architected network topography ensures data integrity and network reliability. Knowing when the

Table 9-13 Input/Output for Asset Location Function

Get Asset Location	Parameter	Value
INPUT	Asset ID	ABC123
OUTPUT	Time Stamp	2/12/2006 2:34 PM
	Location	Room 207

system is experiencing difficulties and getting clues as to why the system is having problems are both necessary to create a system that is readily managed. System management employees have learned that a system that cannot report that it has a problem and why it has a problem is not worth installing because of all the headaches they and the business will endure. Last but not least, all of these layers must conform to the security requirements of the business.

Acronyms

AIM—America Online Instant Messenger

API—Application programming interface

BIW—Business information warehouse

BPI—Business Process Integration

BRML—Business Rules Markup Language

CRM—Customer relationship management

DAL—Data abstraction layer

ERP—Enterprise resource planning

HAL—Hardware abstraction layer

HRMS—Human resources management system

IPSec—Internet Protocol Security

IRC—Internet Relay Chat

LDAP—Lightweight Directory Access Protocol

NNTP—Network News Transfer Protocol

OSI—Open systems interconnection

PKI—Public key infrastructure

PLM—Product lifecycle management

RAM—Random access memory

RuleML—Rule Markup Language

SCM—Supply chain management

SQL—Structured Query Language

T-SQL—Transact Structured Query Language

WRDI—WebSphere RFID Device Infrastructure

10

The Issues of Security and Privacy

The issues of security and privacy, although interrelated, are different. With respect to RFID, we define these issues as follows:

- *Security.* The ability of the RFID system to keep the *information* transmitted between the tag and the reader secure from non-intended recipients. For instance, assume that a third party intercepted a message between tag *T101* and reader *RA*. Assume also that the third party could determine that the message was *"123F4D9C1B."* However, the intercepting party had no way of determining what this code meant. This we would consider a breach of security.
- *Privacy.* The ability of the RFID system to keep the *meaning* of the information transmitted between the tag and the reader secure from unintended recipients. For instance, assume that a third party intercepted a message between tag *T102* and reader *RB* where tag *T102* was affixed to an article purchased by *Bob*. Furthermore, the third party could also determine that the message was *"123F4D9C1B."* and it meant *"Item: Prescription Drug | Brand: PharCo | Drug:Cancergone | Lot:3425B123 | ProdDate:01/15/200."'* In this case, the intercepting party would know that *Bob* just purchased a drug to treat cancer. This we would consider a breach of privacy.

It is very important to understand this distinction because the issues created from each have very different repercussions and solutions. In a given environment, an RFID solution may pose security risks without affecting the issue of privacy. An example of this scenario is where a tag broadcasts its unique identification number in a consistent and unencrypted manner. This opens the tag to be read by any reader that can decode the RF signal. If all that is read is the tag's unique identifier, no association can be made to what that identification means without having access to the backend database system that maintains the relationship between the tag IDs and the objects they represent. However, issues of *traceability* and *inventorying* may remain.

We will use the term *information safekeeping* to signify the combined issues of security, privacy, traceability, and inventorying (See Figure 10-1.) This is necessary because, although these issues are interrelated, there are times when they are discussed in their entirety. is a pictorial representation of which components of the RFID infrastructure are related to the security and privacy aspects.

The purpose of this chapter is to create an awareness of the issues of security and privacy that surround RFID implementations and distinguish what is fact and what is myth. Also discussed are proposed guidelines and technologies for alleviating the problems that exist or may exist.

10.1 Privacy-Related Traceability and Inventorying

Traceability and inventorying are issues that relate to the ability of an unauthorized entity reading the identifiers sent by RFID tags without necessarily being concerned about the item to which the tag is affixed or who/what is carrying it. In other words, by just capturing the signals emitted by an RFID tag, a third party could trace where the tag is or has been (traceability) as well as to what tags have been detected (inventorying).

Two examples are used to explain these issues:

- *Traceability.* Imagine that a consumer, Mary, buys three items from a store that has attached passive RFID tags to all its merchandise. These items include a pair of boots, a blouse, and a purse. As Mary leaves

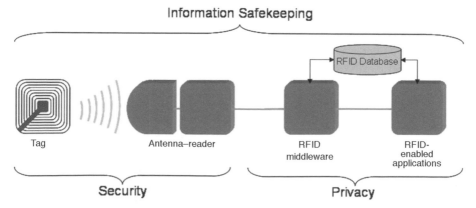

Figure 10-1 Information safekeeping, security, and privacy.

the store with her purchase, the tags can be scanned by anyone having the appropriate RFID reader. Even if the signal being transmitted by the tag and reader is encrypted, the signal is unique and repeatable. This means that as long as the spying reader can pick up the same signal, it knows that it is following Mary. Furthermore, assume that Mary returns to the store a month later. This time however, she is wearing the boots she had bought a month earlier. By picking up the signal from the boots, the store can determine that Mary has come back and may decide to alert a salesperson to invite Mary to see items similar to what she had bought previously. Many people would feel that their privacy had been invaded by this act.

• *Inventorying.* Using our same protagonist, Mary, and assuming that the tags used by the store were EPC tags, a spying reader could determine what items Mary had bought at the store. Perhaps this is not too disconcerting, but the level of concern would be justifiably much higher if the items she bought were medicines associated with a psychological condition. This information could be used by, say, her employer to question the sanity of Mary.

Considering the EPC standard, it is possible to see why these issues are potentially dangerous. A standard EPC tag conveys information associated with a particular item, its model or product class, and its manufacturer. Anyone with a standard EPC reader could get close enough to a shopper leaving a store to determine what products and what quantities were purchased. Furthermore, the unauthorized reader could track the shopper from a distance utilizing a high-power reader.

In a corporate or industrial setting, RFID tag data could be used for espionage. Imagine a situation where an unscrupulous corporation, Corp Spy, sets up a long-distance reader near a competitor's store, Corp Store. By reading the EPC tags that are shipped into Corp Store, Corp Spy could gain information as to what and when inventory is being delivered, thus gaining confidential information about the sales activities of Corp Store. The reason why Corp Spy would be interested in reading what is being delivered to Corp Store as opposed to what is being purchased and thereby removed from the store by the consumers is that Corp Store may choose to kill the RFID tag upon purchasing, thus rendering the tag inactive.

10.2 Issues That Have Been Raised

RFID, as it has been shown in this book, is a great technology component for object tracking. In this case, we can define an object as a physical asset that occupies three-dimensional space. This means that the whereabouts of any physical object (including animals and humans) can potentially be tracked within the scope of the RFID infrastructure. As RFID technology development progresses, this scope can become larger and larger, where eventually it can conceivably be any location on or above the planet (land, sea, or air).

This fact has raised many questions and concerns from people because of the potential invasion of privacy that can be attributed to RFID technology. But before we get deeper into the privacy issues and their repercussions, let's look at a few examples of what privacy advocates and the concerned public claim can go wrong with the use of RFID technology.

10.2.1 Tracking Consumers by the Products They Buy

Consumer and privacy advocates have closely followed the deployment of RFID-enabled solutions in the supply chains of major retailers such as Wal-Mart, Tesco, Target, and others. They contend that by using the same technology adopted by the retailers to track individual items through their supply chains, consumers could potentially be tracked after buying the merchandise and leaving the retail stores. Advocates contend that if a third party could associate the RFID tags of the products purchased by a consumer with the identity of the consumer, the third party could gather potentially harmful information related to the whereabouts of the consumer. This invades the right to privacy of the consumer.

10.2.2 Tracking Travelers by the Passports They Carry

The U.S. government has made a decision to implement RFID chips in U.S. citizen's passports. These chips will contain the passport holder's information as well as a digitized picture of the passport holder. Initially, the U.S. Department of State's proposal did not include any security protocols. The information would be contained unencrypted within the passport's RFID chip. Therefore, anyone with the right reader technology could potentially scan a traveler's passport, perhaps while still in the traveler's possession, and obtain all the personal information transmitted by the passport. This, it is argued, could help terrorists, thieves, or others to determine the traveler's identity, nationality, and even the digitized picture of the traveler.

After much negative feedback from the public and different organizations, the Department of State changed its proposal and added three layers of security:

1. *Encryption.* The information would be encrypted in the RFID chip.
2. *Access control.* The key to decrypt the data would be encoded in the passport and could only be obtained by scanning the passport with an optical reader. The RFID reader would then decrypt the information using that key.
3. The passport covers would contain a metallic mesh that would create a Faraday cage, essentially rendering unreadable the RFID chip when the passport covers were closed.

Security experts still raise a debatable issue relating to the fact that the chip's unique identifier can be read by any reader, since this falls below the layer of protection provided by the encryption methodology. This would create an issue of passport traceability; anyone carrying *that* passport could be tracked.

10.2.3 Tracking Readers by the Library Books They Check Out

Many libraries, primarily in Europe, have started to implement RFID technology in their operation. In the most advanced scenario, the idea is to tag every book in the library with an RFID chip and allow patrons to "automatically" check out the books by means of carrying an RFID tag and making the proper association of books-to-patron as the patrons walk out though the checkout portal. Privacy groups contend that patrons' right of privacy could be violated by someone with the proper technology within close proximity of the patrons. This would allow the malicious person to determine what books have been checked out by the patron.

10.2.4 The Conspiracy Theory

The most aggressive privacy concern groups claim that governments could potentially require access to all commercially controlled RFID databases and therefore have full access to the consumer, travel, and general habits of its population. It is claimed that governments would achieve this by deploying wide area RFID infrastructures where all the activities of its citizens could be tracked, from what they buy to what they read to where they travel to what they watch on videos, and so forth.

10.3 Security

Initially, commercial applications of RFID did not emphasize security. RFID readers and tags communicated with each other using open, unencrypted messages. In fact, even today, most RFID readers and tags just merely transmit information without any encryption.

There are a few reasons why this has been the case so far:

- Use of RFID has been somewhat limited to specialized applications.
- Even today, and for the foreseeable future, major implementations of RFID will be around the supply chain. In fact, the major applications being considered by the big retailers and the U.S. DoD have revolved around their supply chains.
- RFID tags, in the quest for being as inexpensive as possible, have been designed with very limited processing power, thus making it very difficult to implement encryption algorithms or randomized transmission circuitry inside the tags.

- Most of the current implementations still remain at the case and pallet level, not at the individual item level.
- RFID infrastructure is expensive and hard to implement. An implementation covers a very limited perimeter and thus provide a natural deterrent for widely deployable spying activities.

Considering what has been written so far in this chapter, the impression from these statements is that RFID tags are insecure, outdated, and not up to the task. There has been a huge boom in the expected number of applications and areas of spread where RFID will play a major role. Furthermore, it seems more likely that RFID tagging of items and people will become ubiquitous sooner rather than later.

However, the fundamental issue is that in order to create a widespread marketplace for RFID, the cost of its infrastructure (tags and readers) must be kept to a minimum. This fact, on the other hand, limits the amount or complexity that can be put in the tag, thus limiting its capability to process information such as sophisticated encryption algorithms or randomized transmission circuitry. So the dilemma of how to create a *secure* RFID infrastructure remains an elusive hot spot.

For this discussion it is important to remember that for the purposes of this book, *security* deals with the ability to ensure that communication between the tag and the intended recipient is not read and understood by unintended third parties.

As RFID systems become more common, spanning industrial and commercial applications, there will be a need for these systems to guard against security threats that enable the interception and manipulation of the information transmitted between the tags and the readers.

10.3.1 RFID Security Threats

High-security RFID systems should have the ability to guard against the following categorized security and privacy threats:

- *Eavesdropping*. RFID tags are designed to transmit stored information to an inquiring reader. This allows unauthorized users to scan tags stealthily. People can also collect RFID data by eavesdropping on the wireless RFID channel. The unrestricted access to tag data might reveal private information such as personal credit record.
- *Spoofing*. If the security protocol used in the RFID channel is revealed, attackers can write blank RFID tags with the same formatted data that has been collected. For instance, dishonest persons could replace the RFID tag on an item to get a cheaper price when checking out from a supermarket.
- *Relay attack* (also known as *cloning*). Relay devices can intercept and retransmit RFID queries. With this kind of device, offenders can abuse various RFID applications by replaying the data in order to imitate a

genuine data carrier. For example, on an automatic toll payment road, an attacker can record an encrypted code when a car's license plate is being scanned and replay it later to avoid paying the charge.

Many proposals have been put forth that aim to create a secure RFID environment. Some of these rely on encryption algorithms, some on cleverly designed communications schemes, and others on taking advantage of the basic physical properties of RFID communication. The following is a list of some of the proposals:

- Faraday cages
- Limited range transmission
- Kill command
- Sleep command
- Encryption
- Blocking

We will now provide a brief description on each one of these techniques.

10.3.2 Faraday Cages

This is a relatively low-tech approach to the issue of RFID security is a relatively low-tech as described in this chapter. Faraday cages (or meshes, as they are also known) are based on the principle that containers made of certain metals and in a specific physical configuration provide a natural barrier to radio waves. It is the same principle that creates one of the challenges for the application of RFID. While extremely effective, this solution requires a conscious, manual action in which the user must cover and uncover the tag every time he or she wants the tag to function. Also, it makes the user aware of the tag as well as of its placement on the item. Furthermore, this method does not offer any protection when the tag is not within the Faraday mesh.

There are, however, a few limited applications where a Faraday mesh may make sense. The use of a Faraday mesh cover on a passport, discussed in Section 10.2.2, is one that probably works well for most users, since passports are usually only open when they need to be presented. This Faraday mesh, combined with the fact that the information in the passport's RFID chip is encrypted with a key that can only be obtained by optically scanning the inside of the passport, offers some protection.

10.3.3 Limited-Range Transmissions

This method relies on the attenuation of the RF signal so that it can only travel a few centimeters. The assumption is that an unintended reader would have to be in close proximity to the tag and therefore probably easily identifiable. Actually, this is a very weak method for security protection. Imagine a person, Pierre, carrying some articles with limited-range transmission RFID tags at rush hour in the Paris subway. It is probably next to impossible for Pierre to avoid potentially malicious persons with pocket readers getting very close to him. Even if Pierre could somehow create a "circle of privacy," a malicious reader could still enhance the read range from Pierre's chips by specialized methods.

Dr. Ari Juels from RSA Laboratories suggests in *RFID Security and Privacy:A Research Survey* that it makes more sense to think of multiple read ranges as opposed to just a single read range for passive tags (Jules, 2005). He contends that there are four different read ranges that are worth considering:

- *Nominal read range.* This is the intended read range for a tag using standard power readers and standard antenna configurations. For example, the ISO 14443 standard for proximity cards calls for a 10-cm nominal range.
- *Rogue scanning range.* This is the maximum range at which a tag can be read by using a highly powerful reader that may exceed legal limits and a powerful antenna or antenna array. For example, Kfir and Wool showed that by using relay attacks, they were able to read ISO 14443 tags up to 50 cm away; five times the nominal read range (Kfir and Wool, 2005).
- *Tag-to-reader eavesdropping range.* In this case it is necessary to have two readers:
  - The first reader must be very powerful. Its task is to power the tag.
  - The second reader need not emit any signals whatsoever; it just needs to monitor the response from the tag and therefore not announce itself. The second reader may be at a range larger than the rogue scanning range.
- *Reader-to-tag eavesdropping range.* This relies on the fact that under some configurations, the reader transmits tag-specific information to the tag. Since the transmission signal from readers can reach much further distances because of its power, it is susceptible to eavesdropping at ranges greater than the tag-to-read eavesdropping range.

10.3.4 Kill Command

The Kill command renders the tag unreadable. This is a command built into the chip that can be activated from a reader at the point of sale (POS), for instance. In order to execute the Kill command, the reader must transmit a PIN to the tag to ensure that it has the right control access.

Although extremely effective once the command has been successfully executed, this method presents two major limitations:

- It is not effective until the command has been executed. This means that it must be combined with some other solution to provide protection during the life cycle of the tag.

- It prevents use of the tag for future applications after the item has been sold (execution of the Kill command).

To illustrate the second point, imagine the following scenario. Richard, a techno-savvy consumer, chooses to buy the latest model of a washing machine that incorporates RFID functionality. The great thing about the washing machine is that it can use its embedded RFID reader to detect what garments have been placed in it by reading the RFID tags embedded in the garments. This information allows the washing machine to automatically control the temperature settings and washing mode so that the delicate garments are not damaged. However, if the articles that Richard bought at his favorite clothing store implemented the kill commands, Richard would certainly complain about the inconvenience presented by the washing machine not being able to identify the garments and potentially ruining his clothes.

Albeit this is not the most tragic scenario that one could devise, it portrays the issue at hand. The Kill command can severely limit the functionality and applications of RFID downstream from the point of sale—something merchants are not interested in promoting.

10.3.5 Sleep Command

The use of Sleep commands on tags is an attempt to answer the shortcomings cited in the Kill command proposal. The Sleep command is a more commerce-friendly proposal. Instead of killing the tag at the point of sale, this proposal renders the tag temporarily inactive until the consumer physically reactivates the tag. The key here is that the tag cannot be reactivated remotely (via RF). The assumption, however, is that no unauthorized party has physical access to the tag to reactivate it without the consumer's consent. The fact that the tag must provide a way to allow a consumer to reactivate the tag creates problems of its own. For instance, imagine when Richard (from the previous example) returns home after an afternoon of clothes shopping. In order to achieve the benefits of his RFID-enabled washer, Richard would have to physically reactivate each tag as he stores the garment. This is a daunting task, to say the least. Another issue with this proposal is that the cost of the tag is probably higher, since it must provide a way to be physically reactivated.

10.3.6 Encryption

A logical solution to provide RFID security protection is to encrypt the communications between the tags and the readers. After all, cryptology, which is defined by Wikipedia as "the field concerned with linguistic and mathematical techniques for securing information, particularly in communications," has been around for many centuries (Wikipedia, 2007). It can be traced all the way back to the Roman emperor Julius Caesar, who used encrypted messages to communicate with his military field commanders.

Strong encryption, however, requires a high level of processing power that is lacking on present RFID chips. This lack of processing power is due to the cost constraints within which RFID chip manufacturers must operate. As suggested earlier, the proliferation of RFID solutions is directly related to the price point of the RFID infrastructures. In a world where almost every item will be tagged, RFID tags must be extremely inexpensive. After all, who would put a 25-cent tag on a can of soup whose profit margin is 5 to 10 cents?

There are applications, however, where a more expensive tag that allows for the inclusion of more sophisticated circuitry to enable encryption makes sense. These applications involve high-value assets, where the cost of the tag is nominal compared to the price of the object to which it is affixed. For example, most mobile hospital pieces of equipment are high-value assets. It is not rare for hospitals to acquire mobile pieces of equipment that can cost in the tens or even hundreds of thousands of dollars. Another example is the tracking and management of high-value aerospace engine components. Some of these components are very bulky and expensive and require condition-based monitoring to ensure that they are stored in environments with acceptable humidity levels and temperature. In these examples, the criticality and cost of the assets being tracked justify the use of more expensive tags that would allow the use of encryption to ensure a secure RFID infrastructure.

For tags that store information about the outside world (i.e., beyond their unique identification number), it is imperative that the information contained within the tag be encrypted. This does not require such a high level of processing power, since the content is already encrypted and there is no need to perform encryption within the tag itself. The information would be meaningless to any third party that intercepted the communication, since it would appear as gibberish to whomever did not have access to the proper back-end systems to decipher the information intercepted. The identifier of the tag could serve as a pointer in the back-end system to obtain the correct decryption key. Once this key is accessed, the back-end system could unlock the information. The fact that the tag continues broadcast a unique identifier still presents an issue of traceability, since a third party could keep track of the whereabouts of the tag by its ID, even if it didn't know what the message meant.

Many people have argued that Moore's law may apply in this scenario. Loosely, Moore's law states that because of technological innovations and manufacturing improvements, one can expect the capability of microprocessors to double every 18 months or so. If one believes this (and it has proven in the past to be more or less accurate), one would expect that in the near future, the technology would be available to manufacture RFID chips that could entertain encryption at a low enough price point. We believe that in the long run this is true and Moore's law will hold. However, for implementation scheduled for the next two to five years, it is unlikely that the industry will get to that point.

10.3.7 Blocking

This approach was suggested by Juels et al. (ACM, 2003). Under this approach, tags and readers are extended to handle a *privacy bit* in the RFID tag. Also, this approach calls for the introduction of a *blocker tag*. The blocker tag is a special tag that prevents the unwanted scanning of tags whose privacy bit has been turned on.

In a consumer-driven environment, this privacy bit would be turned off from the moment of fabrication until the POS. At the POS, the privacy bit would be turned on, allowing the tag only to be read when it is not in the presence of a blocker tag.

Juels et al. used the following example to illustrate the application of *blocking*:

> To illustrate how blocking might work in practice, consider a supermarket scenario. When first created, and at all times prior to purchase—in warehouses, on trucks, and on store shelves—tags have their privacy bits set to "0." In other words, any reader may scan them. When a consumer purchases an RFID-tagged item, a point-of-sale device flips the privacy bit to a "1": It transfers the tag into the privacy zone. (This operation is much like the Kill function in EPC tags, and may be similarly PIN-protected.) Once in the privacy zone, the tag enjoys the protection of the blocker. Supermarket bags might carry embedded blocker tags, to protect items from invasive scanning when shoppers leave the supermarket. When a shopper arrives home, she removes items from her shopping bags and puts them in the refrigerator. With no blocker tag inside, an RFID-enabled "smart" refrigerator can freely scan RFID-tagged items. The consumer gets privacy protection from the blocker when it is needed, but can still use RFID tags when desired!

The advantage of blocking is that it renders tags unreadable while in the presence of a blocker tag (effectively accomplishing the same behavior as the Kill command) but allows for tags to be reused by other applications, such as smart appliances, when away from the blocker tag.

It is important to note that at this writing, this is only a proposal and no standard or manufacturer has adopted nor implemented this approach.

10.3.8 Clip Tags

This approach, originally proposed by IBM, provides a seemingly simple yet effective solution to minimize tag recognition from standard read distances. The idea is to create a tag with a full antenna that can be clipped at the point of sale by the consumer in order to reduce the span of the antenna and therefore reduce its readable range from a few meters to only

1 or 2 cm. The tag still works and can be read with a proximity reader (a reader that is placed within 1 or 2 cm from the tag) but is not readable from afar. Figure 10-2 shows a pictorial representation of the clip tag.

10.4 Facts and Misunderstandings

Although many other issues have been raised, most of them have a common theme: RFID technology could potentially be used to invade citizens' private lives. Many of the concerns are ill-founded, whereas others are valid. This is due to the confusion that has been created among the public in terms of the real capabilities of RFID.

In an effort to promote this technology, some people in the RFID industry have overstated the capability of the technology to the point that a person who just reads the headlines could potentially believe that RFID is an almost "magical" tracking and identifying solution with global reach. This misrepresentation encourages people to believe that an RFID chip could be read from almost anywhere and by almost anyone. In reality, this concept falls far short of what can actually be achieved today and in the near future. Let's take a look at some of the prevalent myths as well as some of the potential real issues.

Myth. Any item purchased at a retail store that contains an RFID tag can be tracked by malicious individuals or groups that steal the shopper's identity.

Fact. Most of the tags applied to items in retail stores are passive. These have a very short read range (1 to 3 m) and usually transmit only the ID of the RFID tag. A malicious individual or group would have to gain access to the retailer's back-end database to make the correct association between the shopper and the item. If the malicious group could gain access to this information, there are much more serious problems than just the fact that the ID from the RFID tag was intercepted and read.

Myth. An RFID chip could be read anywhere in the world, thus tracking any person's move.

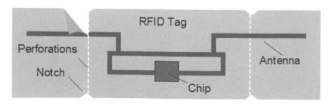

Figure 10-2 Clip tag.

Fact. As we have seen in this book, RFID chips can only be read within a predefined infrastructure. In general, infrastructures are expensive and require a major investment on the part of an entity to read wide areas. Although one could possibly imagine a malicious government deploying such infrastructure, the sheer volume of information gathered by such an infrastructure would be massive and require incredibly sophisticated computer centers to process that information. That infrastructure would have to read chips in metal structures, tunnels, transportation centers, inside buildings, and so on. To track people today, it would be much more efficient to use the cellular network infrastructure that is already in place rather than create an entire new and expensive RFID network. Such an infrastructure would take years to deploy and develop technology to support it. In today's world, passive RFID technology has a reach of less than 10 m, whereas active RFID technology could have a reach as great as 1 to 2 km in the best of cases. This is hardly enough to create a global reach infrastructure, and even if there was a desire to do so, it would be immensely costly.

As an example, imagine that some entity wanted to track every person's movement throughout the United States. According to the CIA's World Facts, there are over 4.1 million km of paved road in the United States (CIA, 2006). The same source cites the United States having a population of over 300 million people. Assuming that this entity wanted to create an active RFID infrastructure that would cover all paved roads of the United States to track its population, roughly 1.5 million readers (assume 1 km read range) would have to be installed. The current price of an active reader is about US$1,500 or about 3 percent of the U.S. median income (according to the U.S. Census,, the median income as of 2003 was a bit over US$65,000). This means that the entity would have to spend over US$2.5 billion in just readers to cover paved roads of the United States. To provide comprehensive coverage, the entity would also desire to set up the infrastructure in buildings, malls, offices, airports, rail terminals, parks, and so on. This could conceivably bring the price tag into the hundreds of billions, if not in the trillions. Considering that the U.S. gross domestic product (GDP) is about US$11.5 trillion, the infrastructure would consume a large chunk of that number.

This does not include the entire cabling and/or wireless infrastructure required to connect the readers, the computing power necessary to process the data, or the people required to maintain such an infrastructure. This is a daunting task at a minimum.

Issue. A retail store could keep a log of all the items a consumer buys by registering the products using the RFID chips.

Fact. This issue is present today even without RFID. When a consumer buys a product and pays with a credit card, the retail store could use that information to make all the data analyses necessary to invade the privacy of the consumer. As stated, there is no need for an RFID infrastructure to accomplish something that is already possible.

In many of today's supermarkets, consumers willingly agree to provide certain information about their shopping habits by signing up for a "savings card." The issue that is justly raised by consumer advocacy groups is that RFID presents a mechanism whereby retailers could obtain this information in secret and without the consent of their patrons. This is a valid concern and one for which technology alone may not have the answer.

It is also very important to recall the distinction between *security* and *privacy*. This distinction can be clearly applied in most of the examples cited as potential issues of invasion of privacy. In most cases, even if an unintended party could read the RFID chip's unique identifier (a security issue), the party still would have to gain access to the back-end database system to make the association between that ID and the person to which it is related (a privacy issue)—a different and much harder issue with which to deal. However, the issues of traceability and inventory are still of concern.

Another important fact is that most RFID chips used in retail business contain a very small amount of memory. This memory is intended to deal with the chip's unique identification schema. Information about consumers is not stored in these chips, making them useless to people who do not have access to the identification schemas.

Some of the issues raised by concerned groups stem from either misunderstanding of the technology and its capabilities or by simple inaccurate facts. Both of these roots are evidence that the RFID community has done a poor job at conveying to the public, in an accurate and understandable form, what the technology is and its capabilities. Education will be a key component in the acceptability, progress, and evolution of RFID technology.

Businesses have a vested interest in creating a publicly accepted corporate image—one that would not be tarnished by any association with the idea of violating the business patron's right of privacy. On the other hand, malevolent governments or unscrupulous businesses could potentially create or promote infrastructures that would allow the gathering of information that could indeed violate the right of privacy. That is why it is so important to truly understand the facts and capabilities of the technology at hand, and the RFID industry should encourage watchful groups to stay on top of the technology by providing open information of its inner workings, its applications, and its limitations.

10.5 Privacy Guidelines Being Considered

As more enterprises get into the business of implementing RFID and more people become aware of these implementations, lawmakers will and are starting to take an interest in RFID activities that involve individual privacy issues. This interaction will force two major thrusts involving the protection of an individual's right of privacy. One will be a self-regulating industry set of guidelines; the other, legislation.

Thanks to the work of many concerned groups, the RFID industry is taking a deep look at its own operations and proactively attacking the issue of privacy. An example of this is the creation of a Kill command that would render an RFID tag useless after a predefined event. That event may be the final purchase from a retailer, a timed event, or the activation of the command by the end user.

The following are a set of self-imposed guidelines proposed by EPCglobal to proactively promote individual privacy protection (EPCglobal, 2005):

1. Consumer Notice
Consumers will be given clear notice of the presence of EPC on products or their packaging and will be informed of the use of EPC technology. This notice will be given through the use of an EPC logo or identifier on the products or packaging.

2. Consumer Choice
Consumers will be informed of the choices that are available to discard or remove or in the future disable EPC tags from the products they acquire. It is anticipated that for most products, the EPC tags would be part of disposable packaging or would be otherwise discardable. EPCglobal, among other supporters of the technology, is committed to finding additional efficient, cost effective and reliable alternatives to further enable customer choice.

3. Consumer Education
Consumers will have the opportunity easily to obtain accurate information about EPC and its applications, as well as information about advances in the technology. Companies using EPC tags at the consumer level will cooperate in appropriate ways to familiarize consumers with the EPC logo and to help consumers understand the technology and its benefits. EPCglobal would also act as a forum for both companies and consumers to learn of and address any uses of EPC technology in a manner inconsistent with these Guidelines.

4. Record Use, Retention and Security
The Electronic Product Code does not contain, collect or store any personally identifiable information. As with conventional barcode technology, data which is associated with EPC will be collected, used, maintained, stored and protected by the EPCglobal member companies in compliance with applicable laws. Companies will publish, in compliance with all applicable laws, information on their policies regarding the retention, use and protection of any personally identifiable information associated with EPC use.

As expected, these guidelines will evolve as the technology and applications evolve. A big effort is being put toward providing the consumer a choice (Guideline 2) that allows consumers to eliminate the tag altogether.

On the other side of the spectrum, governments of many countries are starting to propose legislation to limit future capabilities of the technology. The European Union, for example, has proposed a requirement that retail stores disclose the presence of RFID tags on products and the presence of readers. They also proposed that retailers state how they intend to obtain and control the information, who will maintain and control the data, the purposes for which the information will be used, how to kill or render unusable the tag from the product, how to exercise the right to access the information on the tag, and so on (Sullivan, 2005).

Similarly, legislators in the United States are also proposing guidelines that would require the proper dissemination of information regarding RFID usage. For example, in early 2004, Senator Debra Bowen of California proposed a bill (California's State Bill 1834–SB 1834) that would require any business or state government agency using RFID technology with the capability to track products and people to (Promo Magazine, 2006)

- Tell people they are using an RFID system that can track and collect information about them.
- Get express consent before tracking and collecting information.
- Detach or destroy RFID tags that are attached to a product offered for sale before the customer leaves the store.

Although the bill did not pass in the end, it was marked for consideration for future legislative sessions and shows the interest from government representatives to legislate against potential misuses of the technology.

Many states in the United States are taking proactive measures, even if it is only to study the issue of privacy and RFID in more depth. As the National Conference of State Legislatures states as of November, 2005 (NCSL, 2005):

Legislators in several states, recognizing privacy concerns about the use of this technology, have introduced bills that seek to respond to the increasingly rapid adoption of RFID technology. Three states—Maryland (H.B. 32), Utah (S.J.R. 10) and Virginia (H.B. 1304)—have introduced bills designed to study the issue in more depth and to provide recommendations for future legislation. Two states—Missouri (S.B. 867) and Utah (H.B. 251)—have introduced legislation that would require all products containing RFID tags, to be appropriately labeled. Utah (H.B. 314) has introduced another bill that requires instructions to be provided on how to disable the RFID tag, or a notice that the tag will remain active after purchase. Finally, California (S.B. 1834) has introduced a bill that outlines when it is permissible to use or record personally identifiable information in the context of an RFID transaction. Three states— New York (A.B. 6073), Virginia (H.B. 151, S.B. 107, S.B. 148) and Washington (H.B. 1019)—also have introduced bills that make personally identifiable information collected by automatic toll systems (like EZ-Pass) confidential.

Another well known group, the Electronic Privacy Information Center, has posted general guidelines specifically geared toward the use of RFID in consumer environments (EPIC, 2006):

A. What RFID Users Must Do:

1. *NOTICE.* Give notice to a RFID Subject of:
   a. *Tag presence,* whether through labels, logos, or equivalent means, or through display, either at the place where a tagged item is stored, such as a shelf or counter, or at point of sale, such as a cash register. The notice shall be reasonably conspicuous to the individual and contain information that enables the individual to be reasonably aware of the nature of the RFID system and the data processing in place.
   b. *Reader presence,* whether through labels, logos, or equivalent means, or through display, whenever tag readers are present. The notice shall be reasonably conspicuous to the individual and contain information that enables the individual to be reasonably aware of the nature of the RFID system and the data processing in place.
   c. *Reading activity.* RFID Users must use a tone, light, or other readily observable and recognized signal whenever a tag reader is in the act of drawing information from an RFID tag anywhere on the sales floor.

2. *REMOVAL.* Attach tags to items in such a way as to allow for the easiest possible removal of tags.

3. *ANONYMITY PRIORITY.* Any RFID user—before linking RFID tags to personal information—should first consider alternatives which achieve the same goal without collecting personal information or profiling customers. If personal information must be collected and associated with tag data, the RFID user must satisfy the following five requirements:
   a. *Consent.* Obtain written consent from an individual before any personally identifiable information of the individual, including name, address, telephone number, credit card number, and the like, is attached to, stored with, or otherwise associated with data collected via the RFID System.
   b. *Purpose.* Before obtaining written consent, the RFID User must inform the RFID subject about the purpose of associating gathered data with personal information, and specify that purpose before such attaching, storing, or association.
   c. *Use limitation.* Before obtaining written consent, the RFID User must inform individuals about the scope of use of gathered data, whether the use is limited to the person's own interests or whether the data will be disclosed to third parties. Keep data only as long as it is necessary for the purpose for which the data was associated with personal information.
   d. *No third party disclosure.* No disclose, directly or through an affiliate, to a nonaffiliated third party an individual's personally identifying information in association with RFID tag identification information.
   e. *Data quality.* Keep gathered data accurate, complete and up-to-date, as is necessary for the purposes for which it is to be used.

4. *SECURITY.* Take reasonable measures to ensure that any data processed via an RFID system is transmitted and stored in a secure manner, and that access to the data is limited to those individuals needed to operate and maintain the RFID system.

5. *OPENNESS.* RFID Users must make readily available to individuals, through the Internet or other equivalent means, specific information about their policies and practices relating to its handling of personal information. Any personally identifiable information itself shall be provided upon written request of the individual in a secure manner.

6. *ACCOUNTABILITY.* Designate someone who is accountable for the RFID User's compliance with these guidelines.

B. What RFID Users Must NOT Do:

1. *TRACK.* Track the movement of RFID subjects at any time without their written consent to all tag reading events. RFID users shall not track individuals via tagged items on the premises or outside the premises where an RFID system is employed to obtain individual shopping habits or any other such information obtainable through tracking, even upon suspicion of such activities as fraud or shoplifting.

2. *SNOOP.* Record or store tag data from tags that do not belong to the RFID User for any reason except for the processing of returns or warranty service and upon the consumer's request. RFID users shall not collect RFID data from objects on, or carried by, an individual person for the purpose of generating a consumer profile, even if the profile is assigned anonymously.

3. *COERCE.* Coerce or force individuals to keep tags turned on after purchase for such benefits as warranty tracking, loss recovery, or compliance with smart appliances; and not require individuals to provide unnecessary personal information as a precondition of a transaction. RFID Users must allow individuals who so desire to enroll anonymously in any RFID data-gathering scheme.

C. RFID Subjects' rights:

1. *ACCESS.* RFID Subjects must have the right to access data containing personally identifiable information collected through an RFID system, and have the opportunity to make corrections to that information.

2. *REMOVAL.* RFID Subjects have the right to get tags removed from tagged items.

3. *ACCOUNTABILITY.* RFID Subjects have the right to challenge the compliance of persons employing RFID systems when practice contradicts the guidelines set forth above.

These guidelines are more or less a code of ethics calling for the proper implementation of RFID solutions that deal with individuals' information. Unfortunately, they are only suggestions and must be backed up with the proper technology to provide auditable trails of infractions.

10.6 Information Safekeeping

As stated at the beginning of this chapter, information safekeeping refers to the combination of security, privacy, traceability, and inventorying. As we have seen, no one solution can answer all the questions posed when dealing with information safekeeping.

We have exposed many facts that warrant a true concern with regard to information safekeeping. However, we have also shown that there is a lot of misunderstanding regarding the capabilities of RFID technology. Education and accurate information dissemination will be critical for public acceptance of this technology.

One aspect that is critical to information safekeeping is that of information back-end security. This aspect is not limited to RFID but instead is global to all IT solutions that handle sensitive information. Back-end security deals with two main aspects:

- The ability to prevent unauthorized access to the database systems that contain the information captured, or said in another way, guarantee that *only* authorized access is allowed;
- The ability to authenticate that the information provided by the back-end system is in fact the information *contained* in the database systems.

Because it is not within the scope of this book and plenty of literature is available that dwells in details on how to achieve back-end security, we will not go into the details of how to make a back-end system. However, we point out to the reader that this aspect is critical to the success of information safekeeping, and thus we encourage the reader to consider this aspect of any RFID implementation.

More than just the pure concern for security and privacy, traceability and inventorying are issues that can be exploited more easily by unscrupulous third parties. When considering RFID implementations, designers must take these into consideration and take the necessary steps to either avoid them or find satisfactory solutions for these issues.

Note that no single measure provides "enough" protection. Different combinations of these proposed actions will yield different levels of protection against unauthorized privacy invasion, tracking, and inventorying.

10.7 A Final Point: Decoupling

Decoupling of private information from tag Information is, in our opinion, a very effective way to protect the privacy of individuals. Private information should not be kept in the RFID tag. Instead, the tag's unique identifier should be used as a pointer into a separate, secure back-end database system where the personal information resides.

In most applications, it is the objective of the RFID solution to identify a specific object. There is no value in providing more RFID information than the tag ID itself, as the association of the tag ID and the object upon which it is embedded can be performed by a back-end system that is more secure, does not broadcast the private information, and requires proper user authentication to log in. Another benefit of this approach is that the amount of information related to the tagged object is only limited by the amount of storage provided in the back-end system—usually, this storage can grow as large as necessary in a much more inexpensive way than it would cost to add storage space for the information at the tag level.

The reason why we say that the objective of *most* RFID applications is to just identify a specific object is because there are certain applications where only identifying the object by its tag ID is not enough. Information about the object must be able to be carried, modified, and transmitted at the tag level. An example of such system is an RFID field-maintenance management application. This is a system in which field-deployed equipment contains RFID tags with the intent of providing maintenance history to the technicians that work on this equipment. The peculiar aspect of this application is that the equipment is serviced while it is in the field. Because the deployment field could be anywhere on Earth, there is no RFID infrastructure that can cover this equipment all over the planet.

Therefore, it is necessary for the RFID tag to carry all of the maintenance information so that it is available for the technician when he or she accesses it. As an example, military equipment falls under this type of environment. When equipment is deployed to battle zones, it may not be possible to establish an RFID infrastructure that could cover the area where equipment must be maintained or serviced, yet it is critical for the technical personnel to have information as to what the history of the service has been on a specific piece of equipment to quickly diagnose problems or to provide proper maintenance to ensure the correct operation of the equipment. In this situation, RFID tags must provide the necessary history and specifications of the equipment for service personnel to do the job because it may not be possible to access a backend system.

References

ACM Press. 2003. "Conference on Computer and Communications Security." 103–111.

American Street. 2005. "A Surprising Find in the List of Median Income by State." Available online via www.reachm.com/amstreet/archives/2005/05/02/median-income-by-state.

CIA. 2006. *The World Factbook*. Available online via https://www.cia.gov/cia/publications/factbook/index.html

EPCglobal. 2005. "Guidelines on EPC for Consumer Products." Available online via http://www.epcglobalinc.org/public/ppsc_guide

EPIC.org. 2006. "Guidelines on Commercial Use of RFID Technology. Available online via http://www.epic.org/privacy/rfid/rfid_gdlnes-070904.pdf

Juels, Ari. 2005. "RFID Security and Privacy:A Research Survey." RSA Laboratories. September 28th, 2005. Acquired August 11, 2006, as a PDF.

Kfir, Z., and A. Wool. 2005. "Picking Virtual Pockets Using Relay Attacks on Contactless Smartcard Systems." IEEE/CreateNet SecureComm. Available online via http://eprint.iacr.org/2005/052 (accessed August 11, 2006).

NCSL. 2005. "News from the States." Summer. Available online via www.ncsl.org/programs/lis/CIP/CIPCOMM/summer04.htm#RFID.

Promo Magazine. 2006. "Senator Proposes RFID Privacy Legislation." Available online via http://promomagazine.com/news/marketing_senator_proposes_rfid/index.html.

Sullivan, Laurie. 2005. "The European Union Works Out RFID Privacy Legislation." February 5. *InformationWeek*. Available online via. http://informationweek.com/story/showArticle.jhtml?articleID=59301363.

Wikipedia. 2006. "Cryptography." Available online via http://en.wikipedia.org/wiki/Cryptography (accessed January 18, 2007).

Epilogue

Throughout this book we have attempted to provide a road map for practitioners that are associated with RFID implementations. We explained in Chapter 1 that the stage is set for RFID to grow into our everyday lives; in fact, we showed some examples of ubiquitous RFID applications that already form part of our daily routines such as RFID-enabled toll plazas on our highways and RFID-based systems that provide access control to buildings and offices. We recounted in Chapter 2 the history of how RFID had its beginnings in World War II, when the British military implemented the "identification, friend or foe" (IFF) system to determine if incoming planes were allies or not. In Chapter 3, we presented the basics of RFID, its components, its architecture, and its programmatic capabilities. We showed some of the different types of RFID (passive, active, and semiactive), and we provided a detailed description of what each component is and how it works. We also covered issues associated with frequency ranges and their regulation by different governments of the world. In Chapter 4, we dove into deeper detail concerning the physics behind RFID and the algorithms that make it work. Chapter 5 covered some of the recent advances in RFID technology, both from the hardware perspective and the software perspective.

In Chapter 6, we presented the basic principles necessary to conduct a business case analysis for the implementation of any RFID project. We also presented an approach on how to rationalize, from an economic perspective, the deployment of an RFID solution and presented an elaborate example that demonstrated a business case analysis of the implementation of an RFID solution in a hospital, hoping to seed in the reader parallels that could be used in the implementation of a project.

We provided, in Chapter 7, an overview of the current standards that are helping the proliferation of RFID in the business world, and we conveyed the global importance of these standards and the organizations that are driving them. In Chapter 8, we covered in depth the components of RFID technology and how they interact with each other. This led us to Chapter 9, where we discussed some integration issues of RFID technology into general business applications.

In Chapter 10, we presented a dialogue of very important issues in the user community: privacy and security. We presented the current state of where RFID is in terms of offering adequate privacy and security, as well as the accepted guidelines being used to ensure privacy and security. In Parts B, C, and in Appendix A, you will find RFID applications in selected application areas, some unique applications that are at the forefront of RFID deployments, and the current state of RFID in different geographies of the world. Appendix B lists 10 web sites that provide useful insight into the world of RFID.

Where We Are

As has been shown in this book, we have come a long way in terms of the current state of RFID. However, we perceive that we still have a long way to go. Aspects such as cost, size, coverage area, and security require much more development than what we have available currently. To use the life cycle of a human as an analogy, we believe that RFID has definitely been born and gone through the "terrible twos" stage, but it is just now reaching the childhood state of its growth. The next few years will be critical for the development of RFID and will determine how big it can grow. If the RFID community does a good job at anticipating its growing pains and addressing the different issues presented by the user community, it can almost guarantee that RFID will grow to a healthy maturity, becoming a ubiquitous solution in our everyday life. If, however, the RFID community fails to understand its position in the business world and if it fails to provide enough adaptation for users to embrace the technology, it may lead RFID to a premature death, opening the door to competing technologies that may provide a better adaptation to the user environment.

If we look at current implementations of RFID solutions being discussed in industry journals and at technical conferences, it is clear that there are still many issues that must be resolved to gain full acceptance of the technology. The issue of read reliability has been a problem in some implementations, especially those where asset ownership is to be tracked by the RFID solution. Take, for instance, the case of reusable containers. These containers are used by multiple partners in a relatively closed loop.

As Figure 1, shows, reusable containers move from supplier to manufacturer to customers and back to supplier. Under this scenario, the RFID solution is only trying to determine what containers left which facility, when they left, as well as what containers arrived at which facility and when. In this way, "ownership" of the containers can be established at any point within the loop. If a container is lost, the RFID solution can provide the information necessary to determine which party is responsible for losing the container and, therefore, should pay for it. In principle this is a situation requiring minimal RFID infrastructure—for instance, readers only at the entry/exit gate of each facility. This solution requires 100 percent reliability

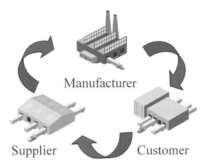

Figure 1 Close Loop Asset Tracking.

of reads, since the accountability of the container "ownership" is based on the read events captured by the RFID infrastructure. However, companies have found that today's technology falls short of providing this 100 percent reliability all of the time. This is due to a myriad of reasons, such as failing tags, tag misreads, and so on. Redundant systems or statistical quality control procedures must be put in place to ensure that this solution performs according to expectation. This is a fairly common picture in today's implementations. Redundant systems and processes must be part of an overall RFID solution to guarantee performance in mission-critical applications.

We have, however, in the recent past seen RFID solution providers bring to market much-improved RFID infrastructures that provide much higher reliability a higher percentage of the time. We believe that as technical issues are solved, RFID infrastructures will reach the point at which the preceding asset-tracking problem will be totally solved by RFID solutions.

One fundamental problem that the RFID industry is facing today is the overwhelming hype of the technology and its capabilities. In an effort to promote the technology, firms and organizations with vested interests have overstated the capabilities of RFID, only to disappoint users when they start working on pilot tests or implementation of RFID solutions. The two primary misleading statements that have damaged the RFID community have been the expectation of a sub-US$0.05 tag and the ability to track anything, anywhere regardless of the environment.

Although the sub-US$0.01 tag is a very real possibility in a few years, it is something that is not economically feasible yet. This limits the types of RFID deployments, primarily in the retail environment, which is the one that would consume the largest number of tags. The typical example of the economically infeasible solution is the tracking of a can of soup where the profit margin may be US$0.02 to US$0.04 per can; a $0.01 tag would still make tagging the can not a very attractive proposition. Even if we assume that an RFID solution could yield a 50 percent improvement in the efficiency of the supply chain of the soup cans, the economical benefits are not yet there. Having said all this, however, some new technologies are emerging that promise sub-US$0.01 tags in the next 12 to 24 months. Inexpensive tags, when they emerge, could eliminate this issue. The problem has been twofold. The first concerns the initial expectation set forth by the industry in its beginning without properly advising of the technology hurdles that it must overcome to make this a reality. Second, the current cost of the tags may make it infeasible for certain types of applications, since the cost of a manual process may still be more economically advisable than the RFID solution.

The second overhyped point is that of the ability of tracking anything, anywhere, regardless of the environment. The fact is that RFID is extremely sensitive to liquids and metals—the physics of RFID are not negotiable! Given that most industrial environments are heavily infiltrated by these two elements, users should expect that RFID implementations will have to mitigate the effect of these elements by ingenious antenna design and physical location of the readers and tags. This is something that has been understated by the RFID community in general and thus has resulted in major disenchantment at the time of implementation.

On the other hand, we believe that the RFID industry is realizing that sensationalist messages do more harm than good and has started a concerted effort to properly educate the user community about the truth behind RFID. There are many publications and web sites, some of which are shown in Appendix B, that provide an accurate perspective of what is going on in the world of RFID. We encourage the reader to make use of these sources to further complement the message that this book is trying to convey. Beyond the written message, the industry has held many conferences and seminars throughout the world demonstrating real-life executions of RFID implementations and helping disseminate the accurate message of what is capable and not capable from RFID solutions. As more companies deploy these solutions, other companies can gauge the level of commitment and results that RFID implementers are achieving using this technology.

Where We Are Going: A Vision of the Future

Where will RFID be in 2 years? In 5 years? In 10 years? In 50 years? Next century? Indeed, it is hard to say. If history is any indication, the rate of growth in technology resembles an exponential curve (within limits) as shown by the well-accepted fact that technology has advanced further over the last 100 years than it did in all of the years combined since the time the pyramids were built in Egypt.

If we assume that the RFID community does a good job at addressing the user community, pays attention to the business issues, and works as a holistic entity considering real-world scenarios and adapting to them, we can expect, in the short-term future (say, two to five years), significant advances in antenna technology, chip circuitry, memory capacity, reading distance, security capability, and standards development—all at lower prices. This will allow us to create smaller, more powerful tags and readers that can be securely and privately detected at further distances. Antenna development is of special interest because antenna design provides controlled coverage of the RF signals, allowing RFID systems to be better suited for special applications that require discrete areas of coverage to provide real-time location (RTL) information. We can also expect to have better integration of RFID devices with other systems such as global positioning systems (GPS) and communication devices that can broadcast the RFID information over cellular, satellite, or other far-reaching communication systems such as ham radio, and so on. This is probably one of the most promising areas of future development, as RFID will be combined with other technologies such as infrared (IR) and laser to provide more versatile solutions.

Higher memory capacity allows a tag to be more self-sufficient, since it can hold more information. Today's tags are quite limited in terms of memory, which makes them less than ideal in situations where there is no connectivity to a backbone system. Field-deployed tags that may need replacement in hostile environments for long periods of time will be able to log and record vast amounts of information to provide mission-critical decision support information to the users. RFID patient bedside assistance will become a reality, supporting the monitoring and administration of the right drugs to the right patients in the right quantities at the right time.

In the medium- to long-term future, say, 5 to 50 years, we can expect RFID technology to be mature enough to be as ubiquitous as microchips are today. We should expect the capability to tag any and all items that are sold today, regardless of their size. One application that is prohibitive today is that of tracking endangered species in the wild. In 50 years, the technology should be available where any animal can be tracked anywhere on Earth—land, air, or sea—to study and better understand the location and behavior of animals, thus allowing the control and survival of these endangered species. Furthermore, because of advances in integrated sensor technology, RFID will be used to monitor the state of hazardous substances on an individual level. We will be able to determine, for instance, that a specific intermediate bulk container (IBC) traveling in the middle of the Pacific Ocean and carrying explosive gases is reaching the critical pressure level inside of it, which may result in an explosion in the underwater carrying level of the ocean cargo ship. The preceding examples have been envisioned by many people today, but current technology does not allow us to put them in place for a variety of reasons, including economical considerations, actual technological development, and lack of communication infrastructure.

RFID will greatly improve the quality of life for all of us. RFID tags will be biocompatible to the point where they will become an integral part of living organisms, monitoring health status and reporting any problems with the state of the organism. RFID tags containing accelerometers and motion sensors will alert medical staff of accidental falls that patients may experience. Tiny RFID chips will travel through the human body, detecting localized problems and communicating their exact position inside the body, allowing medical staff to better diagnose patients.

RFID will allow companies to conduct selective recalls on defective products and determine what parts need to be replaced with minimal effort. RFID will also help law enforcement entities track convicted criminals long after they are released into society. Chips will be implanted in convicted felons and alert law enforcement personnel of the felon's location if he or she tries to remove the chip or if the felon approaches an area that has been designated off limits—for instance, an area in which there is a protective order in a family dispute.

In general, we believe that RFID is an enabling technology that when combined with other technologies can provide a plethora of solutions that require the individual identification of entities. Keep in mind that RFID is normally part of usually bigger solutions with more components, such as communication infrastructures, data management systems, and sensoring devices, that when put together address specific real-life problems. The goal and challenge for the RFID community is to deliver this enabling technology in a form that is economical, secure, accurate, reliable, and efficient.

B

Applications in 10 Areas

RFID in the Automotive Industry

1 Introduction

Electronic tracking and identification technology, which is the predecessor of RFID, has been in use in the automotive industry for around 20 years, but only to a limited extent. The major applications lie in vehicle identification and protection (Borysowich, 2004). One of the rapidly budding applications of the use of RFID technology in the automotive industry is in vehicle immobilizers (Figure 1). Over the past few years, immobilizers have become very common in new cars, and over 40 percent of the new cars manufactured in North America come equipped with RFID-enabled immobilizers (RFID Update, 2006).

The appeal of RFID technology in the automotive industry is the real-time visibility and security protection that it offers the automobile itself, as well as the benefits in the assembly processes of automobiles. For example, General Motors, Volkswagen, and Johnson Controls are already employing RFID tags and readers in their assembly operations, whereas TNT Logistics had deployed RFID technology to optimize the process of just-in-time parts sequencing to its automobile-manufacturing customers. Because of these emerging benefits offered by RFID, it has almost revolutionized the industry.

2 Application and Benefits

RFID technology offers a number of applications in the automotive industry. An RFID-based antitheft vehicle immobilizer is a protective device installed in many cars. RFID also holds great promise for the assembly and manufacturing processes of automobiles, in particular, for flexible and agile production planning, spare parts, and inventory management. The technology not only helps to automate the whole assembly process in which a

Figure 1 Examples of RFID-equipped vehicle immobilizers.

significant reduction in cost and shrinkage can be achieved, but it also offers improved services to automobile users that include more efficient replacement part ordering and automated generation of maintenance reminders. In the text that follows, four major areas are highlighted that include current and potential applications.

Vehicle Immobilization

An automobile immobilizer is a security device that is installed in a vehicle to make it much more difficult for unauthorized use of such vehicle. It is currently the largest segment of RFID usage in the automotive industry. Nearly half of all vehicles manufactured in North America employ RFID-based antitheft systems. Almost US$4 billion in revenue was generated through this application in the year 2005.

A typical antitheft system in an automobile would flash the headlights and sound the horn if there is any attempt to open the doors or hood without a key. A vehicle immobilizer provides a means of theft deterrence where the device immobilizes the engine, cuts the fuel or electric supply, or stops some other moving parts. Thus, it prevents the vehicle from being started and driven without due permission. New generations of immobilizers not only manage the engine but also have RFID-equipped readers installed in the door locks and car ignition to ensure that the right key or device is being used to start the vehicle. Typically, these RFID-based keys or devices are embedded with passive RFID chips that are used to unlock the vehicle doors and to activate the vehicle ignition. A mismatched RFID-based key or device will not allow the mobilization of the vehicle and furthermore, the owner of the vehicle may be alerted via wireless means that the vehicle is being tampered. Because of the effectiveness of such RFID-based antitheft systems, nowadays, most new cars are incorporated with some variant of the device.

Inventory Management

RFID-enabled assembly and manufacturing increases the visibility and accuracy of the inventory control and management of automotive parts and accessories. The technology, when implemented in the production process, could help in the implementation of a just-in-time manufacturing process.

The automotive industry is a high-value, medium-volume operation where one of the goals in the assembly process is to keep stocks and car parts at a low level but without the situation of running out. To accomplish this goal, a highly efficient production planning and stock replenishment scheme is essential and effective inventory management is necessary. This requires careful planning based on production quantities, on-hand stocks, and in-transit parts. Nowadays, more and more components for automotive assembly are delivered just-in-time, and RFID technology is definitely a solution to provide reliable and accurate information concerning inventory in real time.

Moreover, RFID helps to keep track of production resources such as machinery and labor, work in progress, raw materials, and semifinished parts in an automotive assembly plant. It enables the gathering of real-time location information as well the status of these resources. With this information, production planning, scheduling, and quality control can be performed more effectively and in a timely manner, especially in situations where unexpected events such as breakdowns of production equipment occur (KST International, 2005; TNT, 2005). In addition, better allocation and deployment of resources can be more readily performed.

Agile and Flexible Manufacturing

Today's automotive production is already a highly automated business where reliable automatic identification of components and subcomponents enables an even higher level of automation and flexibility. With the integration of advanced robotics and material-handling systems with the power of the auto-identification of car parts using RFID, a more agile and automated assembly operation can be achieved for the automotive industry.

To enhance the agility of automotive assembly, the incorporation of RFID tags in car components and accessories can greatly facilitate a desired mix, given the diverse specification of these components and subcomponents. For the many different models of automobile that are being assembled along the same production line, RFID tags attached to the car components and subcomponents are programmed with their respective recipe information. As these components travel through the assembly process, the production information is obtained by RFID readers to enable workers to perform the required operations. The new status can also be updated on the RFID tags that are attached to the components and subcomponents before going to subsequent assembly stages. Before the parts are assembled or leave the production line, information stored can be verified for quality assurance. With such flexibility in part specification and tracking, the concept of a fully flexible manufacturing system can be readily realized without the need to separate and batch the production operation, which is well suited to the automotive industry.

Moreover, the information stored and captured by the RFID tags that is associated with the components and subcomponents can be relayed to other systems of the assembly plants, including the inventory, warehousing, and quality assurance. It is expected that with the appropriate deployment of RFID technology, significant time and cost saving can be achieved.

Product Life Cycle Management

Automotive assembly is just one of the enterprise processes where RFID technology helps to improve its performance. To improve the automotive enterprise as a whole, product life cycle management (PLM) is a hot issue that is being examined. PLM is an emerging strategic approach for managing the product-related data and information efficiently over the whole product life cycle. To carry out effective PLM, RFID technology provides the capabilities to access, manage, and control product data and information over the entire product life cycle. The technology facilitates the tight integration among operations and even organizations by facilitating data and information exchange in a seamless manner. In this regard, RFID technology assumes an important role and becomes one of the core technologies in the development of PLM systems (TNT, 2005).

3 TNT Logistics and Ford

TNT Logistics, the largest provider of third-party logistics services to the automotive industry, has launched an initiative to deploy RFID technology as part of its logistics solution offered to automotive manufacturers at the end of 2005. The initiative started at the Material Sequencing Center (MSC) operated by TNT Logistics for Ford Motor Company to support their assembly plant in Dearborn, Michigan (Kiritsis, 2006). RFID tags and a network of wireless locating sensors were set up to provide real-time location information shared between the plant and TNT's facility. With the information, MSC can deliver small lot, sequenced, and metered parts to the plant. The system also triggers shipping notices so that the plant knows exactly what material is en route.

When the initiative is fully executed, the system will provide real-time visibility and a synchronized assembly process to deliver an uninterrupted flow of parts from MSC to the assembly plant that even automates the preproduction processes including gate arrival, load and unload of parts to storage racks, validation of part specifications, tracing of parts history, and the like.

Numerous benefits are offered by this initiative. For TNT, asset utilization, rack availability, and thus the spare capacity for storage and shipment are greatly improved. With the availability of real-time information, labor cost is reduced by eliminating the time used to search for racks. For Ford, the solution helps to automate workflow, reduce inventory, and prevent business interruption in the assembly process. Given the complexity of the automotive supply chain, with an RFID solution, all parties within the supply chain benefit from the system.

4 Conclusion

The benefits that RFID offers to the automotive industry, both to the production process as well as to end users, are visibility, traceability, flexibility, and added security. The uniqueness of the industry—where there exists a large variety of models with many different specification and features, but at a modest volume of individual components—makes RFID solutions attractive for sophisticated components and parts tracking, flexible and cost-effective production, and enhanced security protection of vehicles.

Yet there are obstacles to the full deployment of RFID in the automotive industry. One of the most commonly cited obstacles is the relatively high cost of rugged RFID tags for use in automobiles, and the cost of active RFID tags and readers. The technology is still comparatively expensive to be fully applied to all automotive components. As the demand for RFID device usage is ever-increasing, the growth in their production volume will drive the cost down to a break-even point where full implementation becomes viable.

References

Borysowich, Craig. 2004. "The Future of RFID in Cars." Available online via http://supplychain.ittoolbox.com/blogs/featuredentry.asp?i=1749.

Kiritsis, D. 2006. "Automotive Manufacturing Research Roadmap for RFID." RFID Academic Convocation. Available online via http://autoid.mit.edu/CS/forums/storage/16/56/Forum_auto_background%20v0.1.doc.Mathur, R. 2005. "RFID in the Automotive Industry: The Road Ahead." Available online via www.domain-b.com/industry/automobiles/general/20051003_rfid.html.

KST International. 2005. "WhereNet Expands Active RFID Automotive Ecosystem to Include Optimization of Just-in-Time Parts Deliveries From TNT Logistics to Vehicle Manufacturers." November 11. *MoreRFID*. Available online via www.morerfid.com/details.php?subdetail=Report&action=details&report_id=873.

RFID Journal. 2006 "RFID News Roundup." *RFID Journal*. Available online via www.rfidjournal.com/article/articleview/2218/1/1/.

RFID Update. 2006. "RFID Drives into Auto Manufacturing." Available online via www.rfidupdate.com/articles/index.php?id=1078.

TNT 2005. "TNT Logistics Launches RFID Initiative for Automotive Manufacturers." Available online via www.tntlogistics.us/en/press_office/press_releases/archive_2005/20051102_tnt_launches_rfid_initiative_for_automotive_manufacturers.asp.

RFID in Cattle Ranching

1 Introduction

Traditional cattle ranching relies on experienced ranchers, who may have been in the business for generations, to rear, keep track of, and trade their livestock. There is increasing health awareness of consumers, who are demanding quality and information concerning the meat products that they purchase. Therefore, an effective and reliable means of information capturing and storage in addition to product tracking and tracing is needed for the cattle ranching industry.

There is a lack of coordination between links in the production chain of meat products, especially for beef production. From cow–calf operators (where cows are raised, mainly to produce calves) to cattle feeders, meat-packers, and the retail outlets and supermarkets, the current practice makes it very difficult for the industry to convey consumer preferences from the retail market to each link in the supply chain. One of the difficulties comes at an early stage of the supply chain in cattle ranching. There are a large number of cattle ranchers with very different herd sizes that operate in wide geographical locations, making it difficult to track the origin or source of meat products. Furthermore, the competitiveness in the ranching and cattle feeding sector, which is made up of varying herd-sized producers, creates difficulty in coordinating between the various echelons in the supply chain. Currently there is little coordination between feedlot owners and the cow–calf sector (Lamb and Beshear, 1998).

To improve the quality of service and reduce the costs of operation, the beef industry, as an example, must aim to promote better coordination between stakeholders—that is, if the industry wants to remain competitive and wants to better serve the rapidly changing consumer preferences across the supply chain. With the advent of epidemics such as the avian flu, the existence of agroterrorism and occurrences of bovine spongiform encephalopathy (BSE, also known as mad cow disease), the call for better traceability of the origins of food products for their prompt containment against proliferation of epidemics is ever more urgent. These important issues, together with new legislation across the world calling for individual electronic identification of livestock, have become the major driving forces behind the introduction of effective tracking means. A major solution mechanism is the use of RFID technology in cattle ranching. RFID can improve not only business operations but also provide better customer convenience, inventory control and lower costs.

Cattle ranching, being at the head of the livestock production supply chain that directly feeds other industry stakeholders including slaughter and processing plants, sales barns, auction markets, stockyards, veterinarians, pathology laboratories, mobile butchers, customers, and so on, plays a leading role in setting the benchmark. RFID technology has emerged as a very promising solution for satisfying this need. In fact, there are many successful cases where the implementation of RFID on livestock and food products have positive returns on investment.

2 RFID-Enabled Cattle Ranching

Imagine a cattle ranching operation where instead of calling roll by counting each cow, the rancher can just call them with his mobile phone. This is no longer science fiction, because RFID technology is already accomplishing this objective.

An RFID tag is placed on the animal's ear. That tag can store much information about an animal, including its breed and pedigree, its date of birth, its vaccination records, its birth date, and even its temperature profile. The cattle ear tag can then be read at some distance through RFID readers or antennas, and the information can be conveyed to a laptop computer, a personal digital assistant, or a mobile phone via wireless network connections.

Tagging cattle with RFID tags is increasingly common, as the governments of various countries are ramping up their efforts to electronically track livestock. In 2006, over 70 million livestock are being tagged. In 2005, the Canadian government committed C$1.8 million in funding for the Canadian Radio Frequency Identification (CRFID) reader program. The initiative is to facilitate tracking and tracing of cattle across the entire cattle industry, from cattle ranching to auctioning, distribution, butchering, and retailing. The tagging will enable electronic transfer of cattle identification information to the Canadian Cattle Identification Agency and Agri-Traçabilitié Québec, in which RFID tagging of cattle is already mandatory. In the United States, the RFID tagging of cattle will become mandatory in 2009, and the system aims to trace the history of sick animals within 48 hours of diagnosis.

In fact, with the deployment of RFID technology on cattle tagging, the system can track far more information than what various governments will require of the cattle ranchers. These added benefits include better inventory control by keeping track of livestock and cattle that often roam in a large physical space. Such a system will enable ranchers to have better control and assurance in terms of the integrity of their supply chain.

Statistics show that Australia, Canada, the United States, and other countries are strongly progressing with RFID tagging of cattle, some of which comes from a legal push (see Figure 1). The main reason is not, at this moment, because it saves money and increases sales for the large supermarket chains, but for disease control, traceability, and cost reduction at the early stage of the supply chain (see Figure 2). For example, RFID can help with mad cow disease by tracking what was fed to the cattle from birth. In contrast to more urgent health concerns, the use of RFID technology in cattle ranching and food production can sometimes demonstrate the superior quality of products, and information on RFID tagged meat allows customers to hold the meat product near a terminal to display the identification of the rancher and other useful information, for example, nutrition facts and cooking suggestions. This may result in more income for the retailers and suppliers of the meat product. In addition, we can see that RFID tagged meat products can help to combat counterfeiting and the tag can double as an antitheft device in stores and supermarkets.

3 Successful Cases

RFID technology is not new to the food and livestock industry. Some pilot schemes have already been implemented around the world. For example, beef producer Brandt Beef, of Brawley, California, is using an RFID and barcode tracking system to keep track of its cattle, from birth to beef.

A successful application of RFID technology in cattle ranching was found in the Warrnambool Livestock Exchange, a livestock sales yard in Australia. Here, an RFID-enabled tracking system was developed and fully implemented in 2003 (Warrnambool, 2006). This system was the first of its kind in the world that uses RFID technology to allow cattle owners to identify,

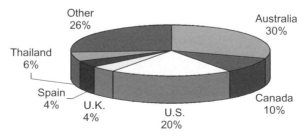

Figure 1 RFID deployment cases for livestock world wide (*Source:* Courtesy of IDTechEx Ltd. 2006).

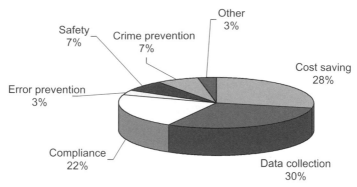

Figure 2 Benefits of RFID for livestock (*Source:* Courtesy of IDTechEx Ltd. 2006).

trace, and capture data for each cow, and at the same time, help the cattle owner comply with Australia's stringent National Livestock Identification System (NLIS). NLIS is the largest and most sophisticated livestock database and management system in the world. It was established to meet livestock identification and traceability requirements mandated by the European Union in 1999.

The system, which is greatly facilitated by RFID technology, uses cattle ear tags with transponders to keep track of and store relevant data. These tags have read/write capabilities, allowing cattle ranchers to add, change, or retrieve details on each animal, such as health information, farm location history, market eligibility, and commercial information.

As the animals move through the weighing system, RFID readers or interrogators installed across a lane or at the entrance or exit to a weigh bridge read their tags to identify the cattle and track their movements. As many as 3,000 cattle can be recorded each day. This can be compared to previous methods that tracked a daily average of only a few hundred animals. With the implementation of the system, Warrnambool Livestock Exchange achieved Quality Assurance and accreditation for the European Union, which enables EU-accredited producers to sell livestock that are RFID tagged through the yards to EU processors without being differentiated from other producers.

4 The Challenges

While successful stories are increasing, there are still challenges ahead for the global acceptance and adoption of RFID technology in cattle ranching. Although the foreseeable benefits are huge, the acceptance of the technology, including resistance from larger ranchers that try to maintain the status quo and the resulting lack of willingness to change, is still a major hurdle to overcome.

In addition, initial investment cost is still high. These costs include the installation of the infrastructure, the cost of the tags, the customization of the system, and the education and training of the ranchers. These are legitimate issues to overcome. For example, cattle tags require special design so that they can withstand environmental conditions. The tags are often biocompatible implants that are installed as pellets in the stomach or in the usual fashion as ear tags. These are long-range RFID tags that are about 10 times more expensive than standard RFID tags used in other products. As a long-range location tracking system, the RFID solution may need to be coupled with GPS and mobile communication technologies to provide an integrated means for cattle tracking. Further technological development is required, and the costs issue is still the major hurdle.

In addition, the industry is still keenly awaiting a worldwide standard for the RFID technology to be developed and endorsed by governments before their full deployment. New technology will require time to stabilize.

5 Conclusion

From the successful cases cited of RFID technology in cattle ranching, together with the push from government legislation worldwide and other economic, health, and safety driving forces as discussed, it is foreseeable that RFID technology can capitalize beyond just cattle tracking and tracing in the early stage of the livestock production supply chain.

In the future, there will be a wide variety of good reasons for using the technology in cattle ranching, and in the food supply chain as a whole. Widespread use of RFID will not only strengthen the competitive advantage of the cattle ranching business but also further support the production of safer, higher-quality meat products.

However, being able to tag a vast number of livestock cost effectively is by no means a simple undertaking. Will robust printed electronics be the key? Will the emergence of an acceptable standard or the acceptance by cattle ranchers and others who are in the business be the ultimate factors for using RFID in the cattle industry? These together with many other challenges and the different pace of legislation across the world will continue to control the adoption of the technology. As in the development of a supply chain, the issue is becoming more global, and perhaps we need to look for a global solution.

References

IDTechEx. 2006. "Food and Livestock RFID: Where, Why, What Next." IDTechEx Knowledgebase Case Studies. Available online via www.idtechex.com/products/en/articles/00000434.asp.

Lamb, R. L., and M. Beshear. 1998. "From the Plains to the Plate: Can the Beef Industry Regain Market Share?" *Economic Review* 4 (Third Quarter). Available online via . awww.kansascityfed.org/publicat/ECONREV/PDF/4Q98Lamb.pdf

Warrnambool. 2006. "Live Stock Exchange: The Place to Sell." Warrnambool County Council, Australia. Available online via www.warrnambool.vic.gov.au/Page/page.asp?Page_Id=295&h=0.

RFID in Health Care

1 Introduction

Health care is an indispensable component of human welfare in our modern society. Health care organizations from time to time spend a tremendous amount of resources to explore and improve their services, facilities, and operational systems. In general, an effective and efficient health care system is achieved through adopting new technologies, improving surgical and medical procedures, and providing comprehensive training to staff across the health spectrum. Technology plays a vital role in enhancing the overall performance of the health care industry. Over the years, the emergence of new technology such as electronic records, database systems, wireless technology, and computerized transaction systems has improved the efficiency and effectiveness of health care systems in different perspectives.

RFID technology has assumed the mantle of the latest and greatest information technology. It is a means of identifying an object or a person using a RF-transmitted identification code and has a wide range of applications in health care systems.

2 An Overview of Health Care Systems

A health care system that is as large and complex as a public hospital can generally be categorized into three main components: accident and emergency (A&E), inpatient ward, and outpatient care. These three components are closely related, as shown in Figure 1. In this figure, the movement or flow of patients between and among the three components is highlighted. When a patient is admitted to either the A&E or the inpatient unit, the patient will be assessed and treated depending on severity of the condition. Usually, the treatment delivered by the A&E is relatively prompt, whereas for the inpatient unit, such treatment tends to be longer term. After initial treatment, a patient admitted to the A&E unit will be further assessed by physicians, and depending on condition, the patient will either be discharged or referred to inpatient wards. For the outpatient unit, patients are

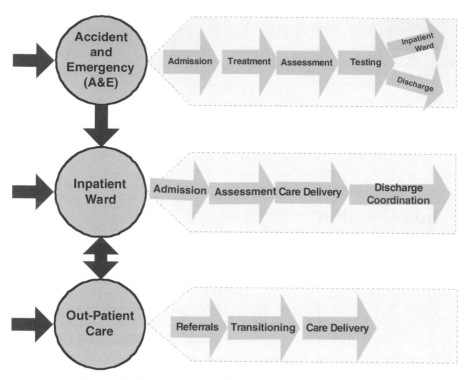

Figure 1 The business model of a typical hospital system.

referred for consultation and same-day treatment. Under this health care model, in addition to the physical flow of patients, information concerning patients' medical history, treatment records, and so on, as well as resources such as medics, equipment, and moneys, are passed within and between the three components, making the system a complex supply chain of service delivery. By studying patient flows and analyzing the problems throughout a patient's journey in one of these components, the health care system can be significantly improved. Here, a business model of a typical hospital system is presented that reveals the main problems that hinder patient's access to a hospital and its services.

Accident and Emergency

The accident and emergency department assesses and treats people with serious injuries and emergencies. This department normally operates 24 hours per day, 365 days of the year. When a patient reaches the A&E department, he or she might be treated immediately or, more often than not, will have to wait for treatment. This depends on the seriousness of the patient's injury and the current condition of the A&E department. After treatment is completed, the patient will be discharged. However, if the injuries or condition of a patient is more serious, he or she might then be sent for further testing, such as X-ray and blood test, or admitted to the hospital for further treatment.

The key issues affecting the performance of A&E are delays in consultations and treatments and transport of patients to the inpatient ward after they have been admitted to the hospital. Quite often, there are no clear guidelines and criteria specifying the eligibility for A&E admission. A&E departments are often confused with minor injuries units, which treat patients with injuries like cuts, sprains, minor burns, cold, and flu. These patients often misuse the emergency services and cause delays in A&E services. Also, delays always occur because of poor and nonsystemic management of patients in the department. Patients might be blocked to access A&E even when service is available. Patient test results often require a long time to be delivered, as no integrated reporting system is available. A majority of reports and medical records are still in handwritten format in thick stacks of files.

Despite delays in the A&E area, the most serious problem occurs after the treatment stage. Patients might need to wait for a long time before they can be discharged. This is mainly due to poor communication between the units in A&E. On the other hand, up-to-date information concerning the inpatient wards such as availability of beds and equipment is not available to A&E when a patient needs further treatment. Delays always occur in moving patients from A&E to the inpatient unit, and accessing porters or nurses to escort patients to wards. These delays are normally caused by lack of communication between different departments and wards.

Inpatient Ward

Patients who need medical treatment are admitted to inpatient wards directly or from the A&E department. Inpatient ward services and consultations use a team care approach and subspecialty expertise. On each ward a charge nurse has overall responsibility for the ward. During the stay of a patient, a doctor and a team will be responsible for his or her medical care. The information regarding the patient throughout the course of inpatient care is held within clinical notes or on computers.

The key issues impacting the performance of the inpatient ward are poor bed management and insufficient discharge planning. There is a lack of systematic approach to identify currently available beds and patients waiting for emergency admission. The role of bed managers is unsupported by technology. As a result, wards frequently tell A&E that a bed is free, but often the admission of a patient is delayed for an hour or more. Patients who will clearly be admitted are unnecessarily held while tests are performed. Guidelines and agreements between units may be informal and insufficiently clear, which sometime causes serial rejection of patients by specialty units.

Patient medical history and test results are frequently transcribed at length into medical records by the medical staff. This is time-consuming. Plans for discharging patients are not integrated and well-defined. The co-ordination of discharge planning is often suboptimal with little prewarning of when a doctor will decide that a patient may be discharged. There is no streamlined discharge where specific arrangements and preferences of doctors would influence discharge planning. This can cause delays in various aspects. For example, without advance notice, pharmacy cannot plan ahead to ensure they are not delaying the treatment and care.

Outpatient Care

Outpatient care concerns patients who have been discharged from a hospital and require further treatment. Patients may either require further medication or be referred to specialists for monitoring.

The key issues impacting the performance of outpatient care are the availability and utilization of post acute services. There is a lack of easily accessible information about what each service offers for further treatment and what the eligibility criteria are. Records regarding a patient may not be fully integrated when passed to out-of-hospital care services. A better control should be implemented to prevent patients who have been referred to outpatient care services from being readmitted to A&E with the same problem. The current control for this preventive issue does not alert staff to intervene earlier and thus increases the potential of patient readmission. This in turn increases the workload of A&E and the patient flows in a health care system.

3 Benefits of RFID in Health Care

An increasing number of health care organizations have adopted RFID technology. There are business cases showing that such technology has great potential to improve performance, accountability, and responsiveness of health care systems. The advantages of RFID technology can be summarized as follows:

- RFID chips do not require a line of sight
- Reusable electronic tags that are active and expensive
- Real-time access to detailed information
- Automatic identification of assets, equipment, patients, and so on without visual contact
- Security control with track and trace capabilities
- Improved resources management

The following paragraphs reveal applications and typical examples of adopting RFID technology in the health care industry and demonstrate how RFID solves the prevailing problems.

RFID Tracking System

With an RFID-based system, all patients, visitors, and staff entering a hospital are issued a smart card embedded with an RFID chip. The card is read by RFID antennas installed in the vicinity of the hospital where these people move around, for example, registration, waiting areas, consultation rooms, operating theaters, and post anesthesia care unit. The smart card records exactly when a person enters and leaves particular areas or departments. Such information is stored in a computer database. This system enables medical staff to keep track of everyone who enters various departments. If anyone is later diagnosed with an infectious disease, a record of all other individuals with whom that person has been in contact can be determined immediately.

For treatment and health care delivered in a hospital, the system enables medical staff to track patients with RFID tags. The system displays a patient's care status on an electronic tracking board that can be configured to the floor plan of the hospital. For example, in the inpatient ward, medical staff will assign patients who are ready to receive surgical operations with RFID-enabled badges. The badge is incorporated into the patient tracking system by entering the badge serial code. The RFID system is therefore able to track the badge and, hence, the patient as this patient moves around the facility. Medical staff can use computer terminals to check the patient's name, location, and time of arrival at each area via the tracking system.

As such, the RFID-based tracking technology enhances the operation and management of a health care system. As an example, the tracking system has helped reduce the A&E department patient stays at the Wilmington, Delaware (United States) based Christina Care (Health Data Management, 2006). The RFID-based tracking system was able to reduce the average length of stay for admitted patients by 36 minutes in the A&E department and to reduce the average length of stay for patient released from the A&E by 14 minutes. Moreover, the system decreases by 24 percent the number of patients who left the A&E without care, resulting in an increase in revenue.

RFID Bracelets

Another significant RFID-based health care development is the RFID bracelet or wristband. It is a plastic band strapped onto a patient's wrist that includes an RFID chip that is incorporated during admission to the inpatient ward. Encoded on the band are patient name, date of birth, gender, and a medical record number, linked to the hospital network that connects the patient record to laboratories, billing, and the pharmacy (Schwartz, 2004). The small RFID chip is able to encode information and data, such as surgical information and medication of a patient, which is more comprehensive than the traditional wristband. Also, the RFID chip can be placed on the back of the bracelet and the information can be displayed on the front.

The ultimate advantages of RFID bracelets are to reduce the risk of misidentifying patients and to access patient records in a timely manner. For instance, medical staff prints a patient's name and surgical site on a tag and encodes the tag with the name of the surgeon, surgery date, and type of treatment or procedure. The tag is scanned prior to surgery to verify the information. After the patient has moved into the operating theater, the tag is scanned again to further verify the data with the information in the patient's file.

RFID under the Skin

A controversial application of RFID in the health care industry is an implanted RFID chip about the size of a grain of rice in a patient's arm. Each of these chips contains a unique verification number that, when implanted, connects to a hospital database. The hospital has specialized RFID readers in order to scan and access the information in the chip. For security and privacy reasons, patients implanted with an RFID chip have control over who can access their information.

At present, patients who have been implanted with an RFID chip are mostly sufferers of Alzheimer's disease, diabetes, and other chronic illnesses. The main purpose of this implanted device is identification. Patients can be recognized with full identity, and their medical records can be provided comprehensively to out-of-hospital care services. Also, patients can be readily and accurately identified by medical staff when the patient is readmitted to the hospital.

Patient Management System

A patient management system that is integrated with RFID technology can collect data from various information systems and provide a real-time, on-screen, virtual floor plan of a hospital. The floor plan has icons representing individual patients. By clicking these icons, medical staff can access patients' medical history, demographic data, and current status, such as if they are scheduled for surgery or discharge.

An RFID-based patient management system provides a clearer snapshot of how patients are moving through the facilities inside a hospital. This in turn reduces the time taken to discharge patients and shortens the overall patient's length of stay.

Resources Management System

The idea behind a resources management system is to gain a better insight of the development of the health care process in and around operating theaters and to achieve an optimally organized logistics flow in a hospital. In achieving this, the management system can benefit from the appealing tracking and tracing properties of RFID technology. This includes checking and updating information regarding all kinds of resources, such as operating theater materials, blood products, the utilization of machines, the administration of blood products, and so on. The objective is to trace the consumption or utilization of resources per patient to optimize stock management.

From a microscopic view, effective resource utilization can be achieved by managing individual resources. The most important and basic resources in a hospital are beds. Bed management can be better controlled by attaching RFID tags to the beds for tracking their availability. This enables medical staff to check and change the status of each room. For example, if a patient is being discharged, the bed can then be earmarked for cleaning after the system shows the patient has been moved.

Equipment and tools for surgical operations are normally supplied in the form of kits, which are tailored and designed for a particular operation. Since the parts have to go through a number of manufacturing and sterilization processes, it is not suitable to label them. RFID technology would be an ideal solution to this problem. By embedding RFID tags in the parts, they can be tracked and thus can easily be reconciled before delivery to the hospital. Moreover, RFID enables medical staff to track each instrument's full history regarding involvement in patient surgical procedures. This can reduce the threat of transmitting infectious diseases and ensure that each instrument is in the right place at the right time.

One concern due to advances in the health care industry is an overabundance of medical waste. The amount of illegal or false dumping of medical waste is growing. To prevent this, health care organizations have started to place RFID tags on the containers that hold waste. Hence, it would be easier to track which person or organization is responsible for the dumping.

An ultimate advantage of an RFID tag is its size. Encrypted data can be placed on a small chip, including items such as patient name, identifying number, address, doctor-in-charge, test type, and results. This development can help to eliminate human error and counterfeiting of test results, and improve quality control and data verification processes.

RFID-enabled labels for drug bottles are designed to help the health care industry, especially those in the pharmaceutical supply chain, to authenticate drugs and to create an e-pedigree using unique electronic product codes providing information to RFID tags. The RFID tags record each drug bottle's distribution history as it makes its way from manufacturer, through the wholesalers, down the supply chain, and, eventually, to the hospital or pharmacist's shelf. The shipment and receipt information of a drug bottle at every point in the chain is stored in the RFID tag, making a "certified chain of custody" that can be verified on demand. Hence, the technology proves a drug's chain of custody and protects against the introduction of counterfeit and fraudulently obtained and resold drugs into the supply chain.

4 Conclusion

From these successful stories about using RFID technology in health care, it is evident that RFID technology is able to boost the efficiency and effectiveness of the industry under several principles. It can enhance the flow of transportation, such as moving patients, beds, and equipment. The waiting or idle time can be reduced dramatically as the procedures for bed assignment, admission, discharge, and searching for patients, medical staff, and documentation are simplified and made more accurate. Better inventory management, such as beds, pharmacy stock, or specimens, can be obtained. Defects such as medication error, incorrect patient identification, wrong procedures, and missing information can be eliminated.

Because of these appealing properties of RFID technology, an increasing number of health care organizations have conducted pilot studies and trials to determine how RFID can work for them. Reports from these organizations always show that RFID has remarkable benefits for the management and operation of a health care system, such as enhancing efficiency, reducing operating costs, improving safety, as well as increasing revenue. Hence, by employing RFID technology or integrating RFID into the existing health care management systems, the health care industry has tremendous opportunities to improve its performance and move a big step forward with the new technology.

References

Correa, F. A., M. J. A. Gil, and L. B. Redin. 2005. "Benefit of Connecting RFID and Lean Principles in Health Care." Business Economics. Working Papers, wb054410. Universidad Carlos III, Departamento de Economía de la Empresa.

Geodan. 2005. "Health Care Sector Starts Test with RFID." Press release. Geodan. Amsterdam. September.

Health Data Management. 2006. "Consultant Launches New Service Line." *Health Data Management* 14(1): 33–35.

O'Connor, M. C. 2005. "New RFID-Enabled Drug Pedigree Solutions." *RFID Journal.* Newsletter. November 15.

Schuerenberg, B. K. 2005. "Keeping Tabs with RFID." *Health Data Management* 13(10):39–46.

Schwartz, E. 2004. "Siemens to Pilot RFID Bracelets for Health Care. *InfoWorld.* July 23.

Sokol, B. 2004. "Medical Instrument Tracking Could Reduce Health Risks." *RFID Journal*, RFID Technology in Healthcare Applications. October 29, 2004.

Sullivan, L. 2005. "Company Introduces RFID-Embedded Medical Test Tubes." *InformationWeek.* March 28.

Treasure, T., O. Valencia, C. Sherlaw-Johnson, and S. Gallivan. 2002. "Surgical Performance Measurement." *Health Care Management Science* 5(4): 243–248.

UPS. 2005. "RFID in Healthcare: A Panacea for the Regulations and Issues Affecting the Industry." *UPS Supply Chain Solutions*. White paper. United Parcel Service of America, Inc.

RFID in Manufacturing

1 Introduction

RFID is considered as an important new technology for the manufacturing industry. Manufacturers are attracted to the benefits that RFID offers. The technology can be implemented in numerous areas of the manufacturing industry. For example, it can be used for work-in-process tracking, quality assurance, parts identification, inventory control, production planning, and replenishment, as well as for reverse logistics tracking.

2 Potential for RFID in Manufacturing

In general, a manufacturing business can be modeled as a three-echelon operation that includes the inflow of raw materials into a factory, production of goods, and delivery of goods to the wholesalers. Figure 1 illustrates the operation of a typical manufacturing business.

Inflow of Raw Materials

When pallets of raw materials are delivered to a factory, their contents need to be verified and allocated to different production lines and units in the factory. RFID technology can simplify and enhance the efficiency of the inflow and acceptance of raw materials. When pallets of raw materials are received from a truck at the truck dock, a handheld RFID reader or an RFID reader installed at the entrance gate can be used to read the RFID tags at the pallet level. This allows immediate verification of all the contents of the incoming load, and the information is directed to the warehouse management system (WMS) or enterprise resource planning (ERP) systems. Using this information, forklift operators can be directed immediately to move the pallets to their respective locations. This will increase the efficiency of material inflow, make the material handling process more streamlined, minimize human error, facilitate information flow in the manufacturing supply chain, and increase productivity.

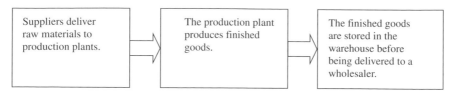

Figure 1 A three-echelon manufacturing model.

At the Production Line

In the production process, raw materials, components, or subcomponents are being modified, assembled, or processed at workstations. However, different products require different manufacturing processes. Conventionally, workers will have to verify the details of manufacturing processes that a particular product requires. Oftentimes, this is time-consuming and error-prone. With the appropriate installation of RFID technology, some of these inefficiencies and potential problems can be alleviated:

- It is often time-consuming for workers to verify the type of manufacturing process or modification that a product needs. However, if a product is RFID tagged including recipe information, workers can immediately verify the manufacturing process that details the modifications and operations that need to be performed on the product at intermediate stages of the process.
- An RFID-tagged item may be programmed with such information as the specification of its components and raw materials; the workers who have handled it; the machines, production lines, and operations it has gone through; and the dates and locations where it is produced—in other words, the entire production history. This information can be readily accessed for quality assurance, product tracking, production management, production planning and control, as well as reverse logistics operations such as product upgrade, maintenance, and recalls.
- As the quality of products relies heavily on the performance of the machinery and equipment in a plant, a proper maintenance schedule is essential. Traditionally, the scheduling of maintenance on machines is performed manually and the maintenance history of individual machines is updated manually. This is time-consuming, error-prone, and often unstructured. In this respect, RFID technology can enhance the efficiency of the maintenance process. By tagging not only the work in process and finished goods but also the production machines, information detailing the maintenance history of a machine, the identification of the technicians involved, parts replaced, and services performed can be readily available. Engineers can effectively collect the necessary information concerning the maintenance history of the machines and determine their corresponding maintenance schedules. Technicians can

obtain the service history at the machine using a handheld RFID reader before the maintenance and then update the information stored in the tag after performing the maintenance. The benefits of saving time, improving quality, and reducing the chance of procedural and human errors are apparent.

In the Warehouse

In most batch production settings, finished products are stored in the warehouse before delivery to the wholesalers or retailers. One of the major tasks in a warehouse is therefore to prepare products for staging—that is, products are picked and gathered before delivery. Using RFID, an automated system such as a WMS, which is a computer-based information system, can be set up to organize storage space, line up cartons of product in the correct sequence based on orders received, and route them for staging. In addition to more effective warehouse management and product tracking; the deployment of an RFID-enabled WMS can eliminate inaccurate order sequencing and incorrect shipment and can increase the overall operation efficiency and service level.

3 Manufacturing Case Files

A successful case using RFID in manufacturing is for manufacturing process tracking by Seagate Technology. Seagate Technology is a leading manufacturer of technology products, in particular, computer hard disk drives, for data storage, access, and management. The company is a market leader in various-sized hard disk drives (Pasquerell, 2006). In order to ensure the quality of its products, Seagate has deployed RFID technology to track its products in real time as they are moving through the entire manufacturing process.

In the Seagate hard disk manufacturing process, each disk is routed via a conveyor system through over 20 production and assembly processes at various locations. Tight quality control in these production processes is essential, as any deviation from the standard work procedures would lead to scrapped hard disks. In this regard, Seagate needs to store information for each disk in the manufacturing process so as to ensure that each hard disk has successfully completed all preceding production processes before going to the next process. With tens of thousands of disks routing through the plant daily, strict product traceability is vital for Seagate to manage its manufacturing operation. Seagate has decided to deploy RFID technology to improve the visibility in its production as well as capitalize on the ability to read and write information that is stored in an RFID tag. In addition, the robustness of the RFID tags that it uses provides added advantages in that these tags are able to withstand rigorous production steps like frequent cleaning.

In Seagate's hard disk manufacturing process, an RFID tag is placed onto each disk, where processing information for the disk is stored. At each decision point along the assembly line, the data stored in the tags is read and sent to the host computer. Based on the information stored in the tags, the host computer then determines the routing of the disks in the manufacturing process. As such, every disk is directed to the right position in the assembly line. Any misplaced disk can be immediately identified before any incorrect processing steps take place. With the appropriate deployment of the technology, the RFID-based tracking system helps to reduce the scrap rate to almost zero, and the system thus offers excellent production control for Seagate.

4 Conclusion

In view of the contributions of RFID technology in manufacturing such as the Seagate case, we can appreciate the benefits gained in the entire manufacturing supply chain. RFID technology enhances the efficiency and accuracy of receiving and allocating raw materials in a manufacturing plant, it improves the management and control of production operations, and it streamlines the handling and tracking of the staging and delivery of finished products in a warehouse.

With the benefits that RFID delivers, there exists a number of persistent issues that prevent its wide implementation in manufacturing worldwide. First, the cost of RFID technology is still high compared with labor costs in some parts of the world, such as in developing countries, where labor costs are rather low. Second, a globally acknowledged standard for RFID tags and technology is still under development. This impedes the worldwide implementation of RFID technology in the global supply chain. Third, organizations are very concerned about security issues, as discussed in Chapter 10. Confidential information about shipments and inventory may easily be tracked by competitors if RFID technology is implemented in the manufacturing supply chain. These problems are yet to be resolved; nonetheless, the driving forces are there and are intensifying. With the rapid advancement of technology and an increasing number of successful cases, RFID technology is on the way toward revolutionizing manufacturing.

Reference

Pasquerell, L. 2006. *"RFID Tracks Critical Manufacturing Processes."* Integrated Solutions. Available online at www.integratedsolutionsmag.com/articles/2006_01/060108.html.

RFID in Marine Terminal Operation

1 Introduction

In some parts of the world such as Hong Kong and Singapore, a marine terminal is the critical interchange between production and sales. Problems and inefficiencies in terminal operations can have a costly ripple effect across the whole supply chain. The United States, as an example, has very large port operations in New York and in Los Angeles, plus some other locations, and port security is a major concern. The importance of terminal operation has driven many marine terminal operators to evaluate and adopt new technologies for improving efficiency, effectiveness, and security. More and more terminal operators are looking toward using RFID as a promising solution to increase efficiency and security, and RFID is being seen as an indispensable technology in the "port of the future."

The strength of this technology is the real-time visibility it offers. Marine terminals have long been searching for technology to solve the classical problem of tracking containers and tractors. RFID can help to locate their position and provide accurate data that helps in orchestrating their deployment. The technology is also seen as a means to comply with various security regulations after the events of September 11, 2001.

In fact, there are terminals already trying out the technology. For example, the Port of Busan (see section later in the chapter) has deployed a trial RFID container-tracking system to improve security and handling efficiency (Collins, 2005); Hutchison Whampoa, Port of Singapore Authority, and P&O Ports have decided to deploy RFID tracking technology in their terminals worldwide (Narasimhan, 2005). As an increasing number of leading container ports and terminals around the world are planning to become RFID-ready, the technology is arriving much faster than we may anticipate.

2 Applications and Benefits

RFID technology offers a number of application possibilities in terminal management, including container and tractors tracking and container security control. The prime reason that RFID can provide such useful functionality is because of its provision of key features such as traceability, efficiency, security, and cost-effectiveness. RFID technology enables terminal operators to have better knowledge of the whole terminal, which could lead to better planning of terminal operations. Active RFID tags are particularly applicable in container terminals. They can be read at distances of over 30 m, greatly improving the usability of the device in terminals.

Within the Terminal

In order to stay competitive, modern terminals where container-handling services including loading, unloading, and storage are provided have to process an increasing number of containers in an efficient and secure manner. A crucial part of this challenge is the ability to locate specific containers at any given time (Scott, 2001). This is a complicated task, as there are thousands of containers moving in a terminal every day. In this respect, real-time visibility is becoming essential for the management, and it can help in the compliance with the new security regulations.

Typically, containers arrive at a terminal via vessels, trains, or outside tractors through the check-in gate. Once a container is moved into the terminal, it may be temporarily parked on a chassis in the terminal, placed atop a stack of containers, or moved around the terminal as a result of operating algorithms. When a container is to be retrieved, it must first be located among thousands of containers in the terminal before it is delivered to a destination, such as another vessel, a tractor, or some specific locations in the yard. It is not uncommon that in the course of delivering a container, human error is introduced where information concerning the particular container is entered, modified, and retrieved.

A solution to the problem is to have a system that is able to automate the real-time tracking and locating of containers. With the fitting of an active RFID tag on every tractor that enters the terminal, the movement of the tractor that is carrying the container can be accurately tracked. Information concerning the current location and prior moves of the tractor can be used by the terminal operators to schedule the loading and unloading process. By also tagging the containers, the movement of a container and the information concerning its content can be tracked at the container level. With the location and meta data of the containers and the tractors electronically recorded in a terminal management system, operators are able to rapidly locate specific containers in the yard and can make more informed decisions on planning and scheduling. This greatly speeds up the loading or unloading operations of vessels or tractors.

In addition, more accurate operations can be ensured where automatic checking of containers can be performed using the RFID-based system. The seal number, contents, loading date, and destination that are stored on a tag can be managed and matched with the vessel manifest, guaranteeing that the right containers are handled and thereby reducing operational errors, paperwork, staff time, and drayage and increasing container throughput (Horowitz, 2005). Other benefits may include the automatic monitoring of container status such as power hookup time and temperature for refrigerated containers.

In terms of security, RFID-enabled containerization can help to combat terrorism in international transhipment, where integrity of a container can be better ensured. As the importance of safety and security in the supply chain has become a major concern, new regulations have been adopted. In January 2002, the Customs Department of the United States launched the Container Security Initiative (CSI) to help prevent containerized cargo from being exploited by terrorists. In 2003, the newly formed Customs and Border Patrol (CBP) Agency under the Department of Homeland Security (DHS) launched its Customs-Trade Partnership Against Terrorism (C-TPAT) program. The program sets the import standards for importers and carriers in ensuring the safety of global supply chains.

With these regulations enforced, there are increasing burdens on container terminals to ensure the integrity of containers. Thus, recording the movement of goods from the point of origin to the point of consumption has become necessary. The functions of automatic identification and data collection facilitated by RFID permit container ports to comply with these regulations. The use of RFID technology for employee ID badges and access control security seals provides added assurances to container integrity. Currently, containers that meet these requirements will be fast-tracked on arrival in the United States, allowing them to move across the terminal faster (Mullen, 2006).

Across Terminals

RFID technology is being explored as a solution to improve security control because of a number of attributes that make it uniquely suited, including a high level of security, non-line-of-sight reading, multiple reads at long ranges, high speeds, large amount of data stored in a small-sized RFID tag, and reliability in super-harsh environments (Horowitz, 2005).

A new generation of "smart seals" has been developed to improve the integrity of containers and their contents (see Figure 1). Traditionally, conventional security seals made from plastic or metal, which could provide evidence of tampering, are used (see Figure 2). Visual inspection is often required. Evidence of tampering is usually discovered long after it has happened. Smart seals with active RFID tags will broadcast messages when they are opened or removed without authorization. Once a container arrives at its destination, authorized personnel read the data from the RFID tag and confirm the integrity of the container. Even during transit, RFID tags can send status information to the customs and port authorities before arrival (Chung, 2005).

Figure 1 An RFID-equipped smart seal.

Smart tags can also be equipped with sensors to monitor environmental conditions within or around the container. The tags can be equipped with radioactive, chemical, and biological sensors to check for weapons of mass destruction (WMD). They can be equipped also with sensors that detect changes in light, temperature, and humidity to ensure that a controlled environment is maintained, especially important for goods sensitive to these conditions. Containers with RFID smart seals will enable shippers and carriers to continuously monitor the security and integrity of their shipment, and to perform "virtual inspection" in advance of arrival (Mullen, 2006).

To further monitor the location, the status and the condition of containers in a global transhipment operation, RFID tags can be integrated with the Global Positioning System (GPS). The U.S. Department of Defense is now using this hybrid technology for high-security containers (LeMay et al., 2001). Complementing the strength of RFID for indoor and information storage with GPS for accurate global positioning, the integrated system provides a complete resolution for tracking assets.

3 Successful Case Examples

A number of terminals around the world have successfully adopted RFID technology in enhancing the efficiency and security of containerization. The following sections highlight some of these success stories.

Figure 2 Conventional container security seals.

Long Beach Port

NYK Logistics at Long Beach Port, California, is a mammoth 70-acre container yard and trans-load facility featuring 1,200 parking slots and 250 dock doors. NYK is responsible for managing more than 50,000 inbound ocean freight containers from the Port of Los Angeles/Long Beach and

30,000 outbound trailers every year. NYK Logistics operates 24/7 and processes more than 1,000 gate transactions daily during peak season, checking in and out containers and trailers from 11 different vessel liners and 12 to 15 domestic carriers (NYK, 2006).

In 2005, an RFID-based wireless real-time locating system was deployed by NYK for better management of its terminal and yard operation. The system enables NYK to automate more than 90 percent of its terminal operations, which has increased dock door utilization, reduced yard congestion, and increased throughput. In particular, upon arrival at the container terminal gate, every container gets tagged with an active RFID device. From this point forward, NYK operators have constant connectivity to terminal assets such as containers and other container-handling equipment wherever they move about the facility. The system enables accurate and automated records of every container entering the terminal to be maintained and tracked. Based on container tractor driver feedback, the system has resulted in a 50 percent reduction in time spent in terminal to complete a transaction.

The Port of Busan in South Korea

The Port of Busan is currently deploying a trial RFID container-tracking system that aims to provide better operational efficiency of the terminal (Collins, 2005). This trial is part of a project to enhance the efficiency and security of its global overseas shipping operations.

Smart containers are employed to streamline the operations by providing automated advanced notification of when containers are scheduled to arrive at the port. Containers are tracked as they enter the port gates and are loaded onto a vessel by crane mounted readers. The information collected is used for scheduling and port management. The system is planned to be used at other container ports in South Korea.

The Port of Rotterdam in the Netherlands

The world's largest active RFID installation is implemented in the Port of Rotterdam (Telematics, 2005; RFid Gazette, 2005). The Broekman Group is deploying an RFID-based real-time locating system at its port. Under the new system, each vehicle is given an active RFID tag where the vehicle identification number (VIN) is stored. The system helps to locate all vehicles that are deployed in the terminal at any given point in time. Currently there are over 250,000 vehicles entering the terminal annually, and the system helps to manage and keep track of these assets. The data collection process for these vehicles is automated to increase the port utilization and throughput, enhance the customer service and hence satisfaction, and at the same time, cut cost.

PSA Singapore Terminals

The PSA Singapore Terminals operates four container terminals handling about one-fifth of the world's total container transhipment throughput. In

2005, PSA Singapore Terminals handled 22.28 million 20-foot equivalent units (TEU) and is a major Asian trading and transportation hub (PSA, 2006).

Early in mid 2004, PSA Singapore Terminals became the first pilot port in Asia under the U.S. Container Security Initiative, and in 2005, PSA is implementing the use of RFID seals for all containers bound for U.S. seaports. It is reported that RFID technology presents new business opportunities for the Singapore information communications sector, and the adoption of the RFID technology gives Singapore an edge as a logistics center and global trading center. The Singapore government believes that the adoption of RFID in its terminals not only increases the efficiency gains and lowers overall operating costs but also demonstrates that Singapore is on technology's cutting edge (RFID Journal, 2004).

4 Conclusion

RFID technology enables real-time visibility of trailers, containers, and even container-handling equipment, imparting significant operational advantages to marine terminals and optimizing their operations. With successful case files, the improved visibility of container movement and content tracking allows better planning and scheduling of resources, hence improving the efficiency of terminal operation. Reduction of errors by as much as 70 percent is evidenced, and as a whole, service is improved and customers are more satisfied. RFID solutions also improve the security control of containers in the global transhipment supply chain, and the technology holds great promise for marine terminal operation and management as a whole.

While leading ports including the Port of Long Beach, Port of Busan, Rotterdam, and PSA Singapore have been aggressively deploying RFID for security control and container tracking, other terminals around the world have started to probe into the technology. Even though worldwide adoption of RFID for containerization will not occur overnight, in the long run, RFID will definitely become one of the core technologies in the "port of the future."

References

AeroScout. 2005. "Yard Management Visibility Application Note." Available online via www.aeroscout.com/data/uploads/AeroScout.

Chung, K. 2005. "Secure Cargo Container and Supply Chain Management Based on Real-Time End-to-End Visibility and Intrusion Monitoring." Avante International Technology. Available online via www.avantetech.com/white%20paper%20on%20container-real-time-locating-monitoring%20system.pdf.

Collins, J. 2005. "Korean Seaport Tests RFID Tracking." *RFID Journal*. Available online via www.rfidjournal.com/article/articleview/1438/1/12.

Horowitz, Z. 2005. "Application of Radio Frequency Identification Technology to Container Security and Tracking." Portland State University. Available online via www.cecs.pdx.edu/~monserec/courses/freight/classprojects/PDF%20-%20 rfid_in_container_security_paper.pdf

LeMay, S. A., R. Cassady, J. Withee, and Viator, J. 2001. "Tracking and Positioning Software: A Market Need, Value, and Cost Analysis." National Center for Intermodal Transportation. Mississippi State University. Available online via www.ie.msstate.edu/ncit/ncit_web_update/Version2LeMayFinalProject. 2001.htm.

Mullen, D. 2006. "The Application of RFID Technology in a Port." AIM Global. Available online via www.aimglobal.org/technologies/rfid/resources/Port-Tech.pdf.

Narasimhan, T. E. 2005. RFID: "Box Ports' Friend." *CII Logistics & Freight News* 1(3): 2–3.

NYK. 2006. "NYK Logistics Case Study." WhereNet. Available online via www. wherenet.com/successstories/NYKLogisticsCaseStudy.html.

PSA. 2006. "PSA Singapore Terminals." Available online via www.singaporepsa. com.

RFid Gazette. 2005. "WhereNet to Track Vehicles at Port of Rotterdam." *RFid Gazette*, Available online via www.rfidgazette.org/2005/09/wherenet_to_tra.html.

RFID Journal. 2004. "Singapore Seeks Learning RFID Role." *RFID Journal*. Available online via www.rfidjournal.com/article/articleview/1024/1/1.

Saxena, M. 2005. "Does GIS and RFID Amalgamation Work?" GeoPlace.com. Available online via www.geoplace.com/uploads/FeatureArticle/0505tt.asp.

Scott, J. 2001 "WhereNet RTLS in Marine Terminals." WhereNet.. Available online via http://www.wherenet.com/pr_10_21_2003.shtml

Telematics. 2005. "WhereNet Deploys World's Largest Active RFID Real-Time Locating System." *Telematics Journal.* Available online via www. telematicsjournal.com/content/topstories/858.html.

RFID in the Military

1 Introduction

RFID is a revolutionary technology that will play an important role in the implementation of a knowledge-enabled logistic support system for military operations through fully automated and visible management of resources. Applications of RFID in military and defense can be divided into two main areas: logistics related and combat related. The application of RFID in logistical supply chains helps to add visibility to item data at every node of the supply network, allowing commanders to visualize movement of materials. This has been a difficult issue to tackle with traditional tracking systems like the barcode.

2 Logistics and Inventory Control

The application of RFID in logistics is no groundbreaking news; the U.S. Department of Defense has employed active RFID in its supply chain for nearly a decade and has successfully provided commanders with in-transit visibility during major operations (U.S. DoD, 2006), such as Operation Enduring Freedom and Operation Iraqi Freedom. The first application of active RFID in the United States was motivated by the occurrence of several serious problems in tracking and obtaining necessary supplies during Operation Desert Storm. A study conducted in 1992 suggested that thousands of containers of materiel did not reach their destination, causing difficulties in field operations.

Active RFID provided by Savi Technology was implemented in early 1990 (before Operation Desert Storm took place) and has been operating since then. The U.S. military compared Operation Desert Storm (late 1990) to Operation Iraqi Freedom (2003) and found that 90 percent fewer containers were shipped in Operation Iraqi Freedom, but the difference in troop strength was only 30 percent less compared to Operation Desert Storm (Savi Technology, 2003). These figures demonstrated the ability of RFID in improving the efficiency of logistics systems by assisting logisticians to visualize large quantities of inventory under a pressing time frame. The Department of Defense estimated that the military had saved US$300 million in Iraq because of the implementation of RFID. With the implementation of passive RFID, logistics systems in the military sector are expected to provide near-real-time in-transit visibility for all classes of supplies and materiel to in-the-box content level of detail. It is also expected that with the adoption of RFID technology to inventory management of military supplies, a nonintrusive means of data collection with item-level visibility can be achieved. All these benefits translate to more efficient management for high quantities of small items such as ammunition and pharmaceuticals.

3 National Security

Apart from inventory control, RFID can be used to prevent international crime (AIM, 2006). In 2004, there were more than 20 million freight containers circulating throughout the world. Countries such as the United States received 7 million containers per year but only about 5 percent of them were physically inspected (Flynn, 2006). While commercial firms are often concerned with missing items in the containers when their customers open them, national security is more concerned about having unwanted items in the containers. Unchecked containers could harbor illegal immigrants or even terrorists (Sopensky, 2005). The spacious container may also contain hazardous materials or weapons of mass destruction that may pose a threat to the stability of a nation. RFID tagging allows tracking of container movement prior to arrival. Security officials may use this information to apply appropriate security measures to individual containers upon arrival at the port. RFID technology can also register unscheduled opening and resealing of containers. Thus, if a container stopped at various ports prior to arrival and was opened and resealed in one or more of those ports, security officials may be alerted to this nonnormal travel history and inspect the container

4 Field Combat

Though customers waiting at the end of a military supply chain are troops fighting in harsh conditions; quite different than typical customers in the commercial world, the benefits from and processes for implementing RFID are similar. RFID has many unique benefits in its potential applications to combat, reconnaissance, and rescue operations.

Implementation of RFID in the military has been successful in logistics and in many other areas that are less familiar to the general public. Future combat systems (Defense Industry Daily, 2006) under research are said to allow soldiers in the field to have access to different equipment, including manned vehicles and unmanned robotic vehicles. In other words, future battles will be fought by robots instead of humans. Better and faster use of combat information will become a key factor to dominate the battlefield. During combat operations, commanders taking charge of tactical and strategic operations at the console are always eager to continuously monitor the terrain and movement of their troops in the field, so that more accurate and responsive command can be given to direct the troops to achieve the mission. During Operation Iraqi Freedom, RFID technology provided exactly what the commanders were looking for. RFID tags carried by troops enabled the radar to detect the troops' location and produce an instant image of the formation at the console. This technology not only allowed commanders to visualize and understand the field situation better; it allowed them also to see their troops closing in on their objective in real time. This remarkable ability was a far cry in operations prior to the implementation of RFID technology. The ability to see the movement of troops in real time helps the commander to make more comprehensive decisions and may decrease casualties.

5 Military Training and Homeland Security

Outside of the battlefield, the same personnel tracking technology can be applied to the training environment. Location-enabled training environments can facilitate more complex and more realistic training exercises. The system is also suitable for urban indoor and outdoor combat training. Movement of recruits in the training environment can be seen in real time on a computer screen and can be captured and replayed for evaluation with the recruits after the session. Senior commanders can be trained under the same system to learn to coordinate troops approaching from different directions. In addition to combat and training, security systems on military bases may employ the same technology to determine unauthorized entrance or exit from specifically defined areas. If all personnel and weapons are RFID tagged, their path of movement can be recorded and analyzed in real time to alert the commander if abnormal behavior of individuals is found (O'Connor, 2005). A scenario illustrating the operation of such a system could be an intruder entering a restricted area with a fake ID. Let's say that the intruder disabled an armed guard and now has the officer's weapon Since the intruder possesses a fake ID, the system will alert the officials when the intruder tries to get through another gate, because the system senses that the tag on the firearm is not moving with the associated tag assigned to the disabled guard. In military access control, tracking the movement of weapons is a useful tactic in addition to human identification.

Highly trained dogs are often used in search operations. These dogs search for explosives as well as for missing personnel. Dogs are trained to locate hidden objects using their sense of smell. Depending on the training provided and special characteristics of different breeds, some dogs are more sensitive to the smell of explosives and others are more sensitive to the smell of humans, dead or alive. The dog is trained to alert its handler by barking when a suspicious object is found. This signaling method may be sufficient in urban operations and in small outdoor areas where the communicating pairs remain in sight most of the time, but when searching in a large area, such as a forest, the reflection of sound and obstacles in sight may make it difficult for the human to locate the barking dog. Installation of RFID tags allows human handlers to locate the dog easier, hence making the search more effective.

6 Friendly Force Identification

Though casualties in war are inevitable and expected, casualties due to friendly fire are a particularly serious matter. For this and other obvious reasons, technology that can identify friendly units in real time on the battlefield has been in great demand. NATO has been testing a combat identity system that employs RFID technology under battlefield conditions (Ranger, 2005). The system consists of RFID tags that are larger than those used by retailers and are more rugged to suit military applications. Energy sent by an aircraft's radar is used to illuminate the tag, which can then send back location information of the reflected signal. The system is relatively low in cost and can be implemented without modifying the radar system. The specially designed RFID tag with a small antenna can be powered by four AA-sized batteries and can return a signal from as far as 125 kilometers to military aircrafts (Ranger, 2005). The tag can be carried by friendly troops and vehicles as well as installed at targets that should not be fired upon, such as hospitals.

The system demonstrates promising potential in fratricide prevention, but there are still issues to be solved before the technology can be implemented. One obvious question is how to make sure that the friendly tag doesn't get into the enemy's hands. If a soldier becomes a battlefield casualty and his or her tag is picked up by an enemy, how can the system differentiate between the two sides? Another problem is how to prevent the tags from responding to enemy radar; if the tags reply to every digital query like those used in retail applications, soldiers can become ready targets for the enemy.

7 Reconnaissance

As discussed elsewhere in this book, semiactive tags contain internal power sources but still rely on RF energy transferred from the reader to the tag to make a response. The internal power source contained is for monitoring environmental conditions. Semiactive tags use an internal power source to operate the electronic components to sense the environment or to relay signals.

The U.S. military is developing semiactive tags with sensors for detecting the sound of a human footfall at 5 to 10 meters' distance. These tags are about the size of golf balls and are camouflaged to look like a rock. They are difficult to spot when placed among real rocks (O'Reilly, 2005). A principal application of these sensor-equipped tags is to place them near base camps or troops in the field to allow intelligence units to monitor the sound of an approaching enemy over a wide area. These "rocks" can also be distributed over a wider field or desert from aircraft to detect enemy movement. For example, trails between the many mountains in Afghanistan can be regularly monitored in real time by dropping a large quantity of these rocks with a number of repeaters to transmit data back to the base camp or via satellite. These tags are to be massively produced at costs so low that they won't require retrieval.

The initial phase of development aims to retrieve signals by a remote sensing device. A more ambitious plan is for these rocks to listen to each other and form intelligence nets. The whole idea is in line with the future combat concept, which is to remove human soldiers from being exposed to danger while at the same time gather as much intelligence and offensive might as possible on a mass scale.

8 Conclusion

As engineers are becoming more aware of the potential applications of RFID beyond logistics, this technology is finding its way into exotic application areas such as security and defense. Innovative use of RFID in homeland and national security enables authorities to effectively monitor abnormal entries and transits at air terminals as well as seaports; hence, dangerous articles and persons can be strategically blocked or monitored as soon as they are spotted. Application of RFID on the battlefield not only helps to strengthen defense by acting as a sensor to detect unregistered movement in a covered area, but it also helps radar networks to differentiate between friend and foe to avoid friendly fire on the battlefield. In addition to defense applications, RFID is also applied to assist search-and-rescue operations. As seen in this section, many possible application areas for RFID are in the idea stage or in the early application stage. Logistics, reconnaissance, search and rescue, field combat, and inventory control are areas with great application possibilities

References

AIM. 2006. "RFID and Homeland Security." Available online via www.aimglobal. org/technologies/rfid/resources/articles/dec03/Homeland.htm (accessed May 24, 2006).

Defense Industry Daily. 2006. "FCS Spin-Out Plans Detailed." *Defense Industry Daily.* Available online via www.defenseindustrydaily.com/2005/12/fcs-spinout-plans-detailed/index.php (accessed May 18, 2006).

Flynn, S. E., and J. J. Kirkpatrick. 2006. "The Limitations of the Current U.S. Government Efforts to Secure the Global Supply Chain against Terrorists Smuggling a WMD and a Proposed Way Forward." Written testimony before a hearing of the Permanent Subcommittee on Investigations Committee on Homeland Security and Governmental Affairs United States Senate on "Neutralizing the Nuclear and Radiological Threat: Securing the Global Supply Chain." Available online via www.cfr.org/publication/10277/limitations_of_the_current_us_government efforts_to_secure_the_global_supply_chain_against_terrorists_smuggling_a_ wmd_and_a_proposed_way_forward.html (accessed May 24, 2006).

O'Connor, M. C. 2005. "Homeland Security to Test RFID." *RFID Journal.* January 28. Available online via www.rfidjournal.com/article/articleview/1360/1/1/ (accessed May 20, 2006).

O'Reilly, Tim. 2005. "US Army to Deploy RFID 'Listening Rocks.'" May 29. Available online via http://radar.oreilly.com/archives/2005/05/us_army_to_depl.html (accessed May 20, 2006).

Ranger, S. 2005. "NATO Tests RFID to Prevent Friendly Fire." October 20. Available online via http://news.com.com/NATO+tests+RFID+to+prevent+friendly+ fire/2100-11395_3-5904392.html (accessed May 23, 2006.)

Savi Technology. 2003. "Case Study: Operation Enduring Freedom/Operation Iraqi Freedom (OEF/OIF)." December. Available online via www.savi.com/products/ casestudies/cs.oif.pdf.

Sopensky, E. 2005. "The Sun, the World and RFID." *Foreign Service Journal.* December. Available online via www.afsa.org/fsj/dec05/sopensky.pdf (accessed May 18, 2006).

U.S. DoD. 2006. "Beginning to See RFID Payback." Available online via www.defenseindustrydaily.com/logistics/ (accessed May 24, 2006.)

RFID in
Payment Transactions

1 Introduction

The contactless smart card with embedded RFID is conquering the market for payment transactions. Smart cards are used as an alternative, or even a substitute, for traditional cash. More and more companies are now offering their own versions of a payment card to their users. RFID has redefined the concept of payment and money. Throughout the world, contactless smart cards are transforming the way people purchase commodities, pay for goods and services, and shop from home, and they are spending more, as well.

The appeal of this technology is its convenience and efficiency offered to both the consumer and the merchant. The embedded-RFID technology also offers the ability to have more than one payment application resident on the same card and the ability to have other applications such as loyalty schemes and access to information facilities incorporated.

In the United States, there are RFID-based payment systems already operating in the marketplace, including the Speedpass offered by ExxonMobil, which is used by customers at fuel pumps and is discussed in Chapter 1. The system allows companies to track metrics such as frequency of customer visits, average purchases, and types of purchase (gasoline, candy, newspapers), and it provides customized opportunities at the point of purchase. Similar payment systems are also offered by Philips 66 and Citgo. In addition, American Express has been testing its ExpressPay RFID payment product with merchants in the Phoenix, Arizona area (Collins, 2004). In addition, the Oyster card is used with Transport for London and the National Rail services. One of the most successful deployments of RFID-related payment system has been used by millions of people in Hong Kong for many years. The Octopus system, discussed later and shown in Figure 1, undeniably captured the Hong Kong market, and it is the role model for a lot of similar payment systems around the world.

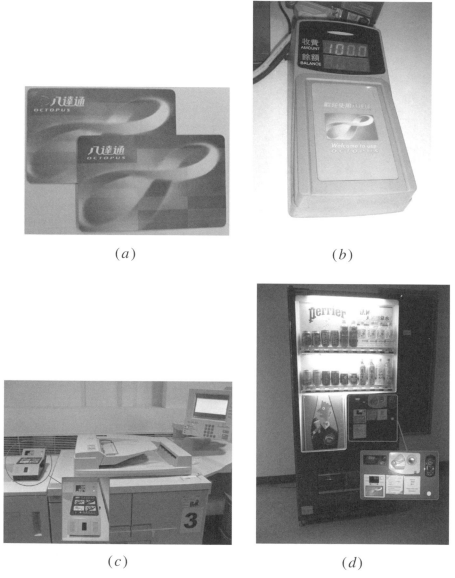

(a)

(b)

(c)

(d)

Figure 1 The Octopus Cards and readers (a) Octopus Cards used in Hong Kong (b) Octopus reader (c) Octopus Card for payment in photocopying (d) Octopus Card for vending machine.

2 Applications and Benefits in Payment Transactions

Payment cards have been in existence for many years. They started as plastic cards printed with the cardholder name, expiration date, and so on, with an authorization signature. These cards may be used at the point of sale to purchase goods or services, and in other cases, they are used as some kind of membership card or discount card. Consumers just need to show their card at the point of sale to obtain the discount offered or to identify their membership for services.

Owing to the limited information stored on these cards, their use is somehow restricted. A magnetic strip was soon developed and introduced as a means for holding more data compared to cards with printed data alone. The magnetic strip allowed stored data to be read electronically with a suitable terminal or card reader so that data verification can be performed with little or no human intervention. However, the contact nature of these cards reduces the efficiency and reliability of the transaction, as it takes time for the terminal/reader to communicate with the cards. To pay with a card that is installed with a magnetic strip in a supermarket, the transaction may even take longer compared to a cash payment. In addition, because the storage space on a magnetic strip is limited, application of the card is constrained. In terms of security, magnetic-strip cards have already been developed to the point where there is little payoff for introducing better anticrime measures (Thales e-Security, 2006). All these factors have driven the market to look for new technologies to develop electronic means for payment transactions with improved security and convenience.

In this regard, contactless smart cards evolved to be a means for next-generation transaction payment with improved security, speed, and convenience. Contactless cards that are incorporated with wireless RFID technology can be directly recognized by the reader without removing the card from a user's purse or wallet. According to Octopus Card Limited (Octopus, 2006), transactions can be completed in less than 1/3 second and according to FreedomPay (Collins, 2004), the entire transaction process can be up to 60 percent faster than it would be for cash payment. Evidently, the transaction payment made by these contactless cards provides a quick payment method for consumers when compared to a cash payment or payment made by a magnetic strip card.

Furthermore, contactless smart cards offer convenience to both the merchants and consumers. Consumers no longer have to fumble with cash and change or worry about having insufficient cash for a purchase; they can just hold their card near a reader and complete the transaction. For example, it can be extremely time-consuming and clumsy to pay the exact bus fare on public transportation that requires taking different denominations of coins and feeding them into the coin slot of the bus. In comparison, by paying through a contactless smart card, the operation becomes swift and easy. For small-sum payments, the use of a smart card has proven to be even more convenient to consumers. With the use of electronic money that is facilitated by these smart cards, merchants can also enjoy lower operating costs and improved efficiency with less effort needed to handle a large amount of cash. As such, the adoption of contactless smart cards can directly benefit both parties in payment transactions.

An RFID smart card that consists of a microchip can handle and store from 10 to more than 100 times more information than a traditional magnetic stripe card (Bansal, 2007). As a result, these smart cards have the ability to handle more than one payment application and even other non-transaction applications on a single smart card. As personal details can be stored, these smart cards can also be used for access control as driving licenses or even personal identity cards. The use of these contactless smart cards is extremely promising because they can provide a reliable, cost-effective, and convenient means to streamline our everyday life.

3 A Successful Case: The Octopus System

Just imagine using a single smart card to pay the fares on all public transportation systems (buses, underground, trains, minibuses, etc.); pay for purchases in convenience stores, supermarkets, and restaurants; pay for commodities in shops; and for many more uses. People in Hong Kong enjoy this convenience using the Octopus Card, a contactless smart card that uses RFID technology (Siu, 2002).

The system was developed by Octopus Card Limited in 1997. Octopus Card Limited was established by a group of public transport operators including the Mass Transit Railway Corporation (MTRC), Kowloon Canton Railway Corporation (KCRC), Kowloon Motor Bus (KMB), Citybus, New World First Bus, and New World First Ferry to provide a simple and convenient way to pay fares. In 2006, there were over 13 million Octopus Cards in circulation, while the population of Hong Kong is approximately 6.8 million. Moreover, there are over US$9.2 million in transactions each day using the Octopus system. A little arithmetic leads to an annual transaction value of HK$25 billion (HK$7.8 = US$1, approximately). The Octopus System is indisputably the world's number one electronic transaction payment system. The system has been awarded the "Asian Innovation Award 1998" from the Far Eastern Economic Review and "2003 Hong Kong Top Ten Brandnames Award" from the Chinese Manufacturers' Association of Hong Kong (Octopus, 2006). The system is a prime example of a successful RFID-enabled deployment. Currently, there are over 50,000 locations where the Octopus card is accepted in Hong Kong. These locations include public transport, car parks, supermarkets, convenience stores, fast-food stands, bakeries and coffeeshops, personal care stores, vending machines, kiosks, photo booths, photocopiers, and recreational facilities. (HKTDC, 2005). Figures 1a through d show examples of Octopus cards and typical readers that are used in public transportation systems, for retailers, and for parking meters in Hong Kong.

Despite the great success of the Octopus Card system, it is not replicated worldwide, as the core technology deployed does not follow the prevailing RFID standards. RFID was still in its infancy, and these standards did not exist when the Octopus Card system was first introduced in the 1990s. Therefore, Europe and the United States are investing in developing RFID-enabled card systems instead of the Octopus Card system.

4 Key Benefits of Smart Cards

RFID-enabled smart cards have greatly facilitated the development and deployment of electronic transaction payment. Such payment systems originally introduced for fare collection in transport systems are rapidly expanding with respect to the scope of service offered the community. In addition to public transport, the system is now used as an alternative to cash in stores, supermarkets, vending machine, and the like. The system transforms the way people buy and pay for goods. A growing number of retailers now accept this means of transaction payment, including large chain stores, supermarkets, pharmacies, convenience stores, fast-food shops, and household stores.

In addition, the system is being used to make payment in many other areas, for example, for admission to public facilities like theme parks, sports events, and museums; and an increasing number of car parks are now accepting the system for payment of parking fees. The system is an efficient, flexible, and reliable means of cash collection that shortens the transaction time for sales of goods and services compared to using cash.

5 Conclusion

RFID technology holds great promise for next-generation transaction payment systems. Their convenience and efficiency has driven the rapid growth for transaction payments around the world. The successful case of the Octopus system in Hong Kong and others similar systems around the world have become role models for many others to seriously consider deploying RFID-based technology in streamlining their transaction operations.

As in the case of Octopus, their success in bringing revolutionary changes to the low-value, high-volume transaction business has further established the value in the deployment of RFID-based technology in payment transactions. Many other operations around the world, including the EZ-Link card in Singapore for its MRT and bus systems, Suica for the JR East Railway and the Nagasaki Smart Card system in Japan, TransCard for the Shenzhen Metro and EasyCard for the Taipei Metro in China, Oyster Card for London Transport, and SmarTrip for the Metro system in Washington, D.C., and Chicago Card on Chicago's CTA, in the United States, are riding on such technology (Wikipedia, 2006).

We see that the growth worldwide is imminent, and what we are waiting to see is standardization of the system. RFID has reformed the way that we make our payments and such handy e-cash will definitely become the money of the next generation.

References

Bansal, Vinay. 2006. Private communication. BrickRed Technologies Private Ltd. Noida, India. February 2.

Collins, J. 2004. "RFID Serves Up Cafeteria Food." *RFID Journals*. Available online via www.freedompay.com/misc/news/RFIDj_825.htm (last accessed January 31, 2007).

HKTDC. 2005. "Octopus Spreads Its Tentacles Worldwide." Hong Kong Trade Development Council. Available online via www.hktrader.net/200502/success/success-EricTai200502.htm (last accessed January 31, 2006).

Octopus. 2006. "Octopus Cards Limited." Available online via www.octopuscards.com (last accessed January 31, 2006).

Siu, L. L.S. 2002. "Octopus and Mondex: The Social Shaping of Money, Technology and Consensus." Available online via www.sociology.ed.ac.uk/finance/Papers/Siu_Octopus.pdf (last accessed January 31, 2007).

Thales e-Security. 2006. "Smart Cards for Payment Systems." Available online via www.thales-esecurity.com/Whitepapers/ documents/Smart_cards_for_payment_systems.pdf (last accessed January 31, 2007).

Wikipedia. 2006. "Octopus Card." Available online via http://en.wikipedia.org/wiki/Octopus_Card (last accessed January 31, 2007).

RFID in Retailing

1 Introduction

RFID is billed as "the next big thing" in terms of information technology advancement for retail business (Benchmark, 2006). It is an emerging technology that is high on the priority list of some international retailers like Wal-Mart in the United States, Metro in Germany, Tesco in the United Kingdom, and Carrefour in France. It is anticipated that this technology will be adopted widely worldwide in retail business by 2015. It will significantly revolutionize the way and the process in which retailers are operated and managed today.

The appeal of this technology lies in the visibility that RFID brings to inventory management and the supply chain (Computer Science Corporation, 2004). It can transmit information even when it is buried under layers of product and materials. Such capabilities provide opportunities to improve the retail operation in terms of efficiency and effectiveness, and also have the potential to significantly reduce the operational cost of bringing products to consumers in retail stores.

Retail leaders, including Wal-Mart and Metro Group, have already adopted RFID in many ways. RFID-enabled solutions were introduced in the Wal-Mart system at the beginning of 2005. Over 300 Wal-Mart suppliers used RFID tags by the end of 2006, and it is expected that another 300 suppliers will be RFID-compliant by the end of 2007, bringing the total to 600 (MarketWatch, 2006). The United States is not the only region to adopt RFID solutions. In Europe, the German retailer Metro Group has taken an even more aggressive approach. Since August 2006, the Group has deployed second-generation RFID tags to the POS cases at the Future Store in Rheinberg and at Real: an important step to further improve the goods availability for consumers. The latter can identify the cases tagged with RFID chips by the EPC logo (Metro 2007). RFID provides not only the retailers but also the suppliers and even the customer many more benefits so that shopping is becoming a lot more convenient and time-saving.

2 Opportunities and Threats

Traditionally, the running of a retail business follows a model with a number of well-defined operations that can be found in a typical retail store. Despite being the norm for many, there is room for improvement, as discussed in the following sections.

Typical Operation in a Retail Store

In a typical retail business such as a retail store or a supermarket, the operation of the retailing process can be viewed from both the suppliers' side and the customers' side. Suppliers are more concerned about maximizing their profit, while customers prefer quality products and services. New products are made to order, but most of the products are shipped from the vendors' warehouses to their distribution centers directly. Upon arrival, products are checked against orders in terms of quality, quantity, and specification; then they are unloaded and stored in distribution centers. Meanwhile, the inventory status of the distribution center is updated. When the retail stores place an order to the distribution center, these centers immediately access the order and send the products requested to the retail store. Some products are sent as full pallets, but the majority of them are being sent as mixed pallets, as a retail store seldom requests a very large quantity for one single product.

Traditionally, when the retail store receives replenishments, most of them are placed in a storage area off the sales floor before placement onto shelves where goods are displayed for sale. Every day, staff tour the store and check the quantity of products on the shelves. If staff spots an empty shelf, they send a replenishment request to the storage area. The responsible staff search the products in the storage area and then replenish the shelves, if the merchandise can be located. If stock runs out, they send a delivery order to the distribution center and wait for the next delivery.

Traditional shopping habits suggest that customers look at products sequentially as they shop and check on the details on the package of these products in choosing what they want to buy. Once they finish choosing all the items they want, they bring the goods to the cashier to check out and make the necessary payment.

Drawbacks to the Current Approach

Despite being the norm for retailing, there are major drawbacks to this mode of retailing, and there is much room for improvement. In particular, staff has no visibility of the actual inventory status, and they have little up-to-date information of the quantity of replenishment stock in the storage area. In addition to being an inefficient means of stock control, serious consequences including missed sales opportunities as a result of sudden out-of-stock situations may occur. Moreover, excess stock may be ordered, as items cannot be located easily when they are needed. Surplus inventory might be located at unknown places while the shelves stand empty (Roberti, 2006). As such, the only way for a store to check for out-of-stock situations on the sales floor is to have employees walking the aisles and taking note of gaps. This means of stock control, however, is inefficient and often cannot detect out-of-stock situations in time. The result is that if an item is not found on the shelf when they want to buy it, customers abandon their purchase. Thus the store not only loses sales but also loses customer loyalty. Analysts estimated that in the United States alone, the retail industry loses approximately US$30 billion annually because of products not being on the shelf when customers want them (IBM, 2004a).

In fact, for most supermarkets, the so-called back-room storage areas are often small in size. For example, on an average day at Wal-Mart, staff often spends almost 20 minutes searching and identifying items on the picking list from the temporary storage area (Roberti, 2006). In today's business environment, this is inefficient and unacceptable, and there is a need to improve this system so that staff can spend more time and effort on serving customers.

From the customer's point of view, when one is shopping in a retail store, particularly a supermarket, he or she wants comprehensive information concerning the production date, shelf life, use-by date, and so forth for a product. In supermarkets, comprehensive product information on individual merchandise is often incomplete. Furthermore, the time that a customer needs to spend on completing a purchase transaction is sometimes too long, especially in peak hours, where shoppers have to wait in long queues at the checkouts counters.

Given the way that typical retailers, such as supermarkets, operate, it is beneficial to enhance the efficiency and the visibility for shopping. That is also one of the reasons why major retail chains around the world are rolling out new processes to improve the efficiency and effectiveness of their businesses.

3 Application of RFID in Retail Stores

In retail business, store operators face a host of problems concerning the tracking and tracing of inventory because of inefficiency and limitations such as real-time visibility of the manual process. With the deployment of RFID technology, we can help ensure that the right product and information is available on the right shelf, at the right time and at the right price. Information accessed and used through RFID solutions can help the store raise its service level, optimize inventory investments, and thus improve efficiency and effectiveness in the operation and management of retail stores.

An appropriate RFID solution, whether it is implemented at the pallet, case, or item level, could have a dramatic impact on many retail operations. Improvements are possible in inventory and shelf management, information dissemination and customer service, shrinkage (i.e., theft) prevention, and security processes. These improvements can lead to increased customer satisfaction and loyalty, which indirectly adds to the bottom line.

Inventory and Shelf Management

The use of RFID increases the visibility and accuracy of the on-hand inventory status. As a result, this technology could help to reduce the labor cost, improve shelf management, and even improve sales potential.

Conventionally, a distribution center (DC) or a retail store receives its shipment on pallets. These are identified manually, and the delivery is checked against the delivery note and the order (Metro, 2004). Pallet-level RFID tagging enables automatic identification of individual pallets, thereby removing the time-consuming manual operation. Quite often, a lot of labor time can be saved in identifying these pallets in the receiving process. Case-level tagging can also be used in mixed-pallet picking. In the retail business, the majority of product that is received is sent as mixed pallets to the retail store. These mixed pallets are picked at the distribution center according to the needs of the retail store. RFID tags allow the exact determination of how many cases are picked. This use of RFID tags could increase the picking accuracy and can dramatically reduce the manual counting effort. Higher accuracy means fewer missing products in a delivery, which in turn increases the product availability and reduces the chance of an out-of-stock situation at the retail store. Real-time automatic replenishment can also be achieved based on the availability of this real-time inventory status. When the inventory level of a certain product dwindles to a certain level, a stock replenishment alert will be initiated and purchase orders automatically generated. For example, in a supermarket, storage area RFID readers could track removal of cases of beverage and send a replenishment alert to the supplier when stock drops below a certain level.

Shelf management can be improved with the use of item-level RFID tags and the installation of smart shelves. Smart shelves have built-in RFID readers to track the presence of products. Traditionally, out-of-stock situations on the shelves are detected by staff upon visual inspection. Smart shelves can be used to monitor the product quantity, placement, and activity on the shelf. Smart shelves are designed to send messages when a shelf needs to be restocked. Shelf replenishment alerts are generated automatically and sent to the storage area to replenish the shelf stock. With this technology, automatic picking lists are generated for items that need to be picked from the storage area and brought out to the sales floor so that the amount of inventory on hand and the respective location of that inventory both on the sales floor and storage area are tracked and recorded. Automatic reordering can also be achieved when the case level for a particular product dwindles and reaches the threshold for reordering.

Furthermore, smart shelves are capable of providing expiration and obsolescence alerts. Items that are approaching expiration date and becoming obsolete should be removed from shelves or moved to the front of the shelf. This condition can be monitored by RFID readers on the shelf.

As the nature of retail shelf replenishment is complex and labor-intensive, the introduction of RFID-enabling technology greatly helps to remove many of the manual operations without major changes in the retail process. The benefits include a reduction in handling and inventory costs, increased inventory accuracy, and the availability of real-time product tracking capability. According to Gillette (Jones et al., 2006), RFID technology potentially saves substantially through better inventory control and management, savings that could be passed on to the customer.

Information Kiosk and Customer Service

Customers can have access to additional services provided by the retailer with the deployment of RFID technology. Comprehensive information would be provided regarding the items in the stores when they carry RFID tags. By presenting the tagged item to the reader at the kiosk located inside the store, a customer can check on the item's information through the kiosk's screen. For example, for a prepackaged chicken, data such as the animal's date of birth, the date and place of its slaughter, the farm where it was raised, as well as the name of the wholesale butcher and perhaps the kinds of food it was fed could be made readily available. These data can assist customers in the buying process, possibly increasing sales. Such information is stored in the database of the retail store and recalled by the unique code that is stored in the RFID tag.

In addition, with information provided by the customer, the kiosk can also provide warnings according to the customers' preference. Ingredients of an item that is stored in the RFID tag can help customers check for substances to which they are allergic and provide further information concerning the type of products that the customer may want to avoid.

In today's supermarkets, the process of checking out is often time-consuming. Customers have to wait often in long queues at the checkout counters. By implementing item-level tagging, customer can choose to use self-checkout instead. Products in the cart are passed through a reader in the self-checkout counter. The reader detects all the tags; the system then records the items being bought and how much customers should pay. Much time is being saved, and RFID technology can also facilitate customers in paying their shopping bills. They may choose to pay by RFID chips that are linked to their credit card where their bills will be automatically charged to their respective card account.

As a result, not only would consumers benefit from more efficient and informative shopping, but also the retailers would save significant amounts on the labor costs. Retail stores can thus have fewer staff and save on operating costs.

Shrink Prevention and Security Issues

Currently, shrinkage is a US$33.1 billion loss in the United States alone (IBM, 2004b). It is an important issue that must be addressed by every retailer. A large portion of shrinkage is due to human error, including unrecorded returns, mistakes at checkouts, incorrect pricing, and inaccurate inventory counts (IBM, 2004a). Shoplifting is another major source of shrinkage. A recent retail security survey report shows that shoplifting accounts for more than 30 percent of retailers' inventory shrinkage (Jones et al., 2006). With the use of item-level RFID tagging, smart shelves, and a portal reader, much of the shrinkage on the sales floor and in the storage area can be prevented.

Today, RFID applications in shrinkage prevention are already being seen in the retail business. Removable RFID tags are used for theft prevention in retailing, especially for luxury products like apparel and jewelry. Tags are attached to products displayed in the store, and readers are installed at the exit doors. Normally, RFID tags of all purchased items will be removed or nullified by the cashier. Then, when the customer exits the store, the reader at the door will not detect any tags. However, if the reader identifies some tags in the customer's possession, that means that some items held by the customer are not yet purchased. This system can help monitor the product and reduce loss from shoplifting.

Item-level implementation can further reduce the effort in theft prevention, and nowadays, the physical removal of tags from the purchased product is no longer required, as tags can be efficiently nullified at checkout. There are numerous examples of successful implementation, For example, the Italian fashion retailer Prada is using RFID in its Epicenter Store in New York as a security measure. Moreover, Gillette's Mach III razor is reportedly the most shoplifted product in the United States. For its European market, Gillette plans to put a half billion RFID tags on individual packages of its razors to track them from the manufacturer to the point where the consumer makes the purchases, and one of the initiatives is to increase its security in the retail process even at a sub-item level (Jones et al., 2006).

Product identification using RFID tags enables real-time tracking of the products from the moment that they are received at the retailer, then displayed on the sales floor, to the time they are purchased and leave the retail store. Product authentication allows the store to verify individual items on the shelves. Some of the products may be just misplaced by the customer. Item monitoring can also eliminate the chance of return fraud.

Customer Satisfaction and Loyalty

To further enhance the efficiency of shopping, RFID-enabling technology can be designed such that when a customer enters the store with a shopping list on a mobile electronic device, such as a personal digital assistant, he or she could transmit the list to the store. The store would then locate the customer and the RFID-tagged items on the list and send back a path to the customer for finding the items (NCR, 2003). With this in place, a customer can find the intended item much easier and conveniently; and at the same time he or she could be alerted to promotions or discounts. Customers could be better informed before making decisions in the store.

With the information that is obtained by deploying item-level tagging and smart shelves, management can analyze the operating efficiency of its retail business on different items, obtain the shopping habits of customers, improve the layout of retail stores, enhance the popularity of products, and achieve many more benefits.

By tagging carts with RFID or the mobile electronic device held by the customer, individual movements through the store could be traced and tracked in real time. Information concerning the customers such as their purchasing patterns, reward preferences, and interests can be captured (National Hardware Show, 2005). Customer characteristics, such as their shopping habits, will be stored on the database of the store. Target marketing exercises could be conducted, and a store can customize its promotions to specific customer groups, providing customers with promotions and discounts of interest to them as well as other customer-centered campaigns.

As target marketing is an effective means of enhancing customer satisfaction, it can help retailers improve their relationships with their customers, which in turn boosts sales. A successful case in applying RFID technology in enhancing customer loyalty is the previously mentioned ExxonMobil Speedpass system. As mentioned, ExxonMobil is the first company adopting a RF-based loyalty application. The system, while providing convenience to consumers, also helps companies track metrics such as frequency of customer visits, average purchases, and types of purchases (gasoline, candy, newspaper, etc.), and it provides customized opportunities at the point of purchase (National Hardware Show, 2005). From successful case files and studies, it is evident that with the appropriate deployment of RFID technology, shopping can become much more convenient to customers, and retailers can have a much more powerful handle to promote their products and increase their sales.

4 Conclusion

RFID technology holds great promise for retail business. It poses great opportunities to improve the operation in terms of efficiency and effectiveness, and at the same time, it drives the operating costs down significantly. However, there are obstacles to widespread implementation. The most prevalent obstacles are probably the tag cost and concerns for consumer privacy. RFID technology is still comparatively expensive to be fully applied to the item level. For some products, the cost of the tag may be even more expensive than the product itself. On the other hand, the use of RFID expands the retailer's ability to monitor consumer behavior. Yet it is also invading the privacy of customers in some manner. Furthermore, certain technical issues still prevail that need time to be resolved. With regard to the introduction of industry standards for RFID such as the Electronic Product Code by EPCglobal (EPCglobal, 2006), it takes time for such standards to be globally accepted and adopted. In addition, hardware issues such as the effects of the ambient environment on the operation of RFID tags may require further attention (Psion, 2004). However, none of these challenges are insoluble, and engineers and researchers are working hard to tackle these issues. A positive indicator is that major retailers are now driving the adoption of RFID technology.

Looking to the future, scenarios that currently seem impossible in the eyes of today's retailers may become practical sooner rather than later. New applications in retailing will expand as the cost of the technology continues to decrease.

References

Benchmark Research Ltd. 2006. "RFID in UK Industry: An Executive Summary." Available online via www.rfidc.com/pdfs_downloads/Benchmark%20Research%20final.pdf.

Blau, J. 2003. "Revolutionary Retailing a Reality." Available online via www.networkworld.com/news/2003/0825store.html?page=1

Computer Science Corporation. 2004. *Shaping the Future of Supply Chain.* Available online via http://se.country.csc.com/COUNTRIESDOCS/se/sv/kl/uploads/886_1.pdf.

EPCglobal, inc. 2006. "The EPCglobal Network." Available online via www.epcglobalinc.org/index.html

IBM. 2004a. "Item-Level RFID Technology Redefines Retail Operations with Real-Time, CollaborativeCcapabilities." Available online via http://www-03.ibm.com/industries/wireless/doc/content/bin/RFID_eBrief_Final_2a.pdf.

IBM. 2004b. "The Path to a Successful RFID-Enabled Store Environment: Integrating Processes to Create Value." Available online via http://www-03.ibm.com/industries/retail/doc/content/bin/rfid_path.pdf.

Jones, M. A., D. C. Wyld, and J. W. Totten. 2006. The Adoption of RFID Technology in the Retail Supply Chain. *The Coastal Business Journal* 4(1):29–42.

MarketWatch. 2006. Wal-Mart Sees More Suppliers Adopting RFID. April 18. Available online via www.marketwatch.com/News/Story/Story.aspx?guid=%7BE9A143E1%2D723B%2D431E%2DA2F7%2D54C264241006%7D&dist=rss&siteid=mktw.

Metro. 2004. "RFID: Uncovering the Value Applying RFID within the Retail and Consumer Package Goods Value Chain." Metro Group Future Store Initiative. Available online via www.future-store.org/servlet/ PB/-s/na222ymo6elzs4wx7pgvk65rorwmn/ show/1002180/RFID_METRO_Broschure.pdf.

Metro. 2007, "Use of RFID on Retail Cases." Metro Group. Available online via http://www.future-store.org/servlet/PB/menu/1011432_l2_yno/index.html (January 2007).

National Hardware Show. 2005. "Retailing Industry Redefining Approach to Customer Loyalty." *National Hardware Show and Lawn & Garden World.*, April 8. Available online via www.nationalhardwareshow.com/images/100184/2005_Press/2005RFIDGatheringandUsingConsumerInformation_FINAL.pdf.

NCR Corporation. 2003. *Fifty Uses of RFID in Retail.* Available online via www.usingrfid.com/features/read.asp?id=3.

Psion. 2004. "Understanding RFID and Associated Applications." Psion Teklogix Inc. Available online via www.psionteklogix.com/assets/downloadable/Understanding_RFID_and_Associated_Applications.pdf.

Roberti, M. 2006. "Wal-Mart Tackles Out-of-Stocks." Available online via www.rfidjournal.com/article/articleview/1551/4/160/.

RFID in Transportation

1 Introduction

It is a delightful experience to drive on a tolled highway, tunnel, or bridge without stopping at tollgates—even slowing down is unnecessary. This is a remarkable benefit of the application of active RFID systems for automatic toll collection that are already in operation around many parts of the world. With these systems in place, toll charges are automatically deducted from a prepaid account. Every day, people around the world move from place to place by various means of transportation, but without much public awareness, more and more RFID-equipped devices have been scattered around, providing travelers more effective and more efficient experiences.

2 Intelligent Transportation

RFID technology can be applied in many different areas in the transportation domain—for example, electronic toll collection (ETC), electronic vehicle registration (EVR), automatic vehicle identification (AVI), fleet management, traffic management, and vehicle positioning. The technology can also be used in car parking, access control, and electronic fare collection, as discussed in association with another area of RFID application in this part of the book.

If an RFID tag has been installed in a vehicle, detailed information of the vehicle can be retrieved from the tag when the vehicle passes a reader installed along a road or at the entrance of a building, car park, or tollgate. Hence, the identity of the vehicle can be read, the location of the vehicle together with the route that the vehicle has traveled can be recorded, and the access right of the vehicle can be detected. Using RFID technology, precise data of actual traffic flowing through a particular road or highway at any period of time can be collected and related, and statistics can be calculated. The analysis of the collected data provides valuable information about the dynamic traffic condition on the road. The information is essential for decision making on traffic control or planning to avoid congestion on highways, tunnels, bridges, or other public-transport infrastructures. RFID is one of the enabling technologies for the development of intelligent traffic management system (TagMaster AB, 2006).

3 Automatic Vehicle Identification

The most common way to identify a vehicle is via the license number printed on the license plate of the vehicle and the main purpose of automatic vehicle identification is to identify a vehicle automatically. This may be the reason that an AVI system sometimes referred to the automatic recognition of number plate on a vehicle. Some AVI systems use optical methods (optical character recognition, or OCR) in the license plate recognition process. However, as RFID technology fits nicely with the application, some countries have already entered into discussions that may lead to using a license plate equipped with an RFID tag for the identification of vehicles. Through identification of vehicles electronically, individualization of services or measures will become more feasible. Services such as ETC, EVR, and automatic access control to buildings or car parks becomes feasible.

Furthermore, with AVI, the role of a vehicle in transportation can be changed from a passive to an active one. For example, when a vehicle has been reported stolen to the police, the traditional way is to use the license plate for tracing this vehicle. However, a license plate needs to be observed in order to determine its location. If the vehicle can be identified electronically, the stolen vehicle can be detected whenever passing a roadside reader. The vehicle will have a better chance to be located by the police. The whole process can be performed efficiently at a lower cost. Furthermore, when a traffic offense is detected, the license plate of the offending vehicle is also used to trace and fine the vehicle's owner. A license plate is easily forged and can be removed readily from the vehicle. However, if a vehicle has an implanted RFID tag that is not part of the license plate, the vehicle is still identifiable even though its license plate has been removed. Security can be further enhanced if the tag is matched against the serial number on the vehicle each time before the vehicle starts operating, and the vehicle will not operate if the tag has been removed or tampered with. Compared to traditional license plate identification, AVI is a more reliable way to identify a vehicle for enforcement purposes.

4 Electronic Toll Collection

Electronic toll collection is one of the most successful applications of RFID technology. ETC is a road transport solution that allows the manual in-lane toll collection process to be automated so that drivers do not need to stop and pay cash at the tollgate (Wikipedia, 2006). In an ETC system, tags are usually mounted on the vehicle windshield at the corner in front of the driver's seat or behind the blind spot of the rearview mirror. Readers are installed at the tollgate pointing down at the center of the lane. When a car equipped with an active RFID tag passes through a tollgate, the tag communicates immediately with the reader. Information from the tag together with its identification number are read. If it is a valid RFID tag, payment is automatically processed at the back-end system. Usually there is more than one lane for toll collection. Different readers are installed to read the tag on the vehicle passing a particular lane. Each reader is turned on and off and synchronized in a way that only one reader is activated and ready for reading at any moment. A reader needs to be turned on for only a few milliseconds to read a tag on the vehicle passing through the lane. The reading range of the readers is also reduced so that tags in the adjacent lanes would not be read. Moreover, multipath reflections that are characterized by reduced power in the received signal could be screened out by the reader.

The ETC system has the advantage of reducing traffic congestion and increasing the speed of passage through the tollgate. It provides a convenient means and better safety to customers with the facility of nonstop payment. In addition, the operating cost for toll operators can be reduced. It is also a reliable system with proven accuracy. Furthermore, since the transaction is being processed at the back-end system without toll operators handling cash, chances of theft are reduced. ETC systems are also traffic management tools that can help government and transport authorities to better control road traffic volume and automate the toll collection transaction to increase transit efficiency.

5 Electronic Vehicle Registration

Almost every country has it own rules and regulations to prevent unsafe, uninsured, or excessively polluting vehicles traveling on the road. Annual registration renewal is required for every vehicle to ensure compliance with the regulations of the national, state, and local government. Manual monitoring is costly and ineffective. Moreover, the vehicle registration fee is an important source of revenue for the government. The government is apparently losing money if a vehicle fails to comply with the annual registration requirement. Also, for national security purposes, there is an increasing demand to monitor and track vehicles, especially in secure areas.

Electronic vehicle registration automates the compliance screening process for vehicle registration requirements. EVR uses RFID technology to electronically identify vehicles and validate the identity, status, and authenticity of vehicle data. EVR replaces labor-intensive and expensive manual, visual-based systems. It also detects and screens vehicles for compliance with regulations (3M, 2006).

With EVR, the efficiency and accuracy of the compliance screening process can be increased. Public transportation security can be enhanced, and the safety of vehicles can be improved. The number of uninsured vehicles can be reduced. Furthermore, the cost of vehicle registration transactions can be decreased.

6 Fleet Management

In a densely populated city like Hong Kong, buses are a convenient and economical means of mass transit. In Hong Kong, there are five franchised bus companies. Among these bus companies, the Kowloon Motor Bus Company Limited (KMB) is the largest, and it is also one of the largest road passenger transport operators in Southeast Asia. In 2005, the total fleet of the company carried 2.77 million passengers a day. The company operates about 400 bus routes, with a licensed fleet of about 4,000 buses serving many routes that pass through each terminal. The fleet management of bus companies on such a scale can be very complicated.

The administration of buses in each terminal is a very time-consuming task. In a typical bus terminal, staff of the bus company has to collect information, sort inquiries, dispatch orders, analyze collected data, and report the analysis. All of these administrative tasks take time and energy, and it is very easy to make mistakes, especially when most of these operations are carried out manually. In addition to the inconvenience to staff and passengers, the most undesirable scenario for a bus company is to have a fleet that is much larger than is actually needed. With an automatic tracking and tracing system, the bus company can optimize the number of buses that are running on the road. The service provided to the passengers can also be faster and more predictable. Moreover, less ground space, which is an expensive resource for the bus company, would be needed for parking buses. The terminal staff can shorten the time needed to handle the complicated and time-consuming administrative tasks.

With a long-range RFID system, the identity number and arrival or departure time of a bus passing through each terminal can be captured by the information system for automatic terminal management without the bus stopping. Departure information can be shown to the passengers on large displays. Dispatch of the buses can be controlled electronically, and statistical reports can be generated automatically. With the aid of RFID tags and readers, equipment utilization can be optimized, asset management can be improved, and security can be enhanced. A fleet management system equipped with RFID technology can automatically and continuously monitor readers, capture data, validate tags, open gates, and update equipment activity databases to provide accurate and reliable real-time tracking and monitoring of the buses and to optimize the utilization of such expensive assets of the company.

7 Railway System Positioning

RFID technology can be applied to automatic identification and positioning in railway systems, such as a train, tram, or other urban rail transit system, to deliver accurate information for traffic and passenger information and onboard management. There are two basic configurations. In the first configuration, tags are mounted directly on the trains, either on the locomotives or on the cars, and readers are fixed to the side of the tracks. This configuration provides accurate and reliable information about where a train is located and is suitable for applications where the identity or position of a passing train is required to update systems external to the train. The real-time positioning information of the train can be sent to the information system and used to update the passenger information displays at stations and terminals.

In the second configuration, readers are mounted directly on the trains and the tags are fixed to the tracks. This configuration is suitable for applications where systems on board the train need to know the precise position of the train. The reader determines the location of the train by reading the tag identity as the train passes over the tag. This position information is transferred to the onboard system and is used to update passenger information, automatically broadcast an announcement, or play a video commercial showing nearby tourist attractions on the onboard displays. Moreover, the technology can also be used for accurate positioning, for example, to control stopping positions of the train when it enters a platform.

8 Car Parking and Access Control

In car parking facilities or any restricted area, RFID technology can be used to identify and track vehicles for secure access control. The technology can also be used to collect parking fees accurately. RFID technology enables solutions for secure and convenient hands-free access control for drivers or parking facility owners. Operators can also save time and money without sacrificing customer service. Drivers can stay safely inside a locked vehicle without the need to roll down the car window, stop to pay cash, swipe a card, or punch a keypad when driving in or out of car parks. The traffic flow through car parks can be improved, especially during peak hours. For car park operators, parking fees can be automatically collected. Entry and exit time with the identity of vehicles can be captured for analysis. Also, more flexible customer services can be provided. Discounts can be offered to frequent car park users, and special privileges can be tailored for VIP customers (TransCore, 2006).

9 Conclusion

Applications of RFID can be found everywhere on the road. Governments are making use of the technology to avoid congestion, to better enforce and regulate transportation. Transportation companies serve their customers better at a lower cost. Most important of all, people moving on the road will have a shorter time to their destination, and travel will be more convenient throughout their journey. Traveling will become more and more enjoyable.

References

TransCore. 2006. "Transportation Systems Management." TransCore. Available online via www.transcore.com.

3M. 2006. "3M Traffic Control Material Division." Available online via www. 3M.com/tcm.

TagMaster AB. 2006. Available online via www.tagmaster.se.

Wikipedia. 2006. "Electronic Toll Collection." Available online via http://en. wikipedia.org/wiki/Electronic_toll_collection.

RFID in Warehousing and Distribution Systems

1 Introduction

The basic functions of a warehouse can be described simply as follows: receive goods from a source, store and protect goods, retrieve goods according to customer requirements, and prepare goods for transportation to the customers. Since the cost of RFID tags is decreasing, RFID technology is gradually becoming a strategic tool in warehousing to defeat competitors by improving the customer service level while keeping the cost of operation to a minimum.

2 Warehousing Objectives

Before we look at how RFID technology can be applied in a warehouse and its benefit, an understanding of the objective of warehousing is helpful (Tompkins and Smith, 1988). An effective and efficient warehouse operation should do the following:

- Minimize the cost of movement of goods within the warehouse.
- Maximize the effective use of space, equipment, and labor.
- Keep track of all items within the warehouse correctly.
- Respond to customer requests or enquiries in a timely manner.

3 Benefit of RFID in Warehousing

The deployment of RFID can be categorized into three different levels: item, case, and pallet. Different benefits can be brought by different levels of deployment, but the constraints are also not the same. Managers should carefully consider the trade-offs before implementation.

Generally speaking, RFID technology can facilitate the automation of all manual processes. As a result of automation, the amount of labor can be reduced. Since labor cost is a major operating expense in a warehouse, its cost reduction is significant. Additionally, by eliminating human error after automation, data accuracy can be improved. This in turn reduces the cost of rework. Using RFID can also speed up the handling process. As the processing time is reduced, overall throughput can be improved. Furthermore, since information can be programmed into the tags or retrieved from the tags at any processing point throughout the supply chain, a more dynamic decision-making process is allowed even without a central controlling information system (Garcia et al., 2003; Alexander et al., 2002).

With RFID technology, more detail and real-time data such as the location of the goods and the status of the movable assets or resources (for example, forklifts, containers, and operators) can be collected. By extracting useful information from the large amount of data collected and integrating the extracted data with the information system, inventory planning can be improved, asset utilization can be optimized, better security control can be implemented, and ultimately, a higher level of customer satisfaction can be achieved.

4 Warehouse Activities and RFID Applications

In a warehouse a lot of activities are related to the movement of goods. Typical movement processes include placing or retrieving goods in and out the storage area, reshuffling goods within the storage area, or transferring goods directly from receiving to shipping docks (cross-docking). Goods may be handled by operators or moved by automatic or manually driven equipment. These movement processes are the major operating costs which should be minimized.

In addition to the movement of goods, there is also a lot of paperwork and supporting activities in a typical warehouse. Verifying the quantity of goods to be delivered, recording the inventory, scheduling the delivery, and planning the storage areas all are back-end activities that are essential to the efficient operation of a warehouse.

Receiving

In the receiving process, goods are accepted from external sources. The accepted goods are then checked against the bill of lading to see whether the correct product in the right quantity has been delivered. After checking, the responsibility of the goods is then transferred from the source to the warehouse. A stock-keeping unit (SKU) may then be assigned to the goods for identification purposes within the warehouse.

If the process is handled manually, it will be very time-consuming and subject to human error. Even if barcoding is used, the received goods have to be scanned individually by the operators. The situation is even worse if the goods contain multiple products in different quantities. On the contrary, if all the received goods are tagged using RFID, the goods are automatically scanned within seconds when the pallet carrying the goods is being moved through the receiving door. Information concerning the received goods can be directly sent to the information system for validation, with instantaneous feedback to the operator in the receiving dock.

The use of RFID technology also removes the process of retagging. Instead of adding a new label or a barcode to the received goods to hold the SKU number, the number can be programmed directly into the RFID tags.

Damaged goods can be easily distinguished by programming an indicator in the tags together with all other information related to the damage such as the inspection result. The damaged goods will then be easily identified by subsequent processes and sent through different handling processes. Sometimes, before the goods reach the receiving docks, the goods may be known to be damaged or just need to be repackaged. If this information has been programmed into the tags, the damaged goods can be identified at the receiving door. The damaged goods can be set aside so that the workers can focus their effort on higher-priority goods. As a result, the throughput of the receiving process will be improved.

Cross-Docking

Cross-docking is a distribution strategy in which goods are distributed continuously from suppliers through warehouses to customers, eliminating all non-value-added activities such as storage. In a cross-docking system, the function of a warehouse is shifted from inventory storage to inventory coordination. Goods move quickly from the receiving docks directly to the shipping docks without moving into the storage area of the warehouse. Successful cross-docking reduces inventory costs by reducing storage space and eliminating labor involved in putaway (i.e., putting items in the appropriate location) and picking, and decreases lead times to the customers.

A key factor in the successful implementation of cross-docking is the visibility of the goods across the supply chain. Suppliers, distribution centers, warehouses, and retailers have to be linked to ensure that all goods can be picked up and delivered within the required time window. This time window requirement sets up a limit such that goods have to be moved quickly from receiving to the shipping docks within a warehouse. Using RFID technology will improve the efficiency and accuracy of this process. After the goods have been moved through the receiving door, their RFID tags are read and the information is sent to the warehouse management system (WMS) to check whether the goods are needed to fill an open order at the shipping docks. The goods are then sent directly to the shipping docks if required.

It is important to emphasize that the cross-docking process should be initiated at the receiving dock. Imagine a situation in which goods are designated for cross-docking but mistakenly are sent to storage and shortly moved from storage to the shipping docks. This is not only a waste of time and labor but also a risk to the order fulfillment within the tight time window requirement of cross-docking. Using RFID will speed up the processes of receiving and identifying the cross-docked goods without sacrificing accuracy; hence, RFID technology is an important tool for implementation of cross-docking throughout the supply chain.

Putaway

After completing the receiving process, goods are then moved into the storage area of a warehouse either manually or automatically by the material-handling system. Different kinds of product may need to be stored in a specific environment and may need different protection levels. Perishable goods—for example, fruit, vegetables, and frozen items—should be refrigerated properly to avoid decay. High-value goods like memory chips may be required to be placed in a secure location. Hazardous goods such as radioactive materials should be placed in a specially designed location. Improper storage of goods may cause damage to the goods and may even be dangerous.

RFID technology can be used to ensure that goods are stored in the proper environment. The environmental requirement information can be stored in the RFID tag itself. The tags are scanned automatically when passing through the storeroom door. The environmental requirement is then checked with the specification of the storage area. If the environmental requirement is not satisfied, an alarm is generated to alert the operators.

RFID readers can be installed on the forklifts to read the tags on the goods when these goods are being moved to the storage area. If the information from the tags is integrated with the warehouse management system, which has access points on the forklifts, forklift drivers can instantaneously obtain the location of the best storage location to which the goods should be moved.

Inventory Control and Stock Location Management

By definition, inventory control is the process for managing the quantity of goods to ensure that the supply of goods meets the demand, whereas stock location management is the process of accurately recording the storage location of the goods and efficiently retrieving the location when required. Both the exact quantity and the exact storage location of the goods are vital to an efficiently operated warehouse. RFID technology is an effective tool for both inventory control and stock location management. For example, if RFID readers are installed on the racks within the storage space, then the item stored with its exact location inside the storage area can be continuously monitored. Labor-intensive work such as physical counting of inventory and manual recording of the location of the goods can be avoided.

Additionally, in a random-location storage warehouse, there is no fixed location assigned for a given SKU. Any SKU can be allocated to any available storage location. In such a system, there may be some unoccupied space within a filled storage area. Such an ineffective use of storage is called *honeycombing*. By continuous monitoring of storage space using RFID technology, storage space allocation can be more effective and can help to minimize honeycombing in a warehouse.

Picking

Picking can be described as selecting the correct items in the right quantity from storage according to the customer's order. Increasingly, orders are being made with smaller quantities but more frequent deliveries to maintain a lower inventory level at the retail sector. Full-pallet shipment to a retailer is rare. Mixed SKUs on a pallet for delivery is becoming the norm. As a result, case-level picking is a necessity that increases the time in picking and the chances of errors being made. To prevent any inaccurate shipments, time and labor cost spent on verification has to be increased. To face this challenge, RFID technology is an ideal tool to reduce the time of the verification process and to remove human error within the process.

Sortation and Conveying

RFID may also find application in the area of sortation (FKILogistex, 2006). For example, after retrieval from storage, goods may need to be sorted according to the destination or the product type before being loaded onto vehicles. Before being moved onto the sortation conveyor system, goods have to be identified individually. If barcoding technology is used, for instance, each item has to be read individually by a barcode scanner or an array of barcode scanners in a high-speed sortation system. However, barcoding requires line-of-sight reading, and the scanning result is also sensitive to the orientation of the goods. This is a limitation to the efficiency of the sortation system. By design, RFID can handle multiple loads simultaneously disregarding the orientation of the loads. If RFID technology is used instead, the limitation of barcoding can be removed and the efficiency of the sortation system can be further improved.

Shipping

The aim of a shipper is to deliver the right product to the customers in correct quantities, free of damage, on time, with accurate shipping documentation. Any deviation from this objective will result in claims, returns, inaccurate inventory, and customer dissatisfaction. To avoid these undesired results, shippers have to verify the goods before delivery. However, verification is a time-consuming process. Additional staging space is needed to hold the goods for verification. Additional labor is needed to verify the goods. All these factors increase the shipping cost and lead time.

If RFID technology is used, all items going out of the shipping door will be automatically scanned and reflected on the shipping documents. Verification can be eliminated from the process, staging space and labor can be reduced, and throughput can be improved. There will be a better chance to deliver an error-free shipping order and to maintain a high level of customer satisfaction.

Asset Management

In a warehouse, there is a lot of important equipment moving around. Expensive equipment such as trucks, tractors, trailers, forklifts and other material handling devices are essential for the movement of the goods within the warehouse. But, over equipping the warehouse is a waste of resources. Sometimes, unitizing load devices may need to be returned to the shipper and there may be a penalty if such devices are lost. Also, containers, pallets and cages need to be managed for handling different kinds of goods. Sometimes, operators cannot move a load simply because the appropriate pallet is not available.

Scheduling jobs for pieces of equipment is not an easy task because equipment locations change. By installing long range active RFID tags and corresponding readers in appropriate locations within the warehouse, these movable assets become more manageable. Real-time location of trucks and forklifts can be fed into the warehouse management system for the operational level decision-making of the managers. Eventually, utilization rates of expensive equipment can be improved, wait time of goods can be reduced and management can be more responsive to changes.

Physical Control and Security

Theft exists everywhere. The warehouse environment with its availability of finished goods makes it a prime area for theft. Item-level tagging with readers installed on racks enables 24-hour continuous monitoring and security control, which prevent or decrease theft in the storage area especially at night, when few managers are available. However, this kind of control cannot prevent goods from theft prior to the goods' arrival at the warehouse. Goods can be stolen by truck drivers who deliberately deliver fewer goods than the shipment required. This in-transit theft can only be avoided by careful counting in the receiving process. With the old way, pallets had to be broken down and cases had to be opened, or at least samples of cases had to be opened, to count the number of items inside the case. This process was extremely labor-intensive. RFID can be applied to replace manual counting and to avoid human errors. However, if the truck driver joins hand in hand with a dishonest receiving dock worker, goods are still easily stolen before going into the warehouse. Similar security threats also exist in the shipping process. This collusion of theft should be avoided by careful inspection and checking, which is also labor-intensive and prone to human error. These inspection processes can be effectively automated using RFID technology.

5 Challenges

Even with the decreasing trend of RFID tag prices, cost is still a major barrier to the widespread application of the technology. Compromises have to be made and applications should be carefully selected to ensure payoff of the investment in the early adoption of the technology. Apart from the return on investment, companies have to consider process changes in every aspect of the whole warehouse operation in order to optimize the benefits brought by the technology. For example, shrink-wrapping is a process commonly found in a warehouse. The wrapping material may cause electrostatic discharges (ESD) that can damage the chip inside an RFID tag. Modification to the process to be performed on an antistatic floor using ESD-sensitive wrapping material can eliminate the problem.

Like all other technologies, RFID also has its limitations. Communication between tags and readers are inherently susceptible to electromagnetic interference, especially when other systems are using the same frequency range within the warehouse. Also, metallic packages, liquid contents, and any other conductive material present in the environment may cause failure when RFID tags are read by a scanner. To maximize the scanning rate, multiple scanners may be installed to detect goods passing a location. This causes multiple reads by different scanners on the same item. The data must then be filtered by middleware before sending it to the central database. As scanners may read any tags passing in their vicinity, the facility and layout should be carefully designed so that any scanner installed to detect goods going through a door will not record those goods that are tagged as they are going through some other door near the designated door.

Moreover, compared with a barcoding system, the data collected are drastically increased after adopting RFID technology. The company has to consider whether the information infrastructure can handle the vast amount of data collected. In addition, since there are many RFID vendors in the market, relying on a single vendor is too risky. Furthermore, it is unlikely that barcoding will be totally replaced by RFID technology overnight, or ever, for that matter. Companies using RFID technology will inevitably face the challenge of handling the environment with multiple RFID vendors of tags, scanners, middleware, and any other RFID components that are mixed together and integrated into the information system, with barcoding technology running in parallel within the company.

6 Conclusion

Although barcoding technology is inexpensive, reliable, standardized, and widely used, limitations such as the line-of-sight requirement, proximity dependence, and orientation sensitivity make barcoding a slow and labor-intensive process that increases the possibility of human error. Efficiency and effectiveness is also constrained by the characteristics of the barcode itself. Moreover, the data stored in a barcode is static and nonrewritable, and the amount of information stored is relatively small. Inconsistent printing quality also causes problems in the application of barcoding in the warehouse environment.

RFID is a wireless technology that promises to overcome these limitations. Applications can be found in most activities in a warehouse, and companies can anticipate benefits brought by applying RFID technology. Receiving, storing, picking, and shipping processes will all become more efficient and effective. The amount of labor and time necessary to complete a task will be reduced. Efficiency can be improved without sacrificing data accuracy by reducing the need to check, audit, or verify the products to be delivered. As a result of the increase in the efficiency of the whole operation, products can be made available for customer orders more quickly. Throughput can be improved, leading to on-time delivery to the customers. With the volume of data that RFID tags provide, RFID is an enabling technology supporting item-level tracking throughout the supply chain. Although there are some outstanding challenges that need to be overcome, RFID is still a promising technology for an efficiently operated warehouse and enables item-level visibility throughout the supply chain in the future.

References

Alexander, K., T. Gilliam, K. Gramling, M. Kindy, D. Moogimane, M. Schultz, and M. Woods. 2002. "Focus on the Supply Chain: Applying Auto-ID within the Distribution Centre." Auto-ID Center. September.

FKILogistex. 2006. "RFID Solutions for Material Handling." Available online via http://www.fkilogistex.com/rfid/default.aspx

Garcia, A., D. McFarlane, M. Fletcher, and A. Thorne. 2003. "Auto-ID in Material Handling." Auto-ID Center. May.

Tompkins, J. A., and J. D. Smith. 1988. *The Warehouse Management Handbook*. Raleigh, NC: Tompkins Press.

RFID Activities in 10 Countries

RFID in Australia

Contributed by BGee Shekar (bgnaan@yahoo.com)

1 Regulation

Australian Communication and Media Authority (ACMA; www.acma.gov.au) is the government agency responsible for the regulation of the use of radio frequencies in Australia. The current class license allowed in the 900-MHz band is to operate between 918 MHz and 926 MHz at a maximum power of 1 watt (W) EIPR (error interrupt pending register).

Following are allowed RFs for various applications:

Class of Transmitter	Permitted Operating Frequency Band (MHz) (Lower limit exclusive– Upper limit inclusive)	Maximum EIRP
RFID transmitters	1. 1.77–2.17	100 picowatts (pW)
	2. 2.93–3.58	
	3. 7.2–10.01	
RFID transmitters	1. 13.553–13.567	1 W (for 920–926 MHz,
	2. 918–926	4 W on experiment)
	3. 2400–2450	
	4. 5725–5795	
	5. 5815–5875	
	6. 24000–24250	
RFID transmitters	5795–5815	2 W

ACMA has issued an Australia-wide scientific license to GS1 Australia (formerly EAN Australia, formed in 1994 and renamed in December 2005) for allowing RFID services to operate at 4 W EIPR between 920 to 926 MHz as opposed to 1 W EIPR. In turn, GS1 Australia will provide third-party authorization to operate under the said frequency. GS1 will monitor the deployment of 4-W readers and rectifies the interface problems. The companies who wish to subscribe to this service must apply directly to GS1 Australia (www.gs1au.org/services/epcglobal/4w/_4w.asp) for each location they wish to use the 4-W RFID readers. This license will be valid until July 12, 2007, with the possibility of one-year extension if necessary. ACMA expects to obtain critical information over this time, which will assist with their decision to increase the class license to 4 W.

As for the licensing, the act confirms that the equipment manufacturer or the supplier must ensure that the minimum EIRP is adhered to as indicated within the respective frequencies.

2 Standards

GS1 Australia is to help Australian business enterprises become more efficient in trade. Its fundamental role is to allocate EAN/UCC (European Article Number/Uniform Code Council numbers and barcodes and maintain internationally accepted trading standards. This in turn allows Australian organizations to adopt world's best-practice supply chain management techniques. *in large global market place*

GS1 Australia has over 14,000 members operating in 18 industry sectors that represent 52 percent of Australia's GDP and account for 55 percent of Australian companies. These companies employ over 70 percent of AtrahDVxlia's workforce. Members from manufacturing and wholesale trade alone compose 88 percent of the total membership, with 60 percent and 28 percent, respectively.

In Australia, GS1 Australia is working closely with ACMA to formulate and administer standards for RFID. EPC Global Australia is an affiliate of EPCglobal and a subsidiary of GS1 Australia, serving subscribers in Australia to help foster the adoption of the EPC Network and related technology. EPC Australia operates out of GS1 Australia's premises.

3 Major Institutions in Developing and Testing RFID

The Government of the State of Victoria (Melbourne being the principal city) has been the forerunner to encourage and develop RFID initiatives in Australia. It has projected Victoria as the RFID capital of Australia. The government made a grant of A$100,000 for forming an RFID group named Vic RFID Action, which subsequently collected A$600,000 from the industry in kind. Subsequently, Vic RFID Action was renamed RFID Action Australia (www.rfidaa.org) and has been actively working on acquiring more memberships from the industry.

The key functions of RFIDAA will be to address technical issues, develop business cases, and communicate with industry. This will become the peak body-driving collaboration between providers, users, and others concerned with research, development, and application of RFID. RFIDAA is located in Port Melbourne, Victoria.

Apart from the government's initiative, many companies are engaged in providing RFID solutions (hardware and software), setting up R&D centers and testing RFID applications. The key companies among them are as follows:

- Sun Microsystems—Planning to set up an R&D center in Sydney
- Visy Industry—First Australian company to sponsor a lab at University of Adelaide—The Adelaide Auto ID Lab
- Sunshine Technologies—RFID in logistics and supply chain solutions
- Microsoft—RFID data management and RFID software launch
- Accenture—RFID solutions across all industries
- Unisys—RFID services
- CSIRO—Managing the national pilot project for RFID/EPC Technology jointly with GS1
- University of Adelaide—The Adelaide Auto ID Lab part of Department of Electrical and Electronic Engineering, includes research on RFID
- Adilam Electronics Pty. Ltd.—Distributor of RFID equipment
- ADT Security Australia—Distributor of RFID equipment
- Allflex Australia—Livestock identification solution
- Barcode Data Systems Pty. Ltd.—Distributors of RFID equipment
- Electro-Com (Australia) Pty. Ltd.—RFID solutions and equipment distributors (Texas Instruments)
- Matthews Intelligent Identification—Coding and labeling specialist
- Peacock Bros. Pty. Ltd.—Distributors of RFID equipment (Zebra)
- RFID Australia Pty. Ltd.—RFID solutions provider
- TCS—RFID technology integration services
- KAZ Group—RFID infrastructure services
- EDS—RFID services consulting company
- Infosys—RFID solutions for retail, manufacturing, and logistics
- HCL—RFID-based asset management solution

4 Current Status in Adoption of RFID

RFID has been a buzzword for many years. However, the early adoption of this technology was mainly in e-tags for electronic tolling on highways, livestock and animal identification, and access control. E-tags have provided a convenient mode of payment for drivers and at the government level to monitor traffic and reduce congestion at the toll plazas.

As of July 1, 2005, the Australian government announced that the usage of RFID tags on livestock was mandatory to track individual animals from the property of birth to slaughter for food safety, product integrity, loss tracking, and market access. This has been implemented through National Livestock Identification System (NLIS) for cattle and sheep. As of January 1, 2006, all transactions must be recorded on the NLIS system.

With the recent concentration on the technology and the considerable cost reduction, there are currently quite a few pilot studies and implementations. Most of the pilots that are conducted are kept confidential. Hence, the real fact and the results are not available in the market. Industry leaders predict that the next few years ahead will be a boom, with the expectation of results published by those pilot studies and those who have adopted RFID technology already.

Companies believe that there are great benefits using RFID technology but are unclear on the exact ROI. The cost that was already spent on barcode technology is included in the calculation of ROI, and this pushes up the total cost of RFID implementation. The well-established barcode technology, with its proven ROI and low cost of implementation, makes organizations think twice about RFID technology. Hence, the implementation of RFID technology remains a concern for Australian adopters.

Among those who sell RFID products, some develop technology and manufacture the products locally, some buy the technology license to manufacture locally, and others import from companies around the world and distribute the products locally. The concentration is more on the equipment and how it can be connected to the existing application. Hence, the real middleware–software concept of repository and the reporting capabilities are in its nascent stage. Sun, Microsoft, and IBM among others are focusing on middleware applications.

Tracking Cyclists in a Race

Victorian ICT companies iCrystal and Victorian Machine Vision teamed with Box Hill Institute to develop a simple and affordable world-class RFID-based product to track cyclists real time in a race. RFID in Sports Event–Cycling (RISE-C) is a radio tracking solution that will benefit race officials, coaches, and cyclist in everyday racing.

RFID tags are permanently attached to the race numbers that are attached to the cyclists' back. High-speed RFID readers around the circuit read the data and then match it with high-speed cameras that provide photo finishes. The middleware software filters the desired data, which is polled by a publisher module. The publisher module sends the data to the events results system and to a database on a Web server through mobile data communication. RISE-C can help publish live information on a computer for display to officials; on a screen for spectators, team managers, and coaches; and even on the Internet (Minister of Information & Communication Technology, 2005).

Australian Defense Force to Track Supplies

Savi Technology Australia Pty Ltd., a wholly owned subsidiary of Savi Technology, USA, was awarded an initial contract of US$ 10.1 million by Australian Defense Force (ADF) to provide a consignment management solution. The solution includes usage of barcode and RFID technologies to improve real-time visibility and accountability of military supply consignments both in-country and of joint-force operations into international theaters of operation. This solution will enable ADF to enhance its In-Transit Visibility System (ITV) and become interoperable with ITV networks already deployed by the U.S. Department of Defense, NATO, and NATO member nations. The RF-ITV network is the world's largest active RFID cargo tracking system, extending across more than 1,500 locations and 45 countries. This RFID-based network is based on ISO 18000-7 standards.

RFID Trial at Australia Post

Australia Post is a member of International Post Corporation (IPC), a Belgium-based cooperative association. The IPC members handle 290 billion pieces of mail per year, which represents 65 percent of the world's postal traffic.

Lyngsoe, a Denmark-based IT company, was assigned with a trial run of using RFID technology by Australia Post to improve the monitoring and management of its operations. In January 2006, Lyngsoe began implementing its Automatic Mail Quality Measurement System (AMQM™), which incorporates its Quality of Service Monitor (QSM) software. Four-hundred RFID readers and over 12,000 actives tags were used and readers were installed at mail sorting and distribution locations across Australia. QSM software was used to store and analyze RFID-generated mail-tracking data.

Research International will manage the panel assigned to send and receive the test mails and provide data to Australia Post. The mail carrier will use this information to better understand performance of its mail network to pinpoint inefficiencies and provide objective service level measurements to the Australian Competition and Consumer Commission that regulates the postal service. The trial was conducted in parallel with the old monitoring system for six months. The new system, using RFID technology, took over completely in July 2006.

RFID-Enabled Credit Cards

MasterCard has announced the issue of a new credit card with RFID PayPass technology to Commonwealth Bank Credit Card customers in New South Wales, Australia. This will enable the customers to make payments up to A$35 without their signature or personal identification check by just flashing their cards on the PayPass reader. This facility will be available at more than 150 merchants, including 7-Eleven and SUBWAY. This technology will help reduce the money handling and quicken the queue movement.

5 Technology Advances

A pilot project on National Demonstrator for RFID/EPC technology, systems, and standards, which was the first of its kind in the world, funded by the Department of Communication, Information Technology and the Arts (DCITA). DCITA has allocated the funds from its Information Technology Online Fund (ITOL). The result of this project was released at Impetus 2006 in July 2006. This project was jointly managed by CSIRO and GS1 Australia. The scope of this project was to expand the examination of all the elements of EPC Global System and not just RFID tags and readers. Metcash, Gillette, Procter & Gamble, Nugan Wines, Capilano Honey, Visy Industries, Linfox, Chep, VeriSign, Sun Microsystems, and the Australian Food & Grocery Council (AFGC) were the other participants to this project. A copy of the report can be from the GS1 Australia web site.

An Australian-based RFID technology developer, manufacturer, and licensor Magallan Technology (www.magtech.com.au/technology) has developed a Phase Jitter Modulation (PJM) technology, which contributed to ISO/IEC 18000 Part 3 Mode 2. Their advanced read–write RFID system operates at 13.56 MHz and enables applications to read many tags that are stacked tightly. The ability of this technology to reliably identify items that are in close proximity to one another will find its way into applications used in pharmaceutical, jewelry, document control, airline baggage handling, gaming, postal, and courier services.

6 Future Potential for RFID In Australia

Packaging, supply chain, and logistics industries are gaining momentum in implementing RFID technology apart from manufacturing. Retail giants in Australia are expected to follow Wal-Mart's lead in the adoption of RFID. The Australian market always follows the USA and the UK markets on any technological development. With RFID climbing the maturity curve, Australia is sure to follow. Moreover, Australia is a product market. Hence, there is a potential for those vendors who are able to offer RFID solutions.

7 Others

There are potential uses of RFID by Australian government agencies that vary from building security, tracking of aircraft parts, and luggage handling to keeping track of books and CDs in public libraries. The State Library of NSW alone stores about 4 million rare books, CDs, paintings, and manuscripts, among other items, which can be a potential target for RFID solution providers.

The Australian government has launched ePassport, a passport that contains an embedded microchip in the center page, with biometric information of the holder such as photograph, name, gender, date of birth, nationality, passport number, and the passport expiry date. The pilot project involved 6,000 passports and received a fund of A$2.2 million from the federal 2004–2005 budget. Since October 24, 2005 all full validity passports issued are ePassports.

E-Toll is becoming more popular and has the potential of being mandatory for commuters on the motorways, bridges, tunnels, and linked expressways throughout Australia. The usage of E-Toll has resulted in significant improvement in traffic flow through toll plazas. Linking up the tags to almost all the toll plazas has provided ease of single-tag usage across tolls.

Australian pie manufacturer Patties Foods is piloting the first Australian trial for RFID usage with frozen foods. Patties is conducting the trial with key players involved in food manufacturing and supply chains. GS1 Australia will oversee the trial, while coding and labeling specialist Matthews Intelligent Identification, IT vendors VeriSign Australia, and cold-storage company Montague Cold Storage will provide support and expertise.

EPCglobal, Australia has released an RFID cookbook. This book is for the mature portion of the RFID audience who are preparing themselves for pilots and testing. It includes information from EPCglobal working groups with an objective of providing practical and timely information. Some parts of this online book are available to EPCglobal members.

8 Conclusion

The year 2006 is expected to be the year of RFID evolution, with many pilots and implementation of RFID and the following years will witness major RFID implementations. It is forecasted that a worldwide spending of A$116 billion by the end of 2008, where about 50 to 100 projects will be under way in Australia alone. More appropriate ROI, reduced cost of implementation, cost absorption of barcode systems, and adoption of technology at all levels of the business chain partners will make the breakthrough. For those companies who pioneer in this technology, the Australian market is a good place to focus their attention to grow their business.

References

Minister for Information & Communication Technology. 2005. December 13. Available online via www.dpc.vic.gov.au/domino/Web_Notes/newmedia.nsf/ 8fc6e140ef55837cca256c8c00183cdc / 2dfe608a7d6e00d1ca2570d70003e9bf ! Open Document.

RFID in China

Contributed by Wang Shujun (wangsj@beic.gov.cn)
Lin Zhuo (lin@bjtsb.gov.cn)
Wang Dong (wangdong@cs.sjtu.edu.cn)
Tan Jie (tan.jie@163.com)
Jason Liu (jason@bjagent.com)

1 Regulations

In China, RF spectrums are controlled by the National Radio Administration Bureau (SRRC; www.srrc.org.cn) under the Ministry of Information Industry (MII; www.mii.gov.cn). RF resources are very scarce, and they are an important strategic resource for China. Just as natural resources, radio frequencies are an important foundation for survival and development of the society. As China takes an active and open attitude toward planning and usage of RFID frequencies, government agencies work with standards and technical organizations to understand and support frequency planning.

At present, China has four widely used frequency ranges for RFID applications. The first is the low-frequency range from 105 KHz to 200 KHz. The second frequency range is 13.553 MHz to 13.567 MHz. China's second-generation ID cards fall in this frequency range, and this frequency range is used extensively for fare collection in public transport systems. The third frequency range is 915 MHz to 928 MHz UHF at up to 2 W power. The identification of China's high-speed railway carriages uses this range of frequency. The fourth is the range from 2.40 GHz to 2.425 GHz.

Internationally, there is also the 433-MHz UHF frequency for RFID technology. In October 2005, SRRC published regulations on short-range devices covering 433 MHz and allowed this frequency to be used for short-range RFID products.

The SRRC Certification Center provides radio-type approval for RFID radio devices where in-country testing is mandatory. The cost of testing is determined by SRRC and charged by the test labs. The major steps to obtain

SRRC radio-type approval on RFID devices are documents submission, in-country product testing, review and approval, and product labeling. There are multiple certification systems in China, and other agency approvals may be required in addition to SRRC approval.

2 Standard

With several Chinese government agencies having competing interest in RFID, it is difficult to understand who is in charge. While China's standardization work is centrally managed by the Standardization Administration of China (SAC; www.sac.gov.cn/english/home.asp), specific standardization work is performed by affiliated relevant technical committees. In September 2005, the SAC issued an officially approved document listing ISO/IEC 18000 in the national standard revision plan. The Article Numbering Center of China (ANCC) and Electronic Industry Standardization Research Institute (CESI; www.cesi.cn/www/en/) assumed the responsibility to convert ISO/IEC 18000 into a national standard.

The Ministry of Science and Technology (www.most.gov.cn/eng) took the lead in creating an association of 14 ministries and commissions to organize specialists all over China to prepare a white paper for China technical policy on RFID. This white paper has been completed and submitted to the leaders of relevant ministries and commissions for examination. The white paper studies and establishes China's technological strategy for RFID, industrialization promotion strategy, and standards strategy, and it will play an important role in China's RFID development.

3 Major Institutions in Developing and Testing RFID

Many technical and demonstration centers on RFID technology have been established by Chinese research institutes. The following are some of these centers:

RFID Research Center. This is the Chinese Academy of Sciences (CAS; http://english.cas.cn/Eng2003/page/home.asp) Institute of Automation's (www.ia.ac.cn/new/english/info.asp?column=191) department for R&D on radio frequency technology. This center conducts research and development and applies the theories and methods that have potential into the industrial ecosystem. Currently, however, the main focus is on RFID testing technology, Internet-based RFID information networks, and RFID applications in typical industrial situations such as production control in the manufacturing industry, supply chain management in the tobacco industry, food safety, forgery prevention, and others.

Auto-ID Laboratory. This laboratory is located within Fudan University. It is one of seven Auto-ID laboratories in the world. Relying on Fudan University's National Major Laboratory for Application Specific Integrated Circuits and Systems, it specializes in research and development, and promotion of automatic identification, intelligent object, and EPC systems. The laboratory conducts basic and applied research related to various industries. It develops EPC systems and tools, promotes the EPC concept, and conducts research on core RFID technology. It participates in the establishment of Chinese RFID standards, promotes RFID applications in China, and provides RFID system training.

EPC/RFID Lab. This lab belongs to the China EPC Working Group (http://www.chinaepc.org). It is an open RFID experiment platform where extensive RFID application systems may be tested, including tests for software systems and label application schemes. This lab is supported by EPC Solutions International, Oracle, Printronix, VeriSign, and Alien Technology.

Shanghai RFID Solution Center. Set up by RFID Research Center of Shanghai Jiaotong University, this center congregates a number of RFID equipments and provides vivid interaction with the public. The center has already implemented several applications that could demonstrate the use of RFID in the entire supply chain, including the manufacturer, distribution center, and retail store.

Microsoft Technical Center (China) RFID Laboratory. This laboratory is for the development of RFID-integrated platform software. A beta version system has been completed, and it is being tested as of this writing.

NEC Academy (China). This academy is for applied research of RFID in supply chains for cold storage of perishable food and forgery prevention.

4 Current Status in Adoption of RFID

China is well aware of the potential of RFID technology for improving manufacturing activities and supply chain operations. The following highlights some of the many RFID implementations that have taken place in China.

China new-generation smart ID card. Beginning in April 2004, China started a project to change 1 billion traditional paper ID cards for its citizens into smart cards. About 200 million new cards will be issued annually from 2006, and a total issue of 900 million cards will be completed by 2008. This could be the largest RFID card application in history. Potential market demand for card readers compatible with the new ID card will be in the range of 4 to 5 million.

China Railway automatic train identification system. RFID has been successfully applied in the China Railway Automatic Train Identification System since 1999. It has been widely used in many railway bureaus, and more than 30,000 locomotives and 600,000 carriages have been installed with RFID tags. RFID is playing a crucial role in real-time track management and is credited for increasing the on-time rate of the train system.

Fixed assets management. RFID labels are widely used in electric equipment management of a transformer substation in Shenyang City, Liaoning Province, China. Each piece of equipment has an attached RFID label for unique identification. This application solves routine inspection and maintenance problems for a great number of large-scale fixed assets in an effective manner through on-site identification using RFID.

Clothes processing industries. In 2004, a Chinese clothes manufacturer installed an RFID system on its production line. The system enabled automatic control and the tracking of all material used in production. The system includes intelligent clothes hangers, each installed with an RFID label. Each workbench has an RFID reader–writer with two antennas. The readers are networked to form an integrated workshop automation system. This system can acquire material-processing information for each procedure and manage the production line in real time to realize dynamic optimization on the production line schedule and enable visible material tracking management.

RFID on containers. The information system in a container wharf has become a bottleneck restricting the development of container transportation. Since the container does not provide any electronic information during transportation, the routing and identification of the contents in the container are recorded manually. To enhance the management level of container transportation, a Shanghai port operator implemented RFID for container identification in 2002. At that time, this application was on the leading edge of RFID technology. After working on the project for more than a year, the company finally turned the concept into reality. This project was highlighted in the Shanghai program of major science and technology solutions in 2004. Five-thousand containers with RFID labels traveled between Shanghai and the Yantai Port over a four-month test period.

5 Technology Advances

A good foundation has been laid for technical development of RFID in China as described in the following paragraphs:

RFID chip design and manufacturing technology. Shanghai Fudan Micro-electronics, Shanghai Huahong, and others have begun the manufacture of 13.56-MHz HF RFID chip. In September 2004, Shanghai Fudan Micro-electronics began production of the first Chinese 915-MHz UHF RFID chip. Tsinghua University and Beijing University also played a leading role in this field. China has the wafer fabrication capability to produce locally designed chips.

RFID reader–writer, antenna design, and middleware. Many companies have carried out the development of LF, HF, and UHF RFID read–write equipment. These companies include Shenzhen Yuanwanggu, Shenzhen Promatic, Beijing Futianda, Beijing Vision, Shanghai Huashen, and others. China has many talented specialists in antenna design, some of which can be found in South China University of Technology, Tsinghua University, and Shanghai Research Institute of Microwave Technology. These locally designed antennas meet the international standard of performance. With respect to middleware, Shanghai Jiaotong University, Fudan University Auto-ID Lab, and SAP developed the first Chinese RFID middleware through a cooperative effort lasting nearly two years. Preliminary field trials have been conducted. This has laid a solid foundation for the development of mature RFID middleware products.

RFID packing equipment technology. At present, most domestic RFID tag converting equipment is imported from abroad. Therefore, development of core manufacturing equipment using independent intellectual property is one of the keys for healthy growth of this industry in China. Packaging equipment is not only used in the RFID technology field but also in packaging of many sophisticated integrated circuits. Some institutions in Shanghai and Shenzhen have already engaged in the development and manufacture of packaging equipment. Their target is to build a fully automatic RFID chip production line that is comparable to the modern lines found around the world.

6 Future Potential for RFID in China

The low-frequency RFID market is relatively mature. Applications include access control, employee attendance monitoring, automobile theft protection, animal identification, parking lot fee determination, and many others. The high-frequency RFID market is developing rapidly. Application areas include all-in-one cards, transportation, bill and note forgery prevention, and others. Thus, there is huge development potential for the high-frequency RFID market.

Ultrahigh-frequency RFID application in the supply chain is the largest expected potential application of RFID. As a global manufacturing center,

China plays an important role in the global supply chain. In a sense, China is at the beginning of the global supply chain—the manufacturer. Wal-Mart and other international retail enterprises mandate that their suppliers use RFID technology. This requirement will pose direct or indirect pressure on Chinese manufacturing enterprises to comply. The wave of global RFID application has inevitably spread to China and will bring the application of RFID technology to Chinese factories. The UHF RFID market has great development potential and will become the largest RFID application market in the future.

It is anticipated that China will become one of the largest RFID application markets in the world. With China's low manufacturing costs, it is anticipated that production facilities of some leading international RFID labels and read–write equipment manufacturers will be transferred to China. In the future, RFID technical development in China will also contribute substantially to global RFID development.

7 Conclusion

A solid foundation for RFID can be found in China. RFID technology is relatively well-known, and RFID applications are popular. The RFID market has developed steadily and is growing rapidly; thus, huge business opportunities exist for RFID technology. LF products and HF products are relatively mature markets. These are the results of the promotion and education provided by various Chinese government agencies, organizations for standardization, technical enterprises, and application enterprises. Its potential influence on production and everyday life have been widely recognized by government institutions, manufacturers, logistics companies, retail enterprises, and the Department of Defense, who are RFID user groups now and in the future.

RFID application projects have shown good results, with the government projects dominating the large-scale RFID application projects. The Chinese government promotes RFID applications in various fields, including urban traffic, railway vehicle identification, dangerous goods tracking, and national defense. Many system integrators explore RFID applications in different industries; new applications are emerging in coal mining, tobacco processing, electric power generation and distribution, food safety management, production process control, and supply chain management. Thus, one can expect innovative RFID applications to emerge from China.

China is not isolated. Thus, frequency allocations, international standards that are developed, public policy of various nations, RFID applications in other regions, and return on investment on RFID projects will influence RFID applications and industrial development in China.

RFID applications have been led by government sectors in the past. However, RFID applications in the Beijing Olympic Games, the Shanghai

World's Fair, and some unusual military RFID applications will raise the world's attention toward China's capabilities in the area of RFID applications. Attention given to these applications will lead to numerous additional RFID applications in China and set the pace for many RFID projects in the years ahead.

RFID in France

Contributed by Hervé Astier (herve.astier@brooks.com)
Brooks Automation, France (www.brooks.com)

1 Regulation

The RF band usage in France is regulated by the Electronic Communications and Posts Regulatory Authority (ARCEP; www.arcep.fr). This authority is responsible for the regulation of RF usage in civil industrial applications, except for audiovisual applications. ARCEP cooperates with European Telecommunications Standards Institute (ETSI; www.etsi.org), based in France. ETSI is an independent, nonprofit organization whose mission is to produce telecommunications standards. ETSI is officially responsible for standardization of Information and Communication Technologies (ICT) within Europe.

The National Frequencies Agency (ANFR; www.anfr.fr) is responsible for managing and allocating the RF spectrum, dealing with interference, and participating in international negotiations on frequencies. The ANFR publishes a national table of frequency bands (called TNRBF) with allocation of frequency bands by application and the delegated authority for each band usage (e.g., Department of Defense, ARCEP, Civil Aviation, etc.).

The only official frequency band in France for RFID is 2.446 to 2.454, GHz, as defined in the TNRBF. However, RFID applications can be included with some other applications within the frequency bands, as shown in the following table. There are also some French RFID companies that can offer technologies and applications using other frequencies such as 5.8 GHz.

	Authorized Frequency Band	Maximum Field Strength/Field Power
LF	125–134 kHz	0.25 W
HF	13.553–13.567 MHz	< 60 dBμV/m at 10 m <11 dBμV/m at 30 m
UHF	869.4–869.65 MHz	< 500 mW ERP
MW	2.446–2.454 GHz	< 100 mW EIRP

Compared to other countries in the world, some frequencies (e.g., 923 to 925 MHz used in the United States) are not allowed in Europe. Other frequency bands such as 865.6 to 867.6 MHz, although recommended by the European Union, are restricted in France, as they are currently reserved for military applications. Unless a company needs a special frequency band or power for a specific application, there is no need for a license in France to use RFID. Special authorization can be provided on request by the ARCEP.

2 Standards

There are two main areas with respect to standards in France. First, there are the RFID "norms" defined by the International Organization for Standardization (ISO). Second, there are the industry standards, the predominant one being GS1's Electronic Product Code (EPC). French institutional organizations are also keeping an eye on Asian standards such as Ubiquitous and Hibiki.

France is very involved in the RFID normalization work closely associated with ISO. In particular, the Traceability Competence Center (www.poletracabilite.com), which is a French government sponsored program. The French Normalization Association (AFNOR; www.afnor.fr) also participates in the standardization effort and distributes the ISO norms in France.

Gencod-EAN France was renamed in February 2005 as GS1 France (www.gs1fr.org), with EPCglobal France under its purview. GS1 France actively promotes RFID and the EPC standard through regional meetings, training, and support for its members. GS1 France also works closely with the national authorities and with international counterparts (EPCglobal action groups) to develop the RFID standards.

For example, GS1 France is working with the French government to open the frequency band for 865.6 to 867.6 MHz UHF RFID at 2 W ERP. GS1 France published a document in June 2005 highlighting the need to open this frequency band according to the European recommendation. For more information, point your search engine to "Standard ETSI 302 208."

3 Major Institutions in Developing and Testing RFID

Various companies and institutions or universities are working on development and testing in different areas. Following is a nonexhaustive list of test and development centers located in France.

Public Institutions and Research Laboratories

The Traceability Competence Center (www.poletracabilite.com), located in Valence, opened in 2002 and receives support from the European Union, the French Ministry for Research and New Technologies, and other local institutions. This center offers a test and development platform to solution providers for product testing and to users for solution validation.

The Conception and System Integration Laboratory (LCIS) from the National Polytechnic Institute of Grenoble (INPG; www.inpg.fr) is carrying out several projects to optimize the design of integrated antennas for RFID tags.

The Laboratory of Electronics and Information Technologies (LETI; www.leti-cea.fr) is conducting research work in emerging technologies such as organic electronics and ultrafine, ultrafast inkjet printing. These research activities will lead to solutions for RFID mass-fabrication processes.

The Center for Innovation in Micro & Nanotechnology (MINATEC; www.minatec.com) is working on projects and joint developments on tools for micro- and nanotechnology production. MINATEC has developed specifications for polymer electronics, RFID, and energy components. The ultimate aim is to invent a new industry focusing on production of low-cost and very large-area active components.

Private Companies

The IBM Industry Solution Center (www.ibm.com/news/be/en/2004/07/01.html), located in La Gaude, was created in July 2004. This RFID testing and solution center has been established to help European companies test RFID solutions in real customer environments.

STMicroelectronics (www.st.com), a French–Italian company, is a worldwide leading supplier of RFID chips involved in the development of RFID technology. In September 2005 it introduced a UHF contactless memory chip compliant with the latest EPC specifications.

Other French companies involved in the development of RFID are ASK (www.ask.fr), Gemplus (www.gemplus.fr), TAGSYS (www.tagsysrfid.com), Balogh, MAINtag, Tracetel, RFID Systemes, and Cybernetix.

4 Current Status in Adoption of RFID

There are many French manufacturers, vendors, and integrators who have implemented RFID projects, especially with LF and HF RFID. Only a few projects have been implemented using UHF RFID.

All the major international RFID companies are present in France along with French companies. Lists of RFID suppliers in France can be found on the GS1 France Web site. There are many RFID applications deployed in France in various industries such as medical and pharmaceutical, transport and logistics, security and access control, textile, fraud prevention, anticounterfeiting, libraries, agriculture, manufacturing, and toll road systems. Some examples are described in more details as follows.

Fraud Prevention and Anticounterfeiting

In the pharmaceutical industry, Pfizer and Paxar are working together to implement an RFID solution to control and validate the origin of boxes for the distribution of Viagra®. The deployment of this solution is at Amboise, France, where there is a production and packaging facility providing Viagra to almost all international markets. Pfizer was facing an increase of counterfeit products and decided to find a solution by tracing its products to validate their origin. Now UHF tags are applied on all boxes leaving the production line. This solution allows Pfizer to deploy a process to register the transportation of Viagra to the United States and to certify the product's authenticity.

Medical

Four French hospital research laboratories (Paoli Calmettes Institute, Hospital of La Timone, Hospital of La Conception, and North University Hospital) are using RFID to identify biological specimens stored in liquid nitrogen. TAGSYS deployed a solution for those four research labs using 13.56-MHz RFID tags able to withstand temperatures as low as −196°C (−320°F) when stored in liquid nitrogen, as well as a rapid temperature rise by as much as 125°C (257°F), when they are removed from storage and exposed to room temperature. This allows the research lab to quickly and easily identify individual test tubes containing biological samples for cancer and stem cell research, enabling more frequent and regular monitoring of pathology samples. The project started in 2004, and at the end of 2005, more than 200,000 test tubes have been equipped with RFID tags. Two RFID readers are deployed at each facility. The read–write tags carry 2 KB of memory. These are used to store a unique serial number as well as a security key. The serial number of each test tube's tag is linked to a database housing critical information on that tube's tissue samples, including patient data, tissue treatments, and other variables. The system uses software, developed by Cybernetix, to manage the readers and the database, as well as to provide an application to pinpoint where a specific test tube is located on the tray being read.

Libraries

Several French libraries have implemented RFID systems to help them manage the books and documents checked out by the public. The RFID solution helps the libraries to manage their item inventory and to ensure better security. Maizières-lès-Metz implemented a solution from CheckPoint in 2003 with 13.56-MHz RFID tags to track 30,000 items. Marseille also implemented an RFID solution provided by ASK, Cybernetix, and STMicroelectronics for the 17 public libraries. In all, 1.5 million items (books, magazines, CDs, DVDs, and other media) are tagged. The system is used to manage, track and secure the library (www.ask.fr/uk/applications_and_references/marseilles_libraries_1.html).

Transport and Fare Cards

The Paris subway system, RATP, uses RFID technology with tags on the trains and readers in different parking zones to automatically guide the trains to their respective parking areas at the end of their daily service. Since 2004, the solution has been implemented by Balogh using 2.45-MHz technology on three different subway lines. All stations on lines 1, 3, and 13 and trains are equipped with 2.45-MHz tags and readers to trigger visual and audio destination information for passengers.

The Navigo pass is a means for payment for public transportation, deployed in 2004. Based on the success of Navigo, RATP began experimenting with an RFID-enabled telephone as a contactless transit card starting in March 2006. Special NEC mobile phones are being used for the trial with a 13.56-MHz passive RFID chip from Inside Contactless embedded in the phone.

Some 15,000 taxis are managed in real time at the Paris Charles de Gaulle airport using RFID technology from Balogh. Each cab is equipped with an RFID tag capable of up to 10 m read range. Implemented in 2004, this system helps manage over 23 million taxi rides per year. It has reduced the passenger waiting time at the airport by 30 percent.

Logistics and Retail Supply Chain

This area has a high growth potential for RFID, with most projects in the pilot phase. The Graveleau transport and logistics company has implemented a 2.45-MHz RFID solution from Balogh to manage the entry/exit of its trucks to the warehouse sites. The Sernam transport and logistics company conducted a pilot test in 2004 to 2005 with IBM, using UHF RFID technology. Sernam published positive results in June 2005. It developed a complete system that is now ready to be deployed in its transport network, depending on the interest of their customers. The transport and logistics group Geodis is also conducting a lot of tests on RFID in different areas. Carrefour also conducted a large pilot test using RFID to track textile products from China to the chain supermarkets in France.

There are many more examples, and the preceding are just some examples to show that France is eager for RFID adoption.

5 Technology Advances

French private and public laboratories are involved in the development of RFID systems. Some areas of development are RFID tags on polymer inked antennas, increased miniaturization, chipless technology, embedded functions, and new types of inks and substrates for RFID printing. A recent conference was jointly organized by sOc-EUSAI to present the current research status in RFID and other topics (see www.soc-eusai2005.org/index. php).

Interestingly, research is also under way to increase the capabilities of HF systems versus UHF systems. This could be promising to overcome the regulation and potential health issues from UHF systems. Still, one key remaining problem is the cost of the RFID tag. Technology advances will drive the cost down, but there will be a limit to how low the price can go.

6 Future Potential for RFID In France

France has been and is involved with standards definition, application development, and implementation. Many projects have been implemented, and more RFID applications are visible in daily life. Clearly this is only a beginning. Further research and investment are planned to continue development and promotion of RFID usage.

According to a study conducted in May 2005 by Pierre Audoin Consultants in collaboration with HP and Microsoft, the main obstacles to the deployment for RFID in France are technology complexity (2 percent), lack of references on the French market (4.9 percent), standards not ready (22.5 percent), and price (71.6 percent). Other factors more difficult to quantify are still the public perception of RFID in term of privacy risks and potential health issues. The numerous players in the French RFID market are addressing these concerns. Standardization is progressing rapidly with the adoption of the EPC. On the regulation side, the limit imposed on the UHF frequency band could disappear soon. In February 2006, the French Ministry of Defense and the French Ministry of Industry jointly asked the army to start talks with ARCEP to relax the constraints imposed on the UHF frequency band as recommended by the European community.

With the rapid development of RFID technology and standards, new large projects should kick off in the next several years, especially in the transport and logistics industries.

7 Others

The adoption of RFID technology is an ongoing process in industry, especially pushed by GS1 France and EPCglobal. For the general public, the technology is more visible without raising too many concerns. An interesting study was published in 2005 by CapGemini on "What European Customers think about RFID and the implications for Business" (see www.gs1fr.org/download/nonprotege/b_outils_ean/rfid/Capgemini-EuropeanRFIDreport.pdf).

Privacy issues posed little barriers because existing RFID applications are not currently infringing on privacy. Eventually, society will see the full potential of this technology and will learn to accept it when it comes to personal data, personal finance, and medical records. Still there are examples where people have expressed concerns. When Navigo was implemented in the Paris subway system, (see www.bigbrotherawards.org/), there were complaints about privacy issues because it was possible to track when and where a person used his or her subway pass, and, potentially, with whom he or she was traveling.

In France, the National Commission for Data Protection and the Liberties (CNIL; www.cnil.fr) is an independent administrative authority protecting privacy and personal data. This commission has published several communiqués since 2004. Four specific privacy concerns were highlighted: the insignificance of data, the priority given to objects (still linked to people), the globalization risk (technology standards based on the American concept of "privacy" without taking into account the European principles of privacy protection), and the risk of individual "nonvigilance" (RFID can be invisible and remotely activated).

The commission considers that RFID data are personal data and fall under the French law of "data processing and liberties." This law includes an access right to personal data that is a challenge in the context of RFID. The only solution offered would be to neutralize the RFID tag (temporarily or permanently), which would require the inclusion of this feature in the tag design. Solutions exist, but they are not yet at the implementation phase. Today this authority is working actively with other French institutions on the specific topic of privacy issues linked with RFID.

Potential health issues due to the increased use of RFID systems in industry (only for UHF and above) are rising. The debate is on the risk due to radiation. This issue has been discussed by the World Health Organization since 1998. WHO created the International Commission on Non-Ionizing Radiation Protection (ICNIRP; www.icnirp.de/) that published different studies and recommendations.

In Europe, the ICNIRP recommendations were translated into a European recommendation in July 1999 (Ref. 1999/519/CE) on the limitation of public exposure to electromagnetic fields (from 0 to 300 GHz). This limitation is effective in France, since a national decree dated May 3, 2002 (Ref. 2002–775). More recently, a new European recommendation was published in the official journal in April 2004 and is available on the portal to European Union law (Ref. 2004/40/CE), giving minimal prescriptions for security and health relative to the exposure of workers to electromagnetic fields. France has to apply this recommendation by the end of 2008.

Those recommendations are then translated into European technical standards by the European Committee for Electrotechnical Standardization (CENELEC; www.cenelec.org). Specific CENELEC standards relative to RFID are, for example, EN 50364:2001 and EN 50357:2002.

Unlike previous public concern for the mobile phone, RFID health issues are not yet a major concern by the general public. Still RFID application providers apply what is called the principle of precaution until limits are clearly defined.

8 Conclusion

This report is certainly only a quick snapshot of the RFID industry in France and not an exhaustive report. To summarize the situation, there are many companies working on RFID including suppliers, manufacturers, integrators, and users.

As of today, most implementations are using LF and HF frequency bands. More pilot tests are done in the UHF bands, which may lead to full-scale implementation in some industries.

As pointed out in this report, the main conditions to increase the deployment of RFID are to continue to reduce costs, to continuously improve the technology, and to help companies start projects as more implementations mean increased visibility, which will lead to economy of scale for implementation across the entire supply chain.

RFID in Germany

Contributed by André Hanisch (andre.hanisch@iff.fraunhofer.de)
Fraunhofer IFF (www.iff.fraunhofer.de)

1 Regulation

The RF band usage in Germany is regulated by the Federal Network Agency (Bundesnetzagentur) (www.bundesnetzagentur.de), which is also responsible for the German electricity, gas, telecommunications, postal, and railway markets, underlying legislation, and important consumer rights in these innovative markets. Since January 1, 2006 the agency's responsibility also includes competition in the rail networks.

The Federal Network Agency for Electricity, Gas, Telecommunications, Post and Railway is a separate, higher federal authority within the scope of business of the Federal Ministry of Economics and Labour, and has its headquarters in Bonn. On July 13, 2005 the Regulatory Authority for Telecommunications and Posts, which superceded the Federal Ministry of Posts and Telecommunications (BMPT) and the Federal Office for Posts and Telecommunications (BAPT), was renamed the Federal Network Agency. Moreover, it acts as the root certification authority as provided for by the Electronic Signatures Act. This agency also works in close conjunction with the European Communications Committee (ECC).

The frequencies classified worldwide as ISM frequency ranges (industrial, scientific, and medical) can also be used in Germany for RFID applications. In addition to ISM frequencies, the entire frequency range below 135 kHz is used to work with high magnetic-field strengths when operating inductively coupled RFID systems. So the frequencies ranges commonly used and allowed in Germany for RFID applications are 0 to 135 kHz, and the ISM frequencies around 13.56 MHz, 27.125 MHz, 40.68 MHz, 433.92 MHz, 869.0 MHz, 2.45 GHz, 5.8 GHz, and 24.125 GHz.

At the end of 1997 the frequency range 868 to 870 MHz was passed for short-range devices (SRDs) in Europe and is thus available for RFID applications in the 43 member states of the European Conference of Postal and Telecommunications Administrations (CEPT; www.cept.org). The band around 915 MHz is not available in Germany (and Europe) mainly because the neighboring frequency ranges are occupied primarily by D-net telephones and other cordless services.

2 Standards

GS1 Germany (www.gs1-germany.de) is actively promoting the EPC standard. Besides EPC, GS1 Germany is also responsible for rationalization of the electronic exchange of business data using XML.

3 Major Institutions in Testing and Developing RFID

In the last few years, quite a few so-called RFID solution centers or RFID labs have been established all over Germany. Some of these centers are still focused on research and development of RFID tags, readers, and middleware. However, the majority of the institutions have put their focus on helping business and industry test and pilot RFID systems before implementing them in their own operations. Some of these institutions are as follows:

- LogMotion Lab—Fraunhofer Institute for Factory Planning and Operation
- Licon Logistics e.V.–RFID Standards/Solutions
- Metro Future Store
- Intel SBS RFID Lab
- openID Center

The LogMotionLab (www.logmotionlab.de, www.iff.fraunhofer.de) at the Fraunhofer Institute for Factory Planning and Operation in Magdeburg, Germany, tests and neutrally evaluates RFID technologies for their suitability for practical application for specific company processes. The lab views itself as a service organization for companies, which do not make any investments in their own systems. Besides testing services, the LogMotionLab also presents various possibilities for applying RFID technology in logistics processes. For example, logistics processes can be mapped and studied in an industry-like environment.

The LogMotionLab provides users many diverse advantages. They can assess the technical potential of RFID technology, calculate their cost effectiveness under field conditions, conduct customized tests—both in the lab and at their own facilities connected to their logistics processes—and develop and produce training scenarios.

Clients and interested parties benefit from the equipment of the Log-MotionLab, the consulting know-how of the Fraunhofer IFF, its partners, and the fundamental knowledge of the University of Magdeburg. No investments need to be made in RFID systems at this stage. If test operation is convincing, then the RFID technology can be integrated in real operations, Siemens, for example, provides support as an experienced consulting and implementation partner.

A major focus of Licon Logistics e.V.–RFID Standards/Solutions (www.licon-logistics.de), a consortium, is the development and promotion of RFID solution scenarios in the area of logistics. The full benefit of RFID technology in logistics can only evolve by implementing applications along the entire supply chain. The global integration of the data flows between companies, and so-called anticipated information on the basis of open RFID systems plays a central role. The same applies to the complete tracking, tracing, and documentation of material and goods flows. Therefore, the Licon working groups examine how the existing systems and process can be adapted to open solutions and systems. Licon has more than 20 members, consisting of hardware producers, software companies, R&D, consulting companies, and logistics providers.

The Metro Future Store (www.future-store.org) in Rheinberg near Düsseldorf has been established, as the name implies, by Metro AG. This supermarket, using the "Extra" brand from Metro's sales division offers hardware and software vendors a platform to test newly developed applications for warehouse and retail management under real conditions. In contrast to the other institutions, the Future Store focuses mainly on the benefits for the customer at the very end of the value-added chain. Providing this service today gives insight concerning the future application of RFID at the retail level.

Intel (www.intel.de), in an alliance with Siemens Business Services (sbs.siemens.com), has opened an RFID lab in Felskirchen near Munich. This lab differs from the above-mentioned Fraunhofer IFF's LogMotion Lab in that the testing and developing of RFID solutions is not the focus. Rather, it offers customers the possibility of gathering information on how to support different business processes with RFID and how to integrate these possible solutions in their existing IT architecture.

The openID Center (www.openid-center.de) in Dortmund offers another test platform for its customers from the industry to not only see RFID in action but also to understand the influence and changes within supply chains. A pilot plant represents different stages of a logistic chain for transponder-equipped transport packaging, from manufacturing to waste disposal.

4 Current Status in Adoption of RFID

Many different projects with the scope of utilizing RFID technology in industry have been successfully conducted. Even though the number of applications is growing every day, there exists the issue that the companies do not publish all of their accomplishments or even their failures This makes it difficult to keep track and see the current penetration of the market. However, some strikingly interesting projects will be mentioned here.

Fraport AG, understands that luggage trolley management is a substantial part of the terminal operation of airports and must therefore be analyzed and represented in a holistic manner. Safety issues and service-level agreements are just two among many other critical aspects to the problem of trolley handling. The operational cycle of the luggage trolley handling is divided into four subprocesses:

- Locate luggage trolley.
- Retrieve luggage trolley.
- Transfer luggage trolley.
- Fill up luggage trolley collection areas.

Apart from these four processes are two further support processes: the quantitative counting of the luggage trolleys furnished by the operational coworkers and the guarantee of luggage trolley functionality and safety.

Until now, the respective trolley management workers went aimlessly all over the place looking for abandoned luggage trolleys to collect and to bring to the nearest collecting area. This procedure was very ineffective because it did not consider the demand for trolleys at a certain time and area and it only considered problems when a worker visually saw them.

The solution was to install an active RFID system. Four-hundred luggage trolleys were equipped with active RFID tags that can be localized with a precision of a few meters. Each RFID tag on the trolley contains a unique identifier and its maintenance history.

At a control center all the trolleys' positioning data are collected and illustrated on a Geographic Information System (GIS) layout. With this visibility, the responsible person can send his or her workers to targeted areas to collect luggage trolleys and transfer these to another predetermined area to satisfy current deficiencies or to prevent their future occurrence. Even more important, instructions and their respective execution can now be monitored and centrally coordinated.

Siemens Power Generation offers a complete product line of 50- and 60-Hz gas turbines ranging from 4 to 278 megawatts (MW) of gas turbine-based power generation, the technology of choice for producing low-cost electricity. Its scope of supply covers gas turbines in various scope packages such as component packages, power islands, and complete turnkey power plants. Its production areas are not only spread over Berlin, Germany, but include several countries such as the United Kingdom, United States, and China. Huge gas turbines parts such as the gas turbine blades are shipped throughout the world from suppliers to Siemens, to subcontracting refiner, and eventually back to Siemens. The whole process can have several iterations. These blades are usually transported in thousands of specially designed plastic boxes and travel from one end to the other, covering Siemens PG's complete supply chain. The problem is to find a specific box. These boxes tend to get lost or come back damaged. The solution to get a more transparent look at the complete box travel cycle was to provide each box with an RFID tag. Furthermore, a series of measuring or reading points were introduced. A measuring point is usually an area where boxes are sent to or received from other areas so that the blades inside the boxes can be stored and handled. At each measuring point a worker scans the box's RFID tag, gives it a status (full, empty, broken, usable), and puts in the sender and receiver information. This information is kept both on the RFID tag and in a control center. With this new infrastructure, Siemens is now able to track every single transport box, check travel times, and pinpoint where boxes are most often damaged.

Airbus was one of the first companies to introduce an RFID tool and equipment handling system. Most of the tools and equipment in the aviation industry are very specific and often quite expensive. Many smaller and also bigger airlines do not buy all of the equipment but instead rent it from Airbus in case they need it. Each of the tools comes with different certificates and all kinds of other information. Now all of this information is put on a single 2-KB RFID tag, which helps improve the handling processes. For example, most of the tools need to be calibrated once they have been used. Before the introduction of RFID technology, each tool would be sent back to the respective Airbus tool rental shop, which would then realize that the specific tool's certificate was expired and needed to be renewed in a repair and calibration shop—most likely on the other side of the world. Hence, the piece was sent out again, consuming a lot of money and time. With RFID and a simple handheld application, each operator can read the status of a tool, write back usage data, and acquire, for example, the address to send the tool. Ideally, the tools go back to a repair and calibration shop first if required before being put back in the storehouse.

VEM Motors GmbH, an electric motor manufacturer, succeeded in making RFID technology usable for electric motors. A usual electric motor becomes an easy-to-service *memory motor* by having a special metal tag embedded into its casing. This tag is considered to extend and perhaps replace the motor's mandatory nameplate. These nameplates contain all kinds of important data. However, these motors are meant to work under heavy conditions in industrial environments. Motors often had their nameplate dirtied, scratched, painted over, or even fall off, which meant that the motor and its technical data might not be identified. The new RFID motor tag delivers many types of information and status data such as power parameters, maintenance schedules, and phone numbers. Information can also be written to the RFID motor tag. Information monitoring and maintenance becomes more efficient, as well as less expensive, and breakdowns are in many instances prevented. Should an incident occur, the available data allow for quick response times and fast action. Furthermore, the use of the RFID technology does not only start at the end of manufacturing but at the very beginning of the assembly to identify a motor, track the assembly progress, and assign a given part to a customer at any time.

5 Technology Advances

Technology advances are not very drastic at the current time. There is steady development regarding antenna design, read and write ranges, special application tags (metal tags), protocols, anticollision, bulk reading, and so on. However, the real innovations such as polymer chips and tags have not passed the laboratory stage. In the future, technology advance can be achieved by opening new domains of applications that require RFID to be mixed with other technologies such as GPS (Global Positioning System), GSM (Global System for Mobile Communications), sensors, and so on.

Currently, there are smart containers with integrated RFID antennas that can permanently keep track of their inventory status. Sensors for shock, temperature, humidity, and so forth measure the status of the container and contents. A GSM unit sends any abnormality to a control center, and an integrated GPS receiver adds geographic positioning data to it. This kind of technology mix is supposed to leverage the real benefit of RFID technology.

6 Future Potential for RFID In Germany

Up to now, several RFID applications have been developed and implemented in Germany. The cost concerns do not only apply to the RFID tags itself but also to the necessary reader hardware, respective middleware, and mandatory IT integration. Further exploitation of RFID in all the different sectors will depend on a cost reduction in these areas.

The next big projects will probably be carried out in the areas of container and vehicle tracking. RFID tags will be attached to items of high monetary values or in circulating logistic systems in order to reuse them several times. Metro's vision of replacing barcodes on every single object in supermarkets and stores with RFID tags is still far off.

7 Conclusion

There are many more examples of RFID activities and application in Germany. A larger picture of RFID emerges by broadening the view to Europe or even the whole world. Since the technology is still quite expensive, the majority of current users are so-called big players that do not act in solely one country. Also, if one looks at the main area of applications where RFID is to revolutionize the flow of information connected to the flow of goods, he or she understands that logistic supply chains can certainly not be limited to only one country. Taking these two points into consideration, this discussion is not meant to be exhaustive but gives a fairly good cross-representation of the current RFID activities in Germany. The more RFID technology penetrates the different sectors from industry and trade, the less it will be used in isolated local projects. RFID will eventually cover global supply chains all around the world and become standard, standing side by side with other identification technologies such as the barcode.

RFID in Japan

Contributed by Tatsuya Inaba (tinaba@sfc.wide.ad.jp)
Jin Mitsugi (mitsugi@sfc.wide.ad.jp)
Jun Murai (junsec@sfc.wide.ad.jp)
Shin'ichi Konomi (konomi@colorado.edu)

1 Regulation

The radio frequency spectrum in Japan is regulated by the Ministry of Internal Affairs and Communication (MIC; www.soumu.go.jp/english/index.html). MIC reviews the radio spectrum allocation plan based on the vision reported by the Japanese Information and Telecommunications Technology Council. MIC changed the usages of several bands recently. For example, RFID was not allowed to use the UHF (952-MHz to 955-MHz) band until 2005. At this point, RFID whose emission level is less than 4 W equivalent isotropic radiated power (EIRP) is allowed with a radio station license for each RFID reader and a UHF RFID system whose emission level is less than 20 mW EIRP is allowed to use without license only if the equipment has passed the designated Technical Regulations Conformity Certification. The following table shows the spectrum bands currently used for RFID in Japan.

Band	Frequency Spectrum	Regulation	
LF	< 135 kHz	Inductive radio communication equipment	< 15 μV/m at wavelength/2π
HF	13.56 MHz	Inductive reading and writing radio communication equipment	< 47,544 μV/m at 10 m.

UHF	952–955 MHz	Specific low power radio station	10 mW carrier power + 3 dBi antenna
	952–954 MHz	Premise radio station	1 W carrier power + 6 dBi antenna
UHF	2.427–2.47075 GHz	Premise radio station	300 mW + 20 dBi antenna
		Specific low power radio station	10 mW + 20 dBi antenna
	2.400–2.4835 GHz	Specific low power radio station	10 mW/MHz or 3mW/MHz depending on the usage of the band + 6 dBi antenna

MIC set the Radio-Radiation Protection Guidelines in 1990 in order to protect the human body from exposure and absorption of radiation. The guidelines were not specifically developed for RFID but for the general impact of devices that use radio waves. The guidelines consist of three parts: exposure limits, measurement and estimation methods, and protection methods. The exposure limits, based on empirical studies, are electric field strength limits, magnetic field strength limits, and electric power density limits. It also made reference to guidelines of other nations, such as the United States and standards such as IEEE and ICNIRP.

2 Standards

Standardization activities in Japan are promoted by three initiatives: ISO/IEC by Japanese Industrial Standard Committee (JISC, www.jisc.go.jp/eng), EPCglobal by GS1 Japan (www.gs1jp.org), and the Ubiquitous ID Center (UID, www.uidcenter.org). Activities of ISO/IEC in Japan consist of many national committees and play a central role in standardization activities in Japan. JISC is a committee organized under the Ministry of Economy Trade and Industry (METI). Some of the standards ratified by ISO/IEC are localized by JISC and become a JIS (Japan Industry Standard).

There are two organizations in Japan that support EPCglobal standardization activities. They are EPCglobal Japan and Auto-ID Labs Japan. EPCglobal Japan is an organization in the Distribution System Research Institute (DSRI), a member of GS1. Since the activities of EPCglobal began in the United States, the number of members were few at the beginning. But manufacturers who supply their products to U.S. retailers that mandate EPC-compliant tags become end-user members of EPCglobal, and the number of members increased gradually. In addition, the fact that a Japanese retailer, Yodobashi Camera, that deals with home electronic appliances and office supplies, recently announced that it would mandate EPC Gen 2 compliant tag applications to its top suppliers also influenced the deployment of the EPCglobal standards.

Auto-ID Lab Japan is a member of Auto-ID Labs, a global network of academic research laboratories. Auto-ID Lab Japan, hosted at Keio University, supports standardization activities at EPCglobal, investigates technical and social problems that occur in RFID deployment, and conducts R&D work on RFID technology.

The ubiquitous ID Center is part of the T-Engine Forum, a nonprofit voluntary organization that is the research and development body of TRON (The Real-Time Operating System Nucleus). The center has proposed *ucode*, a counterpart of EPC, and distributed information service architecture for securely obtaining relevant information for a *ucode* tag. Pilot implementation projects supported by the center ranged from traceability systems for agricultural products, to hospital logistics, to apparel supply chain tracking, and to a support system for handicapped people. The center has certified both tags and readers within RFID systems. The mu-chip (www.hitachi.co.jp/Prod/mu-chip/), a 0.4-mm-square 2.45-MHz RFID chip, was also certified by the center and became one of its standards.

3 Major Institutions In Developing and Testing RFID

There are several development and test facilities operated by the solution vendors. Their business is to provide a total RFID solution, and they use the facilities for customer consultation. These centers include the Sun RFID Design Center, HP RFID Noisy Lab, and IBM RFID Solution Center.

Another category of facilities is owned by the RFID tag, reader, and labeler vendors. In most cases, their business is also to provide a total RFID solution and they use the facilities for their own system development and test. Vendors with such facilities include Dai Nippon Printing, Denso Wave, Fujitsu, Japan Information System, Hitachi, Lintec Corporation, Mitsubishi Electric Corporation, NEC TOKIN Corporation, Nitta, Omron, Panasonic Communications, Sato Corporation, Texas Instruments Japan, and Toppan.

4 Current Status in Adoption of RFID

Among the RFID-based systems that were put into real use, there are three that are outstanding in terms of scale: Suica, Edy, and RFID-chipped mobile phones. These three systems use Sony's FeliCa 13.56-MHz RFID technology (www.sony.net/Products/felica/abt/index.html). Public transportation fare cards the Octopus Card in Hong Kong and the EZ-Link in Singapore also use Sony's FeliCa technology.

Suica is an RFID train pass that is mainly used in the Tokyo/Kanto, Sendai, and Niigata areas. Edy is an RFID "electronic wallet card" that allows consumers to easily make payment at certain stores. RFID-chipped mobile phones, which are informally called *wallet phones*, now incorporate the functionalities of both Edy and Suica.

Suica was first introduced by JR (Japan Railways) East in November 2001, and as of September 2005, more than 13 million Suica passes were issued. Suica passes can now be used for making payment at over a thousand stores. They can be used for checking in for a flight as well. In the last few years, similar RFID passes were introduced in other areas of Japan. For example, Icoca was introduced in the Kansai area in November 2003, and Toica will be introduced in the Nagoya area in 2006. PiTaPa is an RFID pass used for riding trains, buses, and subways in the Kansai area. PASOMO is an RIFD pass for riding trains, buses, and subways that will be introduced in the Kanto area in 2007. Some of these RFID passes are or will be interoperable, allowing a passenger to use a single card for traveling across different regions and different types of transportation.

Edy is a prepaid card that can be used at over 25,000 stores across the nation. The first major rollout of Edy was carried out by bitWallet, Inc. in November 2001, and as of September 2005, over 12 million Edy cards were issued. The Edy service can also be used with RFID-chipped mobile phones.

RFID-chipped mobile phones or wallet phones were first introduced by NTT DoCoMo in July 2004. The company sold over 10 million RFID-chipped phones by the end of January 2006. All of the three major mobile telcos in Japan, NTT DoCoMo, Vodafone, and KDDI, now provide RFID-chipped mobile phones. In January 2006, JR East introduced a service called Mobile Suica that allows consumers to use the Suica service with RFID-chipped mobile phones. This in effect makes an RFID-chipped phone a platform for using most of the major services.

Open-system RFID applications in logistics and supply chain management are still in the development phase. One of the reasons why development of the open system is delayed is the availability of the UHF radio spectrum. The UHF band was not available for RFID until 2005, thus explaining the short history of UHF RFID applications in Japan.

METI (www.meti.go.jp/english/index.html) supported a number of RFID pilot projects through public bidding. Other ministries supported METI as well as ran their own pilot projects. The following table shows the projects selected from FY 2003 to FY 2005.

FY	Projects	Related Ministries
2003	Department stores and apparel (Experimental use of RFID in retail outlets)	

Food industry (Food traceability)	Ministry of Agriculture, Forestry and Fisheries	
Electric home appliances and electronic equipments/devices (Evaluation of readability of applied tags)		
Publishing, bookstores, and libraries (Experimental use of RFID at retail store)		
2004 Electric home appliances and electronic equipments/devices (RFID for recycling)		
Construction machineries, industrial vehicles, and agricultural machineries (RFID for JIT manufacturing)		
Publishing, bookstores, and libraries (RFID for efficiency improvement and theft prevention)		
Medical and pharmaceutical products (Pharmaceutical traceability)	Ministry of Health, Labor and Welfare	
Department stores and apparel (RFID for customer service improvement at retail store)		
International marine and land container transportation (RFID for container security and efficiency improvement)	Ministry of Land Infrastructure and Transport	
CD/DVD media and retail/rental stores (RFID for efficiency improvement)		
2005 RFID for Home Electronic Appliance (RFID for recycling)		
Medical and pharmaceutical products (Pharmaceutical traceability in hospital using RFID)	Ministry of Health, Labor and Welfare	
Peacekeeping operations of the Japanese Self-Defense Force (RFID in defense operations)	Japan Defense Agency	
Autonomous robot control using RFID to support customers at local shopping mall (RFID for customer service improvement)		

Joint RFID pilot project between CD/DVD media and books industries (RFID for efficiency improvement)	
Future store (Evaluation of RFID in retail outlets)	
Logistics and transportation—returnable container project with ASEAN* countries (Evaluation of RFID in logistics)	Ministry of Land Infrastructure and Transport
Cross-border supply chain application— Japan, China, South Korea joint project (Evaluation of RFID in logistics)	

* Association of Southeast Asian Nations

Another financial support from METI is the Hibiki project. The goal of the Hibiki project is to develop technology to enable mass production of inexpensive RFID tags. Through a public bidding process in early 2004, Hitachi and the supporting companies Toppan, Dai Nippon Printing, and NEC won the award. The requirements of this project are as follows:

- To develop a passive UHF tag (860 MHz to 960 MHz).
- Compatible with EPC UHF Generation 2 and ISO 18000-6 Type C.
- Memory capacity larger than 512 bits.
- Reading speed faster than 10 ms/tag and rewritable about 100,000 times.
- Communication range 3 m for reading and 1 m for writing.
- To develop a mass production system that would be operational within two years.
- To develop tags whose cost is lower than 5 Japanese yen at inlet level.

These inlets can be inserted into mediums such as cards, labels, and stickers to produce contactless cards and RFID labels.

5 Technology Advances

As of February 2006, Hitachi had developed arguably the world's smallest RFID chip, with a size is 0.15 mm × 0.15 mm × 0.75 mu. This breakthrough is expected to help increase productivity of RFID chip manufacturing processes.

YRP Ubiquitous Network Laboratory (www.ubin.jp/english/index.html) developed a small active RFID tag called Dice in April 2005, whose size is about 15 mm × 15 mm × 15 mm. Its communication range is about 10 m (when it's connected to a 30 cm copper antenna) and supports DES encryption. Its potential uses include inventory management and secure transportation of containers in logistics. The laboratory also developed UC Watch, a prototype RFID reader that can be worn like a watch. When a user grabs an RFID-tagged object by hand, the device automatically reads information from the tag.

Interesting recent developments besides miniaturization include integration of RFID tags with other devices and materials. Dai Nippon Printing (DNP), for example, sells a multisensor tag called ACCUMODE that integrates temperature, humidity, and light sensors with an active RFID tag. Epson developed an RFID tag with a display that is made of electronic paper. Ricoh's RECO-View RFID Tag Rewritable Sheet integrates an RFID tag with a thermal rewritable sheet that shows the information stored in the tag. Toppan, Nippon Sheet Glass, and Hitachi developed a technology to embed RFID tags and reader antennas in glass sheets. NICT developed an RFID tag that is primarily made of flexible fabric material and can easily be attached to curved metal surfaces.

6 Future Potential for RFID in Japan

One of the characteristics of RFID applications in Japan is that the area of the application is not so much focused on logistics and supply chain management as in the United States but on retail and daily life. Applications at retail stores are tested in the pilot projects, most of which provide value added services to customers. So far, they are experimental and the focus is how to provide new experiences to customers, but if the retailers consider the benefits of RFID not only from customer service improvement but also from marketing and supply chain management, the ROI of RFID investments would become positive soon. Moreover, the success in retail stores may accelerate item-level tagging because retailers deal with items at their storefronts. An existing success case that demonstrates this potential is Mitsukoshi's RFID system at shoes and jeans stores. Their pilot tests revealed substantial benefits of item-level RFID in reducing out-of-stock items at storefronts, and the system is currently used to support the stores' everyday business, leading to better customer satisfaction and increased sales.

In addition, this characteristic may result in two more impacts on RFID deployment. First is the acceleration of source tagging. The more retailers start using RFID at retail stores, the stronger the buying power will get, which may accelerate tagging at the production process. Second is the proliferation of the applications for individual customers. If we can assume ubiquity of RFID tags as has been achieved with the barcode, RFID applications will not only take place in business but also in our daily lives. They are becoming widespread, but the stories that refrigerators with RFID readers will announce the expiration of items inside and washers with RFID readers that will automatically select washing mode based on the clothes inside may become true. Another key to success for RFID mass adoption is to create synergy with smart card applications.

7 Other Issues

Current RFID has several issues, such as relatively high cost of tags and unstable read accuracy, but these are the issues that will be addressed in the future through technology development. To further deploy RFID not only in Japan but also other parts of the globe, privacy issues that derive from RFID applications must be taken into consideration. Although privacy seems to be unfolding differently in Western countries. It has created many fewer instances of disputes and less active discourse in Japan so far, but it is not something that can be ignored. Moreover, since privacy issues in the future may look different from current issues, continuous efforts such as establishing new guidelines, educating people, developing technological solutions, and contriving safe operations will be required to address privacy.

With regard to privacy guidelines, a joint effort made by METI and MIC developed a privacy guideline in 2004. This guideline is specifically developed for the privacy threats caused by RFID. There is an urgent need for this guideline prior to the spread of RFID applications. The guideline consists of eight basic points concerning how privacy is to be protected when RFID applications are used. This guideline together with the Act on the Protection of Personal Information, which was enacted in 2003, is the foundation of safe RFID implementation in Japan. The eight points described in the Privacy Guideline in Japan are as follows:

- Must have indication that RFID tags exist.
- Must guarantee consumer rights to choose activation or deactivation of tags.
- Must share information about social benefits of RFID.
- Must follow the Act on the Protection of Personal Information when private information regarding tags is stored in databases.
- Must obtain individual's permission before gathering information stored on tags.
- Must ensure accuracy of information when private information is stored on tags.
- Must have information administrators.
- Must explain merits and demerits of using RFID to consumers.

8 Conclusion

Japan has already accumulated know-how from the many local RFID system applications. Both the Japanese public and private sectors are contributing to the development of international standards. The Japanese government supports RFID deployment through regulation updates and financial support for pilot projects. With more Japanese companies making efforts to utilize this new technology, increased deployments of RFID applications are anticipated in the near future.

RFID in Singapore

Contributed by Robert De Souza (rdesouza@nus.edu.sg)
Mark Goh (tligohkh@nus.edu.sg)
Wong Tack Wai (tliwtw@nus.edu.sg)
The Logistics Institute—Asia Pacific
(www.tliap.nus.edu.sg)

1 Regulation

The radio frequency band usage in Singapore is regulated by the InfoComm Development Authority (IDA; www.ida.gov.sg) under the Ministry of Information, Communications and the Arts (MICA). The frequencies commonly used in Singapore for RFID applications are shown in the following table.

Authorized Frequency Band	Maximum Field Strength/Field Power
125–130 KHz	0.25 W
13.553–13.567 MHz	< 94 dB μV/m at 10 m
433.79–434.79 MHz	< 10 mW ERP
866–869 MHz	< 500 mW ERP
920–925 MHz	< 500 mW ERP (no license needed)
	500 mW to 2W ERP (license required)
2.4000–2.4835 GHz	< 100 mW EIRP

For nonregistered RFID equipment, entities that intend to conduct trials may apply for a technical trial license from IDA for a period of up to 90 days.

In May 2004, IDA launched a three-year, S$10 million plan to develop RFID technology. Their ABC plan encompasses three key thrusts:

- Alignment of frequency spectrum for global interoperability
- Building of capabilities to develop new intellectual property
- Collaboration to catalyze adoption of RFID in key industry sectors

IDA launched a Call for Collaboration (CFC) in November 2004 to develop more RFID capabilities in the various industries in Singapore. Twelve proposals were short-listed for presentation to an evaluation panel. At the end of 2005, successful proposals were informed of the level of funding to help get these RFID project started. IDA released more information on these projects through seminars and write-ups when they are completed in 2006 and 2007.

IDA recognized the importance of frequency allocation with respect to cross-border trading. As such, it has worked with regulators in the Asia Pacific to harmonize RFID frequency allocation. The result of this work can be seen in Figure 1.

2 Standards

GS1 Singapore Council (www.gs1.org.sg), which was renamed on January 2005 from Singapore Article Number Council (SANC), has been around since 1987, when it was appointed by Singapore Trade Development Board to implement and administer an international article numbering system (EAN◆UCC System) in Singapore. EPCglobal Singapore is under the purview of GS1 Singapore. As at December 2005, EPCglobal Singapore has four members that are issued with a unique EPC manager number. With GS1 actively promoting EPC RFID, this number is expected to grow by several

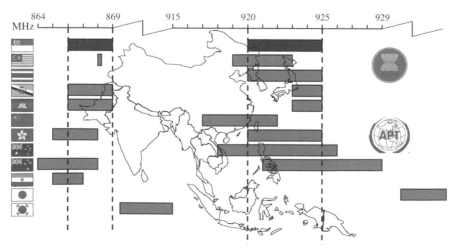

Figure 1 Harmonized RFID Frequency Allocation In Asia Pacific.

fold over the next couple of years as EPC is adopted by more players in the industry.

GS1 Singapore had hosted several key RFID meetings. For example, the Ballot Resolution Meeting (BRM) was held here in June 2005 to incorporate EPC Gen 2 into ISO/IEC/18000-6 Part C. A total of 174 comments were resolved at the BRM. Most were editorial in nature, while others were minor technical changes. The outcome of this meeting is a draft standard incorporating all the comments for voting as ISO standard in February 2006.

The other key meetings were EPCglobal Transport and Logistics Services Business Action Group (TLS BAG) in July 2005, GS1 Asia-Pacific Regional Forum held in November 2005, where a quarter of the two days agenda was taken up by discussions on EPC RFID, and EPC global RFID Singapore Forum in June 2006.

Singapore is actively involved in the development of a standard for RFID electronic seals for freight containers. The working group has expert members from Denmark, Germany, Israel, the Netherlands, Singapore, Sweden, the United Kingdom, and the United States. The proposed standard, ISO 18185, provides a system to identify and present information on freight container electronic seals. When approved and published, this will be the first Singapore-originated ISO standard. The Standards, Productivity and Innovation Board (SPRING, www.spring.gov.sg) Singapore is also working on the implementation of this standard with various industry players, both locally and overseas.

3 Major Institutions in Developing and Testing RFID

Various RFID solution centers have been set up in Singapore. Some centers are focused on R&D, while others are here to help businesses test and pilot RFID systems before implementing them in their own operations. These centers are as follows:

- NOL-Sun Advanced Technology Center (Sun Microsystems and logistics firm Neptune Orient Lines—www.nol.com.sg)
- RFID@NEC Centre by NEC (www.nec.com.sg/bccs/News/2005/050225.htm) and Republic Polytechnic
- IBM-Nanyang Polytechnic RFID Integration Zone (www.ibm.com/news/sg/en /2005/07/IBM_investment.html),
- IBM ASEAN/South Asia RFID Solution Zone (www.ibm.com/ news/sg/en /2005/07/IBM_investment.html)
- RFID Expertise @ A*STAR's Research Institutes (www.a-star.edu.sg):
  - Institute for Infocomm Research (I^2R)
  - The Institute of Microelectronics (IME)
  - Singapore Institute of Manufacturing Technology (SIMTech)

4 Current Status in Adoption of RFID

There is an eclectic mix of RFID vendors in Singapore, ranging from distributors to manufacturers. Many major RFID vendors have offices or have representatives in Singapore. These include Alien, ASK, Intermec, Philips, Samsys, Sato, Symbol, Savi, UPM Raflatac, among others. There are also homegrown RFID expertise such as Smartag (www.smartag.com.sg), manufacturer of smart RFID labels, Kenetics Innovation (www.keneticsgroup.com), developer and manufacturer of RFID readers and antennas, and Wavex (www.wavex-tech.com), an RFID system integrator for libraries. The presence of these vendors are an asset to help any RFID project get started and going in Singapore.

The Singapore RFID Alliance is an industry-led and government-supported initiative with the aim to enhance Singapore's competitiveness by accelerating the development and adoption of RFID among major economic clusters. It has compiled a vendor directory of companies providing RFID related products and solutions in Singapore. The purpose of compiling the directory is to facilitate business and to provide a comprehensive list of companies offering RFID services. The Singapore RFID Vendor Directory can be found at www.ida.gov.sg/idaweb/marketing/infopage.jsp?infopagecategory=factsheet:broadband&infopageid=I3134.

Following are other current applications of the technology.

Arowana Protection

The arowana is an endangered species of fish that is protected under the UN Convention of International Trade in Endangered Species (CITES) of Wild Fauna and Floral. An arowana caught in the wild cannot be sold. The second generation of the arowanas bred in captivity and beyond can be traded. To identify these arowanas, a 125-kHz glass-encapsulated RFID tag is injected into the arowana's body. With this RFID process in place, trade in arowanas bred in captivity was enabled. The first shipment of 200 arowanas with an estimated retail value of US$1 million was sent from Singapore to Japan in December 2004.

Libraries

Although Singapore is a small country with a population of only 4 million people, it has the world largest RFID implementation for public libraries. The first RFID-enabled library was opened to the public as a prototype in 1998, followed by a pilot implementation to another four libraries until August 2000. By then, with all the lessons learned and fine-tuning made to the system, the National Library Board (NLB; www.nlb.gov.sg) decided to roll out RFID to all its remaining 17 libraries, a task that was completed in April 2002. Each library item (books, magazines, videocassettes, and CD/DVDs) is tagged with a 13.56-MHz Philips I-Code I tag. To date, as many as 12 million items have been tagged, and the library continues to tag about a million items a year as new titles are acquired for the libraries.

RFID is used in self-checkout machines where customers place items one at a time on a blue pad (essentially an antenna) for identification without concern for the orientation of the item on the pad. So long as an item is placed on the blue pad, it is identified, checked out, and the EAS (electronic article surveillance) bit in the tag is disarmed at the same time. Besides self-checkout stations, RFID is also used for EAS gates and at 24/7 book drops that immediately identify return items as they slide down the book chute. Behind the book drop, RFID is used to help sort items into 32 categories, representing the respective shelving areas for the item in the library.

RFID has helped reduce queue time to borrow items from two hours to less than five minutes and zero-minute queue time for item return. With a loan rate of 30 million items a year, NLB reported that it has given back 8 million hours back to the customers to do what they want instead of waiting in library queues. With all the productivity gained through the use of RFID, NLB avoided having to employ 2,000 staff to serve the customers' borrowing and returning needs, thus saving $50 million annually in manpower cost.

NLB is committed to the use of RFID in its libraries. The RFID system was extended to 18 Children Community Libraries under its management by August 2004. NLB refreshed the RFID system by upgrading all the RFID hardware, a task that was completed by mid-2006. At the same time, the back-end system was redeveloped from client/server to a .net architecture running Web services.

Eight academic libraries also use RFID, holding an estimated total of another 3 million items, each with an RFID tag. However, six of these libraries use RFID solely for identification but not EAS. These six libraries use a separate magnetic strip for EAS function.

Electronic Road Pricing System

Singapore's Electronic Road Pricing System (ERP), managed by the Land Transport Authority (LTA; www.lta.gov.sg) is the first in the world to use RFID technology to effectively track and manage road traffic volume at different times of the day. Implemented in 1998, this traffic management tool is an electronic toll system that deducts prescribed road price from a stored-value smart card inserted in an RFID based in-vehicle unit (IU) operating at a frequency of 2.35 MHz, powered by the vehicle battery. The same system of having a stored value smart card inserted in an IU has now been extended to collection of car park fees.

Contact Tracing

During the SARS (severe acute respiratory syndrome) outbreak in 2003, Singapore hospitals used a specially developed Hospital Movement and

Tracking System (HMTS) to trace the movements of health care workers, patients, and hospital visitors. Visitors and patients were issued active RFID cards, which contained contact details scanned from their identity cards. The HMTS tracked the RFID cards that emitted radio signals, which were sent to receivers and forwarded to central computers via the LAN. Authorities successfully used the tool to track and identify visitors for quarantine in the event the patients they visited were infected by SARS.

Concrete Testing

More than 4,000 cubes of concrete are being transferred daily from batching plants and project sites to concrete quality test centers in Singapore to determine the strengths of the concrete batch. The entire cube test cycle can be laborious, involving a fair amount of human effort to test and record meticulously all testing results on a daily basis. Now with CubeInfo (www.cubeinfo.com), all testing data on the quality of concrete can be captured automatically with the help of an RFID tag implanted into the cube. During testing, RFID readers installed at the various testing apparatus read the information from the tag attached to the cube and update the test results associated with the tag ID into a server for customers to retrieve.

5 Technology Advances

The Institute of Microelectronics (IME; www.ime.a-star.edu.sg) believes it has developed the world's first integrated RFID tag with an on-chip antenna (OCA) that has read/write capabilities with passive RF power. It also includes an anticollision function. The novel process technology eliminates the need for a separate and costly process for antenna printing and assembly that is needed for a separate "off-chip" antenna, which is many times larger than the chip itself. In comparison with conventional RFID tags typically of a few cubic centimeters in size, this newly developed RFID chip is considerably miniaturized at less than 1 mm^2 and can be produced at a lower cost. The tag opens up new domains of applications that require small and thin tags, such as in biotechnology and pharmaceuticals, and in authenticating important documents or even currencies.

6 Future Potential for RFID In Singapore

To date, several RFID applications have been developed and implemented in Singapore. Going forward, Singapore is expected to further exploit the use of RFID, both in applications and R&D. Large RFID projects are expected for seaports and airports.

7 Other Applications

Besides the cases mentioned, RFID applications are also readily found in gasoline stations (ExxonMobil Speedpass), car locks, and wireless card access systems. On the EPC front, there are several projects in the pipeline. For example, supermarket chains in Singapore will be deploying RFID in their distribution centers for product tracking, and Hewlett-Packard has started EPC-tagging its Intel servers manufactured in Singapore. Local pallet leasing company LHT has started to offer pallets with RFID tags installed. Local logistics operators are using RFID to help manage bonded warehouse operations. Logistics service provider Translink Express has conducted trials on RFID cold chain management. In addition, the library is experimenting with smart shelves.

Privacy issues related to RFID tagging of products that commonly surface in the United States and European countries are not found in Singapore. RFID applications are generally welcome by the public without much concern raised on privacy or health issues.

8 Conclusion

There are many more examples of RFID activities in Singapore. This chapter is not meant to be exhaustive, but it provides a fairly good cross-representation of the many RFID activities in Singapore. Singapore will see increasing adoption of RFID applications. The drivers for this are as follows:

- Reduced prices of RFID tags and equipment
- Advances of RFID technology developments
- Desire to gain competitive advantage
- Desire to improve process visibility and management
- Compliance reasons

RFID in South Korea

Contributed by Yoon Seok Chang (yoonchang@hau.ac.kr)
School of Air Transport, Transportation and Logistics
Korea Aerospace University
(Hankuk Aviation University)
(www.utac.or.kr)

1 Regulation

Use of the radio frequency band in the Republic of Korea (South Korea) is regulated by the Ministry of Information and Communication (MIC; www.mic.go.kr). The frequencies commonly used in Korea for RFID applications are shown in the following table.

Authorized Frequency Band	Maximum Field Strength/Field Power
125–130 kHz*	<500 μV/m for every 1 m
13.552–13.568 MHz	< 47.544 μV/m@10 m
433.670–434.170 MHz	< 3.6 mW EIRP of peak power
908.5–914.0 MHz	< 4 W EIRP
2.4000–2.4835 GHz*	< 10 mW Antenna power

*Even though 125- to 130-kHz radio equipment and 2.4 to 2.4835 GHz equipment were not classified as *radio equipment for RFID and Ubiquitous Sensor Network (USN)*, they follow a notice by the Ministry of Information and Communications (Notice No. 2005-29), Republic of Korea.

Since 2004, MIC has invested millions of dollars on RFID technology development and pilot projects. A summary of pilot, standard, and research activities under the leadership of MIC and NCA are as shown in the following table (details are explained in the RFID/USN roadmap table).

Area	Activities/Investment
RFID pilot service	2004: US$4,000,000 2005: US$3,500,000 2006. US$2,800,000
RFID main service (u-IT initiative)	2006: US$15,000,000
Research	2004: US$7,000,000 2005: US$17,000,000
Frequency (Standard)	Assign 908.5–914 MHz Currently under review—433 MHz
Standard Activities	USN Standard Forum (2004.3), TTA Project Group

RFID pilot service is a government-supported pilot project to drive process innovation and to improve process efficiency in public sectors by adopting RFID supported processes. MIC and NCA have supported 16 projects from 2004 to 2006. Those projects include air baggage-tracking service, ammunition management system, port logistics service system, U-Museum, and F15K part management system.

Based on the results of some pilot service projects, MIC and NCA have just started RFID main service in 2006. The aim of RFID main service is to drive a wide adoption of RFID in industry. Currently there are four projects: ammunition management project, port logistics improvement, hazardous waste management project, and RFID-based logistics at Gaesung Industrial Complex (North Korea).

Figure 1 briefly shows the roadmap till 2012 for RFID and the Ubiquitous Sensor Network (USN) presented by the National Computing Agency (NCA; www.nca.or.kr).

2 Standards

The Korean Agency for Technology and Standards (ATS; www.ats.go.kr) is a government institute that leads the development of industrial standards and technical evaluation in the Republic of Korea. The key missions of ATS include promoting the conformity of Korean standards with international standards; endorsing international mutual recognition agreements for standardization and conformity; conducting research for standardization; evaluating components, materials, and reliability; and certifying new technologies and quality of products for industries in Korea.

The Telecommunications Technology Agency (TTA; www.tta.or.kr) established the RFID/USN project group. There are five areas of activity: standardization of RFID air interface technology, standardization of RFID/USN

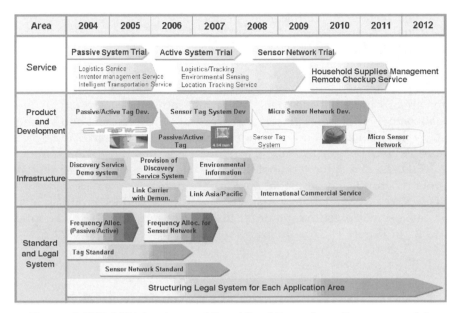

Figure 1 RFID/USN Roadmap of Republic of Korea (http://www.nca.or.kr).

test and certification, standardization of network technology and middleware system based on RFID, relevant information security technology, and standardization of USN architecture and reference model. Work items being conducted by this project group are as follows:

- Air interface RF comformance test standards for Mobile RFID.
- Air interface conformance test standards for 900-MHz RFID.
- Mobile RFID privacy guidelines.
- Adult certification for mobile RFID service (to verify the age of users for specific content).
- Security requirements for mobile RFID services.
- Standard on radio specifications for mobile RFID reader.
- Object Directory System model and Object Directory Service interworking interface specification. (This system is developed by the National Internet Development Agency in Korea. It is similar to Object Name Service [ONS] developed by EPCglobal.)
- RFID privacy protection guidelines.
- Numbering scheme for identifying RF tags.
- Common protocol for RFID readers.
- Application requirement profile.
- Application interface specification.
- RFID system security and encryption technology.
- RFID–Internet Protocol version 6 (IPv 6) interworking specification.

- RFID Testing and certification specification.
- RFID code specification (e.g. EPC, Ucode).
- RFID air interface protocol.

The Korean Standards Association (KSA; www.kis.or.kr) is a public organization with 4,300 members, including companies, associations, and organizations. It includes groups that work in RFID planning and strategy, quality management, education, industrial standards, Korean Standard certification, and ISO certification. Currently, KSA runs three subcommittees for RFID standards: the terminology and roadmap group, the air protocol standards group, and industrial application group.

GS1 Korea (www.gs1kr.org) has started an RFID leaders' group. The aim is to host senior executives in order to increase substantially the adoption of RFID in Korea. The group has been hard at work since early 2006.

3 Major Institutions in Developing and Testing RFID

Various RFID-related centers have been set up in the Republic of Korea. Some of the centers are focused on R&D, while others help businesses test and pilot RFID systems before implementing them in operations. Some of these centers are as follows:

- The Electronics and Telecommunications Research Institute (ETRI; www.etri.re.kr). Established in 1976, ETRI is a nonprofit government-funded research organization that has been a leader in information and telecommunication research. It has several fields of research that include IT fusion components, future technology, mobile communication, radio and broadcasting, digital home, intellectual robot, telematics, USN, broadband, digital contents, information security, information and communication service, and embedded software.
- The Korea Electronics Technology Institute (KETI; www.keti.re.kr) has contributed to the reinforcement of international competitiveness of the electronics, information, and other related components industries, by fostering the R&D necessary for technological innovation and support of small and medium enterprises. It has three big main areas of research: electronics component–materials, nano-fusion technology, and digital convergence.
- The Institute of Information Technology Assessment (IITA; www.iita.re.kr) is a leading R&D promotion institute specialized in information and communication technology sector. Its areas of focus include R&D demand research and technology forecasting, technology assessment, project management, funds management, human resources de-

velopment, technology policy research, information analysis and service, promotion of technology transfer, and so on.
- Ubiquitous Sensor Network Center at National Computing Agency has four main roles: policy support (e.g., national policy of USN establishment support), standardization (e.g., operate USN standardization forum), trial service (e.g., RFID/USN pilot service), and cooperation (e.g., operate a strategy council, host seminars and exhibitions).
- The Korea Association of RFID/USN (KARUS; www.karus.or.kr) is an industry-based organization to enhance Korea's competitiveness and to bring wide adoption of RFID/USN. The purpose of KARUS is to efficiently foster the RFID and USN industry through strengthening cooperation and solidarity by the members and to rapidly usher in the ubiquitous network society. Currently there are over 230 members companies. It hosts/cohosts several forums including the Mobile RFID Forum and the Ubiquitous-Work Forum. It also operates an annual international exhibition and conference, called RFID/USN Korea, which in 2005 attracted 30,000 participants from all over the world.
- The main activities of the National Internet Development Agency of Korea (NIDA; www.nida.or.kr) are creating ubiquitous service infrastructure, leading the development of the next-generation Internet, and creating conducive environment for active Internet use.
- The major activities of the Telecommunications Technology Association (www.tta.or.kr) include setting up plans for standardization, establishment of standard, and testing and certification of standards products.

4 Current Status in Adoption of RFID

Currently there are wide adoptions of RFID technology in the public transport system (e.g., bus, subway) and some key industries such as the automotive manufacturing industry and the semiconductor manufacturing industries in Korea. Some of these are describe in the paragraphs that follow.

Public Transport System

RFID technology has been implemented for payment of fares on the bus and subway in the two biggest cities in Korea, Seoul, and Pusan. Currently most riders are using an RFID smart card for payment of transit fares. Recently as a pilot test, some cars have been equipped with RFID devices that periodically report the car's location (from an onboard GPS). In the case of buses, a central agency accesses this data and allocates buses to areas depending on traffic requirements.

Automotive Industry

Currently, major automotive manufacturers in Korea are using UHF RFID technology for tracking vehicles during the assembly process. In addition,

HF technology is being used to check part supplies by applying RFID to the pallets received from suppliers.

RFID Pilot Service by National Computing Agency (NCA)

NCA has been supporting RFID adoption through pilot projects in public sectors since 2004. The objectives of these pilot projects are to create an initial market and infrastructure, to establish platform standardization among pilot projects, to verify R&D results of domestic companies, and to expand application areas. Some of the trials in public sectors supported by NCA are as follows:

- *Air Baggage Tracking Service Implementation.* The Korea Airport Corporation has a project under way with the objective of improving customer service, reliability, and efficiency of airports by applying RFID to checked baggage. Six local airports are involved, including Jeju Airport, Gimpo Airport, Busan Airport, Daegu Airport, Gwangju Airport, and Cheongju Airport.
- *Property Management System Implementation.* Public Procurement Service (PPS) is a central government procurement agency that purchases and provides goods and services for the operation of various government organizations. PPS has a project for testing real-time property management at its main office, 10 local offices, a central warehouse, and three branch offices using RFID to reduce inaccurate information caused by the delayed update of information (mainly due to manual entry), to improve operational efficiency, and to have transparency in their operations.
- *Ammunition Management System Implementation.* The Ministry of National Defense has a project for testing real-time management of ammunition warehouses where RFID is used for tracking inventory levels of ammunition combined with optimizing storage space using 3-D simulation and automatic calculation of ammunition replenishment.
- *National Infrastructure Implementation for Export–Import Logistics.* The Ministry of Commerce, Industry and Energy has a project for reducing waiting time in manual import–export management. Specifically, this project will enable real-time management of supply chain from shipping to warehouse by applying tags with frequency ranges of 433 MHz and 900 MHz. The RFID tags are applied to automotive parts and containers.
- *Imported-Beef Tracking Service Implementation.* The National Veterinary Research and Quarantine Service in Korea finished a project to ensure the safety of imported beef and to enable real-time input of origin/quarantine information, with immediate withdrawal of the beef if necessary. It applies RFID to trace the supply of beef and to manage the life cycle of the beef after import into Korea.

- *Port Logistics Services Implementation.* The Ministry of Maritime Affairs and Fisheries Service has a project that applies RFID to containers transported from inland cargo base to overseas terminal. The goal of the project is the improvement of traceability and efficiency.
- *Hazardous Waste Management.* The Ministry of Environment has a project to improve safety/reliability of waste treatment from hospitals by applying 900-MHz RFID tags on boxes containing used syringes and contaminated gloves.
- *Air Cargo Management.* The Incheon City and Incheon Airport Corporation has a project to improve efficiency in air cargo logistics by tracking and controlling of containers and pallets using RFID. Currently the implementation is in the export area only.

5 Technology Advances

The Electronics Telecommunications Research Institute (ETRI; www.etri.re.kr) is a nonprofit government-funded research organization that has been at the forefront of technological excellence since its establishment in 1976. ETRI has successfully developed information technologies such as TDX-Exchange, High Density Semiconductor Microchips, and Digital Mobile Telecommunication System (CDMA). As a leading electronics and telecommunication research institute in Korea, ETRI is also leading research in the field of RFID and USN. It believes that it has initiated the world's first UHF-based mobile RFID research and development. The UHF Mobile RFID System on Chip (SoC) can be embedded in the mobile phone, and compared to HF-based Mobile RFID, UHF-based Mobile RFID (i.e., RFID SoC-embedded mobile phone) has a read range of more than 1 m. Many application service models are currently being developed to support Mobile RFID hardware (e.g., SoC).

6 Future Potential for RFID in Korea

To date, several RFID/USN applications have been developed and implemented in Korea. Going forward, Korea is expected to expand the activities of RFID and USN, both in applications and R&D. Many industry-led projects are in the planning stages, with strong government support anticipated for several years.

Since 2005, there have been tremendous government drives for the Ubiquitous City (also called u-City). This is a locale where all major information systems (residential, medical, business, governmental, etc.) are integrated to provide seamless, wireless access/service from anywhere. Some of the key technologies to be implemented in the Ubiquitous City include broadband network, RFID, USN, home networking, wireless broadband (WiBro), digital multimedia broadcasting, telemetry, geographic information system (GIS), location-based system (LBS), smart card system, videoconference technologies, and others. Many of these technologies were developed in research laboratories in the United States, but because of fewer social and regulatory obstacles to implement them, Korea became the ideal test bed for their implementation. The Ministry of Information and Communication, in collaboration with the Ministry of Construction and Transportation (MOCT), set up a task force for the project beginning in November 2005.

In February 2006, MIC and MOCT signed a memorandum of understanding on the construction of u-City. Through the MOU, the two ministries agreed to cooperate with respect to the legal system for the construction of u-City, the development of standardized u-City models, the conduct of pilot projects for u-City, and the exchanges of information and manpower related to u-City projects. New Songdo is included in plans for u-City. It will be the world's largest ubiquitous city. The anticipated budget is US$25 billion for implementing the plan.

7 Conclusion

There are many more examples of RFID/USN activities in Korea. For many years, Korea has proven to be the test bed for new information technology. It will never stop until it achieves its ultimate vision of creating a ubiquitous society where people can connect to the network and other services any time and any where. For this to come true, RFID is one of the key technologies employed to connect people and things to a network.

RFID in Spain

Contributed by Andrés García Higuera (andres.garcia@ualm.es)

1 Regulation

Spanish legislation tends to closely follow European standards and copy legislation coming from the EU. Therefore, any law allowed in the rest of Europe that could eventually affect the implementation of RFID systems in Spain is expected to be quickly adopted.

The Spanish legislation approved the National Table of Frequency Assignment by means of "Order ITC/1998/2005 of 22 June 2005 (B.O.E. number 153 of 28 June 2005)." In this table, eight frequency bands are established that can be used for industry, science, and medicine purposes in a relatively open way. The bands are named ICM bands, for "Industrial, Científico, and Médico," These ICM bands are as follows:

ICM 1: 13,553–13,567 MHz

ICM 2: 26,957–27,283 MHz

ICM 3: 40,660–40,700 MHz

ICM 4: 433,050–434,790 MHz

ICM 5: 2.400–2.500 GHz

ICM 6: 5.725–5.875 GHz

ICM 7: 24,00–24,25 GHz

ICM 8: 61,00–61,50 GHz

These ICM frequencies are designated as being of "common usage," which means that they are regulated but their use does not require specific permission. However, the services using these bands must not generate interference nor apply any special protection against authorized services of a different category. ICM services operating in these bands must always keep the radiation restrictions established in "Royal decree 444/1994, of 11 March 1994."

For RFID purposes, this closely matches what exists in other European countries. However, some concerns were expressed by companies with interests in RFID about specific restrictions on electromagnetic radiation that were recently passed that seemed to affect frequency ranges and could be used for RFID.

The history of this regulation came from the discovery of several cases of leukemia among children attending a school whose playground was in the proximity of a power line and a telephone antenna. Public opinion was mobilized which eventually resulted in the passage of new laws by the government such as "Royal decree 1066/2001" and "Order Ministerial CTE/23/2002."

These regulations on electromagnetic radiation set a limit on human exposure, in terms of, for example, specific absorbed radiation, or SAR, typically from cell phones, and specific energy absorption rates. Some tables are included that specify the levels of radiation that can be tolerated at different parts of the body and the allowed emissions from antennas in populated areas. However, it is not in the spirit of the law to be specially restrictive for RFID purposes, and the power levels contemplated are far higher than what is normal for RFID. As an example, in practice, the only effective limitation existing in Spain for the emission of signals at 13.56 MHz is the European Norm "EN 300 330–1," which establishes a maximum field for this frequency of 42 dBμA/m at 10 m—the same as anywhere else in the EU.

2 Standards

Spain has so far been a rather passive country with regard to the development and adoption of standards for RFID. There is a high level of awareness regarding the new possibilities of RFID for logistics and a certain interest in the possibility of replacing barcodes at the supermarket. However, there is not an active body interested in fostering the specific implementation of this technology by companies in this country at present.

EPCglobal has been lately represented in Spain by the Spanish Association of Commercial Codification (AECOC; www.aecoc.es). With over 20,000 member companies, AECOC is one of the largest business associations in Spain. The association has diversified its offer to incorporate a broad range of companies of all sizes dedicated to manufacturing and distribution in different sectors such as food, textile, hardware, pharmacy, sports, and health care. The combined annual revenue of all associated companies is over € 150 million and translates to approximately 20 percent of the Spanish gross product. Originally, AECOC began as an organization for the regulation of barcode usage in Spain. But at present, it has assumed consulting roles in different activity areas such as logistics, marketing, e-commerce EDI, codification and product identification, and food safety.

The activities of AECOC regarding RFID and the introduction of the EPC have primarily been to raise awareness by means of conferences and seminars. This can be justified by the late involvement of Spanish industries in the use of tracking systems. This posed a serious problem in the year after the passing of European laws enforcing the use of tracking in the EU, mainly for food and beverages. This regulation affects both ascending and descending tracking, meaning the requirement for companies to be able to track products from the manufacturing process to the consumer and from the consumer to the manufacturing process in terms of lot, date, time, and production line. Nowadays the standard procedure for companies to guarantee tracking is considered to be the use of code EAN 128 at the pallet level for the whole of their production. EAN 128 is a label of a considerable size that incorporates different barcodes identifying the product, its manufacturer, and the lot number. The EAN 128 barcode label is usually attached to pallets once they have been wrapped in plastic for storage and distribution.

Most Spanish companies with interests in logistics and distribution have been busy enough, during the last couple of years, incorporating EAN 128 as well as the data management systems that take full advantage of it to guarantee tracking at the pallet level. AECOC has been involved closely in supporting its associated companies with the incorporation of this standard. This, to some extent, justifies the passivity with which RFID has been received by Spanish companies to date.

During 2005, EPCglobal interest in Spain seems to have been reactivated with the creation of a new center attached to AECOC, the EPC Competence Centre (EPC CC; www.epcglobalsp.org). The EPC CC aims to be the meeting point between supply and demand of RFID/EPC needs in Spain, providing all necessary services to support and help Spanish companies develop and implement EPC with RFID equipment, tags, and software applications on display at the center. The Technology Demonstration area is focused on the supply chain, point-of-sale, and home applications. The installation of demonstration kits provides a clear vision to its members of the capability of EPC technology in different environments where supply chain processes are running, such as factories, warehouses, and logistics systems.

Besides EPCglobal-related institutions, there are other similar initiatives in Spain such as IDtrack (www.idtrack.org). IDtrack is the European Association for Sure & Secure Identification, headquartered in Barcelona. Its mission is to communicate, guide, and coordinate activities for the reliable and secure implementation of new technologies of identification and traceability. IDtrack claims to have, as its major objective, the task of ensuring that Southwestern Europe reaches the same level as the United States in the implementation of the technologies of secure identification. This association has been quite active lately in developing reports about the deployment of RFID related technologies in Spain and in organizing conferences and seminars on the subject.

There are other initiatives, also based in Barcelona, concerned with raising awareness about RFID, such as www.RFID-Spain.com, which is part of Bi-Spain.com, a set of Internet sites providing information in Spanish about new computer technologies, with a focus on industry.

Some consulting firms are also offering RFID solutions to their clients as an alternative to barcodes for tracking. This, however, is always restricted to an internal use within their client companies while the standardization process achieves greater consolidation.

3 Major Institutions in Developing and Testing RFID

From the technology development point of view, there are no major Spanish firms in the sector. It is also the case that R&D has always been one of the great weak points in this country. This is the result of a critically low government budget for R&D and a university establishment with old-fashioned structures that can hardly support the pressures of fast technology changes.

Some university research groups, however, are beginning to react to the heightened level of awareness raised worldwide on RFID-related issues. But so far it is in companies, even small or medium sized, as they are in this sector, where the most interesting developments are being conducted. An example of this is the case of LipSoft Electronics (www. lipsoftelectronics.com), with its own set of tags and readers for specific applications, including RFID tags that incorporate temperature or other sensing devices.

4 Current Status in Adoption of RFID

While the main concern for retailers is still deployment cost, RFID adoption has experienced great advances during 2006, as this is a sector with one of the biggest growths in industry, over 30 percent in Spain. Although one in three retailers still does not know about RFID technology, this situation is rapidly changing, as one of the main sources of awareness involves new requirements placed on companies as a result of new EU regulations about traceability for food and beverages.

Most supply-chain-related companies are convinced that production costs for this technology are bound to drop as, with the deployment of the second generation of RFID standards, a reliable tag will appear that will be applicable to many different sectors.

Another factor that is beginning to produce some effects is the approbation of the new standard by the European Telecommunications Standards Institute (ETSI), which will foster the usage of UHF tags in Europe. This new standard, ETSI 302 208, will allow RFID readers installed in Europe to use more power and to operate in a broader band of frequencies, from 865 to 868 MHz.

5 Technology Advances

The recent increase in awareness from possible users is also having the effect of beginning to generate some interest in RFID technology developers. Even so, a problem remains in the structure of this strategic sector, where R&D has been historically underfunded, not reaching 1 percent of the GNP until 2002 and reaching just 1.22 percent in 2005. This has resulted in the virtual nonexistence of technology developers with a competitive size that can have an impact on standardization of new RFID products for generic purposes. There are, however, some small companies and research groups that are developing and commercializing interesting specific applications, like tags with sensors for temperature and conductivity, and the installation of specifically designed RFID systems, mainly for access control and security.

6 Future Potential for RFID In Spain

In 2005, IDtrack presented a survey indicating that 98 percent of Spanish companies have a traceability system in place. However, the survey showed that the systems used were rudimentary in most cases, with 61.6 percent of them using labels that did not even include barcodes. Even so, 86.9 percent of companies claim to be following EU legislation on traceability. However, it must be considered that 70 percent of them have concerns about the lack of clarity in this legislation.

One of the biggest improvements that this survey compared to the one performed in the previous year is a rise in the awareness concerning the traceability regulation. Thus, 99 percent of companies say that they know about the legislation versus 58.8 percent making the same claim as the previous year. Also, 85.7 percent agree on the convenience of having these norms, mainly for food safety issues. But just one company in four is following EU recommendations in the way traceability is being implemented.

In a survey, 87.6 percent of companies that responded believe that the consumer is the most benefited by traceability being compulsory; less benefited are manufacturers. Of the companies surveyed, 71 percent agree that traceability helps improve quality at the consumers' end. In fact, 91.8%

named traceability as one of their most pressing concerns, but among distribution companies that are much less aware of the issue, the percentage falls to 82.6 percent. In spite of these improvements, the survey also brought to light a series of deficiencies, such as the fact that just 4 in 10 companies would be able to react to a crisis in less than four hours.

The use of barcodes for traceability has only reached a level of 52.2 percent. Information interchange among companies remains very low, with just 44.7 percent of companies having compatibility with the system in use by their supplier. In addition, just being compatible doesn't mean that the companies take advantage of it; in most cases they do not. Therefore, companies are mainly relying on traditional paper delivery manifests, invoices, bills of lading, and so forth for documentation purposes. Lastly, it can be said that the use or RFID is restricted to very specific cases within single companies.

7 Other Factors

Another factor to be considered regarding the deployment of RFID is the level of acceptance it is bound to have among consumers. This acceptance will be greatly influenced by recurring privacy issues related to RFID. Even as public concern related to privacy with RFID are as high in Spain as anywhere else in Europe. However, no specific legislation has been passed that can effectively pose a problem for RFID deployment. This is quite understandable, as the pressure groups active in this respect do not have a very realistic idea about the true possibilities of RFID—their views being based more on science fiction than on anything else. The scenarios that they pose have the possibility of spreading discomfort and suspicion among future users.

The European Union has reacted to this concern by putting in place sweeping privacy laws. Article 29 of Directive 95/46/ec is Europe's data protection regulation, and it is the platform on which each country builds its own privacy and data protection laws. Under European law, any company that uses RFID must notify the consumer that the tag is on the product and provide details on how to discard the tag and access the information held on it. The company must also disclose how any information will be collected and used.

More than half of the 2,000 European consumers who participated in a recent online survey say that they are concerned about privacy with regard to RFID. However, this same survey, conducted by Cap Gemini and ORC International, a global research unit of Opinion Research Corp., also found that respondents are more likely to buy RFID-tagged products if there are laws protecting their privacy. The ability to disable RFID tags at the store after purchase, a customer opt-in/opt-out choice regarding information collected, and clear labels that state that the tag is RFID enabled follow in importance.

8 Conclusion

Regulation in Spain is similar to that existing in most other members of the EU. Manufacturing companies, as well as others with interests in distribution and logistics, are well aware of the growing requirements for better ways of tracking their products and know of the benefits that RFID can offer. Different associations such as AECOC (and now EPC CC), IDtrack and others have succeeded to some extent in raising awareness on the issue of tracking, the advantages of RFID, and the possibilities of new standards such as those provided by EPC.

However, the real situation is that these same companies are in many cases involved in short-term projects aimed at upgrading their tracking systems to more matured technologies such as the tracking of pallets by using EAN 128. This somewhat perturbing situation has, however, the advantage of bringing most companies to a point where they are putting in place relatively powerful information management systems that can, in the near future, be the basis for more sophisticated tracking systems.

Unfortunately, from the technology development and from R&D points of view, Spain is still behaving as a rather passive country. Some initiatives coming from small and medium companies and, to a smaller degree, from public research centers such as universities can still allow for some degree of optimism concerning the possibility of improvement in this situation in the near future.

RFID in the United Kingdom

Contributed by Gabriel Fregoso (gabriel.fregoso@brooks.com)
Brooks Software (www.brooks.com)

1 Regulation

Radio and telecommunication terminal equipment, including RFID in the United Kingdom, is regulated in accordance with the European Parliament and the Council of the European Union, which adopted in 1999 a directive defining the rules for any electronic equipment sold or put into service in the United Kingdom and other European countries (www.rtte.org/documents/dir99-5.htm#Article%2015). Any electronic device that is sold in the United Kingdom, including RFID equipment, has to conform to European regulations, and products should be identified with the CE mark (www.ceproof.com/ european_directives.htm) to prove that they comply with the European Product Directives, intended to create a single legal structure for all member states.

The organization responsible for enforcing the legal use of the radio spectrum for the UK communications industries is Ofcom (Office of Communications; www.ofcom.org.uk). Currently 500 mW regulation (EN 300 220) is available for use in the United Kingdom and across most Europe. 2 W regulations (EN 302 208) have been exempt from licensing since November 2005. Other countries in Europe may require local government adoption and a special license.

There are different companies that offer services to equipment suppliers for compliance management, regulatory support, and radio performance testing to enable bringing products to market faster with CE certification, such as Radio Frequency Investigation (RFI Global; www.rfi-global.com).

2 Standards

Regarding standards, GS1 UK is the UK provider of the EPCglobal Network (www.gs1uk.org) and has created an RFID interest group to promote and develop adoption of cross-sector, global supply chain standards. The GS1 organization gives independent advice and information regarding supply chain solutions and services not only on the different aspects of RFID deployment but also for barcoding, electronic business messaging, and data synchronization.

According to GS1 UK, the EPCglobal standards are driven by the user community and the main focus now is on C1-Gen 2 for UHF (865 to 868 MHz), due mainly to the amount of interest from the large retail users. There are already RFID readers certified for Gen 2 from different vendors. Everything is in place for companies to start exchanging data with their partners through EPC Information Services. Gen 2 will allow interoperability among different EPC certified readers and tags from multiple vendors.

HF and LF are not standardized yet. However, there is one group within EPCglobal that is looking at item-level tagging, and they may come out with a standard for HF in the near future.

Standards and regulation for the use of RFID in aerospace is determined by the International Air Transport Association (IATA). These standards are also applicable and followed by aerospace companies in the United Kingdom.

3 Major Institutions in Developing and Testing RFID

The RFID Centre (www.rfidc.com) in Bracknell permanently exhibits and promotes a large range of applications of the technology from the main suppliers for various industries. It also provides education, services, and independent advice. It has reported that the main interest of companies visiting the center since it was opened in January 2005 has been in supply chain management, logistics, vehicle tracking, and retail, followed by asset management. This evidence is concluded from their visitor registration analysis report that shows that up to 50 percent of the visitors are from the retail supply chain. It has also experienced recent interest in pharmaceutical, health care, and asset management applications. However, the RFID Centre is still sceptical about the ROI in applying RFID tags at item level, especially when the tagged object cost is low.

In the United Kingdom there are suppliers of advanced logistic services, such as Unipart Solutions (www.usp.uk.com) in Oxford, that are actively promoting RFID technology for supply chain management, from raw material suppliers to the retail sector. The services include the design and development of end-to-end business process scenarios that can be tested in real time in a controlled environment for companies that want to test the technology. The demo area in their distribution center is dedicated to running RFID trials, pilot tests, and education for their customers. In this type of environment, different solution partners can provide complete advice and trials of the technology that is part of the supply chain evolution to enable supply-to-order.

There are also different RFID interest groups focusing on standards and research for specific industries such as aerospace in the Auto-ID Lab at the University of Cambridge. The Auto-ID Lab at the Institute of Manufacturing from the University of Cambridge (www.autoidlabs.org.uk) is part of a network of seven independent academic research labs that share a common vision and goal.

4 Current Status in Adoption of RFID

Supply Chain Management

RFID activities in the United Kingdom have been increasing in the last couple of years, driven commercially by expected improvements in supply chains with the major retail companies such as Tesco, Marks & Spencer, and so on, attracting attention and driving implementations. RFID technology is now considered to be out of its infancy after several early-adopter companies have used RFID in different parts of their production. Major IT companies such as Microsoft, Sun, Oracle, SAP, and others are partnering with RFID hardware suppliers such as Symbol, Intermec, and others to provide complete solutions to meet customer needs and capture market.

Asset Management

According to Wavetrend (www.wavetrend.net), Thames Port is using active RFID technology to locate containers in the yard to enable scheduling the transportation of product by knowing the exact location of the container and when the driver is expected to pick up the container by using active RFID tags. The Royal Academy of Arts is also using active RFID to enable the tracking, monitoring and protection of all assets.

Carlsberg, Coors, and Scottish & Newcastle have outsourced beer keg management to TrenStar (www.trenstar.com). This relieved the brewers from managing the cleaning, maintenance, and return logistics of the kegs, enabling them to focus on their core business of brewing, marketing, and selling beer. TrenStar RFID tagged 3.5 million beer kegs to help them keep track and manage these assets.

Aerospace and Defense

Adoption of RFID technology in aerospace is in the improvement of supply chain activities in the assembly of aircraft, in order to efficiently manage the cost of labor and material. The Auto-ID Lab in Cambridge has recently launched the Aero ID Technologies Programme (http://www.aero-id.org), driven by the needs of the main aerospace companies such as Boeing and Airbus. One of the program's main activities is the development of a "track and trace" requirements model, examining methods of integrating RFID technology in track-and-trace environments that can provide data in real time of the history and the presence of tagged objects.

In defense, according to the publishers of "MoD Defence Contracts Bulletin" BiP Solutions Ltd., there are talks within the Ministry of Defence (MoD) regarding wider adoption of RFID technology in a similar way to its counterparts in the DoD in the United States.

5 Technology Advances

Most of the development in RFID has been focusing on how to apply the technology to resolve common problems in innovative ways, such as developing new hardware form factors to adapt to the different environments, as well as software applications that resolve some of the issues and improve business processes in new industries. Advances can also be seen in overcoming existing limitations of the technology, such as accuracy of readings with metal and liquids or in harsh environments, and in finding ways to drive down the cost of the technology in general.

The Auto-ID Lab in Cambridge is an example of very diverse research programs. It divides its research projects into three main business blocks: Hardware, Software & Network, and Business Process & Applications. The Auto-ID Lab is leading the way in investigating new business cases and applications in RFID, with a clear focus on business processes and industries such as aerospace (using RFID technology to enable ubiquitous computing environment for aircraft maintenance), automotive manufacturing, retail supply chain, networked RFID systems, the impact of RFID in shelf replenishment, and other potential future applications.

6 Future Potential for RFID in the United Kingdom

According to Intermec, by 2010, "customer intimacy" information enabled by RFID is expected to drive "supply to order." In addition, integrated networks and systems are expected. It also envisions, a long way off, item-level tagging, significant cost reduction in tags and readers, and more inbuilt RFID capability from existing ERP/WMS vendors.

Another area where RFID has seen recent interest and growth in the United Kingdom is in pharmaceutical and health care companies, who are looking to prevent counterfeiting, protect patients, track equipment and staff, and improve supply chain and inventory management.

The potential future applications described by Hodges and McFarlane are in the retail store of the future, where RFID will enable "checkout-free" stores with antitheft shelves, continuous shelf inventory checking, and more frequent replenishment. According to them, Sainsbury's in the United Kingdom opened Future Stores as a means of demonstrating the type of facilities that might be expected in an Auto-ID-enhanced retail outlet.

Other examples of new applications of RFID under consideration are in extending product visibility and information content over its entire life cycle, and at home for continuous inventory that may give a new generation of home appliances the ability to know their content and act on the information.

7 Conclusion

The activities in the United Kingdom are reflected in the large attendance at the various RFID marketing events throughout the year. These events generate interest, promote suppliers, encourage pilot implementations, and support RFID education in general.

There has also been an increased push toward adoption of EPCglobal standards among major retailers that eventually will get into other parts of the supply chain and to manufacturing. However, there are still companies using proprietary codes on their products, arguing that this method protects customers from privacy concerns. In the long term, it appears that these cases will be isolated because of the cost incurred in having custom specific products. Companies will lower the cost by using standard solutions that can be interchanged from different suppliers.

Although there has been general interest in understanding RFID technology and the benefits for the different industries, the reality today is that only a few large-scale corporations have fully embraced implementations. They are still waiting for other parts of the supply chain to cooperate, and very often these supply chains extend outside the United Kingdom. There are expectations for the medium and small enterprises to also fully embrace the technology, and as RFID gets proven, standardized, and somewhat commoditized, this will lower the barriers to entry for most companies in the United Kingdom. Furthermore, as innovative niche applications develop, there may be a need to expand the frequency spectrum assigned to RFID to avoid potential oversaturation when all companies start using RFID in the near future.

RFID in the United States

Contributed by Gisele Bennett (gisele.bennett@gtri.gatech.edu)
Georgia Institute of Technology (www.gtri.gatech.edu)

1 Regulation

There are two federal agencies in the United States that manage the RF spectrum: the Federal Communications Commission (FCC) and the National Telecommunications and Information Administration (NTIA; www. ntia.doc.gov). The FCC regulates RF band usage for nonfederal (private, state, and local government) users. The FCC is an independent U.S. government agency that answers directly to the U.S. Congress. The electromagnetic spectrum for federal users is managed by the NTIA. Although there are two entities that recommend frequency allocations, these organizations signed a memorandum of understanding on spectrum coordination in January 2003. Coordination is necessary, since 93.1 percent of the spectrum below 30 GHz is shared among federal and nonfederal users, while 54.2 percent is shared below 3.1 GHz (for details see *Spectrum Policy for The 21st Century: The President's Spectrum Policy Initiative: Report 1* at www. ntia.doc.gov / reports / specpolini / presspecpolini_ report1_06242004.htm#_ Toc74447274).

The FCC was chartered in 1934 to regulate interstate and international communications by radio, television, wire, satellite, and cable. The RF spectrum is partitioned into 450 frequency bands from 9 KHz to 300 GHz. The bands typically associated with RFID along with their allocated power are shown in Table 1. RFID tags generally operate at low frequency (LF), high frequency (HF), or ultrahigh-frequency (UHF). There is no global RF standard, although some users and countries may designate the 13.56-MHz band as the RFID band.

Table 1 Common RFID Frequency Bands in United States

Band	Typical RFID Frequency Spectrum (Standard Range)	Regulation	
		Bandwidth	**Limit**
LF	< 135 KHz	~ 1 MHz	< 15 μV/m at $\lambda/2\pi$
HF	13.56 MHz (3–30 MHz)	14 MHz	< 10,000 μV/m at 30 m
UHF	433 MHz (300–1,000 MHz)	1 MHz	< 55,000 μV/m at 3 m
UHF	915 MHz (300–1,000 MHz)	26 MHz	< 4 W EIRP*
MW	2.400–2.4835 GHz (2.4 GHz–L Band)	83 MHz	4 W EIRP

*Effective Isotropic Radiated Power (EIRP) is the apparent power transmitted toward the receiver, assuming the signal is radiated equally in all directions.

Each frequency has advantages and disadvantages. The FCC regulation for transmitters operating from the LF to UHF bands is governed by Part 15 of Title 47 of the Code of Federal Regulations of the FCC rules (see www.fcc.gov/oet/info/rules/part15/part15-2-16-06.pdf). Depending on the frequency, the requirement to be compliant can be exhaustive with complicated RF measurements. Part 15 allows for operation of transmitters without a license (unlicensed band). The operating conditions must not cause harmful interference and must accept any interference received.

A listing of advantages and disadvantages of using a given frequency band is shown in Table 2. As illustrated, there are specific applications that are more appropriate for the different frequency bands. The read ranges are a function of not only frequency but also power output and the directional sensitivity of the antenna. LF tags are common in proximity applications such as point of sale and access control. HF tags are used for item-level tracking. The 433-MHz UHF band is primarily seen in active tags achieving read ranges of over 100 m, while the 860- to 930-MHz UHF bands are common for supply chain applications and have read ranges of 3 m. The UHF band has faster data transfer rates than HF tags. However, unlike the LF tags, these HF and UHF frequencies will not pass through items with high water content. The UHF band is not universally available at the same power level and frequency. The microwave (MW) band (2.45 GHz) moves data faster than the UHF tags, with a read range of 1 m for a passive system and 15 to 20 m for an active system. The specifications (e.g., power and frequency spread) for this MW spectrum, like the HF band, varies depending on the country. Other considerations for selecting a frequency to use for RFID application include the affects of materials on the RF band.

Table 2 Advantages and Disadvantages for Frequency Bands

Band	RFID Frequency Spectrum	Advantages	Disadvantages
LF	< 135 KHz	Typical range for passive LF tags < 10 cm, active LF tags up to 5 m. Has ability to read on (or near) wet or metal surfaces.	Higher cost, slower data transfer, short range when passive LF tags are used.
HF	13.56 MHz	Reasonable range of up to 0.5 m for a 4 × 4 cm passive tag, reasonable propagation, low cost, faster data transfer than LF, performs better around liquids than UHF.	More power usage.
UHF	433 MHz	Range < 100 m (with active tags), moderate data speed, low liquid penetration, works well around metals.	Poor water and tissue penetration.
UHF	860–960 MHz	Range < 10 m (for passive tag). Low cost, fast data transfer, effective around metals allowing antenna integration, concurrent read of < 100 items, smaller dipole antennas.	• Signal attenuated by objects (e.g., shadow effect—one tag may obscure another). • Attenuation by water. • Subject to reflection.
MW	2.400–2.4835 GHz	Good range (up to 20 m for active tag), very high data rates, effective around metals.	• Shared spectrum with other applications, e.g., microwave ovens. • More susceptible to noise.

A material or object can be classified as RF lucent or absorbent. An RF lucent object lets the waves pass through without affecting them, while absorbent or opaque objects can limit the usage and reliability of the tags.

A band that is commonly used is the Instrumentation, Scientific, and Medical (ISM) band in the United States that includes unlicensed frequency bands 915 MHz, 2.4 GHz, and 5.725 GHz. These bands are typically used by wireless LANs or Bluetooth devices. The transmitter must have an output power less than 1 W and a maximum EIRP of 4 W. There are other restrictions depending on the FCC 15.XXX parts of regulations that spell out operating frequency, output power, spurious emissions, modulation methods, transmit duty cycles, and antenna gains.

2 Standards

Although the FCC and NTIA regulate frequency usage, there are numerous organizations that determine the plethora of standards for RFID. These standards focus on technology (includes tags and readers), data content, conformance (testing and print quality), and application standards (includes packaging and shipping labels). In the United States there are two governing bodies: American National Standards Institute (ANSI; www.ansi.org) and the National Institute of Standards and Technology (NIST). The primary international governing bodies are the International Organization for Standardization (ISO), GS1 (incorporating EPCglobal; formerly called Uniform Code Council, or UCC), and Healthcare's B2B Standards Development Organization (HIBCC) standards. ISO is a network of national standards groups from 156 countries working in partnership with international organizations. GS1 (see www.gs1.org) has the charter to establish and promote multi-industry standards for product identification. HIBCC is an industry-sponsored nonprofit organization that is ANSI-accredited with the function to facilitate electronic communication through standards for information exchange among healthcare partners. The application standards range from GTAG™ for supply chain (EAN/UCC) to ANSI MH10.8.4 and MH10.8.8 for containers and pallets to parcels and packages, respectively. ISO 18185 focuses electronic seals on freight containers, while other application standards look at automotive and airline industries.

ISO has three technical committees (TCs) that deal with RFID technologies and has formed the Joint Technical Committee (JTC1), consisting of groups within ISO and the International Electrotechnical Committee (IEC). The IEC is a global organization that prepares and publishes international standards for electrical and electronic-related technologies. JTC1 SC31 (SC stands for "subcommittee") is responsible for automatic identification and

(Special thanks to Craig Harmon for the various discussions that are the basis of this overview.)

data capture technology (AIDC). There are five working groups (WG) with WG4 focused on RFID for item management. Within the subgroups in SC31, IS0/IEC 18000, with seven parts, is a standard that is managed by this group. ISO/IEC 18000 series are technical standards that define how tags and readers communicate through the airways with one another, with the various parts defining the frequency bands of operation as shown in Table 3. ISO/IEC 18000-5 Part 5, which focused on air interface communications at 5.8 GHz, was withdrawn due to lack of global acceptance. ISO/IEC 17363 to ISO 17367 are application standards.

GS1 reached an agreement with the Auto-ID Center at MIT to license Electronic Product Code (EPC) technology developed at the center. The EPC was proposed by MIT's Auto-ID Center as a standard for identifying products by adopting the Global Trade Item Number (GTIN) embedded in an RFID tag. GTIN in an EPC RFID tag is similar to the Universal Product Code (UPC) on barcodes and is the next generation of product information.

The 860- to 960-MHz band is in the ISM band, with the ISO/IEC 18000-6 Part C supporting the EPCglobal UHF Gen 2 specification. Existing users include ANSI MH10.8.4, which addresses returnable containers. Users of the 433 MHz (18000-7) include the U.S. Department of Defense (DoD) for container tracking and non-DoD freight containers, supply chain applications, and container seals. ISO 18185 is a current work item for container e-seals and was expected to become a standard by the end of 2006. ISO/IEC 15418 and ISO/IEC 15434 address standards for data semantics and data syntax, respectively.

Although there are other professional organizations involved in providing guidelines for RFID, the most active is probably the Association of Automatic Identification and Mobility (AIM), which formed the RFID Experts Group (REG). The REG was originally formed in January 2004 to assist the DoD with RFID implementation and in July 2004 was rolled under the AIM

Table 3 ISO 18000

Band	Frequency Spectrum	ISO Designation
—	Defines parameters to standardize that determine the Standardized Air Interface Definition in the ISO/IEC 18000 series	ISO/IEC 18000 Part 1
LF	< 135 kHz	ISO/IEC 18000 Part 2
HF	13.56 MHz	ISO/IEC 18000 Part 3
MW	2.4 GHz	ISO/IEC 18000 Part 4
UHF	860–960 MHz	ISO/IEC 18000 Part 6
UHF	433 MHz	ISO/IEC 18000 Part 7

Global activity. Members of the REG consist of industry and academia. There are working groups within the REG to address issues from interrogator system implementation and operations to security to software and middleware. There are currently 14 activities within the REG.

3 Major Institutions in Developing and Testing RFID

Both companies and universities have opened RFID centers with focus areas ranging from RFID certification to RFID animal research. The activities listed in this section are by no means a comprehensive list but highlight applications areas representing sectors that are utilizing or plan to utilize RFID. Most of the standards in RFID that include label placement, recycling, security, data formats, and so on are activities that are lead by the MIT Auto-ID Lab, AIM, and ISO. Following is a listing of these centers and their research activities:

- The University of Arkansas–RFID Research Center focuses conducting research in technology deployment and data analytics and developing business cases for deploying RFID.
- Auburn University Detection and Food Safety (AUDFS) combines RFID with sensors to detect pathogens in food.
- Baylor University is looking at RFID and the use in supply chain management.
- University of Florida's Packaging Science Laboratory is using RFID for the food industry to develop industry-specific best practice, research, and Auto-ID applications and is designing a system for cold chain solutions.
- Georgia Institute of Technology Logistics and Maintenance Applied Research Center (LandMARC) has developed active RFID systems with integrated sensors for environmental and location monitoring. In addition, at Georgia Tech there is research activity in radio frequency integrated circuit (RFIC) design, localization, antenna design, and logistical use of RFID data.
- Johns Hopkins showed that encryption for RFID might not be foolproof (see www.jhu.edu/news/home05/jan05/rfid.html).
- University of Kansas RFID Alliance Lab provides tests on RFID technology to determine RFID equipment performance in a variety of realistic scenarios.
- Massachusetts Institute of Technology's Auto-ID Center is actively involved in working with EPCglobal to develop standards.
- Ohio University's Center for Automatic Identification (AI) is conducting research and education in various automatic identification and data capture (AIDC) technologies.

- University of Pittsburgh's RFID Center of Excellence is focused on research in active remote sensing.
- North Dakota State University and the state have invested in RFID research and manufacturing capability, with applications that include animal tracking.
- University of Texas Arlington's RFID Systems Research Center was recently formed through a collaboration of UT Arlington, UT Dallas, University of North Texas, and North Lake College. Their mission is to provide research and development of new RFID projects and education on RFID adoption.
- Villanova University's RFID Lab provides capabilities for the development of new RFID technologies and prototype designs specializing in tag localization and tracking, collision avoidance, and innovative antenna designs.
- University of Wisconsin-Madison's RFID Laboratory is researching tag readability, packaging, interference, and reader designs.

4 Current Status in Adoption of RFID

Vendors in the United States are as diverse as a two-person shop operating out of a garage to companies with venture capital funding over US$100 million. The regulating standard for tags used in the United States is the EPCglobal definition, with varying levels defining tag functionality and characteristics (passive to active integrated sensors). There are five components in an RFID system: tags, reader, encoder, middleware, and application software.

Although a comprehensive list of players in the RFID space cannot be achieved without consuming an entire book, following is a sample of those who have been in the market since the flurry of RFID started after the Wal-Mart and DoD announcement mandating the use of RFID. A Google search results in tag manufacture listings that are greater than 250, greater than 30 for reader suppliers, and endless middleware and system integrators. A sample listing of tag manufacturers involved in development in the early stages of the RFID flurry include Matrix, Alien Technology, Avery Dennison, Texas Instruments, Zebra Technologies, and Intermec Technologies. Reader manufacturers include Intermec Technologies, Symbol Technologies, and ThingMagic. Software developers that are incorporating RFID data into the logistics and manufacturing process include Manhattan Associates, SAP, and Red Prairie, while other large companies such as IBM Global Services, Accenture, and Intel are working as system integrators. Then there are the thousands of small companies that have started to integrate RFID installation into their portfolio of skills.

Since the announcement of RFID mandates by Wal-Mart and the DoD in 2003, there has been a flurry of activity by other companies joining in the requirement that their suppliers prepare for RFID-enabled goods. Soon after the announcement of RFID and its benefits, other retailers joined the mandate, including Best Buy, Albertsons, Target, Procter and Gamble, and many more firms. With over 550 billion different items per year that pass through the supply chain, it is not surprising that so many have joined in the RFID rush. However, the supply chain is not the only vertical that has requested, has mandated, or is reviewing the uses of RFID. In November 2004, the Food and Drug Administration (FDA) promoted the use of RFID for drug tracking and authenticity. In a report released on combating counterfeit drugs, the FDA speculated that it should be feasible to use RFID to track all drugs by 2007. In 2004, the FDA approved implantable RFID chips for humans for applications in 2006 ranging from easy access to cars and homes to patient tracking with medical history stored on the chip. Other uses for implantable chips include the Digital Angel bio-thermo RFID microchip that can sense temperature for monitoring an animal's body temperature. This has created interest in tracking bird flu cases by monitoring the body temperature of birds. Like the vendor listing, the applications are almost endless. Table 4 shows a sample of the adoption and applications of RFID in the various frequency bands.

5 Technology Advances

With over 350 patents on RFID, the advances in technology continue to grow at a rapid rate. Research in RFID is truly a multidisciplinary field, requiring skills in materials, electrical engineering, physics, chemistry, paper science, packaging, logistics, and policy, to name a few. In electrical

Table 4 U.S. RFID Applications

Band	Typical RFID Frequency Spectrum	Applications
HF	13.56 MHz	Smart labels, access control, library item identification cum antitheft detection, transport fare cards, and e-passports.
UHF	433 MHz	DoD asset tracking (pallet level), automatic asset identification (active tags for containers).
UHF	860–960 MHz	Asset tracking and management, tire tags, e-toll collection.
MW	2.4–2.4835 GHz	Industrial tag readers, tag readers for multiple reads for higher read rates and distances, Bluetooth applications.

engineering, the understanding and advancement of ICs for low-power usage is critical in the development of active RFID tags. Power scavenging for extended life of active RFID tags and readers is critical to applications such as container monitoring and people and livestock tracking. The design of robust reader antennas and the exploitation of software radio technology will be critical to global acceptance of RFID because of the different frequencies in use globally. It would be difficult to achieve an acceptable return on investment if the infrastructure requires multiple readers to achieve 100 percent data accuracy.

The business case is still in its infancy for the use of RFID data for decision and logistical process improvement. There are middleware companies that claim to use RFID data to improve processes, but how can this be true if it has yet to achieve read rates greater than 80 percent reliability? You might ask whether 80 percent is good enough. The answer is it depends. Take, for example, 10 read points throughout the logistical pipeline. If you can read each package at least once through the 10 point, is that enough information to plan, react, or change processes? Some companies might claim 80 percent is good enough for them, but unless it is the right amount of data, it is not good enough. Advances in materials will aid in solving the problem of recycling all the tags and readers that will end up in our landfills. For example, RFID tags that use copper as the antenna component will wreak havoc in conjunction with use on steel pallets during recycling in the steel industry. The copper-based tags in aggregate would adversely change the chemical and structural properties of new steel. A revolutionary improvement in tag development will be the ability to spray on a tag, making application in a high-rate production system feasible and eliminating or reducing the current issues of tag application rate in an assembly line.

Policy will have a significant role in the deployment and application of RFID. We have already discussed standards and recycling issues, but what we have yet to discuss is the policy associated with tracking people and consumer goods purchased. There has probably been more media coverage on privacy due to RFID tracking than there ever was on using cell phones, WiFi-enabled devices, or even OnStar by GM for locating people. The privacy debate has escaladed to various activist groups requesting a moratorium on RFID. Recently the approval of implantable RFID chips by VeriChip has entered the controversial debate of use in tracking immigrants. However, when you factor manpower, visibility, and management of our immigration population, tracking people is not as far-fetched as one might imagine. Of course, the tracking of what someone buys or has in the home is up for privacy debates, but that can be overcome through education of what is technically possible and what is an unfounded concern.

In health care, numerous research topics must be addressed for full deployment. These topics include the effects of RFID frequencies in a hospital environment on other operating equipment, such as the triggering of automatic drips or interference with life support equipment or even alternating the composition of pharmaceuticals and/or vaccines (biologics) with brief or extended exposure to radio frequency. Another example is the impact of RF radiation on biologics (e.g., vaccines) and liquids used in pharmaceuticals. MIT has conducted preliminary research in this area by analyzing the impact on thermal and nonthermal effects. The results are preliminary and will require further research to determine the effects of RF radiation. Other topics include the use of UHF versus HF characterization for health and life sciences applications, the use of sensors—for example, for temperature or for blood monitoring—the use of IEEE 1451 and IEEE 802.11g interface for data transmission, and even the newly introduced IEEE 1902.1 protocol standard, aka RuBee.

6 Future Potential for RFID in the United States

The future potential of RFID is endless. RFID could bring conveniences to businesses such as operational visibility and process improvement that could result in cost savings to the consumers. We will have constant monitoring beyond just portal monitoring, other business verticals such as insurance companies will start to reap the benefits, and privacy will become a design constraint. We have seen applications in the supply chain, health care, homeland security, and immigration, to name a few. The concept we are discussing is the impact of monitoring the movement of objects, animals, and people. RFID is not the only modality for monitoring and tracking. Whatever the platform, more research along with results of deploying of RFID will need to be conducted and analyzed to determine the real benefits to offset the total cost of implementation. We have a research agenda that was outlined in Section 5 that will drive the future deployment and use of RFID. The immediate obstacles to overcome will require the reduction in deployment cost (tag, readers, and infrastructure) and utilize RFID data for an acceptable ROI. To achieve an acceptable ROI, RFID performance must be improved. As part of the improvement in performance, privacy and security must be achieved.

To achieve an ROI that is attractive to end users, we will need to improve the reliability, read rates, accuracy, and overall general performance of RFID. Advances in the development of physical layer designs that incorporate and leverage the benefits of multi-antenna architectures are leading candidates for this performance improvement. Multi-antenna designs can provide (1) increases in signal strength through adaptive coherent combining, (2) diversity to help combat channel impairments, (3) interference suppression to mitigate unwanted noise, (4) capacity enhancement through space and/or beam multiplexing, and (5) improved reliability through these and other mechanisms such as space–time coding. The integration of smart antenna technology into devices will mandate the need for the development of protocols that can support and exploit the new capabilities offered by multi-antenna architectures. Some work in wireless communications ad hoc networks is beginning to focus on cross-layer (i.e., physical layer/medium access) designs to determine appropriate protocols that will take advantage of the capacity enhancement potential afforded by multi-antenna architectures. Similar considerations for Automatic Identification System (AIS) protocol designs are applicable to networks of RFID readers/tags that incorporate smart antenna designs.

Similar to developments in wireless communications systems (e.g., cellular, public safety, and military systems), it appears certain that a one-size-fits-all standards solution for RFID is unlikely and that devices with diverse (and incompatible) physical layers and protocols will be the rule rather than the exception. On the upside, this circumstance tends to promote ingenuity and can yield a wide range of system capabilities to help effectively address varying operational requirements for projected AIS applications. However, it also presents problems with compatibility and interoperability. Hence, although the systems engineer can potentially draw on multiple standards to address different portions of the system design, the overall system design effort may be hindered by physical layer and protocol incompatibilities associated with heterogeneous systems architectures, not to mention the high cost of having to build up an infrastructure for each standard to be deployed. A key technology that can be leveraged to overcome these limitations is software radio technology, which is being pursued and developed for public safety, military, and commercial communication sectors in the United States. Software radio is a technology whose time appears to have come in the wireless telecommunications industry. Software radio technology is based on programmable hardware in the radio that can be configured to achieve different radio characteristics. In correspondence with Dr. Tom Pratt, Georgia Tech Research Institute, the flexibility of the frequency tuning could provide a solution to the multifrequencies that are used globally.

Privacy and security are significant issues that have both technological and policy components. Both are areas that require further advancement that includes educating the public about what is feasible with RFID. For example, someone driving a car with a reader along the street is not going to be able to read what is in a home with a very strong emitter, and if that is the case, there are health issues that should be focused on instead of privacy. Security could be handled through data encryption, but that alone will not solve the problem. The safe handling and integrity of data resides with the overall process, from ensuring that the codes on a tag are not changed to protecting the data as it is synchronized with the logistical system. There are groups such as the IEEE 1363 Working Group for Standards in Public Key Cryptography, Consortium for Efficient Embedded Security, and Zigbee (a communication standard with an industry alliance definition of a network stack architecture composed of the IEEE 802.15.4 physical and medium access control, or MAC, layers, as well as network and application layers) that could be useful for encryption. There are also security standards such as Federal Information Processing Standard—(FIPS) 199 that are used to protect the information and systems. The primary reasons for security include confidentiality, integrity, and availability of information. This will be one of our greatest challenges.

7 Conclusions

We could only provide a glimpse at the applications, technology components, users, developers, and research into RFID. There are business cases that can be made for the components of an RFID system and numerous companies that focus on one or many of the following RFID system components: tags, readers, encoders, middleware, and application software. It will take time, research, and more data before RFID could be considered a ubiquitous technology, as the cell phone is today. RFID is a technology that has shown promise in revamping our asset visibility where an asset could be a product, people, or equipment. The increased asset visibility has promise for improving the logistical process and business practice. The markets of use are numerous and include basic consumer goods, health care, food and animal supplies, and homeland security. However, we cannot loose sight of the policy, privacy, technological, and implementation hurdles we must overcome to fully utilize the potential of RFID, which lies somewhere between the current hype and a fully productive end state.

Appendix A
10 Unique Applications

In many walks of life businesses are finding value and return on investment for their RFID deployments. In this appendix we examine some of the more unusual, and maybe less mainstream, RFID implementations that are happening.

1 Baja Beach Club—Injected at the Door . . .

One visit to the Baja Beach Club in Barcelona, Spain, unveils a crossroads where high-energy nightlife meets techno-geek. RFID technology has provided a means where Spanish nightclub goers may have never had it so convenient. Scantily clad club patrons wearing a microskirt or skintight clothing don't always have a comfortable location to carry something superfluous. After all, who wants to carry a bothersome handbag or wallet on the dance floor of one of Europe's hottest nightclubs? This is why many who frequent the Baja Beach Club have received RFID microchip injections. For the adventurous and willing, the establishment uses a syringe to inject an RFID chip under the skin. The body-aware atmosphere attracts a superficiality where an under-the-skin technology is accepted. Bikini-clad waitresses and topless male waiters lend reminders that it is important to pay attention to the body. Those who are willing to inject the RFID chip are elevated to a new elite status at the club and are able to gain free access to select VIP areas.

Once the RFID chip is implanted, clubbers' identities are recognized as they pass through various portals. Passing certain portals automatically opens doors to exclusive areas at the club for these VIPs (Jones, 2004). They may also purchase food and beverage by simply waving their hand near the proper RFID reader. The purchased amount is simply added to the customer's tab and is treated like a club credit card. Credit balances are easily tracked through the information provided on the RFID chip. Injected customers of the Baja Beach Club, which can accommodate approximately 3,000 on the dance floor at a given time, are able to jump lines and enjoy the freedom of faster navigation around the club (Gossett, 2004). Why wait in long queues when there are so many beautiful people to meet? No longer needing to carry euros or a credit card means that the injected customer's risk of theft or loss is virtually eliminated. Voluntary RFID usage is a matter of consumer convenience for patrons of this popular nightspot.

With tattoos, body piercings, or silicone implants the norm, an RFID chip is considered merely another body accessory for men and women who frequent the nightclub scene. The RFID chip may be placed anywhere on the body as long as it is able to be read when passing through the portal or by another RFID reader. The most common location to insert the chip is under the skin in the hand. The 10-digit unique identification number can be read at distances over a meter. For most it's no big deal to get this 12-mm RFID chip implanted (Graham-Rowe, 2004). It comes in the shape of a glass capsule with a tiny embedded antenna (Maney, 2004). At one point the club instituted Tuesday as Implant Night, which provided an opportunity for guests to be injected with a chip before drinking and dancing. The Baja Beach Club has a medic on hand to perform the injection. Most implants are generally injected early in the evenings, as the procedure is only performed on a patron who is in a sober state. Customers pay 125 euros for the implant, although initially they were injected at no cost (Jones, 2004). The life span for this type of RFID chip is expected to be approximately 20 years.

The Baja Beach Club selected RFID chip usage for two primary reasons. First, it was original, which differentiated Baja from their competition. Other clubs had ways of identifying their valued customers and promoting their nightclub. Baja found RFID very unique. Second, it used the latest technology, which was appealing to the ownership of the establishment. The Baja RFID system was implemented by Applied Digital's VeriChip Corporation, who introduced the first human-implanted ID technology offering. This convention of RFID usage is based on a similar use of RFID for cattle and other animal and pet tracking (Gossett, 2004). Implanting is painless with no side effects. There is no pinching or pulling. Extraction can be achieved almost as easily as removing a small splinter.

For many close to the nightclub, the chip implant represents a signal of what's to come in the future. Skeptics also abound in the debate of tracking humans. A detouring aspect of the implanted RFID chip is that it doesn't go away or isn't deactivated once one leaves the club. This means that the person could continue to be identified by compatible RFID technologies in other environments, a concern among privacy groups. The concept of tracking people outside of a controlled and consented-to environment may slow down the adoption of similar types of systems. But keep all eyes open for the implanted RFID chip. It may be coming to a club near you.

2 Off-the-Street Genetics Biologist

By day a mild-mannered student or employee, but upon a single visit to the Tech Museum of Innovation, presto! A scientist is born. As an amateur genetics scientist, you are able to insert a bacteria sample with the DNA of a jellyfish (see Figure 1). The experiment is conducted in a petri dish. After a 24-hour incubation period, the bacteria will begin to glow green (O'Connor, 2005). For several days the progress of the experiment is monitored on the Internet by you from the comfort of home. This exercise is similar to the medical development of insulin or growth hormones, which occurs by placing human genetic material into bacteria. Listen as real patients struggle with personal decisions about new genetic treatments. Join a discussion on ethical issues surrounding the new genetic technologies. Such experimentation can be discovered at The Tech Museum of Innovation (often referred to as The Tech), located in San Jose, California, at the Genetics: Technology with a Twist interactive exhibit. RFID plays a key role in this advanced learning experience.

The Tech selected RFID technology to help enhance and then extend the learning encounter of visitors. As individuals and families enter the museum, they are provided with a wristband with an embedded RFID tag. Traversing the exhibits in the facility becomes interactive as different exhibits interact with visitors. The Tech is the first museum of its type to make use of the interactive exhibits with disposable RFID tags (Hitachi, 2006). What makes the exhibits unique is that the education doesn't end when visitor's walk out the door. The RFID tag is precoded with a 16-character identification that is also printed onto the wristband (O'Connor, 2005). This may be used at a later time to create a personalized Web page. At home or

(a)

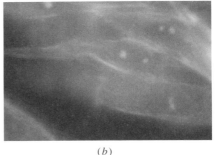

(b)

Figure 1 Jellyfish DNA [*Source:* ©Courtesy of the Tech Museum of Innovation. (*a*) Randy Wilder Photography. 2004. (*b*) John Pedersen University Biomedical Engineering Dept. 2002].

school a visitor may log on to his or her own Web page at The Tech across the Internet, using the 16-character identifier as a personal login. This allows monitoring the experiment conducted and continuing to extract other information from the museum.

RFID at The Tech aids the museum as its exhibits come to life. To activate the exhibits, a user simply waves a hand (with the RFID-enabled wristband) near the readers that are embedded at the various stations. This motion initiates a series of events in the museum. RFID is a also key element of the trendy new NetPl@net exhibit, where participants are able to compete online with visitors of other museums across the Internet. A popular example of NetPl@net is the ability to remotely arm wrestle using a wooden arm with someone at a different location (The Tech, 2007; O'Connor, 2005). Readers and antennas sit behind wood and other materials within each display as patrons patrol the exhibits. At key points in the facility, guests are able to select the language in which a description of the exhibit will be explained.

The Tech selected the wristbands over RFID-enabled smart cards and barcodes for its visitor identification. The microchip used at The Tech is provided by Hitachi. It is 0.4 mm square in size and can read at a distance of about 30 cm to 40 cm (Hitachi, 2006). It operates at the ultrahigh frequency of 2.45 GHz, and read rates are at the high speed of 20 microseconds (O'Connor, 2005). The Hitachi-supplied RFID tags operate as read-only transponders. Is individual identity a concern for visitors? Not a problem at The Tech. At The Tech there is no tracking of people or their information (an e-mail address isn't even required when accessing the experiments from home). Further, the communication protocol between the reader and the chip is proprietary and is not compliant with international standards. This relaxes concerns over privacy and virtually eliminates the potential to have the tag read outside of the four walls of The Tech.

The Tech started its implementation with 40 reader stations and is adding more all the time (The Tech, 2007). At different points in the museum, visitor photos may be taken. In the GeneKids exhibit, visitors can see pictures of themselves interacting with the station. Again at home the activity, located at the museum can be viewed. The Tech has many other such interactive exhibits in the Genetics: Technology with a Twist family of exhibits. Guests may return with their Tech wristbands and use the same identifier for additional exhibits.

Museum visitors are commonly distracted by the breadth of goings-on in the museum, which may prevent them from studying a topic in the depth to which they would like. The Web capability provides later review of the museum material and enables guests to walk the floor without having to hold descriptions and pamphlets. This is believed to enhance the museum learning experience. Other museums around the world are also beginning to adopt RFID for tracking collectable items. They are able to streamline the inventory process, enable self-guided tours, and reduce damage to priceless items. The Tech is providing a new age of opportunity to learn that is enabled by RFID technologies.

3 RFID Hits the Main . . . Stream

One of the largest RFID systems in the world lies in the Columbia River basin. Waters originating in the Canadian Rockies traversing through five states in the northwestern United States and feeding the Pacific Ocean are filled with fish that have embedded RFID tags. For nearly a hundred years the salmon population has been declining in the Great Northwest, which covers 250,000 square miles. Of economic importance and historical significance, the salmon reduction has been a major concern of fisherman, local industry, and ecologists in the region.

A variety of factors are interrupting the spawning cycle and contributing to the situation. The region has become dotted with man-made adjustments to the water system. Periods of overharvest in the early 1900s and habitat changes such as farming, mining, roads, and pollution have impacted the fertile waters of the Columbia River and lower Snake River areas. These ecological changes disturb the environment and affect the river temperatures. Temperature variance alters a fish's behavior and habits, nutritional change has an impact on good fish health, and slower water speeds invite new predators. These factors have all played a role in varying ecological conditions in these rivers and streams.

A young salmon will typically hatch in freshwater, where it remains for one to two years. This is followed by a journey downstream as it migrates to the ocean. The ocean is a spot where the salmon will mature for a two to five-year period. An adult salmon then embarks on a return to its spawning grounds.

Dams in the region bring particular value to humankind by providing a major source of power, flood control, recreation, water supply, and irrigation benefits. With the good comes the challenge of managing wildlife, including the fish habitat. A dizzying array of over 400 waterways and hydropower dams along the Columbia River basin are believed to be a primary contributor to the situation (Lombardi, 2005). For a thriving salmon population, it is necessary to have safe passageways around power turbines and through tumultuous waters. Fourteen of the different subspecies of salmon that once populated these rivers have been identified on the endangered list. It has been commonplace for these fish to be chopped, mangled, and destroyed in the water system.

RFID technology has become a key element in understanding the nature of activity of these salmon. Each year approximately 2 million salmon receive an RFID tag that holds 64 bits of data, forming a unique identifier for each fish (Lombardi, 2005; Swedberg, 2005a). They then are injected with a full duplex passive RFID tag into their abdomen (see Figure 2). The tags

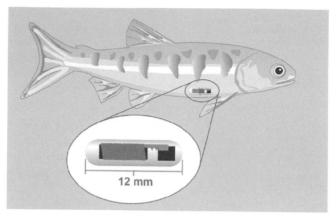

Figure 2 RFID tag injected into the salmon (*Source:* Army Corps of Engineers, 2006).

are very small, comparable to the size of a grain of rice (measured to be approximately 12 mm in length). This allows the fish to continue to be traced without adversely affecting its weight and ability to navigate the streams and lakes. Juvenile fish are sedated in fish tanks in salmon farms or in spawning areas. The RFID tags embedded in the fish are then read to confirm proper injection. The salmon require three days of recovery before they are released from the tanks. Detailed information about each fish such as size and weight is captured and maintained in a large data system called a pit tag information (PTI) system. Individual salmon data is made available as necessary as each fish is tracked through the network of rivers.

Making their way on a course downstream, the salmon are often guided in their migration through either a juvenile fish bypass or over the spillway. Portaging sometimes occurs, which transports the fish by barge or truck in some areas where the ice has formed, making the area more treacherous for the fish. A protective screen is placed in front of large turbines in an attempt to protect the salmon. However, some salmon can't avoid the powerful turbines that reside in the dams despite this protective screen. Installed in the through-water passage chutes are RFID antennas that are over 5 m by 5 m. The giant antennas are connected to a reader that is required to read the tagged salmon at speeds up to nearly 100 km per hour as they travel down the chutes (Lombardi, 2005). Low-frequency tags of 134 kHz are used to read the tags while in the presence of water (Swedberg, 2005a).

The RFID readers are able to process hundreds of tags simultaneously because of the large antenna. The salmon's RFID tag can be read up to 1 m away from the antenna surface. Moving upstream to return to their hatching place is more of a challenge for the salmon with the dams in place. Spawning ladders have been built to assist the adult salmon as they journey up the river system to return to their spawning grounds (see Figure 3).

Since 1986 the Bonneville Power Administration (BPA), whose headquarters is in Portland, Oregon, has been using RFID to track salmon. These

Figure 3 Spawning ladders (*Source:* Army Corps of Engineers, 2006).

include steelhead and the anadromous species of salmon (chinook, coho, chum, sockeye, and pink). Learning more about the behavioral patterns and migration paths with RFID technology is helping to stem the tide of waning salmon population. By understanding details about these fish, death in the salmon has been reduced by 15 percent to 20 percent according to Scott Bettin, a BPA freshwater biologist (Lombardi, 2005). The BPA has demonstrated a commitment to continuous understanding and improvement in the region. In an attempt to restore fish and wildlife to the region, the BPA expends US$600 million annually to help fortify the salmon supply and to understand further how to identify where and how salmon are being lost.

By understanding the natural tendencies and activities of several salmon species that colonize the region, the many dam operations are able to take steps more proactively to minimize the impact on the fish in the network of waterways. Scientist now know how long the salmon take to move from dam to dam and where they cease to cross. Recently more information about fish that are eaten by birds and the affects of the salmon as they go to sea is being collected.

Information can be observed on the project's activity as interactive reports can be run based on a variety of criteria at the PTAGIS Web site (www.ptagis.org/ptagis/frame.jsp?menu=1&main=main.jsp?menu=1, 2007). The salmon-tracking projects are one of the best kept RFID secrets going today. For many years it has been proving its worth in the Columbia River basin.

4 Up, Up, and Away

RFID hits the friendly skies in a major way. While rolling down the runway on course to your favorite destination, knowing and understanding the technologies that assist an on-time safe departure are likely the last things on your mind. Listening to the flight attendant drone on with the safety descriptions, the public doesn't learn that the life vests may be tagged with RFID. Breaks on the aircraft may be identified and tracked with RFID. The very seat you sit in may be RFID enabled with a passive transponder. RFID helps make air travel safer and eases the burden of the maintenance process. Because an aircraft has millions of parts, the industry is attracted to radio frequency technology. Savings is realized by validating that an oxygen mask, for example, is properly placed above the traveler without the need to remove the ceiling panel. Reducing the time of airplane inspection will make employees more efficient and improve the data accuracy of the report created. Leading airplane manufacturers Airbus and Boeing are active in the use of RFID technology and are further expanding their day-to-day RFID operations in search of reaping a variety of business benefits.

Airbus started tagging and tracking with barcodes in the mid-1990s. In 1999, it rolled out its inaugural RFID tracking implementation, which tracked tools and toolboxes. The opening objective of Airbus, with manufacturing facilities in France, Germany, Spain, United Kingdom, United States, China, and Japan, was simple: to maximize tool usage. After being tagged, the tools are traced through their life cycle. All Airbus tools with a manufacturer's serial number are equipped with RFID tags. Data regarding the history of the tool, where it has been, and customs information is maintained on the microchip. A typical operational scenario with an RFID-enabled Airbus tool includes the following steps (Airbus, 2006):

- The shipment is prepared.
- When ready, the ERP (enterprise resource planning) system initiates an RFID tag write about the shipment (synchronized with data system).
- The supply chain can get data immediately regarding the shipping status.
- Delivery of the tool is acknowledged (more efficient shipping and routing).
- The tool is used and returned.
- Upon tool receipt verification, it is inspected and then made ready to send back out.

Results garnered by Airbus included a 25 percent reduction in turnaround time in tools. Supply chain acceleration began to add to the business value. Improved tool availability has reduced error rates and administration costs. Airbus has realized greater accuracy of information, enhanced ability to trouble shoot, improved parts inspection, and increased visibility of the logistics cycle, enabling reduced spares inventory while offering higher rates of spares availability. Reduced paperwork, higher data accuracy, faster, and easier information flow are also measurably improved (Airbus, 2006). By having full part traceability from cradle to grave, faster and more accurate loan invoicing has also been realized. Each of these benefits leads directly to an improved bottom line.

The new Airbus A380 aircraft uses RFID on many of its removable parts. It has been the stated vision of Airbus to someday carry over 10,000 tags on an airplane at a given time. The A380 double-decker aircraft seats up to 555 passengers and made its maiden flight for Singapore Airlines in 2006. The debut of cargo configuration of the A380 follows the passenger rollout in partnership with FedEx®.

Boeing and Airbus share approximately 70 percent of the same suppliers. Because the two rivals are collaborating with their suppliers, implementing RFID in the aircraft assembly supply chain can be a huge benefit to the end consumer. For Airbus and Boeing, supply chain collaboration is a matter of survival in the challenging industry of air travel. RFID is enabling this with cost reductions and increased accuracy.

Boeing's strategy is very deep-rooted with their supply chain. RFID plays a fundamental role in the relationship with their providers. Cutting the historical cycle time of aircraft manufacturing and assembly on the Boeing campus from 18 to 30 days down to 72 hours (Gillette and Porad, 2004) is no small feat. The use of RFID and the ability to track parts and subassemblies through their manufacturing and assembly process then out the door will help reduce the time necessary to build the aircraft. Process reengineering and tight collaboration with suppliers are enabling Boeing to embark on this new vision.

Boeing started receiving tagged parts near the end of 2006. After receipt of these parts, the Federal Aviation Agency (FAA) must perform an inspection of them. This takes precious time. Boeing's use of EPC-compliant Gen 2 tags (see Chapter 7 on industry standards) with 64 Kb of capacity provides ample storage space for recording data regarding the tagged airplane part. Many of these tags will be attached to metal. They are required to be durable enough to withstand extreme temperature changes, vibration, chemical liquids, humidity, electrostatic discharge, and salt sprays. Boeing is identifying 1,750 parts in the 787 (formerly the 7E7 Dreamliner) (Porad, 2005). Some data will be necessary to maintain for many years. Because each aircraft has such a long life expectancy, target lifetime of the tags is 20 years. Total overall aircraft weight of the new Boeing 787 is a driving concern that will assist decisions on where and how to use RFID. Up-front validation of supplies with RFID will help reduce the entry of counterfeit parts into the process.

Airline industry compliance and standards bodies are starting to take note of the RFID movement. The Air Transport Association (ATA) Spec 2000 is a key document, as it defines regulations and guidelines on RFID as part of its e-business applications for aviation parts. The specification is called out in the Radio Technical Commission for Aeronautics (RTCA) DO-160 standard. The FAA provided a policy guidance memo for RFID in 2005 regarding 13.56 MHz (high frequency), though new UHF frequencies are starting to penetrate the industry. The same is expected from the European Aviation Safety Agency (EASA). Aviation objectives are to promote safety and easy part traceability, including the ability to retrieve information at any time.

Historically the inspection and quality programs are laden with mountains of paper documents tracking supplier parts. Airbus is using RFID to identify the quality status of a part in order to eventually eliminate its Yellow Tag paper-trail program. The RFID data is captured and the history maintained in a centralized location for quick and accurate retrieval. Among other values during the inspection process, unapproved engine parts will be identified. For each part, information is maintained regarding where it came from, where it is installed, how long it was in operation, who received it, who installed software for it, calibration information, certification data, and authorized documents. For this purpose Airbus uses an RFID tag that is 8 mm in diameter and has a 4-KB capacity and will be mounted on metal.

Virgin Atlantic Airways is also getting into the RFID fray. It expects to save money spent searching for missing airplane parts of high value. Virgin attaches a label to a container after initial inspection of the part. When the part is loaded onto the aircraft, it is removed from the container as it is placed onto the aircraft. The tag is recycled for future reuse. RFID activity is captured in a centralized database where business analytics are generated from the RFID data, providing real-time data for Virgin to initiate its improvement processes (Swedberg, 2005c).

The cost of lost baggage has become a major contributor to the bottom line at Delta Airlines. Over 7,300 flights to nearly 500 destinations across 87 countries causes logistical challenges. Over 800,000 pieces of luggage are lost annually, costing Delta tens of millions of dollars each year (Rary, 2004). Using RFID to reduce human error will enable Delta to recoup some of the lost revenue. Bags are tracked at time of receipt from the passenger through sorting and onto the aircraft. Correct baggage is checked again at unload time prior to placement on the carousel. It is also expected to provide more customer satisfaction and loyalty. Broader rollout, expected to provide tracking of individual passenger luggage, will yield great savings to the airlines industry.

Airlines and airline suppliers are taking note of RFID technologies. The industry seems destined to struggle financially while they provide a progressively higher quality of safety and greater visibility of operations. The opportunity to extract more business value from RFID implementations is being tested and found in several areas in the industry.

5 Luck Be an RFID Lady

Eight the hard way! Double down? Split the pair? Lay it all on black? Let it ride? Whatever the decision is, the house may be able to predict the outcome probabilities in advance. In an effort to market and promote to their customer base, casinos are expanding their tracking of gambling behavior of their customers. Tendencies of gamblers—amateur, professional, or beginner—are being learned over time with the use of RFID. Sound like the deck is stacked against casino goers? Don't be quite so fast to pass judgment; the jury is still out on the topic.

New blackjack tables that cost in the range $8,000 to $15,000 a pop are enabled with RFID read capability (Keefe, 2005). Embedded in the betting chips is an RFID transponder (a chip in a chip). RFID is bringing these betting chips, which are commonly made of fired clay or plastic, to life (Gambling Magazine, 2005). Readers are positioned beneath the table, upon which the gambler makes his or her wager. The RFID tag is read when each bet is laid down on the table. Some tables have optical readers. Pit bosses can actually see cards, bets, and all table activity electronically from another location in the facility. Every card, every bet, and each player at the table are known by the house data systems. The data is transferred to a database and evaluated with a table management system that profiles an individual's gambling tendencies and habits. Casinos know how often players win, how often they lose, how much they normally spend, and how often they are playing.

What do they do with all that data? The primary objective is to maintain good customers. Bad gamblers are given comps (discounts on rooms, meals, etc.) and other freebies in an effort to entice them to stay and play a little longer (Keefe, 2005). Average or mediocre gamblers and regular customers are treated with loyalty programs encouraging them to return. Gamblers who repeatedly win or are on a lucky streak are finding themselves more ignored and receive minimal comps intended to encourage them to move on to the next casino. The same type of model has been used for several years with computerized slot machines. The goal is to keep the player at the table as long as possible. It's big business for high rollers.

How does tracking begin? Tracking isn't novel for the gaming industry, but the use of RFID is new. Casinos have always offered coupons and perks for customers. Often this is done by providing a card that identifies them at different locations in the establishment. The Flamingo Hotel was the first casino in Las Vegas to publicly acknowledge the adoption of the RFID-enabled smart blackjack table. The new US$2.7 billion Wynn Hotel and Resort is tracking casino activities with RFID chips (Keefe, 2005). In addition to tracking activity, the Wynn hotel uses RFID chips to assist in the accounting of players it issues credit to. If chips are cashed in by players other than those who were lent them, it is an initial sign of possible interplayer loans. This is a risk casino operators want to avoid. Both the Wynn Hotel and the Hard Rock Hotel & Casino have stated that they use RFID gambling chips (Keefe, 2005). There are a several other casinos and cruise ships across the world who are using the RFID technology in their gaming area. Adoption is expected to grow rapidly in the near future.

Critics claim casinos gain a greater advantage over their patrons with these intelligent blackjack systems. Casino owners maintain that it is simply a rewards program for desired and loyal customers, similar to supermarket chain saver cards. Casino owners state that everything is above board. All cards are still shuffled in front of the players with no manipulation of the game itself. Game play can't be affected. Gambling halls are merely anxious to identify players of value. A precedent-setting suit brought against the Alliance Gaming Corp., a major supplier of gaming supplies, claimed that real-time data in the pit could be used to fix games. The potential use of RFID readers feeding data to software threatened game credibility and questioned whether there could be a level playing field on the gaming floor. As a groundswell of concern arose, Bally Gaming agreed to implement a delay of the information such that it couldn't be used in the midst of a game.

Gamblers are often hesitant when they first learn of the RFID technology in gaming. Casinos must be quick to educate their customers on the concept, attempting to put fears to rest. The technology will be helpful to gain a bird's-eye view on wagering and play. Players will no longer be able to sneak extra betting chips onto the table once the hand has been dealt. It will also be used to identify gamblers who are proficient at counting cards.

In addition to customer information, casinos gain a variety of other benefits from the system. They use the system to evaluate dealer's performance. It is also projected to be a deterrent for misdealing and collusion that sometimes can occur between dealer and gambler. Further, it can essentially eliminate counterfeit chips, which is a regular problem in the gaming community. Accounting for chips at the end of a shift has historically been error-prone and time-consuming. With the table management system, validating chip count accuracy improved. RFID-enabled betting chips once cost several dollars apiece. However, steadily dropping prices for chips over recent years make using RFID much more affordable. Read rates have also improved dramatically and are achieved in milliseconds. All in all, RFID chips are providing a strong value proposition to the gaming industry in a variety of ways.

6 Smoke Diver Rescue Missions

RFID is finding a home in one of the dirtiest environments of the day. Digging deep into the mining industry, RFID is found playing a vital role in improved safety and productivity. Smoke divers rely heavily on RF signals during emergency evacuations to locate people and assets. RFID technologies' capacity to work in dirty and greasy environments make it a valuable tool in the field of extracting resources from the earth. Maintaining the necessary safety precautions has become more efficient throughout a mine's complex network of underground tunnels with RFID.

The geographical zones in a Norwegian mine are charted out in a centralized control room. The facility's security has the ability to track employees' and visitors' movement through the mine from the control room. Employees, suppliers, and visitors who enter the mine are registered and equipped with an RF tag (Haagensen, 2004). As they move in and out of the mine shafts, their whereabouts are known back in the control center. Vehicles are also tagged with RF tags and tracked as they navigate through the tunnels. Upon entry into particular areas, the RFID tag is read and access validation is granted where necessary throughout the mine. Visually each person and every vehicle is represented by a red LED on the control screen for positive identification throughout the facility. A control room supervisor also can retrieve additional data about an individual by drilling down on the LED representation on the control screen. This procedure enables all people and assets that are tagged to be found in the case of an emergency.

When an accident takes place, such as a truck engine breakdown, finding those who are injured or trapped can be extremely difficult. Often visibility is very inadequate in the mine. Ventilation is typically poor, making the time to execute a rescue of paramount importance. Smoke divers are dispatched to the proper location in the accident zone based on the RFID position tracking information. This permits a much more effective search in a time-critical situation. The rescue personnel are equipped with handheld devices that assist in locating the RFID tagged workers or visitors in the accident zone. During the rescue mission, individual LED representations on the devices guide the smoke divers to the target.

RFID provides the necessary positioning information for a safe and quick extraction from the scene. RFID technologies are durable and rugged enough to withstand the severe environments of a mine. Automating these procedures in these harsh environments allows mining operations to be safer and more effective with the use of RFID.

7 Dolls' Ailments . . . Cured with RFID

Is it a sideshow at the circus? Or a scene from the space cartoon *The Jetsons*™? Is it integrated with RFID chips? And just how is it restored to health? It's a doll? What will they think of next?

A toy doll created and introduced in Japan named Naoru-kun is able to recover from a sickness through RFID technology. As a child plays with the doll, over time it may develop tendencies. When becoming ill Naoru-kun starts to cough and sneeze. In the course of normal play, when these symptoms are discovered, the child can tend to the doll's medical needs by giving it medicine or placing a syringe in its mouth. The doll is able to recognize it has been given the treatment. This is done as Naoru-kun reads RFID transponders. The doll is able to show signs of feeling better and eventually become cured as it recognizes the correct type of medical treatment. The toy is able to read RFID tags on different articles (food, clothing, toys, etc.) and interpret what kind of item is near. It then reacts to the particular item with one of five sensors in its body. Naoru-kun is also able to communicate, as it speaks 150 different phrases informing its child friend what it can do next (Ubiks web site, 2007). The doll is able to expresses a level of emotion through its phrases. It also has the ability to use other senses such as taste. When Naoru-kun is treated to candy, it will respond positively as a child would. It will also react to bitter tastes.

The objective of the toy, in addition to the age-old enjoyment of playing with dolls, is to promote the notion of caring for the doll. It will assist in teaching a child the art of caring and having a simple responsibility. At times Naoru-kun will request to play and express information about itself. It needs love and attention, similar to the popular Tamagotchi (a simplified handheld computer-based doll), as it reacts to being hugged and taken care of. The doll is being produced and promoted by Japanese toy giant Bandai Corp. Naoru-kun represents a new type of interactive toy that may become the wave of the future.

8 RFID on the Fast Track at NASCAR

Moving at speeds averaging near 190 miles per hour (306 kilometers per hour), RFID is racing around the track in one of the United States' fastest-growing sports in popularity. The NASCAR® racing circuit is using RFID-enabled tires starting in 2006 for all official events. This includes all races at the Nextel Cup Series, Busch Series, and Craftsman Truck Series (Swedberg, 2005b).

Each NASCAR race is made up of 43 drivers, where drivers will use 10 tires on average per race (Psion Teklogix, 2005). Managing over 400 tires in a racing format has its challenges. For the giant tire manufacturer Goodyear, using RFID will ensure valid inventory records and confirm that the tires were properly returned from each driver. NASCAR is benefiting by having tighter controls of race preparation to ensure that no driver has an unfair advantage by using tires built for another type of race track. NASCAR also has future plans to include the tire data in the technical inspection prior to each race. With the Goodyear stamp of approval on each tire, the inspection phase could become simplified and shortened at the racetrack.

The RFID tags are embedded into the sidewalls of each tire made available to these races. Handheld readers are used to interrogate the passive RFID tag, which operates at an ultrahigh frequency (915 MHz) (Psion Teklogix, 2005). The tires are initially scanned as they leave the storage warehouse, and the movement of the tires is tracked through their racecourse and back to the warehouse again. Information regarding each driver and the car driven is maintained in a database of information through this process. This concept was tested during the 2005 season at the Homestead–

Miami Speedway race, which is part of the Craftsman Truck Series (Sullivan, 2005).

Historically, racers were required to purchase the tires for time testing. NASCAR recently released new controlled testing procedures sanctioned by its organization in order to even out the competition. Specific rules surrounding preparation for each race have not always been adhered to by the racing teams. The use of RFID will enable tighter controls for the time tests and promote a level playing field on the track (Sullivan, 2005). RFID will ensure that every tire that comes to the track leaves the track. It will enable race organizers to identify if a car is exceeding its allotted time for testing. NASCAR and Goodyear, the world's largest tire company, have entered a tire-leasing option in order to streamline the process.

The Goodyear™ Company is the sole supplier of tires to the NASCAR racing circuit, providing 200,000 tires each year. Managing the inventory of outgoing tires as well as returned tires has been a challenge for the company. Attempts to use barcodes have been futile, as they are damaged or destroyed during the competition. Characteristics of RFID are naturally more suited for a more rugged environment like racing. Goodyear has been exploring RFID technology since 1984 in an effort to improve inventory management. Trials were conducted as early as 1993. Goodyear is further motivated to use RFID because some of its large retail customers are demanding that RFID-tagged products be supplied.

9 Riding the RFID Wave

Flying down the chute on an inner tube or floating with the man-made waves at the Wild Rivers Waterpark in Southern California is a favorite pastime for many locals and visitors. However, enjoying leisure and fun can turn cloudy when there is a lost child in a crowded amusement park. With 40 different water attractions, wave pools, slides, inner tube rides, and other relaxing areas, it is easy for youngsters to become distracted or lost. Missing meeting points and times is the norm for parents, kids, and family members at the water park. This is why Wild Rivers was so anxious to install a park tracking that is based on RFID technology. Providing parents and patrons with peace of mind through immediate and accurate visitor identification is generating positive results at the amusement park.

In the past, locating a lost child or family member at the water park would typically consume 10 to 20 minutes of time for multiple employees as they canvass the premises, where they communicate with two-way radios. Losing track of a child is a traumatic experience for a parent even for a short period of time. The research firm IntiMetrix reports that over the last 12 months, 27 percent of families lost at least one child for a period of time in amusement parks during their visit (SafeTZone, 2006). This is no longer a problem at Wild Rivers. Real-time identification of those in your visiting group is fast and accurate. Members of any group can be identified immediately at any station strategically placed throughout the facility. Knowing where others in your group are located at any point in time is a huge advancement for those who enjoy fun in the sun at the popular Irvine, California, water park.

Each visitor can get an RFID-enabled waterproof tag that fits around the wrist upon entering the park. Throughout the park, readers are strategically located in order to identify all who are near the antenna. Touch screens are also positioned throughout the water park to identify others in the group. If one wants to locate others in his or her party, he or she may simply wave a wristband near the touch screen. Over 30 antennas are located throughout the park, providing full coverage for the entire facility. Each of those associated with the party are displayed on the screen by the nearest antenna in the park. And all of this is done in real time.

Wild Rivers gained immediate public acceptance of the tracking system, as the number of visitors made an immediate jump following the implementation of the RFID system. Having a high volume of customer is very important to Wild Rivers, since it is only open 120 days during the summer. Its attention to detail and customer service is a focus that management stresses at the amusement water park. Wild Rivers Waterpark reports that it hasn't had a single incident where it needed to sweep the park for lost patrons since instituting the RFID-based system.

10 Wine Flavors Perfected with RFID

In the Santa Rita Hills of Lompoc, California, lie lush hillsides where the soil and climate are ideal for growing pinot noir grapes. This is where Sea Smoke Cellars is gaining global acclaim for its new wines. Growth in leading fine wines such as Ten and Botella from these hills near Santa Barbara is making Sea Smoke Cellars one of the fastest growing wineries of the day.

Wine flavors are highly dependent on the barrels in which they are stored. Sea Smoke's wine barrels are made of French handcrafted oak. The selection of oak material at the company is significant, as the barrel's characteristics contribute to the taste profile. Each barrel is able to provide a degree of impact to individual wine flavors for approximately a two-year period. They typically can be used in some storage capacity for five years. Each barrel costs in excess of US$800 and holds approximately 60 gallons to be aged. This is equivalent to 24 cases of finished wine, with 12 bottles to the case (Hartman, 2005). Sea Smoke bottles are priced between $26 and $66 (Sea Smoke Web site, 2006). For Sea Smoke, understanding the barrel's characteristics and attributes at any given time during wine making is critical in determining the flavor. Knowing supplementary details regarding the wine-making process allows Sea Smoke to make more efficient adjustments.

This is why Sea Smoke has started a complex tracking strategy that is based on RFID technology. Using RFID, it tracks the activity from the hand-sorted grapes extracted from one of its 23 vineyards through shipping the cased bottles. It also uses process data to manage the barrel history. Sea Smoke uses a 125 kHz (low-frequency) RFID tag provided by Omron® that holds 240 bytes of data (Hartman, 2005). The round-shaped coin-sized RFID tag is encased with a plastic resin. Each tag ID is unique. It is attached to the end of each barrel with a silicone adhesive. The RFID readers are fastened on the end of a lightweight wireless handheld device about 45 cm in length. Attached to the device midpoint is a PDA where data related to the RFID tagged item is displayed. The BarrelTrak™ application software, manufactured by TagStream, Inc., runs on each PDA. RFID tags that reside on the barrels are read and supplemental information is entered onto the PDA, which is all later uploaded to a server that manages the data related to the steps in the wine creation process.

Tracking each barrel through the process enables Sea Smoke to better predict and control the taste of its wines. Sea Smoke is now able to know in real time exactly what is in every barrel, from which vineyard the grapes come, and the blend of grapes in each barrel. Available at its fingertips is an analysis of the specific grape harvest, date and time of the harvest, and which additives are put into the barrels. Prior to the RFID rollout, Sea Smoke was only able to manage its product at lot level (groups of barrels), with much less precision of data during the 18 to 20 months of aging. Tracking the barrel movement was performed by marking barrels with chalk (an age-old wine-making process), endless paper instructions, stacks of clipboards, and uncontrolled sets of notes. The notes and paper trail were then manually entered into the company's wine-producing management system.

The new RFID system provides instant visibility at the barrel level. As the critical taste test results are captured, immediate action can be taken. In some cases, early racking (storing) is appropriate, possibly increasing the sulfur dioxide content, or running additional tests on the properties of the wine. Beginning in 2005 the U.S. Food and Drug Administration (FDA) requires that producers of beverages report the origin of all ingredients and additives. As Sea Smoke tracks the aging and fermenting process at this comprehensive level, recently adopted legislative requirements are being met. The sturdy nature of RFID technology was necessary at Sea Smoke because of the environment where the tag is used. Damage to paper labels and mold deterioration makes paper labels unreadable and marginally usable.

In addition to tracking the process, Sea Smoke now has individual barrel profiles, allowing it to be much more predictive in its taste management.

As wines mature, the barrel's oak properties evolve. Different additives are necessary to generate the proper flavor. Through the management of the historical activity of an individual barrel's life cycle, the barrel can be allocated at the appropriate time for the optimal wine product. This predictive capability enables the company to optimize the use of its assets.

Sea Smoke has gained significant publicity when featured recently in the movie *Sideways*. The increased demand created has made its wines more difficult to find. Tracking the process is becoming more imperative for Sea Smoke as the company grows. When it expands operations, process control is crucial to continuing to produce a high-quality wine.

Sea Smoke Cellars is saving time and money by having its RFID system integrated into its business processes. The expensive, labor-intensive record keeping is more efficient. Latency of human decisions due to lack of data has been improved. The chance of human error has been greatly reduced. The days of misread IDs are in the rearview mirror. This means that misplaced barrels are reduced. Wasted wine due to unplanned interruption to the wine-making process has been minimized. Sea Smoke's RFID system has been in operation since 2003. It provides accurate data visibility for quick decision making in a paperless environment.

Acronyms

FDA—Food and Drug Administration

PTI—Pit tag information

BPA—Bonneville Power Administration

ATA—Air Transport Association

RTCA—Radio Technical Commission for Aeronautics

FAA—Federal Aviation Administration

EASA—European Aviation Safety Agency

PDA—Personal digital assistant

References

Airbus. "FAST36." 2005. *Airbus Technical Magazine.* July.

Airbus. 2006. Corporate Web site. www.airbus.com/en/ (accessed February 7, 2006).

Gambling Magazine. 2005. "Betting Chips Meet Silicon Chips as Casinos Integrate Technology." *Gambling Magazine.* January 29.

Gillette, Walt. 2004. Presentation at Boeing. Aerospace and Defense Conference. November.

Gossett, Sherrie. 2004. "Paying for Drinks with the Wave of the Hand." April 14. Republished by *WorldNetDaily.* November 25, 2006.

Graham-Rowe, Duncan. 2004. Clubbers Choose Chip Implants to Jump Queues. May. Republished by NewScientist.com. November 25, 2006.

Haagensen, Sven. 2004. "Using Active RFID Down the Mines." *Intelligent Systems.* February.

Hartman, Laura R. 2005. Tracking wine bottles through RFID. *Packing Digest.* September 2005.

Hitachi US. Home Web page. 2006. www.hitachi.us.com (accessed February 1, 2006).

Jones, Violet. 2004. "Baja Beach Club in Barcelona, Spain, Launches Microchip Implantation for VIP Members." Published on Prison Planet.com Newsline April 7.

Keefe, Bob. 2005. "Technology Lets Casinos Spot Profitable Losers." *Atlanta Journal-Constitution.* September 25.

Lombardi, Rosie. 2005. *IT World Canada.* "Fish and Chips: RFID Chips Track Salmon through River Network." November 17.

Maney, Kevin. 2004. "Get Chipped, Then Charge Without Plastic: You Are the Card." *USA Today.* May 12.

O'Connor, Mary Catherine. 2005. "RFID Works Like a Charm at The Tech." *RFID Journal.* June 27.

Porad, Ken. 2004. Boeing. Presentation at EPCglobal Conference. September.

Psion. 2006. Psion Teklogix Provides RFID Solutions to Goodyear. Psion Teklogix Press Release. May 2.

PTAGIS. 2007. Web site. www.ptagis.org/ptagis/frame.jsp?menu=1&main= main.jsp?menu=1 (accessed January 23, 2007).

Rary, Patrick. 2004. Delta Airlines. Presentation at RFID World Conference. April.

SafeTzone Technology Corp. 2006. "Wild Rivers Waterpark Increases Guests' Peace of Mind with SafeTzone." SafeTzone Technology Case Study. May 2006.

Sea Smoke Cellars. 2006. Web site. www.seasmokecellars.com (accessed January 26, 2007.)

Sullivan, Laurie. 2005. "RFID Rolls into NASCAR Races." *Information Week.* November 28.

Swedberg, Clare. 2005a. "RFID Antenna to Catch Fish." *RFID Journal.* November 3.

Swedberg, Clair. 2005b. "RFID Tracks Tires at NASCAR." *RFID Journal.* November 25.

Swedberg, Claire. 2005c. "Virgin Uses RFID for Plane Parts." *RFID Journal.* August 16.

The Tech Museum of Innovation. 2006. Web site. www.thetech.org/exhibits/ permanent/index.php?sGalKey=gtwt&galKey=lt. (accessed January 23, 2007).

Ubiks.net. 2006. "RFID in Japan." http://ubiks.net/local/blog/jmt/archives3/ 003334.html/ (accessed January 23, 2007).

Appendix B
10 Useful Web Sites

Access to online information via the Internet has helped tremendously in spreading RFID knowledge. At the same time, the Internet has allowed the sharing of both good-and bad-quality information that can help or misguide users eager for helpful reference material.

In this section we provide 10 Web sites that by no means represent the only useful sites on the Internet. There are many others that were not included. However, the reader will find that the 10 sites featured make important contributions in the sharing of news and information to the RFID community. Also, the ordering of the sites does not imply any kind of ranking.

1 RFID Journal

URL: www.rfidjournal.com/

Founded/launched: 2002

Subject: News, opinions, case studies, FAQs, vendor profiles, and more for business users of RFID

This Web site offers insight on RFID news and industry trends. It provides access to use cases, business news, white papers, events, advertising, and a daily newsletter to each of its subscribers. The benefits of being a member include a bimonthly printed magazine, discounts for job postings and events, among others (job postings can be either individuals or companies posting a job). The Web site can be useful as a means for exposing managers to business news and technology. It also provides a buyer's guide. As indicated in the following list, a subscription is required to use services beyond the basics. This Web site provides the following services to its members:

- *RFID news.* It offers the latest news in the marketplace and the news can be categorized by industry.
- *Experts opinion and views.* It allows its subscribers and readers to see the opinions and views of RFID experts. It also allows readers to interact with these experts.
- *White papers and case studies.* Only for paying members. It offers information about RFID business implementations and technologies.
- *Vendors directory and profiles.* It offers a free vendor directory search utility, and paying members can access vendor profile papers.
- *Buyer's guide.* The *RFID Journal* publishes an annual buyer's guide available to members only. It includes hardware as well as RFID software providers.
- *Other utilities.* RFID search utilities, job seeking and job opportunity postings, event calendar, and bulletin boards are part of the many utilities that the Web site offers for free.
- *RFID webinars.* Web based seminars are presented by RFID subject-matter experts. These seminars offer a convenient way to ask questions and discuss the topic with the presentees. Listeners can share questions with other attendees. Seminars are recorded and can be accessed online.

2 RFID Update

URL: www.rfidupdate.com/

Founded/launched: 2004

Subject: Daily briefing newsletter on RFID

This Web site offers news and a space for RFID users to interact for free. A subscription is required in order to use all of its services. Subscribers can:

- Read RFID news.
- Search articles by industry and date.
- Participate in discussion forums and browse companies advertising their technology.
- Receive a daily update on RFID news via e-mail.
- Purchase a yearly marketing strategies report electronically.

Its main objective is to attract executives involved in RFID decisions and involve them in daily updates about the technology as well as to provide a discussion forum where chats can take place.

3 Spychips

URL: www.spychips.com/

Founded/launched: 2002

Subject: Focuses on the drawbacks of RFID technology and why it should be stopped

This Web site offers the latest news in legislation and RFID business implementations that may place consumer's privacy rights at risk. It encourages readers to join its founder on its mission to stop invasion of privacy using RFID technology. Benefits to members include

- Receive a daily newsletter via e-mail.
- Contact governmental agencies or representatives.
- Support the CASPIAN group (Consumers Against Supermarket Privacy Invasion and Numbering).

The Web site is a source for legislation, regulations, and risks presented with RFID technology.

4 RFIDa

URL: www.rfida.com/

Founded/launched: 2002

Subject: Educate the business community about RFID

This Web site offers RFID business and technology news. It also offers a special section for the Wal-Mart RFID experience where specific articles and news are posted about this major RFID implementation.

This Web site categorizes every section into four subsections:

- Introduction
- Discussion
- Knowledge base
- References

It offers a compilation of articles, news, and business cases, and it also references books and other Web sites to add value to its content. It includes links to the following:

- Job postings
- RFID career references

- Hardware and software references
- U.S. government regulation references

5 RFid Gazette

URL: www.rfidgazette.org/

Founded/launched: 2005

Subject: RFID news and commentary

RFid Gazette's Web site is part of a network of Web sites owned by Dot-marketer (www.dotmarketer.com), a search optimization engine. It offers RFID news and allows visitors to post comments. It categorizes its published news in two ways:

- By focus group
- By date

Comments are open to members and nonmembers, and they can be freely submitted.

RFid Gazette is free and no registration is required. It offers also a free RFID monthly newsletter.

6 RFID Weblog

URL: www.rfid-weblog.com/

Founded/launched: 2004

Subject: Views and information about RFID technology with a focus on business uses

This Web site is part of a large network of Web sites of special interest. It is part of creative Weblogging (www.creative-weblogging.com), a Web company focused on wireless and mobile technology in various industry specialties. The services offered in this Web site include the following:

- Recent RFID news in RFID.
- Top five technology news items.
- Case studies in several industries.
- Interviews with experts in the field.
- News that gives the reader an idea of market size.
- Articles specific to the retail industry.
- A weekly newsletter sent to subscribers.

All these services are free. The news case studies and market size articles are recent and give the reader information on RFID industry trends. However, this Web site refers the visitor to other Web sites for full reports on each of the articles posted, and sometimes a paid subscription to the referred site is required to get the full story. The Web site creates a sense of community where readers can express their comments about each of the articles posted.

7 RFIDswitchboard

URL: www.rfidswitchboard.com/

Founded/launched: 2006

Subject: Buyer's guide, discussion forum, requests for proposals (RFPs) for implementation of an RFID system

This Web site targets buyers rather than researchers. The Web site offers the latest news in RFID technology with comments and views by one of its founders. The site is free but requires registration to use its services. The site allows members (i.e., possible purchasers) to

- Distribute RFPs to providers.
- Receive proposals and implementation advice.
- Enter into a dialog with providers.

All these services can be used anonymously.

The list of providers is limited. However, it does allow members to explore opportunities in areas that perhaps were not considered in initial RFPs or implementation designs.

This Web site provides RFID information such as:

- RFID hardware, software solutions and Web site guide index.
- Advice on RFID considerations and implementations.
- Hardware, software, and consultancy buyer's guides.
- Technology and infrastructure considerations when designing an RFID solution.
- Managing RFID data components, guides to unique identification, when to read and field location.
- RFID International standards and regulations.
- Dictionary of terms.
- RFID news and events.
- Comments and views (available on this Web site and via e-mail to members).
- Forum with two main topics: implementation issues and FCC certification.

In summary, this Web site offers potential for communication between buyers and providers.

8 RFID News

URL: www.rfidnews.org/

Founded/launched: 2003

Subject: News and a library of articles on RFID

This Web site provides members with news and a library of articles categorized by industry. The site is free, and most of the information is also free. However, members can purchase an annual membership to have access to articles older than 60 days. The services of this Web site include the following:

- News.
- RFID articles.
- Access to its network of providers.
- Vendor profiles.
- Event information.
- RFID advertising.

9 RfidXchange

URL: www.rfidexchange.com/

Founded/launched: 2004

Subject: Specializes in providing RFID news as well as independent advice and consultancy

The objective of this Web site is the provision of objective advice on RFID technology. This Web site is a compilation of news and RFID-related information and provides the visitor with a supply of referred Web sites with RFID content related to solution providers, technology, and events. From RFID information and white papers to hardware and applications, this Web site provides the user a method for gathering sources of information to expand his or her knowledge of RFID. The Web site is free, and it does not require registration in order to access all of its content. Another objective is to create an interactive community capable of exchanging information and ideas about RFID.

In summary, this Web site provides the following services:

- Quick RFID overview.
- News.

- RFID company directory (categorized by industry).
- Reference to white papers and their content.
- Summary of applications of RFID and companies (categorized by industry).

10 Using RFID

URL: www.usingrfid.com/

Founded/launched: 2003

Subject: News and RFID Resources

This Web site is completely free. Its main objective is to provide visitors and members with a single source of resources to learn, inform, and conduct research on RFID technology. It requires registration to access the full content of every posting. The Web site has the following sections:

- Information center.
- Daily news (major stories) and articles by company and by country.
- Book reviews.
- Events diary.
- Links and resources.
- Directory of manufacturers, suppliers, and integrators.
- Research center.
- Data by research topic.

The Web site allows members to contribute to a probe of market trends and learn about what other members think about the state of the RFID market. This tool can foster member interaction.

The Web sites mentioned in this section offer news, information, and references to obtain quickly the resources that the RFID industry provides.

Oftentimes, a free Web site indicates poor quality. However, in the case of RFID Web sites, free is also a synonym of interest and goodwill among researchers and entrepreneurs to bring the RFID community together.

Index